Gender, Policy and Educational Change

Gender equality has been a major educational theme for the past two decades and has become interwoven with other policy themes, including those of marketisation and managerialism. Contributors to this strong collection are key researchers in their fields and seek to address a variety of questions. What patterns are discernible in the educational attainment of girls and boys over the past two decades and to what extent are changes attributable to gender equality policies? The form that gender equality policies have taken in different parts of the UK is examined together with the impact of European equality policies. Also considered is the way in which gender equality policies have been experienced by particular groups including pupils from minority ethnic and working-class backgrounds.

The book aims to take an overall look at how significant have been the changes in the experiences, aspirations and culture of girls and boys and male and female teachers. It explores how attempts to improve equal opportunities in education have fared and examines the tensions and contradictions in recent policies.

Jane Salisbury is Lecturer in Education at the University of Wales, Cardiff. **Sheila Riddell** is Professor of Social Policy at the Strathclyde Centre for Disability Research, University of Glasgow.

Gender, Policy and Educational Change

Shifting agendas in the UK and Europe

Edited by Jane Salisbury and Sheila Riddell

London and New York

First published 2000
by Routledge
11 New Fetter Lane, London EC4P 4EE

Simultaneously published in the USA and Canada
by Routledge
29 West 35th Street, New York, NY 10001

Routledge is an imprint of the Taylor & Francis Group

© 2000 selection and editorial matter, Jane Salisbury and Sheila Riddell
© individual chapters, the contributors

Typeset in Galliard by RefineCatch Limited, Bungay, Suffolk
Printed and bound in Great Britain by Biddles Ltd, Guildford and
King's Lynn

British Library Cataloguing in Publication Data
A catalogue record for this book is available from the British Library

Library of Congress Cataloging in Publication Data
Gender, policy, and educational change: shifting agendas in the UK
   and Europe / [edited by] Jane Salisbury and Sheila Riddell.
       p.   cm.
   Includes bibliographical references and index.
   1. Educational equalization – Great Britain.   2. Sex discrimination
in education – Great Britain.   3. Educational equalization – Europe.
4. Sex discrimination in education – Europe.   I. Salisbury, Jane.
II. Riddell, Sheila.
LC213.3.G7G48   1999
379.2′6 – dc21   99–22988
                                                                CIP

ISBN 0–415–19433–4 (hbk)
ISBN 0–415–19434–2 (pbk)

Contents

Introduction: educational reforms and equal opportunities programmes   1

SHEILA RIDDELL AND JANE SALISBURY

PART 1
Gender and educational reforms: the UK and European context   17

1 Gender equality and schooling, education policy-making and feminist research in England and Wales in the 1990s   19

MIRIAM DAVID, GABY WEINER AND MADELEINE ARNOT

2 **Equal opportunities and educational reform in Scotland: the limits of liberalism**   37

SHEILA RIDDELL

3 **Beyond one border: educational reforms and gender equality in Welsh schools**   55

JANE SALISBURY

Figures

Tables

Contributors

Madeleine Arnot is a Lecturer in the School of Education in the University of Cambridge and a Fellow of Jesus College. Recent publications include *Gender Equality and Educational Reforms* with M. David and G. Weiner (EOC, 1996); *Feminism and Social Justice: International Perspectives* (edited with K. Weiler, Falmer Press, 1997). Forthcoming books are *Gender and Educational Performance* with J. Gray, M. James and J. Rudduck (OFSTED) and *Closing the Gender Gap* with M. David and G. Weiner (Polity Press). Dr Arnot held a Leverhulme Research Fellowship in 1997 to continue working on gender and citizenship and is currently engaged on *Project Arianne Broadening Adolescent Masculinity*, a project involving collaboration with eight European countries.

Jacky Brine is Professor of Education at the University of the West of England. She previously lectured in European education and training policy within the Department of Educational Studies at the University of Sheffield. She has researched and written widely on European policy and on its interpretation and implementation within the UK. A recent publication, *(Under)Educating Women: Globalizing Inequality* (Open University Press, 1998), explores the education and training policies of regionalised blocs such as the European Union within the context of globalisation and neo-colonialism.

Robert J. Cormack is Professor of Sociology, Co-Director of the Centre for Research on Higher Education, Pro-Vice Chancellor and Acting Secretary to Academic Council at the Queen's University of Belfast. His research interests include the sociology of education (particularly higher education); equal opportunities policies and practices (particularly the operation of fair employment legislation in Northern Ireland); and education and labour market links.

Linda Croxford is a senior research fellow at the Centre for Educational Sociology, University of Edinburgh. Her research interests include the effects of social inequalities on young people's curriculum, attainment and experiences of school. She is currently involved in a project funded by the ESRC which compares the post-compulsory education and training systems in the UK.

Miriam David is Professor of Policy Studies in Education at Keele University. She was previously Dean of Research at the London Institute. Formerly she was

Director of the Social Sciences Research Centre at South Bank University, managing and conducting research on families, education, health and social care. She has an international reputation for her research on families, gender, education and policy. She was a member of the sociology panel for the RAE in 1992 and 1996. Currently she holds two ESRC research grants: one jointly with Dr R. Edwards at South Bank University on Children's Understandings of Parental Involvement in Education and the other jointly with Dr Diane Reay and Professor Stephen Ball of King's College London on student choices of higher education.

Rosemary Deem is Professor of Educational Research, a member of the Institute for Women's Studies and Director of the Social Science Graduate School at Lancaster University. She was Chair of the British Sociological Association from 1994–96, and is currently directing an ESRC funded project on the management of UK universities. Her other research interests include gendered leisure and feminist methodologies. She is a governor of Central Lancaster High School, a staff member of the Council of Lancaster University and was chair of governors at Stantonbury Campus (a mixed comprehensive) from 1981–91.

Jill Duffield has been an educational researcher at Stirling University's Department of Education since 1991. She has worked (with Sally Brown, Sheila Riddell and others) on a number of projects relating to educational policy formation and implementation, and to equality issues of gender and special educational needs. Before joining the department, she was a teacher of Media Studies in Edinburgh and Fife secondary schools.

Anthony M. Gallagher is a Reader in Education at Queen's University, Belfast. His research on equality and education has focused on the dimensions of social class, religion, gender, 'race' and disability. Currently he is completing a major project on education and achievement for the Northern Ireland Economic Council, and on the role of education in ethnically divided societies for UNICEF.

Philip Heaton is Principal with Deloitte & Touche and a regional head of human resource and change management consultancy. Previous studies include research into organisational culture and equal opportunities for women in the senior Northern Ireland Civil Service, and equal opportunities and employer-provided training.

Gwynedd Lloyd is Senior Lecturer in Special Education in the Department of Equity Studies and Special Education, University of Edinburgh. Her current research and teaching interests include gender and deviance, exclusion from school, gender and special educational needs, and traveller children in school.

Lyn McBriar is Human Resources Executive for Compass Group (UK) Ltd. She was formerly a consultant in human resource management with Deloitte &

Touche and has extensive experience in survey work and studies on equal opportunities.

Sheila Macrae is a research fellow at King's College London. She was previously a secondary school teacher in Scotland and inner London. Her current research interests include post-compulsory education and training, transitions to adulthood and social exclusion.

Meg Maguire teaches at King's College, London. She is currently researching post-16 choices and transitions with Stephen Ball and Sheila Macrae. Her research interests include social justice, teacher education, older women in education and ageism as well as contemporary politics and policy matters.

Pat Mahony is Professor of Education at Roehampton Institute, London. She has worked for many years in the areas of 'equal opportunities' and teacher education and has published widely in these areas. She is currently directing an ESRC research project exploring the impact on teaching of the National Professional Standards and Qualifications currently being introduced by the Teacher Training Agency.

Patricia Murphy is Director of the Centre for Curriculum and Teaching Studies in the School of Education at the Open University and was previously Deputy Director of the Assessment of Performance Unit Science project. Her research into assessment and gender is well known. Her publications include *A Fair Test? Assessment, Achievement and Equity* (Open University Press, 1994), and *Equity in the Classroom: Towards Effective Pedagogies for Girls and Boys* (Falmer/UNESCO 1996), both with Professor Caroline Gipps, London Institute of Education.

Robert D. Osborne is Professor of Applied Policy Studies, School of Public Policy, Economics and Law, University of Ulster and Co-Director of the Centre for Research on Higher Education (a joint Centre of the University of Ulster and Queen's University, Belfast). Recent publications include *Higher Education in Ireland: North and South* (Jessica Kingsley, 1996).

Teresa Rees is Professor of Labour Market Studies at the School for Policy Studies, University of Bristol and a consultant to the European Commission on equal opportunities in education, training and labour market policy. She is the Equal Opportunities Commissioner for Wales. Recent publications include *Women and the Labour Market* (Routledge, 1992), *Our Sisters' Land: Changing Identities of Women in Wales* (co-edited, University of Wales Press, 1994) and *Mainstreaming Equality in the European Union* (Routledge, 1998).

Sheila Riddell is Professor of Social Policy and Director of the Strathclyde Centre for Disability Research, University of Glasgow. She previously held a Personal Chair in Education at the University of Stirling and was Dean of Arts and Social Science at Napier University. She has researched and written extensively on special educational needs, disability and gender.

Jane Salisbury is Co-ordinator of Post Graduate Studies at the School of Education, University of Wales Cardiff, where she lectures in education policy, qualitative research methods and post-16 education and training. She has published papers on classroom ethnography, vocational education and training along with the Sociology of work and professions. Recent research for the EOC examined gender equality and educational reform in Wales.

Lyn Tett is Head of Department of Community Education at Moray House Institute of Education, University of Edinburgh. Her research and teaching interests focus on the ways in which policies and practice serve to include or exclude oppressed groups, with a particular emphasis on adult participation in education.

Carol Vincent is a senior lecturer at the Institute of Education at the University of London. Her main research interests include issues of social justice and education, and specifically the relationship between parents and the education system. Her book, *Parents and Teachers: Power and Participation* (1996) was recently published by Falmer Press. She is currently directing two projects: one looking at relationships between refugee families and primary schools in collaboration with Simon Warren, and the other a study of parental 'voice' in school, in collaboration with Jane Martin and Stewart Ranson at the University of Birmingham.

Simon Warren is currently a research officer at the Institute of Education at the University of Warwick. His research interests include the relationships between parents and schools, and issues of social exclusion and education. He is currently completing a PhD looking at the construction of masculinities in primary schools.

Gaby Weiner is Professor of Education at Umeå University, Sweden, having moved there in 1998 from South Bank University, London. Involved with feminist issues since the late 1960s, she has researched and published widely on social justice, equal opportunities and gender issues in education, writing and editing a number of books and research reports. She is currently co-editor (with Lyn Yates and Kathleen Weller) of the Open University Press series 'Feminist Educational Thinking'.

Heather Wilkinson is a Research Fellow in the Centre for Social Research on Dementia, Stirling University. Her research interests include dementia and social policy, participatory research with people with learning difficulties and dementia, gender issues and family support.

Acknowledgements

For permission to reproduce material in this volume acknowledgement is due to the following sources:

The Open University Press for the use of Figure 2.1 from *Young People and Social Change* by Andy Furlong and Fred Cartmel (1997). The Controller of Her Majesty's Stationery Office for providing a licence to reproduce Crown Copyright items from *Statistics of Education 1996*, namely Tables 22b and 31 and from *Statistics of Education: Teachers 1996*, for 'Distribution of male and female teachers in 1994'. The Department of Education Northern Ireland (DENI) for permission to use six tables from *Women in Teaching: Equal Opportunities*, Final Report by Deloitte & Touche, Belfast, DENI (1999). Crown copyright is reproduced with the permission of the Controller of Her Majesty's Stationery Office and may be reproduced elsewhere provided the source is fully acknowledged. These data are used by the actual authors of the report Teresa Rees, Philip Heaton and Lyn McBriar in Chapter 11.

As editors we have ensured that contributors to the volume acknowledge sources, research funders and sponsors fully via end notes or within their text. This explicit referencing and citation will allow academics and students to trace data and research materials efficiently and perpetuate sound scholarship.

Finally, acknowledgements on a more personal note. Editing a volume between Cardiff and Edinburgh, even with the advantages offered by electronic mail has been a challenge and we would like to thank all our contributors for their patience and enthusiasm over the last year. Helen Fairlie and Jude Bowen at Routledge provided solid assistance throughout the various stages of production and we are appreciative of their availability. Jackie Swift's professional expertise in the preparation of the manuscript also deserves a special mention.

Increasingly these days with the demands of university working life, families become drawn into various support roles. Both of us wish to express our gratitude to those with whom we live who share and witness the ups and downs connected to research outputs! A special thank you to these backstage teams – in Scotland, Ken, Annie and Bella and in South Wales, Alan and Anna.

Jane Salisbury and Sheila Riddell

Abbreviations

ACCAC	Qualifications, Curriculum and Assessment Authority for Wales
APU	Assessment of Performance Unit
CCEA	Curriculum, Examinations and Assessment
CCMS	Council for Catholic Maintained Schools
CCRU	Central Community Relations Unit
CCW	Curriculum Council for Wales
CDT	Craft, Design and Technology
CRENI	Commission for Racial Equality in Northern Ireland
CSE	Certificate of Secondary Education
CTC	City Technology College
DE	Department of Employment
DENI	Department of Education Northern Ireland
DES	Department of Education and Science
DfEE	Department for Education and Employment
EBP	Education and Business Partnerships
EC	European Commission
ECER	European Conference on Educational Research
EIS	Educational Institute for Scotland
ELBs	Education and Library Boards
EMU	Education for Mutual Understanding
EO	Equal Opportunities
EOC	Equal Opportunities Commission
EOCNI	Equal Opportunities Commission, Northern Ireland
EO-pathway	The Equal Opportunities Pathway of ESF Objective 3
EP	Educational Psychologist
ERA	Education Reform Act
ERO	Education Reform Order, 1989
ESF	European Social Fund
ESF/3	Objective 3 of the European Social Fund
ESRC	Economic and Social Research Council
EU	European Union
FE	Further Education
FEA	Fair Employment Agency

FEC	Fair Employment Commission
FECSS	Further Education Council Scottish Sector
GCE	General Certificate of Education
GCSE	General Certificate of Secondary Education
GIST	Girls into Science and Technology
GMS	Grant Maintained Status
GNVQ	General National Vocational Qualification
GTC	General Teaching Council for Scotland
HEFCE	Higher Education Funding Councils
HEIs	Higher Education Institution
INSET	In-service Education and Training for school staff
INTO	Irish National Teachers Organisation
ITT	Initial Teacher Training
KS3	Key Stage 3
KS4	Key Stage 4
LEA	Local Education Authority
LEC	Local Enterprise Council
LGR	Local Government Reorganisation
LMS	Local Management of Schools
MGWI	Ministerial Group on Women's Interests
NACETT	National Advisory Council for Education and Training Targets
NC	National Curriculum
NCER	National Consortium for Examination Results
NCVO	National Council for Voluntary Organisations
NICER	Northern Ireland Council for Educational Research
NICIE	Northern Ireland Council for Integrated Education
NPM	New Public Management
NPQH	National Professional Qualification for Headship
NPS/Q	National Professional Standards and Qualifications
NTA	Non-teaching Assistant
NTET	National Education and Training Targets
NUT	National Union of Teachers
NVQ	National Vocational Qualification
OFSTED	Office for Standards in Education
OHMCI	Office of Her Majesty's Chief Inspector of Schools
PAFT	Policy Appraisal and Fair Treatment Guidelines
PCO	parent-centred organisation
PRU	Pupil Referral Unit
PSE	Personal and Social Education
PSI	Policy Studies Institute
QTS	Qualified Teacher Status
Regulation	The ESF Regulation of the European Commission
SACHR	Standing Advisory Commission on Human Rights
SATs	Standard Assessment Targets
SCAA	Schools Curriculum and Assessment Authority

SCOTVEC	Scottish Vocational Educational Qualification
SCRE	Scottish Council for Research in Education
SDA	Sex Discrimination Act
SEN	Special Educational Needs
SES	socio-economic status
SOEID	Scottish Office Education and Industry Department
SPD/94	The UK Single Programming Document for 1994–99
SPD/97	The UK Single Programming Document for 1997–99
TEC	Training and Enterprise Council
TGAT	Task Group on Attainment Targets
TODTW	Take Our Daughters to Work Initiative
TTA	Teacher Training Agency
TVEI	Technical, Educational and Vocational Initiative
UU	University of Ulster
VA	Value Added
WISE	Women into Science and Engineering
WTN	Women's Training Network

Introduction

Educational reforms and equal opportunities programmes

Sheila Riddell and Jane Salisbury

Introduction: the reform of education

Following its electoral victory in 1979, the Conservative government placed at the centre of its agenda the mission of tackling the 'crisis' within the welfare state. The discourse of crisis suggested that the post-war social democratic settlement had turned into an unwieldy bureaucracy which was failing to deliver high standards of service due to its control by the producers rather than the consumers. Furthermore, it encouraged dependency and was too expensive for the tax payer to afford. A few on the Right advocated the abolition of state welfare altogether, but a more commonly suggested solution was the introduction of the discipline of the market into the public sector along with the management practices of private industry. Deakin (1994: 162) comments that despite a widespread recognition within the Conservative Party of 'the need to break the hold of teachers over the manner and content of teaching', there were few ideas of how to break into 'the secret garden' of the curriculum. Duncan Graham, subsequently to become responsible for the implementation of the National Curriculum, suggested that in the early 1980s, the Conservative Party had been captured by:

> lobbyists who were continually ringing (sic) their hands, saying how awful it was that none of the country's children – apart from their own – could read or write, and that something had to be done, without having the slightest idea what it was that had to be done, or how intractable the problems were.
>
> (1993: 6, cited by Deakin 1994: 162)

It was during the Conservative government's third term of office that their resolve to tackle education was finally put into action. In England and Wales, the most sweeping measures were contained within the Education Act of 1988. In Northern Ireland and Scotland, the reforms were enacted differently but were none the less drawn from the same policy repertoire (see David *et al.*, Riddell, Salisbury, and Gallagher *et al.*, this volume, for accounts of the reforms in different parts of the United Kingdom). As with other third term measures, the main consequences of the educational reforms were a simultaneous concentration and diffusion of power. Control of the curriculum, which teachers had long valued, was wrested from them despite a struggle. In Scotland, where the curriculum was already more tightly controlled from the centre, the curricular measures of the 5–14 programme were generally accepted as embodying 'good practice', but national assessment was defeated by an alliance of parents and teachers, who feared that it might foreshadow a return to the unpopular qualifying examination, taken by pupils at age twelve prior to comprehensive reorganisation. In terms of the diffusion of power, the Conservative government committed itself to the empowerment of parents, assumed to be the consumers of education. Parental choice of school, given to Scottish parents under the terms of the Education (Scotland) Act, was granted to English and Welsh parents by the Education Act 1988. The establishment of governing bodies in England and school boards in Scotland, along with the delegation of financial management to schools, removed power from local authorities, investing it instead in schools and parents, thus contributing to the weakening of local government. Crucial to the 'empowerment' of the consumer was the role of information on a range of performance indicators. Particularly crucial to this was the publication of information on pupils' performance in public examinations. This was used to draw up league tables of schools, and became the main currency within the quasi-market of education. The focus on attainment in examination results also fuelled the growth of the school effectiveness research movement, which claimed that by controlling for social class, known to be the biggest determinant of educational outcome, it could offer a picture of how well a school was performing relative to others. School effectiveness research became enormously popular with government because, by demonstrating that schools could make a difference to pupil outcomes, it concealed the far greater power of social class as a determinant of educational outcome.

The 1990s, then, might be seen as the decade in which, despite the rhetoric of choice and diversity, state schools were compelled by law to offer the same programme in terms of curriculum and assessment and had the same yardsticks in the form of raw results applied, regardless of their circumstances. Parents were encouraged to seek out what was best for their individual child, without necessarily considering the effect this might have on the wider system and choices available to others. The language of reform was cast in terms which were neutral with regard to social class, gender and ethnicity, and, according to David (1993: 207), social scientists were themselves sometimes complicit in perpetuating this view of the world. She maintains that: 'despite both the gender-neutral and race-neutral language, reforms and research have been constructed around gender and racial divisions'. Furthermore:

> our understandings and our strategic policy developments and reforms, given this framework, have been and will remain narrow. They do not, and perhaps will not, take into account the full complexity of social and economic changes and their effects on men's and women's lives, inside and outside the family and whether black or white. In other words, we can only fully understand both the past complex developments and their implication for the

future if we adopt a critical perspective which includes both gender and race.

(1993: 207)

The aim of this book is to cast light on the way in which the educational reforms, despite their apparent neutrality, shaped not only the gender relations of pupils in school, but also those of parents and teachers. Our focus is primarily on gender, but its complex inter-relationship with social class, ethnicity and disability are highlighted.

The educational reform programme of the late 1980s and early 1990s was not implemented in a policy vacuum. Throughout the UK during the late 1980s and 1990s, equal opportunities programmes were moving from the grassroots into the centre of the policy arena and were exerting some influence on the national scene. Stemming from the second wave women's movement of the 1970s, these equal opportunities initiatives were bottom-up rather than top-down, with minimal central state involvement, unlike, for example, the situation in Australia where successive Labour governments were formally committed to equality programmes (Yates 1993). To the extent that equal opportunities initiatives received any formal legitimation from the centre, this tended to come from Europe (see Brine, this volume) rather than central government in the UK. Before turning to issues and questions raised by particular contributors to this volume, we comment on the history of gender struggles within education and subsequently provide a brief sketch of some key features of the relationship between feminism or feminisms (Weiner 1994) and education.

Gender struggles within education: the historical context

Debates over how girls and boys should be educated have a strong historical lineage because they relate directly to beliefs about appropriate roles for men and women in society. The idea of women and men operating within different but equal spheres, reflected in differentiated school curricula, was endorsed by middle-class Victorian feminists. Corr (1990) described the campaign for the inclusion of domestic science as a central part of the Scottish school curriculum for girls in the latter years of the nineteenth century. Middle-class women worked through voluntary cookery schools and school boards 'to establish a separate power base from men by stressing the special virtues which women could offer in education and in the home' (ibid.: 38). The argument of these women was that the way to improve the nation's health was not to question the domestic division of labour, but to value women's work in the home as a science. Ailsa Yoxall, for example, argued that it was not poverty that starved the family but the wife's thriftlessness and slatternly habits: 'Only a few enlightened minds could perceive the close connection between the misery in which so large a part of the working classes lived and the generally prevailing ignorance of the simplest facts of common life' (*c.* 1913: 64 cited by Corr 1990: 40).

These middle-class feminists were highly successful in installing domestic science as a major linchpin of the curriculum for girls. This is evident, for instance, in a book entitled *Real Life Arithmetic for Girls* by Olive I. Morgan, published originally in 1935 and reprinted five times over the following three years. Aimed at girls in 'Senior schools of the non-selective type', the book is prefaced with the following quote from the Board of Education on Senior School Mathematics:

> Any large expenditure of time on Mathematics unassociated with applications and for practical work is perhaps more greatly to be deprecated for girls than for boys. With a small time allowance it becomes all important to scrutinise carefully the contents of the syllabus and to ask what Mathematics is essential for girls, how this may best be treated and how far it is desirable or possible to go beyond this utilitarian minimum.
>
> (Morgan 1938: 2)

The first exercise in the book reads as follows:

> Joan earns 15s a week, of which she gives her mother 10s. With the rest she pays 1d tram fare to and from work for six days, and puts 1s in the Post Office Savings Bank. Her mother buys all her clothes except stockings and gloves. How could she spend the rest of her money (a) wisely, (b) foolishly?
>
> (ibid.: 5)

Ultimately, Corr maintains, the domestic science campaign by middle-class feminists was counter-productive since it was not supported by working-class girls who found the type of knowledge gleaned at school irrelevant to their experience at home (and would probably have enjoyed the foolish ways of spending money more than the wise!). The bracketing of femininity with the domestic sphere persisted, reflected in official reports as late as the 1960s. The Newson Report of 1963 on the 'average' and 'below average' child, for example, stated:

> A boy is usually excited by the prospect of a science course . . . he experiences a sense of wonder and power. The growth of wheat, the birth of a lamb, the movement of clouds put him in awe of nature; the locomotive he sees as man's response; the switch and throttle are his magic wands . . . the girl may come to the science lesson with a less eager curiosity than the boy, but she too will need to feel at home with machinery.
>
> (1963: 142, cited by Deem 1981: 136)

These attitudes, supported by some middle-class feminists at the turn of the century, were challenged by feminists in the 1970s. The 'separate spheres of activity' arguments advanced by Victorian feminists also had detrimental effects on women in teaching. During the inter-war period in Scotland, a marriage bar operated so that female teachers were expected to sign a clause agreeing to resign on marriage. The overt justification of this, according to Adams (1990: 90) was that:

Making better mothers was the best strategy for improving the nation's health. Paid employment outwith the home was seen by well meaning middle class councillors as only a passing phase for girls as it was seen as a hindrance to a girl's understanding of her true career as wife and mother.

The same argument was used to justify differential rates of pay for male and female teachers, which persisted until the 1960s (Fewell 1990). Women teachers, it was maintained, were only engaged in teaching as a diversion until embarking on their proper role in life as wives and mothers. In the 1920s, higher salaries for male graduate teachers were introduced to tackle the dearth of men in the teaching profession. Ironically, the marriage bar and the introduction of differential pay for men did not have the effect of preserving teaching as a male profession. Women who went into teaching often preferred a celibate life to giving up their work, partly because of their desire to be able to offer financial assistance to the families who had supported them through their education, but also because they valued their financial independence. Differential pay remained a thorny issue in teaching for many years. Local authorities were not deterred from hiring women teachers, who might well prove a cheaper long-term option, but the rankling inequality of unequal pay for equal work was keenly felt. The institutionalisation of low expectations among women teachers is still evident in Scotland, where women make up 90 per cent of primary school teachers but only 73 per cent of head teachers, and in secondary schools, where women represent 50 per cent of teaching staff but 7 per cent of head teachers. Half of Scottish education authorities (16 out of 32) have no female head teacher at secondary level. Such figures remind us that even though the official language of edcuation is couched in strictly neutral terms, the institutionalised gender discrimination on which the present system is based still casts a long shadow.

Feminisms in education and the construction of 'equality'

Equal opportunities initiatives in school, which struck a chord with many women teachers, was inspired by the second wave of feminism which grew in the United States out of the 1960s' civil rights movement. This brand of feminism drew on a range of earlier traditions and was strongly influenced by liberalism. Middleton (1984: 43) summarises the essential features of liberal political philosophy thus:

> As a social theory which developed with the breakdown of the feudal system, the rise of the bourgeoisie and the onset of commodity production, liberalism is the legitimating ideology of capitalist free enterprise, emphasising the rights of the individual to own property and to accumulate wealth. No longer determined by birth, one's position in the social hierarchy is seen as resulting from 'merit' and hard work. Liberal feminists demand the extension of the liberal ideology to women.

The first wave of feminist thinkers such as Mary Wollstonecraft (1792) and John

Stuart Mill (1869) did not wish to change the capitalist social order, but felt women should have formal equality within it. Some feminists of the second wave, taking a similar position, have been subjected to the criticism that 'all they want is a slice of the capitalist action without changing its structure. All women's rights wants, and all it will get, is a change of the genitalia of the people at the top' (Bunkle 1979, part one, 27). This has been termed a weak liberal approach. A strong equal opportunities approach, by way of contrast, would assume that challenges to the distribution of power would bring about social transformation.

Radical feminist theories differ from liberal approaches in their stronger emphasis on the need to change existing structures before other sorts of change becomes possible. Radical feminists see patriarchy as the main source of oppression while Marxist feminists confer this role on capitalism and socialist feminists seek to identify the complex relationships between patriarchy and capitalism. Black feminists see racism as the principal underlying source of their oppression, while lesbian feminists accord this role to heterosexism and homophobia. As pointed out by Phillips (1992), these approaches share in common a desire to pinpoint the origins of oppression, believing that the social superstructure must change before things can be any different on the ground. However, the final point of women's oppression proved remarkably difficult to identify and there was a gradual realisation that this was probably not the right question to be asking in the first place.

In line with this move away from ontological questions has been a recognition that the endless splitting of feminisms may be limiting rather than liberating. Weiner comments:

> As post-structuralism rightly identifies, it is proving ever more difficult to categorize the amoeba-like changes in feminism, due to the shifting nature of terminology, say of 'woman' or 'feminism' or 'femininity' and the discursive frameworks which have helped shape the 'normalizing' processes for generations of women.
>
> (1994: 52)

Reviewing new directions in feminist thought, Phillips (1992) suggests that these differ both from 1970s' feminism (emphasising equality and assuming a homogeneity among women) and 1980s' feminism (characterised by its emphasis on difference both between and among women and men). The binary divisions between, for instance, radical and liberal feminism are crude and limiting and even the notion of woman as a unitary category is increasingly likely to be questioned. In the work of Phillips (1992, 1997) and Fraser (1997) there is an unease with the standpoint politics of feminists such as Young (1990). Phillips (1992), for instance, argues that a notion of social justice is dependent on groups of individuals seeking to understand the perspective of others rather than simply pressing their particular claims. There is a sense, Phillips suggests, that in rejecting the Rawlsian idea of degendered, objective justice, feminists may have undermined the basis for any notion of social justice at all. She suggests:

What I call the aspiration to universality none the less remains. In the reworking of contemporary political theory and ideals, feminism cannot afford to situate itself for difference and against universality, for the impulse that takes us beyond our immediate and specific difference is a vital necessity in any radical transformation.

(Phillips 1992: 28)

Fraser (1997) has also suggested that the focus on identity has undermined the agenda of redistribution, so that many groups who fail to achieve recognition as an oppressed minority are denied both economic power and access to justice.

Work on the development of equal opportunities policies in the UK suggests that it is not possible to draw a clear-cut line between liberal and radical strategies, since policies are extremely fluid and given aims can produce unexpected outcomes. None the less, some policies are clearly associated with a wider political project of economic redistribution, some with recognition of group identity, while others are concerned at a very minimal level with formal legal compliance. As Power *et al.* (1998) noted, equal opportunities work is currently under attack from those who claim it is responsible for boys' underachievement. It is therefore important that feminist researchers do not entirely abandon the political agenda because of its complexity. By the same token, it would be a pity if debates about boys' underachievement forced feminist thinking back into a binary divide from which it was emerging.

Educational reforms and equal opportunities: multiple policy agendas in action

Let us now look more closely at the contributions to this edited collection, each of which endeavours to provide a particular insight on the sometimes jarring, sometimes smooth coalescence of educational reform and gender equality policies. Part 1, 'Gender and educational reforms: the UK and European context' brings together work in different parts of the UK and reminds us of the European context in which they are located. Three of the chapters, those by David *et al.*, Riddell and Salisbury, are based on studies funded by the Equal Opportunities Commission on gender and educational reform. There is a marked similarity in the central messages of these chapters; girls are tending to perform better than boys in public examinations, but the origins of these changes pre-date the implementation of the reform programme. Despite the gender-neutral language of official discourse and the hostility of the previous Conservative government to what it termed 'egalitarianism', equal opportunities policies are increasingly being adopted at local authority and school level and are no longer restricted to a small number of Labour-controlled metropolitan authorities. The impact of local government reform, particularly in Wales and Scotland, where large regions have been replaced by a greater number of single tier authorities, is not yet clear. There are also, however, different nuances in understandings of gender equality programmes. David *et al.*, for example, maintain that their study reveals that 'the gender cultures of schooling have been transformed in the ten years covered by the study', with wider opportunities opening up for girls. Riddell and Salisbury introduce a more salutory note. One effect of the marketisation of education has been the general decline of schools in peripheral housing estates and poor inner city areas. The loss of pupils to more popular schools has resulted in a reduction of resources and an impoverishment of the curriculum, including gender equality programmes. Riddell's case studies reveal that the focus of the public gaze on one particular performance indicator, raw examination results, has meant that those schools with other strengths, such as strong equality policies, have been left, in the language of the market, with an unmarketable commodity. According to pure market theory, the remedy is simple: the school must either alter its product or close. However, in the world of education, the market does not operate as simply as this and the losers in the system tend to get stuck in a cycle of decline which damages pupils, teachers and parents. The Scottish, Welsh and English studies also reveal persistent tensions between aspirations and outcomes of pupils from a range of ethnic and social class backgrounds. 'The problem of boys' is a recurrent theme in schools and may lead to the recasting of equal opportunities programmes to focus on boys' rather than girls' difficulties. Although promulgating a cautious policy of redistribution (£56 million is to be distributed to schools in Education Action Zones in England), New Labour shows no signs of abandoning the agenda of performativity. We await to see the effect of devolution on central government policies in a range of areas including the management of educational markets, the measurement of performance and the promotion of equal opportunities.

Structure of the book

Chapters in this volume also illustrate the way in which different equality issues achieve prominence in different parts of the UK, depending on which aspects of social identity are seen as having greatest salience. In Wales, the importance of Welsh culture and identity is reflected in the concern to promote Welsh medium schooling. In Northern Ireland, the chapter by Tony Gallagher and colleagues alerts us to the focus on equality for those from different religious groups, leading to a programme of research which has contributed more widely to knowledge of social relations based on social class and gender as well as religion. In Northern Ireland, as elsewhere in the UK, girls are performing better than boys and for that reason gender has not been problematised. However, some practices have been clearly discriminatory. For instance, between 1982 and 1985, girls and boys were treated as separate populations for the Eleven Plus examination. The effect of this was that more boys than girls were awarded the top grade (conveniently since more places were available for boys in grammar schools), despite the fact that girls performed better in verbal reasoning tests. The justification for this, according to Gallagher *et al.*, was that

> as girls matured earlier than boys, they tended to perform better on verbal-reasoning type tests at age eleven years. However, when both sexes had gone

through puberty to achieve maturity, the academic performance of boys 'caught up' with that of girls. On these grounds it was felt that to treat boys and girls as a single population at age 11 years would unfairly disadvantage boys, despite claims by the EOCNI that this practice might be illegal under article 24 of the Sex Discrimination (Northern Ireland) Order 1976.

When a legal challenge was brought, it was successful and as a result an additional 860 girls were given qualified status. This case reveals the way in which biological arguments may still be used to disadvantage girls. In the past, the fact that girls menstruate was used to debar them from higher education on the grounds that it would lead their reproductive organs to atrophy. During the 1980s, the onset of menstruation apparently gave girls an unfair advantage over boys which justified compensatory measures. Such practices existed in the post-war period in England, but were long since abandoned on the grounds of unfairness. It is interesting that they persisted for so long in Northern Ireland. Gallagher *et al.* also illustrate the difficulty of establishing a 'fair' test. When boys and girls were treated as one population between 1990 and 1993, more girls than boys qualified for a grammar school place. The verbal-reasoning test was abandoned in 1993, in part because it appeared to favour girls, and was replaced by attainment tests which produced variability in the comparative rate at which girls and boys were assigned the top grade. Teachers complained that these tests required an excessive amount of reading, with the implication that they might favour middle-class pupils with greater access to books in the home. According to Gallagher *et al.*, media speculation was that the tests were geared towards producing an appropriate number of pupils to fit the available grammar school places. The debacle over assessment for selective purposes in Northern Ireland illustrates the point made eloquently by Murphy, in this volume, that assessment should be treated with a great deal of caution since it is a cultural product and any form of assessment will favour one group over another. Finally, the Northern Ireland chapter reminds us that religious tensions in Northern Ireland have led to the production of very strict equal opportunities policies in relation to employment. The Policy Appraisal and Fair Treatment (PAFT) Guidelines, if enshrined in statute, would represent the strongest from of equality legislation in the UK, applying not just to religion but also to gender, ethnicity and disability. It will be interesting to monitor the extent to which state intervention in the field of equal opportunities, which characterises the Northern Ireland approach more than anywhere else in the UK, will succeed in changing hearts and minds.

Jacky Brine's chapter on the nature and interpretation of European equal opportunities policies under the previous Conservative and present Labour government reminds us of the wider political agenda which may play an increasingly important role in the shaping of domestic policy, particularly if the EC continues to play a central role in the funding of post-16 education and training. However, her chapter also provides fascinating insights into the way in which language is used as tactic in struggles over power and resources. Both the EC and the previous Conservative UK government used a common language in relation to equal opportunities and the mainstreaming of equal opportunities policies. However, while apparently acceding to EC policy directives, the UK government succeeded in conveying to local training providers that equal opportunities was no longer a policy priority and only minimal compliance with equal opportunities funding criteria was required. Brine's chapter also illustrates some of the perils of adopting a generic approach to equal opportunities, in which ethnicity, social class and disability are addressed simultaneously. The result of moves in this direction may be a loss of focus on the particular issues faced by women, for instance, combining work outside the home with the care of small children. Theoretical moves away from categories advocated by post-structuralists and referred to above may have some negative consequences in terms of blunting the political agenda.

Part 2, 'Structures and processes in schools and classrooms', shifts attention to the ways in which particular aspects of the reform programme have worked out in relation to gender equality. Croxford draws attention to the double-edged nature of national curricula. On the one hand, introduction of national curricula in state schools may be seen as the tightening of central control over what is taught and what goes on in the classroom. This was certainly the burden of argument advanced by commentators such as Lawton and Chitty (1988) when the Education Reform Act 1988 revealed the government's intention to break into the 'secret garden' of the curriculum. However, an alternative view was advanced from a feminist perspective by Kelly (1988) and by Galloway (1990) in relation to children with special educational needs. Galloway's argument, in his paper 'Was the GERBIL a Marxist mole?', was that a Left-leaning government might have implemented the same curriculum proposals as the Conservative government in the interests of equity and entitlement. Croxford demonstrates in the Scottish context that the possibility of choice within the eight Standard grade modes enables pupils to separate into gender-differentiated areas of the curriculum in critical areas such as science. The remedy, she suggests, might be to expand the compulsory part of the curriculum for the last two years of secondary schooling. This suggestion might be anathema to those who see pupil choices as central to their ongoing commitment to education, but, as Croxford reminds us, individual freedom is ephemeral and most choices that individuals believe they make voluntarily are socially structured.

Assessment, the focus of Murphy's chapter, is of critical importance to the judgements that are made of schools and of the performance of individual pupils. League tables of school performance and comparisons of girls' and boys' performance are based on the assumption that something 'real' is being measured. Murphy reminds us of the many factors which render assessment a social and cultural artefact. Rather than abandon the quest for equity in assessment, she suggests there is a need to explore the use of complementary modes of assessment, while at the same time recognising that 'assessment, like pedagogy, needs to be understood as an art that is in the process of evolution'. Retaining a sense of assessment as offering a provisional rather than absolute picture of pupil performance might be salutory for those arguing that the battle over gender equity has been won since girls appear to be gaining better examination results than boys.

The last two chapters in Part 2, by Duffield and Macrae and Maguire, give pause for thought in relation to some of the more optimistic suggestions by David *et al.* that the gender culture of schools has been transformed over the previous decade. The study reported by Duffield was intended to unearth some of the processes at work in schools identified as more and less effective and which also varied in relation to social class. School effectiveness research has had very little to say about gender differences in schools, simply because all schools appear to be more effective for girls than boys. The absence of differential effects means that gender, like social class, becomes a background variable, part of the statistical noise to be controlled for rather than understood. Duffield demonstrates the continued resonance of studies of the 1970s and 1980s which looked at gender and classroom processes. In the case study classrooms she describes in the 1990s, girls were still achieving more, but featuring less in classroom encounters and in teachers' awareness and knowledge of pupils. The major losers appeared to be lower achieving girls, who were less likely to receive learning support or the attention of mainstream teachers. Duffield notes that these patterns were common to all four schools, irrespective of socio-economic status or level of measured effectiveness. Some school effectiveness and improvement researchers have suggested that the way to improve standards in school is to identify processes operating in more effective schools and apply these to less effective schools. If this strategy were to be pursued, then gender equality would disappear since differential effects cannot be identified. In the 1990s, school effectiveness and improvement research has enjoyed something of a heyday, fitting neatly with the agenda of performativity and apparently offering neat policy solutions. Duffield's chapter is useful in alerting us to the need for a somewhat broader agenda to tackle issues of social exclusion which are influencing the new policy agenda.

The chapter by Macrae and Maguire also acts as a reminder of the gender issues which remain unresolved and are not as readily described as external examination results. The girls in their post-16 cohort are, at one level, emerging powerfully from their school experience, performing better than their male counterparts despite the persistence of divisions based on social class and ethnicity. And yet, differences and inequalities persist. Despite their ability to compete successfully with boys, young women continue to move towards traditionally feminine areas of the labour market in the later years of secondary education. Sexuality emerges as an area where boys continue to exercise control, possessing young women and policing their behaviour, with girls often complicit in such relationships. One explanation for this clearly lies in the elasticity and adaptiveness of patriarchy and capitalism which demand ongoing analysis and political engagement. At another level, such writing raises uneasy questions about unresolved tensions between culture and biology, which feminists believed had been laid to rest. It is interesting that at a time when women are demonstrating their ability to undertake the same work at the same level as men, there should be a rash of media coverage such as the television series *Why Men Don't Iron* suggesting that hard-wired biological differences between men and women are such that separate gender roles and behaviours will inevitably emerge even when society attempts to override these. Such arguments demand clear responses which do not seek to erase biology, but point to the complex, iterative and changing relationship between biological and cultural influences.

Part 3, 'Delegation and the new managerialism', explores the gendered effects of moves to divert power from local authorities to parents and schools. Deem explores the gendered processes which have informed the practices of governing bodies, intended to give parents and local businesses a major say in the running of schools, thus shifting power from the vested interests of the educational establishment. Financial management, in particular, has tended to be an area in which men rather than women have become involved, thus accentuating rather than challenging conventional gender divisions. A central irony emphasised by Deem is that whereas progressive management is now de-emphasising hierarchy and bureaucracy, governing bodies have tended to reflect 'the bureaucratic, formal, hierachical organisational structures, which are a legacy of local authorities'. Further cultural shifts will be necessary if governing bodies are to reflect gender, social class and ethnic differences more accurately.

The following two chapters provide insight into changes effected by educational reform on women as school managers. Rees *et al.* undertook a survey of the views of teachers and governors of the role of Principal and the involvement of governors in appointments following the introduction of local management of schools (LMS). Northern Ireland has a relatively high proportion of women in management positions in schools, particularly in comparison with Scotland. None the less, Rees and colleagues alert us to the extent to which school headship remains a gendered activity from which women may be further distanced in the future. Women are most likely to be appointed to the post of Principal in primary schools or small rural single-sex grammar schools, but even in these areas there is a perception that the nature of the job is changing and becoming less attractive to women. Chill factors include the perception that the role of the head teacher is becoming tied up increasingly with the management of external relations, human resources and financial matters rather than dealing with the day-to-day running of the school, including close contact with children. Headship is perceived as a more technical and increasingly stressful occupation and women, who already have significant domestic responsibilities, judge that the financial rewards and status may not be sufficient compensation for the added pressure. Governors tend to assume that men are able to enforce better standards of discipline and most of those involved in senior appointments had not participated in equal opportunities training. Given that women are already under-represented in the area, Rees *et al.* point to the danger of education becoming increasingly an arena in which women teach and men manage.

Mahony's chatper highlights the way in which the reshaping of the head teacher training curriculum in England may hasten these developments. Committed to freeing teacher training from a liberal ideology associated with progressivism and, implicitly, lax standards, the Teacher Training Agency (TTA) has striven to establish a new teacher training curriculum based not on theory but on competences required to do the job to an adequate standard. Mahony suggests that the image of the manager in popular texts draws on images of 'competitive, conquering, aggressive and power-seeking masculinities' and these values are reflected in the National Professional Standards and Qualifications developed by the TTA. In order to achieve success in school management, women are expected to prove themselves able to compete unflinchingly on this masculine terrain. They may react, suggests Mahony, either by turning their back on educational management or by adopting the worst aspects of masculine behaviour. So, although there are some signs of a growing number of women in educational management, this may be at great personal cost. Overall, the three chapters in this section present a somewhat pessimistic view of management changes, suggesting that the gains for some women entering previous male preserves might be offset by the establishment of hierarchical, competitive and depersonalised forms of working which most women are likely to find uncongenial and alienating. As Deem notes, it may be that schools are busy implementing a form of management which progressive businesses already regard as lumbering and outmoded.

The final Part, 'Groups at the margins', explores the cluster of education reforms from the perspective of those at the periphery. In her discussion of the learning society, which has become one of the buzz phrases of current education, Tett shows how it has been construed in gender-neutral terms which tend to exclude educationally disadvantaged women. Under the previous Conservative government, education and training came to be seen largely in terms of their potential contribution to economic competitiveness, with the unwritten assumption that those who were most likely to contribute to the economy should be at the front of the queue for investment. Inevitably, this consigned other groups, particularly older people, women with childcare responsibilities and disabled people to the back. Older forms of community education, which had valued informal learning and had nurtured grassroots educational initiatives were starved of resources. For the emancipatory potential of the learning society to be realised, and for disadvantaged women to be included within it, suggests Tett, education which promotes social as well as human capital must be nurtured. Just as the learning society is often treated as a neutral rather than a gendered topic, the gendered nature of school exclusion also tends to be ignored. Gwynedd Lloyd problematises the tendency to exclude far more boys than girls and explores the different ways in which girls' and boys' disturbing or disturbed behaviour is construed.

The position of parents of children with special educational needs as consumers of education is the topic of Heather Wilkinson's contribution. The rhetoric of parental power envisaged the educational consumer as the parent of a 'normal' child whose actions would stimulate schools to compete with each other. Responsibility for the education of children with special educational needs falls disproportionately on women and the choices they make may be unpopular and expensive. Wilkinson reveals the paucity of real alternatives available to this group and the hostility they may evoke when seeking to exercise the promised power. Parents of children with special educational needs in many ways illustrate the limits, as well as the possibilities, of parental empowerment.

Choice is again the topic of Vincent and Warren's chapter, which explores the actions of a self-help support group of African Caribbean mothers. To adopt the terminology of Hirschman (1970), parent centred organisations (PCOs) are concerned with exercising powers of 'voice' rather than 'exit', in accordance with a social democratic rather than consumerist conceptualisation of power. Vincent and Warren consider the extent to which this group is able to exercise a radical rather than conformist influence and point to a range of complexities. At one level, by offering each other support and assistance in negotiating the system, the PCO could be seen as defusing pressure. On the other hand, partly because of its social mix and access to conventional forms of expression, the organisation is able to promote the demands of black women whose voices might otherwise be unheard. This group, it is suggested, must be seen as providing simultaneously individualised solutions, without ruling out the possibility of wider structural change. Overall, the four chapters in this section point up the ambiguities with the reform programmes, which at one level disempower women who form a part of a range of groups at the margins. None the less, the rhetoric of empowerment is not entirely empty and chinks may open up, offering some leverage to those seeking change.

In conclusion

We hope this collection will illuminate some of the hope as well as the disappointment which women experienced over the past two decades. In education, as well as other spheres, the scene altered immeasurably, as the social democratic post-war settlement was undermined by the onslaught of market forces and new forms of management. These developments intersected with another stream of social change emanating from the second wave of the women's movement and advocating gender equality, despite a growing awareness that this in itself was a contested notion. The chapters in this volume illustrate the complex outcomes as supposedly gender-neutral educational reforms were implemented alongside equal opportunities policies. Sometimes, the two sets of policies appeared to be working in harmony, for instance, the emphasis on examination attainment may well have encouraged middle-class girls whose values were already attuned to academic achievement. On the other hand, the focus on measurable outcomes and the neglect of classroom processes meant that many aspects of patriarchal culture continue unchallenged. Similarly, the new models of school management adopted motifs of individualistic competitiveness which were incompatible with women's values and ways of being. On closer scrutiny, then, both educational reforms and equal opportunities turned out to behave with a certain degree of plasticity and ambiguity, and in their implementation there is much evidence of mutual influence and interaction. That is not to deny, however, the negative effect of some of the educational reforms on schools in poorer areas. As the 1980s progressed, these institutions found that their work in combating poverty and promoting equality could not be measured or valued in the climate of performativity.

Reading through this collection, we are struck not only by the breadth of ground that our contributors have covered, but some of the areas which remain to be investigated further in the future. The interactions of gender, social class, ethnicity and disability are considered, but much remains to be explored. We are also struck by the wealth of possibilities which will unfold over the coming years. The New Labour Government, condemned by some as being too imbued in the market-driven values of its predecessor, none the less promises interesting developments in its attempt to rework the equation between social and economic goods. Devolution of power from Westminster to Scotland, Wales and Northern Ireland also holds out opportunities and threats for the future development of gender equality policies. In addition, the EC may have increasing or diminishing influence in the new political order. In reading these chapters, we hope that the reader will be alert to the questions which remain unanswered or unexplored.

References

Adams, K. (1990) 'Divide and rule: the marriage ban 1918–1945', in F.M.S. Paterson and J. Fewell (eds) *Girls in their Prime: Scottish Education Revisited*, Edinburgh: Scottish Academic Press.

Bunkle, P. (1979–80) 'A history of the women's movement', *Broadsheet*, Part One, September 1979, 24–8.

Corr, H. (1990) 'Home rule in Scotland: the teaching of housework in Scottish schools 1872–1914', in F.M.S. Paterson and J. Fewell (eds) *Girls in their Prime: Scottish Education Revisited*, Edinburgh: Scottish Academic Press.

David, M. (1993) *Parents, Gender and Educational Reform*, Oxford: Policy Press.

Deakin, N. (1994) *The Politics of Welfare: Continuities and Change*, London: Harvester Wheatsheaf.

Deem, R. (1981) 'State policy and ideology in the education of women, 1944–1980', *British Journal of Sociology of Education* 2, 2: 131–43.

Fewell, J. (1990) 'The protection racket: the occupation of the teaching profession', in F.M.S. Paterson and J. Fewell (eds) *Girls in their Prime: Scottish Education Revisited*, Edinburgh: Scottish Academic Press.

Fraser, N. (1997) *Justice Interruptus: Critical Reflections on the Post-Socialist Condition*, London: Routledge.

Galloway, D. (1990) 'Was the GERBIL a Marxist mole?', in P. Evans and V. Varma (eds) *Special Education: Past, Present, Future*, London: Falmer Press.

Graham, D. (1993) *A Lesson for Us All*, London: Routledge.

Hirschman, A. (1970) *Exit, Voice and Loyalty*, Cambridge, MA: Harvard University Press.

Kelly, A. (1988) 'Towards a democratic science education', in H. Lauder and P. Brown (eds) *Education in Search of a Future*, Lewes: Falmer Press.

Lawton, D. and Chitty, C. (1988) *The National Curriculum*, Bedford Way Papers 33, London: Kogan Page.

Middleton, S. (1984) 'The sociology of women's education as a field of study', *Discourse* 5, 1: 43–62.

Mill, J.S. (1869) *On Liberty, Representative Government, the Representation of Women: Three Essays*, London: Oxford University Press 1948 edition.

Morgan, O. (1938) *Real Life Arithmetic for Girls*, London: Gregg Publishing Co Ltd.

Paterson, F. and Fewell, J. (eds) (1990) *Girls in their Prime: Scottish Education Revisited*, Edinburgh: Scottish Academic Press.

Phillips, A. (1992) 'Universal pretensions in political thought', in M. Barrett and A. Phillips (eds) *Destabilizing Theory: Contemporary Feminist Debates*, London: Polity.

—— (1997) 'From inequality to difference: a severe case of displacement', *New Left Review* 224: 143–53.

Power, S., Whitty, G. and Edwards, T. (1998) 'School boys and school work: gender identification', *International Journal of Inclusive Education* 2, 2: 95–118.

Weiner, G. (1994) *Feminisms in Education; An Introduction*, Buckingham: Open University Press.

Willms, J.D. and Kerr, P.D. (1988) 'Changes in sex differences in Scottish examination results since 1976', *Journal of Early Adolescence* 7, 1: 85–105.

Wollstonecraft, M. (1792) *A Vindication of the Rights of Women*, Harmondsworth: Penguin (1975 edition).

Yates, L. (1993) 'Feminism and Australian state policy: some questions for the 1990s', in M. Arnot, and K. Weiler (eds) *Feminism and Social Justice in Education*, London: The Falmer Press.

Young, I. M. (1990) *Justice and the Politics of Difference*, Princeton, NJ: Princeton University Press.

Part 1

Gender and educational reforms

The UK and European context

Part I

1 Gender equality and schooling, education policy-making and feminist research in England and Wales in the 1990s

Miriam David, Gaby Weiner and Madeleine Arnot

Introduction

In this chapter we address a number of issues relating to gender and education policy-making: more specifically, the period of UK educational reform at the end of the 1980s and early 1990s, its impact on gender equality and policy-making and feminist quandaries concerning researching gender.

Our discussion draws on a year-long, research project funded by the Equal Opportunities Commission for England and Wales (EOC) which explored educational reform and gender equality in schooling over a ten-year period from 1984–94. We locate this research project in the wider context of education policy-making and commissioned and funded research in Britain today and the range of feminist research perspectives available to us. We argue that policy-oriented research is too limited to identify the reasons for cultural shifts in gender equality, although we reflect on what these reasons might be. First, however, we consider the context of specific policy change and its relationship to gender.

Gender and policy-making

Equality has been a target of British government policy-making at various stages in the twentieth century, though rarely as a high priority. From the 1944 Education Act onwards, 'equality of opportunity' was included in the rhetoric of schooling, whether in the 1940s focused on education appropriate to perceived levels of intelligence, or in the 1960s concerned with eradicating social class differences, or on increased gender and racial equality from the 1970s onwards. Indeed, the 1960s and 1970s were most influenced by concerns about equality of opportunity, both in the political arena and in education.

Before 1979, policies under both Labour and Conservative governments were oriented towards the twin goals of greater equality and increased economic growth – with the former seen as contributing to the latter. The main legislation associated with equal opportunities at this time were the Equal Pay Act (1970, coming into force in 1975), the Sex Discrimination Act (1975) which specifically included education, and with respect to 'race' issues, the Race Relations Act (1976). This set of legislation led to a range of policy strategies instituted by individual teachers, schools and local authorities, many of whom were anxious to see enacted the spirit as well as the letter of the legislation.

However, by 1979, partly as a consequence of Prime Minister James Callaghan's speech at Ruskin in 1976 which signalled the end of the post-war boom period and an increasing concern for value-for-money in education, a debate began to develop about the extent to policies aimed at increased equality might be at odds with those aimed at economic growth and individual accountability (David 1980).

At the same time, a number of consistent research findings began to emerge, pointing to inadequacies in schooling for girls. In terms of the formal curriculum, syllabuses and content were found to exclude the experiences of girls and women (whether white or black). At secondary level, where choice was available, girls tended to opt for humanities, languages and social science, and boys for Science, Mathematics and technological subjects (Pratt *et al.* 1984). Also, students tended to be directed into traditionally male and female subjects and careers, and in the main, girls' careers were believed to be less important than boys' (Arnot and Weiner 1987).

In terms of performance, girls were generally found to be achieving well at primary level although they tended to slip back at secondary level, particularly in Mathematics and Science (Kelly 1985; Burton 1986). Boys' poor performance in English and Languages in primary and secondary school was seen to be offset by their increasingly better performance in examinations as they reached school-leaving age (Spender 1980). In general, young men were seen to have an advantage in the labour market because many young women had low occupational aspirations, tending to opt for low status and low paid 'feminine' jobs to bridge the gap between leaving school and marriage.

The hidden or unwritten curriculum of schooling was also found to exert pressure on students (and staff) to conform in sex-specific ways; for example, there were different rules on uniform and discipline for girls and boys, and sexual harassment and verbal abuse were found to be common features of school life (Lees 1987).

As a consequence, by the early 1980s, some teachers and advisory staff (and the HMI, see Orr 1984) began to develop a range of strategies in order to counter these inequalities. These included: persuading secondary students to opt for non-traditional subjects such as physics for girls and modern languages for boys; encouraging wider career aspiration through non-discriminatory careers' advice; revising reading schemes and school texts to be less sexist and more inclusive; 'de-sexing' registers and 'uni-sexing' school uniform; appointing female senior staff as positive role models for female pupils; establishing equal opportunities working parties, policy statements and posts of responsibility, and so on (Weiner and Arnot 1987).

The main concerns at this time were: at primary (or elementary) levels, helping girls to become more assertive and removing sexist practices from the formal and hidden curriculum; and at secondary schools, raising the profile of young women in the labour market, persuading girls into Science and Mathematics (there was little focus on boys at this time), and the perceived decline of girls' performance and self-confidence during adolescence (Whyte 1983; Millman 1987; Chisholm and Holland 1986; Whyld 1983).

Towards the mid-1980s, however, the scenario began to change as municipal socialism in the form of a number of labour-controlled Local Education Authorities (LEAs) adopted increased support for equality initiatives as part of their challenge to New Right policies. More sharply focused, or perhaps, 'simplistic' (Gillborn 1995: 75) policies were produced which first sought to identify and then to combine different facets of gender policy-making. Connections were made, for example, between gender, race, class and ethnicity as different feminisms began to make an impact on education (Minhas 1986).

Equality began to be viewed as a political football or signifier of the fight between the political Left and Right: in which the principal losers were the metropolitan left-leaning LEAs, whose powers were sharply curtailed by the 1988 Education Reform Act and subsequent legislation (David 1993). At the same time, feminist and equality activists more generally were confronted by what seemed to be a fragmentation of political effort with the emergence of identity politics around different forms of feminist, masculine, black and minority ethnic voices (Weiner 1994). Simultaneously, concepts of equality of opportunity and justice (recast as 'entitlement') continued to be promoted within New Right discourses, but in individualistic and weak forms: for instance, the rough justice of the market and the aspirations of the individual were superimposed over post-war welfarism and equality initiatives targeted at identified social groups and communities.

The period from the mid-1970s until the mid-1980s, thus, might be viewed as one where equality issues had a voluntary dimension, of interest mainly to committed politicians, teachers and local authorities. Gender policy development, hence, might originate from local political allegiance, individual teachers or head teachers, an 'awareness raising' incident or involvement in one of several funded curriculum development projects (Whyte *et al.* 1984; Millman and Weiner 1985). Initiatives were often short-term, small-scale, temporary and local, and the national picture was difficult to ascertain. Also, there was little opportunity to evaluate the long-term effects of any policies and practices, though short-term evaluations suggested that the perceptions of some teachers (and pupils) were changing (Whyte *et al.* 1984; ILEA 1986a, b).

By the late 1980s, as the Conservative government increased emphasis on achievement and standards, interest in gender shifted from policy and practice towards patterns of difference in examinations, and between girls and boys of different social groups (Gipps and Murphy 1994). This coincided with the beginning of the educational reforms when analysis focused on the significance and likely effects of the Education Reform Act and of the National Curriculum (see for example, Arnot 1989; Burton and Weiner 1990; Miles and Middleton 1990; Shah 1990; David 1993).

The set of reforms introduced in the UK between 1988 and 1994 were sweeping and extensive, aimed at destabilising and breaking up the post-war professional culture of schooling which was perceived by some in the New Right as mediocre, collectivist and self-serving. Briefly, the key curriculum reforms affecting curriculum shifts outlined in this chapter are:

- The Technical, Educational and Vocational Initiative (TVEI) in 1983 which was initially a pilot experiment in fourteen LEAs aimed at stimulating curriculum development in technical and vocational subjects for the 14 to 18 age range in schools and colleges, later extended in a diluted form across all LEAs.
- Changes in examinations for 16 year olds at the end of secondary school, particularly the introduction of GCSE (1985 for implementation in 1988), which combined GCE O level examinations with the more recently introduced CSE. These changes provided new criteria for examination and assessment and increased use of coursework.
- Creation in 1986 of a new set of vocational qualifications namely, National Vocational Qualifications (NVQs) and General National Vocational Qualifications (GNVQs).
- The Education Reform Act in 1988 and particularly:
  — implementation of the National Curriculum (Core subjects: English, Mathematics and Science, and Welsh in Welsh-medium schools; Foundation subjects: Art, History, Geography, Modern Foreign Language, Technology, Physical Education and Religious Studies.
  — introduction of new forms of assessment for the National Curriculum i.e. Standardised Assessment Targets (SATs).
- Education Acts of 1992 and 1993, and particularly:
  — abolition of HMI and the creation of the Office for Standards in Education (OFSTED) as a relatively autonomous body;
  — introduction of a new system of regular, statutory inspections for schools, conducted by members of OFSTED;
  — increased emphasis on the role of parents;
  — the introduction of statutory requirement for performance tables of school examinations, particularly at the end of compulsory schooling (16+) and for A levels.
- Dearing Report (1994) which led to a more streamlined National Curriculum with the introduction of curriculum choice at KS3 (at 13+).

The EOC study: educational reforms and gender equality in schools

We responded to an invitation to tender for a research project from the Equal Opportunities Commission late in 1993. The main task of the proposed research was to collect and collate evidence and information on educational reforms, gender patterns in examinations and assessment, and equal opportunities in schools in England and Wales. Significantly, the EOC's research division had not collected such information since the mid-1980s. We identified three different methods of data collection for mapping policy and educational changes over a ten-year period, from 1984 to 1994:

- analysis of examination performance data of school leavers especially at 16+ (GCSEs), 18+ (GCE A levels) and 16–18 (vocational qualifications);
- surveys of the perspectives of all LEAs and a sample of primary and secondary state-maintained schools;
- case studies of a small number of LEAs and schools.

Our proposal was based upon our prior knowledge, as feminists, of education although we each brought differing but complementary areas of expertise to the research – involving theoretical, policy, professional and practitioner perspectives. This led us to choose, within the constraints of the terms of reference, a set of questions and a methodology which would produce both a statistical picture and illustrative qualitative examples. However, because of the nature of project funding, we found ourselves unable to adopt an explicitly feminist methodology but, rather, were able to utilise our prior experience of the issues to suffuse the research questions – and to do feminist research *covertly*. In other words, we were not able to address directly what might be called 'women's oppression' in education or to develop an approach from 'the standpoint of women' but rather to look at the relations between the sexes in education (Acker 1994). Moreover, we were required to map trends in gender equality and schooling over a ten-year period, and the contexts in which they occurred rather than to provide wider explanations for the patterns that we might uncover. This mapping exercise was required by the funder, since the EOC needed a basis for recommending new policies, rather than developing a more detailed theoretical explanation. Thus, emphasis was on strategic rather than pure research, and the research was also constrained by limitations of time, money and scope, imposed by the funder.

Evaluating and reflecting on the research

Implementation was also problematic because we had underestimated the extent of the changes in political and policy context. These affected how we could go about mapping change in a *national context*, given that Wales was experiencing changes that were different from those in England. Scotland had its own separately published study (Turner *et al.* 1995) and a separate publication was also produced on Wales (Salisbury 1996). Thus gathering data on examination performance and selecting LEAs and schools for the surveys and case studies proved more complicated than anticipated. Additionally, we needed to translate questionnaires to Welsh LEAs and schools into Welsh. Also due to the complex definitions of different databases, data sets available to us often included some students from Scotland and Northern Ireland.

Furthermore, changes in the definitions of characteristics of schools, part of the changing policy context which promoted marketisation and 'choice', rendered the sampling frame of schools problematic. Changes in status were particularly notable in the case of newly opted-out schools which had been awarded grant maintained (GMS) status. At the time of research, no comprehensive national database existed for all types of school from which we could draw our sample. For this reason and because of insufficient funding for a more wide-ranging survey, we were compelled to exclude from the study all private/independent schools (not directly funded by government), special schools, and sixth form colleges for 16 to 18 year olds. On reflection, the removal of special schools from the study was unfortunate since investigation of the gender patterns and cultures of such schools would have done much to illuminate the overall analysis. In addition, government strategies to fracture previous LEA–school relations affected access to LEAs and schools, and to their perceptions of the nature of changed perform-ance indicators for schools. Nevertheless, such problems were a salutary reminder of the characteristics of the public policy shifts over time, and strongly informed our policy analysis.

The research approach adopted would have been different had the project had a different sponsor (the Economic and Social Research Council (ESRC) rather than the EOC). On the other hand, as an official government organisation, the EOC gave the research the legitimacy to study these issues and aided access to a range of organisations, schools, LEAs, examination boards, etc. Similarly, it afforded us the opportunity, at a critical juncture, to do important and funded research on a topic of interest to us, at a crucial time in the changing context of gender relations. Nevertheless, there were clear limitations of the study, in terms of the funding time-frame and the overarching political sensitivities to gender issues, both of which should not be underestimated.

Research findings

We report below three sets of findings, which cover gender issues but which may not necessarily be related to each other. They draw attention to changes over the ten-year period under investigation: in particular, improvements in examination performances by gender, advances in equal opportunities policy-making and shifts towards what we have called a 'gender-fair' culture.

1 Improvements in examination performance

First, we found clear evidence of schools' success and achievements. The intro-duction of a National Curriculum in 1988 formalised and strengthened the set of core subjects (to which science was added) and foundation subjects taken by all students. Also regular and public forms of testing were introduced. There appeared to be fewer possibilities for gender-specific subject choice at thirteen plus though, as a consequence of the Dearing Report (1994), the number of compulsory subjects in the initial National Curriculum were reduced, and this has reintroduced sex-stereotyping alongside increased choice.

Primary assessment

At the time of the research, regular assessment of primary school children had not yet been instituted. However, pilot assessments had been carried out in the core subjects (English, Mathematics and Science), the results of which suggested that for primary schools in the mid-1990s, girls were achieving at higher levels overall, especially in English. However, boys remained more likely to perform at the extremes – as the best and the worst of the student population.

Examinations at 16 plus

For secondary schools, the introduction of GCSE (in 1985, first examinations in 1988) has led to higher examination entry and performance patterns of both boys and girls, particularly girls. This change more than any other, in our view, has caused the shifts picked up by the media and others. Since 1985, moreover, there has been an increase in the proportion of year eleven pupils (16 plus) entering public examinations (from 91 per cent to 96 per cent). However, the changes in the cohort sizes of the entries for English Language GCSE reveal a drop in the numbers of male students from nearly half a million to just over 304,000 in 1994 and the number of female students has dropped even more proportionately – from outnumbering males by over 30,000 in 1985 to 2,000 fewer female students than males in 1994. Thus there has been the following consequences:

- An increased entry and a closing gender performance gap in most subjects at GCSE apart from Chemistry and Economics which are largely taken by boys, and Social Studies, largely taken by girls.
- Male students continue to achieve relatively less well in English and the Arts, Humanities, Modern Foreign Languages and Technology.
- There has been a *reversal* of the gender gap in GCSE Mathematics and History with near equality in male and female performance in Mathematics, and girls consistently outperforming boys in History.
- Single sex girls' schools continue to be particularly successful in examination performance.

Significantly, both girls and boys are doing well in terms of entering and passing examinations, and both sets of standards are improving not declining as Woodhead (1996) assert.

Examinations at 18 plus

Between 1984 and 1994 (the ten-year period of the study) the numbers of young people aged between 16 and 19 years old increased by 12 per cent overall. The male cohort rose from just over 73,000 in 1985 to just under 78,500 in 1994, and the female cohort, from just under 67,500 in 1985 to just over 87,500 in 1994. The increased numbers of young women entered for A levels has been steeper than for young men, so that by 1994 females outnumbered males for A level entry by over 9,000. However, sex-stereotyped patterns of subject choice and examination performance persist as follows:

- There is a higher male entry into Sciences (Physics, Technology, Computer Studies, Geography, Chemistry, Mathematics) and the level of male entry into English and Modern Foreign Languages is also higher than previously.
- There is a higher female entry for Arts and Humanities.
- Males gain higher A level grades in nearly all subjects, especially Mathematics, Chemistry, Technology, History, English and Modern Foreign Languages. (They also gain the lowest grades.)
- This grade superiority is gradually being eroded with a marked improvement in female performance at A level, particularly in Biology, Social Studies, Art and Design. In the last two there has been a reversal of performance trends in favour of young women.

For those students seeking vocational rather than academic qualifications, subject and course choice has remained heavily sex-stereotyped with boys and girls choosing different subjects, and girls less likely to gain higher awards. Young men are more likely to achieve traditionally 'male' vocational qualifications and young women are more likely to take the NVQs and GNVQs. Such patterns show vocational education as reflecting the 'strong gender bias' associated with the labour market (Felstead *et al.* 1995: 55).

Thus the ten-year period covered by the research is associated with a *considerable rise* in achievement of all compulsory and post-compulsory qualifications, especially among young women. School leavers' data suggest that although young women leave school more qualified than young men, there are important national, regional, ethnic and social differences in gender patterns. Gender differences remain in relation to subject entry in post-compulsory qualifications, although there has been a marked improvement in performance of female students in almost all subjects at A level, especially those where male students have a high level of entry.

2 Equal opportunities policy-making

The research also focused on the context in which the above changes in gender performance in examinations had taken place. We surveyed primary and secondary schools and LEAs to obtain a picture of their perspectives on educational reforms and equal opportunities. What we found was a relatively high profile for equal opportunities policy-making nationally. Hitherto, equal opportunities policy-making had achieved a high profile only in certain metropolitan and urban areas. An unanticipated finding of the project, given the apparent hostility, or at least lack of commitment, of government to equality issues from 1979 onwards, was that by the mid-1990s, two-thirds of schools surveyed had equal opportunities policies on gender, the majority of which (83 per cent) had been developed after 1988. Interestingly, policies tended to focus on curriculum practice and employment concerns rather than on pupil or student performance or on parents.

Thus, a quarter of LEA policies were applicable to staff only and only two out of five policies included parents. Significantly, the main impetus for the development of equal opportunities policies and practices had come from LEAs and head teachers in the case of primary schools, and from LEAs, head teachers, committed teachers and TVEI in the case of secondary schools. English and Welsh LEAs generally reported an increased role in the development of gender equality in the primary sector since the period of reform with neither parents nor parent governors seems to have played an active part in the development of equal opportunities policy-making. Equality issues tended not to be viewed as a high priority by most schools and LEAs and less than 10 per cent gave gender issues a high priority. There was also evidence of wide variation in awareness and application of equal opportunities or understanding of changed performance trends relating to girls and boys.

Significantly, where equal opportunities initiatives developed, they tended to be locally focused and addressed mainly inspectoral requirements of the Office for Standards in Education (OFSTED), indicators of 'value addedness', such as raising performance, governor training, and male underachievement. The reduction in the role and influence of LEAs also led to relative isolation in policy-making with little attempt to disseminate beyond the immediate school cluster group or the individual school staffroom. The equal opportunities culture of the mid-1990s has been one that has tended to have a narrow focus, and to fuse social justice issues with performance standards and improvement, with a greater emphasis on the latter.

3 Gender fair culture

Project evidence points to the fact that the gender cultures of schooling have been transformed in the ten years covered by the study. The aim of much early feminist educational work was to encourage a school culture in which girls could prosper and raise their aspirations and achievements (e.g. Byrne 1978; Whyte *et al.* 1984; Weiner 1985). A sign of its success perhaps is that students in the 1990s seem more aware and sensitive to changing cultural expectations, with many girls and young women exhibiting confidence about their abilities and future, especially in terms of employment, and boys and young men more sensitive to gender and equality debates. Labour market and cultural transformation has led to changed vocational aspirations for both boys and girls, with girls tending to see the necessity for paid employment and their improved employment possibilities, particularly in the expanding service sector. The availability of part-time work, though lower paid, tends also to fit in with women's traditional family commitments. On the other hand, the employment opportunities of young men have contracted as conventional male manufacturing jobs have disappeared, leading to a higher degree of uncertainty about what the future has to offer, particularly for working-class youth.

However, while schools have seemed to benefit from changing pupil and student cultures, the management of education exhibits no equivalent changes. In fact, schools and LEAs (and also government education agencies, political parties, education quangos, higher education institutions etc.) continue to be shaped largely by cultures of (white) male management (in staffing, governing bodies and other institutional hierarchies) which have demonstrated little interest in equality issues. Unexpectedly, given the high ratio of female staff, this has been a particularly noticeable feature of primary schools.

Feminist research for educational change

Mapping change in relation to gender equality and schooling can be seen from an analytical and an academic perspective, broadly concerned with enhancing knowledge *about* schooling or from a policy perspective broadly concerned with enhancing knowledge *for* schooling. In the latter case, developing strategies for policy development or change are likely to be a higher priority, though both perspectives are susceptible to a range of research methodologies. However, feminist research perspectives do not easily map onto such broad distinctions which polarise 'pure' or 'fundamental' research and strategic or policy research.

Feminist approaches, in our view, are both analytical and strategic – concerned with social justice, social change and reflexivity. Indeed, feminist research is crucially about locating and providing the necessary evidence to bring about improvements in girls and women's educational, social and economic situations. Thus feminist research can be defined in a variety of ways, linked to wider social contexts. The classic definition of a feminist research perspective was provided more than twenty-five years ago by Ann Oakley (1974): 'A feminist perspective consists of keeping in the forefront of one's mind the lifestyles, activities and interests of more than half of humanity – women.' Whether research by a feminist is necessarily feminist research is a question raised by Sandra Acker as follows:

> feminist research, like other research, is shaped by its surroundings, and . . . in certain circumstances the best that can be expected is work that is *covertly* feminist . . . we might think of feminist work as that which is informed at any point by a feminist framework
>
> (1994: 55: author's italics)

Acker further points out that feminists, more than others, 'have been fruitful in the production of scholarship and research; moreover they have engaged in unusually extensive reflection about what it is they do' (ibid.: 56–7). In the last decade, feminism has been influenced by post-structuralism and postmodernism, which focus on discourse analysis to understand the shifting nature of public policy debates on the public versus the private, and also to explore the complexities and power/knowledge relationships that constitute women's lives.

Some feminists have thus offered a new interpretation of standard feminist social analysis, emphasising the value of discourse analysis as a way of knowing or understanding. As Skeggs puts it, however, this has resulted in:

> a move away from the principles of social democracy that informed feminist educational theory and practice . . . It is now realised that social democratic principles only reinforce individualism and the sexual divisions within and between the public and private domains.
>
> (1994: 87–8)

In the changed contexts of higher education and academic research in the 1990s, academic feminists have extended their analysis of women's experiences by taking into account women's material realities *and* diverse identities. For feminists, centring equity and social justice in their work has become inextricably bound up with struggles for power within academic fields (David *et al.* 1996). As Ladwig and Gore point out, reflexivity demands that any discussion of social privilege and power needs to pay attention to 'questions of *academic* power and privilege, competition and contestation' (1994: 236).

Given these changing contexts and definitions, how are we to understand the changing nature of policy and gender relations and of feminist research? There are several interrelated issues. Can feminist research merely consist in self-styled feminists asking questions about gender relations or does such research entail particular methodological approaches? If feminist research is principally about setting initial questions, does prior active involvement or immersion in the issues constitute at least a prerequisite? Is feminist research about taking a particular perspective such as Dorothy Smith's 'standpoint of women' (1987) or Donna Haraway's (1988) 'situated knowledge'? Haraway suggests that feminist research seeks to know more from those with a partiality of vision who both understand the nature of multiple truths and retain a sense of structural inequality:

> We seek those ruled by partial sight and limited voice – not partiality for its own sake, but, rather, for the sake of connections and unexpected openings situated knowledges make possible. Situated knowledges are about communities, not about isolated individuals.
>
> (Haraway 1988: 590)

Can such feminist research be conducted for public bodies such as, in Britain, the Equal Opportunities Commission, which has its own strategic policy aims and responsibilities? Would such research be so constrained by the terms and conditions set by the funding body as to render research evidence and/or analysis problematic? On the other hand, would a feminist perspective preclude immersion in externally funded strategic or policy oriented research, such as that defined by the EOC? Or to take Acker's point, might feminists be compelled to take a *covert* research position?

Shifts in research context: taking a critical stance

The question of the relationship between research and policy has been a concern for social and educational policy researchers in the UK for the past thirty years or so, who have become increasingly involved in the policy process. But that greater involvement has been patchy, and has been affected also by changes affecting the academic and research community and also those determining government stances and priorities. Moreover, a number of researchers (including feminists) have taken a critical approach to the overtly right-wing policy stance of British government between 1979 and 1997 (e.g. David 1993; Bowe *et al.* 1994; Skeggs 1994).

The stance of the New Right was responsible for a shift over the last decade, from 'pure' academic research to research that is, in the terms of the British Research Councils, particularly the Economic and Social Research Council (ESRC), 'policy-oriented and/or relevant'. British academic research whether funded directly through the Higher Education Funding Councils (HEFCE) or the Research Councils now has to be designed to be of use both to academic and to non-academic communities. Moreover, the shifts in research funding (whether pure or strategic/policy oriented) to customer/contractor types of research and to tendering have altered the landscape of research, especially that of social scientific research. If the contractor's main aim now is to get value for money, the nature of research and the knowledge generated are bound to be different, given the discursive shifts in the characteristics of research. Research has become an 'industry'; in which 'pure', 'policy-oriented' and 'strategic' research are entangled, enmeshed and difficult to separate.

This shift in research funding and focus has resulted in questions about the nature and purpose of policy research. Particularly from a feminist point of view, policy research has needed to adopt a dual role of exploring *and* promoting gender equality in education. There are no easy answers to such questions and given the changes in the political landscape of the 1980s and 1990s in Britain, many of those concerned with social justice issues, such as feminists, may have been compelled to shift to a more critical stance on policy and practice involvement as Skeggs (quoted above) has noted, and to put less emphasis on action and change.

Designing a feminist research project in a cold climate

Thus, the question of an appropriate research approach regarding gender equality needs to be contextualised within the changed research arena involving evidence about the nature of policy shifts. A useful instance of the shifting nature of policy-making and policy research is the current interest in male academic performance and 'underachievement', an issue claimed to be 'the most disturbing problem we face in the whole education system' by Chris Woodhead, head of the Office for Standards in Education (OFSTED). Woodhead argues that solutions to the problem of male underachievement are not dependent upon 'all-encompassing psycho-social theory' but on a range of educational policy changes such as raising standards of literacy and numeracy, curriculum developments and education for parenting. According to Woodhead, this is especially important for boys living in single-parent families who have no male role models. A main argument is for strategies and/or policies to restore boys' sense of self-worth as the foundation of their desire to learn; in other words, it is believed that there is currently 'a crisis in masculinity' (Woodhead 1996: 55). This discourse of male underachievement has sharply affected the agenda for feminist researchers of gender.

For policy-makers such as Woodhead, such issues are self-evident and political, assumed to be a crisis by use of phraseology such as 'the most disturbing problem', rather than raised by careful explication of research evidence. The so-called crisis surfaced in Britain in 1994 as a consequence of increased government and media emphasis on comparisons in school and individual examination and performance levels. In the press and media in 1994, typical headlines included 'The trouble with boys'(*The Sunday Times*, 19 June 1994); 'Girls trounce the boys in the examination league table' (*The Times*, 3 September 1994); 'Can girls do better without boys?' (*Daily Express*, 11 November 1994); 'Brainy girls are top of the class' (*Today*, 22 November 1994). Similar debates about a moral crisis have surfaced in other countries: for example, in Australia, Foster (1995: 54) identifies a recent 'backlash period' against gains made by girls as a result of a decade of policy-making deliberately aimed at girls and young women, as has Faludi (1991), in the USA.

In the main, however, media debates about education tend not to foreground the question of gender. Woodhead's approach may be contrasted with the British journalist, Will Hutton's full-page analysis (1996) of 'the looming crisis in education' and his 'recipe for change' written at about the same time. In his left-leaning (New Labour) account, no attention is given by Hutton to issues of gender equality or equal opportunities generally. The problem, as constituted by Hutton, is one involving a relatively crude social class analysis, and a reversion, in terms of policy solutions, to the recognition of 'differing abilities' and different educational solutions for different social groupings. In this respect, not focusing on strategies to reduce gender inequality may be seen to be equally problematic. However, both men identify a crisis in education: Woodhead asserts that it has to do with masculinity whereas Hutton presents a gender-neutral approach but provides a recipe for change that would, implicitly if not explicitly, also promote new forms of masculinity.

There is confusion, however, about whether boys' performance has indeed deteriorated as girls' performance has improved or, whether educational standards are falling or improving and the contribution of shifting gender relations to these patterns. How to map and explain these patterns as a basis for developing new strategies, as we found, is complex and fraught with problems of definitions, politics and analysis. Moreover, there are other questions to consider, which focus on processes rather than on outcomes of equal opportunities policies and/or educational reforms. A feminist perspective, as we have noted, would want to investigate the policies, processes of policy-making and implementation around equal opportunities in order to promote change as well as uncovering the reasons for differential patterns in girls' or boys' performances in examinations. Given then the confused nature of the public debates, we suggest a number of key issues concerning research on gender equality and schooling:

- the significance of changing gender patterns in examination performance for both academic and vocational qualifications;
- the impact of policy changes on gender relations in the processes of schooling;
- the consequence of explicit policies for equal opportunities on both the practices and performances of girls and boys in school;
- the effects of wider social changes on what happens in schools;
- the nature of changing gender relations and their sources and influences in families and in schools.

These issues emerged before and during the research project and profoundly affected how we carried out the research and our ability to explain change.

Problems of explaining change

As we have seen, the EOC project was a mapping exercise of gender patterns and trends in education over a ten-year period. Three different sets of evidence were produced – on examination performance, the extent of equal opportunities policy-making, and cultural shifts in approaches to gender in schooling. In the three domains, there have been some shifts and improvements, but we cannot claim a relationship between them. Nor, as feminists, are we able to claim that any changes may be attributed to feminist or equal opportunities activity. We can speculate nevertheless on the wider changes, in which women and feminists especially have played their part, particularly socio-economic trends and changes which may have contributed to some of the shifts identified.

First, we have found evidence of improvements in examination performance of both boys and girls, but particularly of girls 'closing the gender gap'. However, as we have noted, the picture is not as stark as many political and media pundits would have us believe. Girls are not outperforming boys overall. They are now performing equally as well as boys at GCSE, and in a small number of subjects, better than boys. They have closed the gender gap in many subjects at A level, but there remains evidence of considerable sex-stereotyping in subject entry and in performance. In vocational qualifications, sex-stereotyping is an enduring feature, and boys on the whole still do better. Nevertheless, we would want to acknowledge the achievements of teachers and schools in realising students' potential and in producing these kinds of successes.

This is particularly important since the schools in England and Wales which we studied have been implicated in a continuously changing social and political context in which the schools and teachers have been subjected to what Ball (1990) has called 'a discourse of derision'. Our data suggest, however, that curricular changes, especially those associated with the National Curriculum, have enabled more students to participate in the wider curriculum; sex-stereotyping tends only to emerge in post-compulsory courses when greater subject choice is available. Moreover, moves towards the use of performance indicators and the monitoring of gender patterns in schooling have enabled us to identify and present these patterns. The development of systematic data collection and the monitoring of educational processes as well as performance are urgent priorities. For instance, establishing the part that different types of school play in equality of outcome has been singularly difficult in such a changing environment.

We found pockets of good practice in schools and a changing climate towards what we have called a 'gender-fair culture', where girls and boys have shown greater tolerance towards each other and greater awareness of gender issues. However, given the changing political and policy climate which has also suffused the contexts in which research is now conducted, this particular study has not been able to account for changes in gender performances or practices in schools. We remain puzzled by some of the evidence that we have uncovered; in particular, the fact that there is a changing climate in schools – a gender-fair culture – with respect to the equal treatment of pupils, if not all staff. We are unable to account for improvements in examination performance either in relation to educational reforms or in relation to equal opportunities policy-making. Many of the changes that the project identified had already begun to emerge before the main period of educational reform (1988 to 1994). And in fact, the effects of the reforms themselves will not be able to be fully evaluated until the decade is over.

However, it seems clear that a feminist approach which foregrounds gender has enabled us to be explicit about changing gender relations and what happens in schools and to acknowledge the successes of many schools, especially in the context of heavily constrained resources. We suggest that girls are doing well and boys are only falling behind relatively, not absolutely. The future, however, remains a concern. Our research did not enable us to detect which girls and boys are succeeding and which are failing, though this will be explored in a future publication (see Arnot *et al.* 1999). And the shift towards 'male underachievement' in gender research on education, seemingly, masks a reversal towards research on male-as-norm and away from broadening exploration of gender relations.

Despite the constraints of externally commissioned research, we have been able to apply feminist perspectives and approaches to the consideration of our material. Indeed, we have been provided with an opportunity to explore changes in equal opportunities and gender patterns and processes in schooling, and to update and extend debates within education feminism (Stone 1994). However, constraints on project time prevented the development of wider explanations for the three sets of changes that we have identified. Neither have we been able to make linkages between girls' improved examination performance, increased equal opportunities policy-making and shifts towards a gender-fair school culture.

What would constitute an adequate explanation for the changes that we have witnessed? Inevitably we draw on feminist perspectives to seek an explanation, and also on shifts observed in the wider social and economic arenas, such as the labour market, the family and the influence of feminism as a new social movement. It may well be the case that the broader changes in labour markets and especially women's work and new employment patterns can explain why girls currently opt to take more public examinations. Girls may also be influenced by their mothers', teachers' and other women's lives, seeing labour market participation as a better 'career' choice compared with marriage, motherhood and dependence on a male wage.

For us, then, a feminist perspective on education, society and culture provides a means of explaining the what, why and how of policy and practice shifts in schooling. Such a perspective suggests that the motor of cultural and sexual change is driven by wider social movements and understandings, and not by specific education policy-makers or politicians, themselves inevitably reflecting the ideologies and concerns of the world they seek to change.

References

Acker, S. (1994) *Gendered Education: Sociological Reflections on Women, Teaching and Feminism*, Buckingham: Open University Press.

Arnot, M. (1989) 'Consultation or legitimation? Race and gender politics and the making of the national curriculum', *Critical Social Policy*, 27, 3: 20–39.

Arnot, M. and Weiner, G. (eds) (1987) *Gender and the Politics of Schooling*, London: Hutchinson.

Arnot, M., David, M.E. and Weiner, G. (1996) *Educational Reforms and Gender Equality in Schools*, Manchester: Equal Opportunities Commission, Research Discussion Series No. 17.

—— (1999), *Closing the Gender Gap*: Post-war Education and Social Change. Cambridge: Polity Press.

Ball, S. J. (1990) *Politics and Policy Making in Education*, London: Routledge.

Bowe, R., Ball, S. and Gewirtz, S. (1994) 'Captured by the discourse? Issues and concerns in researching "Parental Choice"', *British Journal of the Sociology of Education* 15, 1: 63–78.

Burton, L. (ed.) (1986) *Girls into Maths Can Go*, East Sussex: Holt, Rhinehart and Winston.

Burton, L. and Weiner, G. (1990) 'Social justice and the National Curriculum', *Research Papers in Education*, 5, 3: 203–28.

Byrne, E. (1978) *Women and Education*, London: Tavistock.

Chisholm, L. and Holland, J. (1986) 'Girls and occupational choice: anti-sexism in action in a curriculum development project', *British Journal of Sociology of Education*, 7, 4.

David, M.E. (1980) *The State, the Family and Education*, London: Routledge and Kegan Paul.

—— (1993) *Parents, Gender and Educational Reform*, Cambridge: The Polity Press.

David, M.E., Davies, J., Edwards, R., Reay, D. and Standing, K. (1996) 'Mothering and education: reflexivity and feminist methodology', in V. Walsh and L. Morley (eds) *Breaking Boundaries: Women in Higher Education*, London: Taylor and Francis.

David, M.E., Edwards, R., Hughes, M. and Ribbens, J. (1993) *Mothers and Education Inside Out? Exploring Family-Education Policy and Experience*, London: Macmillan.

Dearing, R. (1994) *The National Curriculum and its Assessment: Final Report*, London: SCAA.

Faludi, S. (1991) *Backlash: The Undeclared War against Women*, London: Hodder and Stroughton.

Felstead, A., Goodwin, J. and Green, F. (1995) *Measuring Up to the National Training Targets: Women's Attainment of Vocational Qualifications*, Research Report, Centre for Labour Market Studies, Leicester: University of Leicester.

Foster, V. (1995) 'Barriers to equality in Australian girls' schooling for citizenship in the 1990s', *Lararutbildning Och Forskning I Umea* 2, 3/4: 47–60.

Gillborn, D. (1995) *Racism and Antiracism in Real Schools*, Buckingham: Open University Press.

Gipps, C. and Murphy, P. (1994) *A Fair Test? Assessment, Achievement and Equity*, Buckingham: Open University Press.

Haraway, D. (1988) 'Situated knowledges: the science question in feminism and the privilege of partial perspective', *Feminist Studies* 14, 3: 575–600.

Hutton, W. (1996) 'The looming crisis in education', *The Guardian Outlook* 2 March, p. 21.

Inner London Education Authority (1986a) *Primary Matters*, London: ILEA.

—— (1986b) *Secondary Issues*, London: ILEA.

Kelly, A. (1985) 'Changing schools and changing society: some reflections on the Girls into Science and Technology project', in M. Arnot (ed.) *Race and Gender: Equal Opportunities Policies in Education*, Oxford: Pergamon.

Ladwig, J.G. and Gore, J.(1994) 'Extending power and specifying method within the discourse of activist research', in A. Gitlin (ed.) *Power and Method: Political Activism and Educational Research*, London: Routledge.

Lees, S. (1987) 'The structure of sexual relations in school', in M. Arnot and G. Weiner (eds) *Gender and the Politics of Schooling*, London: Hutchinson.

Miles, S. and Middleton, C. (1990) 'Girls' education in the balance: the ERA and inequality', in M. Flude and M. Hammer (eds) *The Education Reform Act 1988: Its Origins and Implications*, Basingstoke: Falmer Press.

Millman, V. (1987) 'Teacher as researcher: a new tradition for research on gender', in G. Weiner and M. Arnot (eds) *Gender Under Scrutiny*, London: Hutchinson.

Millman, V. and Weiner, G. (1985) *Sex Differentiation in Schools: Is There Really a Problem?*, York: Longman.

Minhas, R. (1986) 'Race, gender and class: making the connections', in ILEA (ed.) *Secondary Issues*, London: ILEA.

Oakley, A. (1974) *The Sociology of Housework*, London: Martin Robertson.

Orr, P. (1984) 'Sex bias in schools: national perspectives', in J. Whyte, R. Deem, L. Kant and M. Cruickshank (eds) *Girl Friendly Schooling*, London: Methuen.

Pratt, J. Bloomfield, J. and Scale, C. (1984) *Option Choice: A Question of Equal Opportunity*, Slough: NFER–Nelson.

Salisbury, J. (1996) *Educational Equality and Gender Equality in Welsh Schools*, Cardiff: Wales EOC.

Shah, S. (1990) 'Equal opportunity issues in the context of the National Curriculum: a black perspective', *Gender and Education*, 2, 3: 309–18.

Skeggs, B. (1994) 'The constraints of neutrality: the 1988 ERA and feminist research', in D. Halpin and B. Troyna (eds) *Researching Education Policy: Ethical and Methodological Issues*, London: The Falmer Press.

Smith, D. E. (1987) *The Everyday World as Problematic*, Buckingham: Open University Press.

Spender, D. (1980) *Man Made Language*, London: Routledge and Kegan Paul.

Stone, L. (ed.) (1994) *The Education Feminist Reader*, New York: Routledge.

Turner, E., Riddell, S. and Brown, S. (1995) *Gender Equality in Scottish Schools: The Impact of Recent Reforms*, Manchester: Equal Opportunities Commission, Research Discussion Series.

Weiner, G. (ed.) (1985) *Just a Bunch of Girls*, Milton Keynes: Open University Press.

—— (1994) *Feminisms in Education*, Buckingham: Open University Press.

Weiner, G. and Arnot, M. (1987) 'Teachers and gender politics', in M. Arnot and G. Weiner (eds) *Gender and the Politics of Schooling*, London: Hutchinson.

Whyld, J. (1983) *Sexism in the Secondary Curriculum*, London: Harper and Row.

Whyte, J. (1983) *Beyond the Wendy House: Sex Role Stereotyping in Primary Schools*, York: Longman.

Whyte, J., Deem, R., Kant, L. and Cruickshank, M. (eds) (1984) *Girl Friendly Schooling*, London: Methuen.

Woodhead, C. (1996) 'Boys who learn to be losers: on the white male culture of failure', *The Times*, 6 March.

2 Equal opportunities and educational reform in Scotland
The limits of liberalism

Sheila Riddell

Introduction

This chapter is based on work funded by the Equal Opportunities Commission and carried out at the University of Stirling between 1994 and 1995 with Sally Brown and Eileen Turner (see Turner *et al.* 1995, for a full account of this work). The chapter begins by outlining the ways in which a range of feminisms have found expression in equal opportunities work in schools. In the 1980s, as the second wave of feminism began to lose its initial impetus, tensions emerged between liberal and radical approaches both in the wider field and in the educational arena (Middleton 1984; Acker 1994; Weiner 1994). More recently, in education and other social arena, debates have surfaced between what has been termed the politics of recognition and the politics of redistribution (Phillips 1997; Young 1990). Within the context of these ideological tensions, the nature of gender equality strategies adopted in Scottish education at national, regional and local level are analysed. Subsequently, the impact of educational reforms of the 1980s and 1990s, driven by marketisation and new managerialism, are investigated, with a particular focus on two case study secondary schools in one region. It is argued that at national level in Scotland, equal opportunities discourse has tended to be liberal in nature, based on the assumption that women and girls must compete with men and boys in a gender-neutral system. This apparent neutrality has at times concealed a desire to control and limit women's sphere of activity, reinforced by strong Calvinist elements in Scottish culture. At regional and school level within Scotland, gender equality policies have tended to be more variegated, reflecting a range of interpretations of national policy and not necessarily accepting the male as norm. The focus of this chapter is an exploration of the specific impact of educational reforms on two schools with well-developed, albeit distinctively different, approaches to equal opportunities policies within an authority which had also adopted a positive approach to gender equality work. These schools, which differed with regard to socio-economic status (SES), exemplified what the region regarded as 'good practice' in the area of equal opportunities and were deliberately selected in order to provide an acid test of the effect of educational reforms on gender equality policies. Had we selected schools and an authority where little equal opportunities work had taken place, the impact of a range of educational innovations would have been more difficult to pinpoint. The higher SES school interpreted equal opportunities in terms of identity recognition, while the lower SES school focused more closely on economic redistribution. Within these differing contexts, it is possible to explore the impact of a range of educational changes and to speculate about the future of a range of approaches to equal opportunities.

Scottish education and gender equality

Before exploring national, regional and local approaches to gender equality in Scotland, an outline of some features of national culture, of which education plays a major role, is provided. Maclean (1994) argues that a powerful myth in Scotland concerns the excellence and democratic nature of its education system. For example, Anderson (1985a: 82) quotes a popular history of Scottish education from 1912 which described: 'the sons of the laird, the minister and the ploughman, seated at the same bench, taught the same lessons and disciplined with the same strip of leather'. The myth suggested the gifted 'lad o' pairts' could, by dint of hard work and native ability, attain educational success and subsequently high status within a profession. This belief in equality of access and meritocracy, according to Paterson (1983), arose as a result of the struggle for survival in a poor country where both individualism and collectivism were essential to 'winning a share of the few resources available'.

Maclean examines the extent to which the idea of the lad o' pairts stands up to critical scrutiny, concluding that the myth is not entirely without substance but conceals significant and enduring underlying inequalities. The egalitarian view of Scottish education is supported by the existence of a public school in every parish in the seventeenth century, in contrast with England's tardiness in developing a system of mass education. During the eighteenth and nineteenth centuries, some working-class students were able to gain entry to university – in the 1860s, 33 per cent of students were the sons of professionals, 16 per cent the sons of the commercial and industrial middle classes, 15 per cent the sons of farmers, 6 per cent the sons of shopkeepers and white collar-workers and 23 per cent the sons of the skilled working classes. Very few students, however, made it to university from farming, fishing or labouring backgrounds and since the working class was much larger than the middle class, it has been calculated that 'a minister's son was about a hundred times more likely to go to university than a miner's son, and that the sons of artisans had five or six times the chance of university attendance than labourers' sons' (Maclean 1994). According to Anderson, 'the inclusiveness of Scottish secondary schooling was at a high but not exceptional level within the essentially elitist norms common to all European countries at the time' (1985b: 466).

Developing these points, Paterson argued:

> the school's narrow definitions of 'talent' and 'success' corresponded to a
> Calvinistic view of an elite with god given ability and, together, these two

ideologies were sufficiently powerful to convince the unfortunate lad without 'pairts' that it was all his own fault and that he had no option but to rest content with second or third place.

(1983: 20)

As well as excluding poorer people, the Scottish system also excluded women; as Fewell and Paterson (1990) pointed out, there is no tradition of the 'lass o' pairts' and women in Scotland continue to play a relatively circumscribed role in public life. For example, they make up 51 per cent of all teachers but only 7 per cent of head teachers in state secondary schools. To summarise, despite Scotland's belief in its excellent and egalitarian educational tradition, in reality it offered a type of equality of opportunity which 'could serve inequality by acting as a safety valve preserving social stability' (Maclean 1994).

Although the problems encountered by girls within the Scottish education system have been largely ignored, since the early 1970s their education performance has improved relative to that of boys and overall they now perform significantly better at both Standard and Higher grade (Scottish Qualifications Authority 1997). Social class differences appear to be deeply entrenched and intertwined with the effects of gender (see Figure 2.1). An important reason for the narrowing of social class differences may be attributed to significant improvements in the performance of girls in social classes III, IV and V, coupled with the fact that boys in social classes I and II have failed to improve their performance to any great extent.

It should be borne in mind that even though the performance of Scottish girls may outstrip their male counterparts, this does not necessarily imply the existence of a system which recognises their achievements. Hills (1990) condemns the 'Senga Syndrome' (the name Senga is Agnes spelt backwards, used for working-class girls on the west coast of Scotland), whereby a bright working-class girl obtains an ordinary degree and a teaching certificate before moving back into the classroom, without ever considering other possibilities which might offer wider horizons. The competitive liberalism that characterised Scottish education was built on the assumption that girls could be allowed a foot in the door of the academic establishment, but must simultaneously be taught that overt ambition was unbecoming in a woman. In the next section, the development of equal opportunities initiatives in Scotland in the 1980s and the 1990s is traced, in tandem with the advent of market-driven reforms.

The development of national and regional equal opportunities policies in Scotland

As in the rest of the UK, before the 1970s it was assumed in Scotland that girls and boys were being educated for different roles in life, with girls working prior to marriage and child-rearing and boys adopting the role of principal breadwinner. In 1975, the Scottish Education Department published an HMI report on gender divisions within the curriculum, noting that a common curriculum was

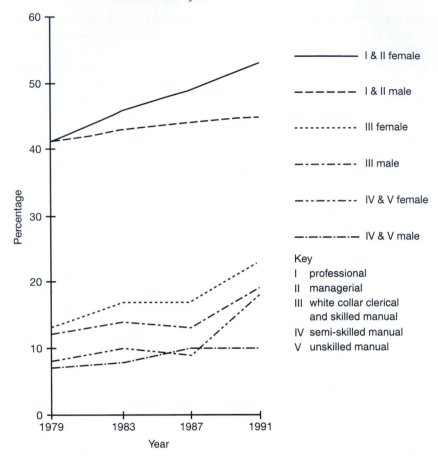

Figure 2.1 Young people in highest attainment band (gaining three or more Highers), by class and gender

Source: Data from the Scottish School Leavers Survey in Furlong and Cartmel (1997)

generally offered to boys and girls in the first two years of secondary school, except in physical education and vocational subjects, where boys and girls were still educated separately. HMI noted the emergence of gender divisions in S3, particularly in Physics and Biology, the former dominated by boys and the latter by girls, but rather than attributing blame to the school, HMI felt that parents were principally responsible since:

> [they] assume the continued existence of 'boys'' subjects and 'girls'' subjects. As parents, they wish to protect their children from what they fear to be the 'notoriety' or ridicule attaching to unconventional subject choices. They are, it appears, afraid of the vocational implications of departure from well-known curricular norms.

> (SED 1975: 28)

HMI also drew attention to schools' hesitancy in allowing pupils to cross gender boundaries:

> The practice in all schools was to examine thoroughly the motives of each pupil opting abnormally and to test the views of parents in the matter. Where pupil motivation appeared to be strong, vocational requirement was established and parents were in support (as well as fully aware of the possible implications), schools were prepared to accept the position and make arrangements accordingly.
>
> (SED 1975: 29)

Although the practices described above scarcely count as equal treatment, HMI was careful to apportion no blame to the school for the persistence of gender divisions, concluding with some sanguinity that there was 'no evidence of schools acting deliberately on unproved educational assumptions (e.g. that girls have less mathematical ability than boys) or educational prejudice'.

The passage of the Sex Discrimination Act in 1976 saw the publication of a circular which drew schools' attention to the fact that it was now illegal to prevent girls from joining 'a course or class to which boys are admitted and vice versa' (SED 1976). However, it was evident that despite the fact that HMI appeared to have identified the existence of gendered disourses in schools, these were regarded as simply common sense rather than problematic.

The tendency to identify but then justify unequal treatment of males and females within the Scottish education system was also evident in a report published by Strathclyde Region entitled *Sex Equality in the Education Service: The Report of a Regional Working Party* (Strathclyde Regional Council 1988). While noting marked inequalities in the position of women and men in the teaching force in Strathclyde, the report maintained that rather than blaming features of recruitment or appointments procedures: 'the relative absence of women from promoted posts must be attributed to their lesser incidence of application' (1988: 24).

The overall message, then, from the early HMI and Strathclyde Region publications was that the education system was beyond reproach in terms of reproducing inequality and the problem was located outwith the school in the wider society. A rather more critical approach was evident in policy documents and statements produced by the Educational Institute for Scotland (EIS) (1989) and the General Teaching Council for Scotland (GTC) (1991). The EIS, the largest teachers' union, produced a series of leaflets 'as a positive assertion of action against sexism', designed not to make girls into surrogate boys but to question the basis of male behaviour. In classrooms, it stated:

> boys demand and receive a generous share of teacher time;
>
> they receive a disproportionate share of hands on experience (e.g. in science or computing);

they receive apologies from teachers when asked to undertake non-traditional tasks;

they are rewarded for being assertive;

they are advised not to act like girls;

they receive a disproportionate share of coveted class materials.

(para 3.2.5, p. 5)

This perspective was clearly far more radical than that of either Scottish HMI or Strathclyde Region, but it is none the less interesting that the NUT in England had been producing publications on equal opportunities since the 1970s.

Scottish local authorities were similarly sluggish in introducing gender equality policies. Whereas English municipal authorities placed gender alongside ethnicity at the forefront of their political activities in the 1980s, most Scottish authorities did not introduce gender equality policies until the early 1990s, in the case of one large Labour authority only weeks before its abolition under Local Government Reorganisation (LGR) in 1996. Turner *et al.* (1995) located the twelve Scottish authorities in existence prior to LGR in a continuum. Two positions on the continuum, *laissez-faire* and open door, might be equated with weak equal opportunities positions, while the positive action and structural transformation positions drew on strong equal opportunities discourses (see earlier discussion). Most authorities, particularly those in rural areas, clustered in the weak equal opportunities positions, while in Labour-controlled urban areas, there was a greater tendency to adopt a strong equal opportunities position, promoting wider access but with an understanding that this would necessitate wider social change. Before looking closely at the development of equal opportunities policies in two schools during a time of rapid policy innovation, let us look more closely at the characteristics of educational reform in Scotland.

The nature of educational reforms in Scotland

Within the research specification provided by the EOC for the study (Turner *et al.* 1995), no indication was given as to which reforms should be ruled in or out of the frame. The researchers decided it was necessary to take account of a broad range of changes introduced during the lifespan of the Conservative government which came to office in 1979. It is important to bear in mind that some of these changes had their ideological origins in the previous Labour government which was concerned with widening access to the curriculum and assessment. Table 2.1 summarises some of the central reforms and their English equivalents. Some of these reforms, such as technology academies and opted out schools, having their origin in the English context, failed to transplant north of the Border and swiftly died a death. Others, such as parental choice of school, were tried out in Scotland

Table 2.1 Scottish educational reforms and their English counterparts

Scottish reforms	English equivalents
Self-governing schools (abolished by Labour government after 1997 election)	Grant maintained schools
Parental choice of school	Parental choice of school
5–14 programme	National Curriculum
Standard Grade	GCSE
TVEI (Technical and Vocational Educational Initiative)	TVEI
Performance Indicators + publication of school performance records	League tables
Technology academies	City technology colleges
Devolved school management	Local management of schools

before its introduction in England and was taken up with some enthusiasm by parents, notwithstanding the fact that their consequences were not necessarily regarded as an unalloyed good (Adler 1997). Yet other reforms, such as the implementation of school boards in Scotland and governing bodies in England, were intended to work differently but their outcomes were not necessarily radically different (ibid.). A unifying theme of the reforms, introduced during the third term of the Conservative government, was to subject the public sector to the discipline of the market by harnessing the power of the parent as consumer (Deakin 1994). However, while power was handed to parents and the school, other powers, notably over the curriculum and with regard to the monitoring of performance, were centralised. Let us focus now on the impact of these reforms on gender equality policies which, as we have seen, were in their infancy at national and local levels.

Curricular reforms and equal opportunities

The discourse of gender equality was very slow to appear in curricular documents. Standard grade, the Scottish equivalent of GCSE, arose as a result of the Munn and Dunning Reports (SED 1977a, 1977b). These did not explicitly mention gender equality, but established the principle of a common curriculum entitlement for all in the last two years of compulsory schooling. Although all pupils were obliged to take a subject in each of the eight curricular modes, the choice of subjects meant that pupils were still able to divide along traditional gender lines and by and large chose to do so (see Croxford, this volume).

The first major source of innovation was the Technical and Vocational Education Initiative, piloted in 1984 and extended to all education authorities by 1987.

Funded by the Manpower Services Commission, it was treated with considerable suspicion north of the Border since it was regarded as introducing the values and practices of the private sector into education (Weir 1988; Turner *et al.* 1994). However, once teachers recognised it as an additional source of funding which could readily be domesticated, the take-up was enthusiastic. One of the criteria for TVEI funding was the ability to demonstrate that equal opportunities policies were being pursued and people who had not previously engaged with these ideas undertook audits of examination outcomes, subject choices, and so on. Some of these audits were perhaps over-optimistic in their assessment of success. One undated document from the Department of Employment, for instance, announced that 'particularly encouraging is the virtual elimination of traditional gender imbalances in the take-up of science'.

The 5–14 Programme, Scotland's national curriculum, also made reference to gender equality issues. A small pack of materials dealing with cross-curricular themes was published alongside the main 5–14 documents (SCCC 1993), with one section devoted to gender awareness, providing advice to teachers on the use of non-stereotypical materials, appropriate language and positive action to combat sexist language or behaviour. The curricular documents published by the SOEID had rather less to say about gender equality, although the document on Reporting (SOED 1992) had a page on equal opportunities. The 5–14 Programme in Scotland did not arouse passions in the same way as the English National Curriculum. This was partly because of the disposal of formal testing at an early point, but also because the curriculum appeared to be less tightly circumscribed and was promoted to teachers as what they were doing anyway. Some felt that gender issues could have been given greater prominence, but generally any hint that these had been brought in from the cold was welcomed.

Management reforms and equal opportunities

As noted above, the reform of school management in Scotland spanned more than a decade, with parental choice enshrined within the 1981 Education (Scotland) Act, school boards implemented in 1988, while devolved school management and the publication of information on a range of Performance Indicators did not come on stream until the early 1990s. None of these reforms made explicit mention of gender although all of them had particular consequences in terms of schools' response to the education of girls and boys. However, the particular consequences of the reforms were often closely associated with the social composition of the school. For instance, parental choice tended to produce a more segregated school system in urban areas (Willms 1997, but see Gorard 1998 for a counter-example), schools in more disadvantaged areas often failed to appoint school boards and devolved financial management led to the reduction of funding to schools in poorer areas as a consequence of their dwindling rolls. The differential effect of educational reforms on more and less advantaged schools, and on different groups of pupils within these schools, is relatively unexplored. It is to the experience of educational reform in two case study schools that we now turn.

The impact of the reforms at school level

The argument in this chapter is that within the same region, different schools implemented equal opportunities policies in different fashions and that the raft of educational reforms had contextual effects, suggesting both the relative autonomy of schools and the malleability of the programme of reform. In order to illustrate this point, two schools are discussed in some detail. Both were in Region C, whose equal opportunities strategy might be located within a strong equal opportunities framework.

McDaid High School

McDaid Community High School, a solid stone building with a grey harling facade, was built in 1926 to accommodate 700 pupils. As a junior secondary school, its remit was to provide education for the children of local artisans and labourers. The future occupations of its pupils were reflected in its early emphasis on cooking and laundry for girls and woodwork and metal work for boys. Although situated in the heart of a relatively wealthy East coast city, after comprehensive reorganisation it had failed to develop the academic reputation of the former senior secondary schools in the city and had continued to attract a different sector of the population. In 1980, it was designated a community school with the remit of providing a curriculum relevant to local people, not just those of school age. However, throughout the 1980s its roll fell and in the early 1990s, having failed to win support from the Region for essential upgrading of its amenities, the school faced closure. Following a successful campaign by local parents, the school remained open but the continuing fall in the school roll led to uncertainty about its future (in 1994/95, at the time of the research, its roll stood at 425: by September 1996, this had fallen again to 386). The declining roll meant that cost per pupil was relatively high; for the academic year 1996/97, this was £3,736 (Scottish Office Audit Unit/HMI 1998), compared with an authority average of £3,036 and a national average of £2,760. The pupil population of the school was described as low income multiple deprivation, with 15 per cent of pupils coming from minority ethnic groups. With regard to examination results, in 1995, 6 per cent of the McDaid S4 roll gained grades 1–2 at Standard Grade, compared with an authority average of 29 per cent and a national average of 27 per cent (ibid.). Some 13 per cent of the S4 roll gained grades A–C at Higher Level in S5. Leaver destinations showed that in 1995, less than five pupils went into full-time higher education, compared with an authority average of 24 per cent and a national average of 27 per cent.

These statistics convey a picture of a school which, compared with its more socially advantaged neighbours, was performing relatively poorly. However, presenting the school in this way would convey only a limited picture of its culture and activity. Throughout the 1980s and 1990s, the school enjoyed a national reputation for its radical approach to equal opportunities work, spanning not only gender, but also ethnicity and social class as well. A former head teacher was well known for her feminist views and at the time of the research, unusually for a Scottish secondary school, women made up the majority of the senior management team and principal teachers. An annual lecture was held, in which a local academic gave a talk on some aspect of equal opportunities, thus drawing an academic audience into the school and ensuring that the school was informed of current policy and research. The overtly political nature of the school's approach to equal opportunities work, stemming from grassroots political activity among the staff rather than top-down management from the authority or the SOEID, was conveyed in its policy statement, which declared: 'Racism and sexism are profound social oppressions which affect women and black people in every area of their lives'.

Teachers were seen as the central mediators of the school's policy and were encouraged to offer:

> an explanation of the unfairness of sexist oppression and a description of its pernicious effects. It is particularly important to demonstrate that it is not mere slagging or unpleasant forms of personal behaviour that are being dealt with but rather a deeply embedded societal oppression which affects every area of women's lives.

The school produced a separate pupil policy document which conveyed a similar message. To help pupils to experience discrimination as a real rather than an abstract concept, during their first year at the school, pupils participated in an equality game. This was described as a sophisticated form of snakes and ladders, with social characteristics attributed to pupils which contributed in a positive or negative fashion to pupils' progress in the game of life. Those designated as middle-class white males advanced rapidly while those identified as working-class women were held back. Efforts were made to convey to the pupils that inequality was a problem 'with the system rather than individual pupils within it'. The existence of a range of family cultures in the school sometimes gave rise to problems, for instance, not all parents of Asian girls encouraged their daughters to be ambitious. There were also difficulties in keeping boys on side:

> There are tensions, but we just try to be careful. When we introduce ideas around gender to classes of adolescent boys, we inevitably encounter conflict because any attempt to give the girls more attention is read as discrimination against them.
>
> (Equality co-ordinator)

Most teachers in the school had a strong personal commitment to social justice work and were also active in the union and in the authority's Women in Education Group. A former head teacher had been active in championing gender equality issues, writing a number of book chapters about equality work in the school. However, a vociferous minority challenged the status of equal opportunities activities, seeing them as too political and distracting attention from the school's major difficulties:

I think there has been a feeling that it has gone too far. There has been tremendous discussion about the use of certain words like 'hen' [a term of endearment], whereas the actual bad language that you hear around the school needs far more strenuous treatment.

(Male maths teacher)

This teacher also felt that efforts to boost girls' confidence had had some positive effects, in that the best girls had 'blossomed', but the downside was that the problems of boys were being overlooked. Indeed, the move towards individualised teaching favoured girls rather than boys:

In maths, they have a scheme of work which they work through and they just approach the teacher if they are having difficulty. The girls seem to respond quite well to that, the boys are hopeless and their behaviour is awful and they are a continuous nuisance. By the end of the first year the girls have advanced and the boys have probably gone backwards so it seems to me that our systems are operating to the benefit of girls and the positive disadvantage of the boys.

(Male maths teacher)

This teacher's perceptions that boys were much more likely to experience difficulty were reinforced by data relating to referral to the year head, formal exclusions and proportion of pupils receiving learning support. For example over a two-month period in 1994, four girls and fifty-eight boys in S1 were referred to the year head in connection with a disciplinary matter.

Curricular reforms were perceived by the staff of the school as having had a largely neutral effect. TVEI had provided much needed cash for equality initiatives, but its agenda had been largely concerned with access and thus it had lacked a cutting edge. The 5–14 curriculum and Standard grade, although based on the principle that the curriculum should be accessible to all, had failed to alter the gender balance in such key areas as Biology, still dominated by girls, and Physics, a largely male preserve. Higher Still, although still under discussion at the time of the research, was seen as threatening because the proposed Advanced Higher, taken the year after Highers, would prove very difficult to teach in a small school with tiny numbers in the sixth form. If it became apparent that only some secondary schools were offering Advanced Highers, then the idea that all comprehensive schools were of equal status offering a common curriculum would be undermined. Already, the school was torn between offering SCOTVEC modules, which might be attainable by a larger proportion of pupils, and Highers, which could not be staffed for the small number of pupils who wished to take them.

Management reforms were seen as much more threatening to the school. The policy of parental choice, in place since the early 1980s, had eaten away at the school roll and middle-class parents in particular had taken their children elsewhere. Formula funding was also seen as threatening; McDaid depended on receiving a relatively generous financial allocation per pupil and the erosion of pupil numbers meant that it was unable to support the number of staff required to teach the full curriculum. Various fund-raising measures had been explored, including the letting of parking spaces in the school yard to local businesses. It was felt that this enterprise culture sat oddly with the values of the school, 'but if that's the only way you're going to get funding then so be it'. The publication of examination results and other performance indicators by the SOEID was also seen as threatening. The quality of the equal opportunities work for which the school was known would not be captured in any of these metrics and the harsh comparisons which would be made could only exacerbate parents' anxieties, leading to further flight of educationally conscious parents and a further exasperation of the school's financial difficulties. Target setting, which was not in place at the time of the research, might well be seen as a further pressure to reorientate the values and focus of the school. The chair of the school board, an unemployed man whose sons attended the school, was inclined to focus on these measurements of performance as indicating that the school was not doing well enough for its working-class pupils. Middle-class teachers, he felt, wasted time on equal opportunities work instead of firing up pupils to perform well in examinations. At the end of the day, he felt that a good crop of examination passes would do more to challenge inequality than gaining an understanding of the roots of inequality. He also felt that girls and minority ethnic pupils were favoured and white boys were disciplined more harshly.

McGovern High School

In contrast with McDaid High School was McGovern, also located in an inner city area but with a more socially advantaged catchment than McDaid. A former selective girls' school, it was originally endowed by a legacy from a tobacco and snuff manufacturer. In 1966 the school moved to its present site, consisting of modern buildings and a sixteenth-century house. McGovern was a consistently over-subscribed school. One pupil who was interviewed commented tellingly:

> It's probably one of the best schools. It's got a private school name for a state school. If anyone ever says if you go to a private state school you've got a better chance in life, you can fight against that with the name. If I say to people 'I go to McGovern', they automatically assume that's a private school. It's quite a balanced school. You don't get excessive bad behaviour.

At the time of the research, the school roll was 1,078 and by 1996 this had risen to 1,110. In 1996–7 the cost per pupil per annum was £2,781. Like McDaid, about 15 per cent of pupils were from minority ethnic backgrounds. With regard to examination results, McGovern regularly featured as one of the highest performing schools in the authority. Thus in 1995, 44 per cent of S4 pupils gained five plus grades 1–2 at Standard grade and 38 per cent of pupils on the S4 roll gained three plus grades A–C at Higher Level in S5. Some 40 per cent went on to full-time higher education on leaving school.

The school had an active equal opportunities policy and in the hall pupils had painted the statement: 'We respect and care for each other and value the diversity which exists among people.' While McDaid's policy committed itself to working towards the redistribution of wealth, McGovern's policy was closer to the politics of recognition, seeking to value cultural diversity without blurring the boundaries between groups. Its staff policy statement hinted at a stronger attempt to challenge inequality, seeking to promote 'a pro-active policy which will reverse disadvantage and promote equal opportunities regardless of gender, race, disability or class.'

Emphasis was also placed on the right of all to feel safe in the school. When staff were asked about their experience of equal opportunities in the school, there was some cynicism, since none of the senior management team or guidance staff was a woman and men occupied the majority of principal teacher positions. The failure of women to be promoted in the school was seen as 'a real disappointment'. The view of the head teacher was that the school should empower pupils to take action if they felt their rights were being infringed. At the moment, he felt 'there is a lot of talk about equal opportunities and multi-cultural work and not much reality'. Since the school had begun its life as a selective single-sex institution, some teachers felt that little had changed. The atmosphere was conducive to the achievement of academically able girls, but others, including girls from working-class families, received less attention. The options for them were, according to one female teacher, 'to become very quiet or become slags'. Another teacher felt that it was relatively easy in a predominantly middle-class school where minority ethnic pupils were in a minority to imagine that discrimination had been beaten: 'In some respects, it's easier for pupils in a more middle-class type school to accept they're not racially prejudiced. The most open prejudice in this school is class prejudice.'

This point was reinforced by the Deputy Head, who spoke of the use of negative terms such as 'schemies' or 'Nids' to refer to children from peripheral estates. There was also a danger that adopting a generic equal opportunities policy embracing gender, ethnicity, social class and disability, might lead to the neglect of gender since it was easy to think that 'gender has been done'. It was suggested by a number of teachers that the focus should now shift to addressing boys' rather than girls' problems, since the former rather than the latter appeared to be disadvantaged within the school.

Pupils themselves were inclined to be impatient with crude representations of gender equality and felt that if the case were over-stated there was a danger of alienating rather than inspiring. A group of sixth year girls felt that a film shown in guidance classes was somewhat heavy-handed:

We used to have some videos like male air hostesses and women in factories. Annie Lennox singing 'Sisters are doing it for themselves' and stuff like that.
   If they started making too big a thing of equal opps then everyone might get fed up with it . . . you still get boys who say 'Ha, ha, ha. Girls should be

kept in the kitchen'. You get annoyed with it. But I don't think anyone believes that.

With regard to curricular reforms, TVEI was seen as having a major impact and had supported a number of initiatives over time, including the release of a member of staff to engage in equal opportunities work and the production of the hall mural. Other reforms were seen as neutral, although there was a tendency to believe that new forms of assessment such as investigation and problem-solving were radically favouring girls. Although girls were performing better than boys, social class divisions were much more significant. A number of teachers, however, believed that boys were 'massively underachieving' and the task of equal opportunities initiatives should be to tackle the problems experienced by boys rather than girls. As at McDaid, the introduction of a common curriculum had made little impact on gender divisions within key areas of the curriculum (see Croxford, this volume).

Although Higher Still was seen as non-threatening, and the school was confident of its ability to provide a suite of Advanced Higher classes, there was some concern about the future of its A level provision. McGovern was the only state school in Scotland to offer A levels, although these were often taken by pupils in the independent sector. This anomaly had arisen because a previous head teacher had decided that offering A levels would attract middle-class parents, particularly those from south of the Border and with university connections to the school. Although the principle of deregulation should have allowed such diversity to flourish, there was some uncertainty about whether it could co-exist with the restructuring of the curriculum for the later years of secondary education. In addition, some staff questioned the reason for providing English qualifications in a Scottish state school. The resources tied up in this, they maintained, should be redirected to lower achieving pupils.

Management reforms were also seen as largely, but not wholly, positive for the school. Parental choice had increased pressure for places, enhancing the perceived desirability of the school. There was a sense, however, that some of the pupils from disadvantaged areas who obtained a place in the school did not necessarily flourish. One teacher commented:

> There is a major class issue in that some parents from housing schemes think they're going to help their child by sending them to McGovern. So they get them the uniform and send them across town by bus and the poor children sit here and are miserable and finally sink without trace. They've lost their peer group and they speak differently and they just don't fit in . . .

The climate of consumer awareness also meant that the school had to be wary of not losing its middle-class elite to the private sector, catering for 25 per cent of city children and with growing numbers. Efforts were made to provide supplementary classes for 'gifted' children and time was taken at parents' evenings and other occasions to assure wavering parents that their child would not suffer by attending a state school. The policy of parental choice, therefore, could have undesirable consequences for the school in terms of diluting its middle-class composition and alienating its traditional constituency. On the other hand, rising numbers meant that, under formula funding, more money would flow into the school coffers, theoretically providing more cash for equal opportunities work.

The greater involvement of parents in the running of the school through the establishment of school boards was again seen as offering cautious support for equal opportunities work, but was likely to curb any attempts to promote positive action too enthusiastically. The male chair of the school board, who worked in higher education, commented: 'Amongst staff and parents there would probably be very diverse views. Some people would be quite unhappy about the idea of positive action.' The concern of the school board was also likely to highlight the position of boys as well as girls:

> I think we are still trying to find our way to understanding these issues. We're concerned that it's still mainly girls who are taking particular subjects like home economics. We're also concerned about the growing divergence between the performance of girls and boys in examinations. I don't pretend to understand it but I can observe it informally. We're constantly having to hassle our son to do homework and other people we know have to do the same thing.

In maintaining the allegiance of such parents, the school saw the publication of exam results as providing it with something of a boost, although the head teacher had written to a national paper, along with a head teacher from a school in a socially disadvantaged area, highlighting the strong association between social class and examination performance. Despite points of tension, McGovern High School was able to exist relatively happily in an environment where management responsibility was moving from authority to school level, but responsibility for the curriculum was retained centrally.

Discussion: the fate of equal opportunities strategies in the two schools

A neat ending for this chapter would be, having characterised the nature of the equal opportunities approaches adopted in the two schools, to compare the out-come for each as the educational reform programme of the 1980s and 1990s began to bite. At one level, McDaid could easily be characterised as pursuing radical strategies, with the goal of effecting some form of radical social transform-ation. McGovern, by way of contrast, might be seen as pursuing a more liberal agenda, attempting to pursue equality issues without altering the status quo. The conclusion would thus be that the liberal equal opportunities agenda were more resilient in the face of the onslaught from market-driven educational reforms. However, closer scrutiny of the schools suggests that to characterise them in this way would be to lose some of the complexities within them. There was also a greater focus at McGovern in celebrating individual identity and diversity, in contrast with McDaid's focus on structurally based social divisions. However, although McGovern generally emphasised individual high achievement, repairing structural disadvantage was also on the agenda.

Perhaps more salient than the schools' particular take on equal opportunities was the effect of their socio-economic status. At McGovern, the powerful school board influenced strongly the brand of gender equality work which was allowed to flourish in the school, with influential middle-class parents supporting the idea that girls should be encouraged to fulfil their potential, but not at the expense of boys. Too great a focus on issues such as sexual harassment, for example, would not have been welcome in the school and the equality game played at McDaid might have been seen as an unnecessary distraction from instructional time. The working-class chairman of the McDaid school board had anxieties about the distraction posed by the gender equality agenda, but these were not regarded as particularly important by the staff. The most damaging influence on equal opportunities work at McDaid, however, was the focus of the public gaze on raw examination results, which represented a crucial part of the government's agenda of marketisation. As confidence in the school declined, the combination of formula funding and falling rolls meant a year-on-year reduction in resources, to the extent that the school was struggling to provide a comprehensive curriculum, particularly for pupils in S5 and S6. As staff became increasingly worn and demoralised, the enthusiasm necessary to keep equal opportunities work alive tended to diminish. By way of contrast, confidence at McGovern was much higher, although some anxieties were evident in relation to a possible dilution of its middle-class clientele through the loss of growing numbers of pupils to the private sector and the replacement of these pupils by children from peripheral estates. At both schools, anxieties were expressed about boys' performance, but at McGovern the equal opportunities work was being reorientated to focus on their needs. Although less radical than McDaid, it was clear that gender equality work, in whatever form, would survive at McGovern, whereas at McDaid there was the danger that it might disappear altogether. Although McGovern and McDaid have been presented in case studies, with emphasis on their particularity rather than generalisability, they clearly reveal an irony that at the very time when gender equality has reached the mainstream agenda through TVEI and the 5–14 programme, the combined effect of performativity imposed by the educational reforms is likely to squeeze out the most radical equal opportunities policies and practices deriving from grassroots activity rather than top-down management.

References

Acker, S. (1994) 'Feminist theory and the study of gender and education', in S. Acker (ed.) *Gendered Education*, Buckingham: Open University Press.

Adams, K. (1990) 'Divide and rule: the marriage ban 1918–1945', in F.M.S. Paterson and J. Fewell (eds) *Girls in their Prime: Scottish Education Revisited*, Edinburgh: Scottish Academic Press.

Adler, M. (1997) 'Looking backwards to the future: parental choice and education policy', *British Educational Research Journal* 23, 3: 297–315.

Anderson, R. (1985a) 'In search of the "Lad o' Pairts": the mythical history of Scottish education', *History Workshop Journal* 19: 82–104.

—— (1985b) 'Education and society in modern Scotland: a comparative perspective', *History of Education Quarterly* 25: 459–82.

Bunkle, P. (1979–80) 'A history of the women's movement', *Broadsheet* Part One, September 1979, 24–8.

Corr, H. (1990) 'Home rule in Scotland: the teaching of housework in Scottish schools 1872–1914', in F.M.S. Paterson and J. Fewell (eds) *Girls in their Prime: Scottish Education Revisited*, Edinburgh: Scottish Academic Press.

Deakin, N. (1994) *The Politics of Welfare: Continuities and Change*, London: Harvester Wheatsheaf.

Educational Institute of Scotland (EIS) (1989) *Report of ad hoc Committee on anti-sexist policy*. Minute no. 559 for Annual General Meeting 8/9/10, June, Edinburgh: EIS.

Fewell, J. and Paterson, F. (1990) 'Girls in their prime: the Scottish education tradition', in F.M.S. Paterson and J. Fewell (eds) *Girls in their Prime: Scottish Education Revisited*, Edinburgh: Scottish Academic Press.

Fraser, N. (1997) *Justice Interruptus: Critical Reflections on the Post-Socialist Condition*, London: Routledge.

Furlong, A. and Cartmel, F. (1997) *Young People and Social Change*, Milton Keynes: Open University Press.

General Teaching Council for Scotland (1991) *Gender in Education*, GTC Policy Document, Edinburgh: GTC.

Gorard, S. (1998) 'Schooled to fail? Revisiting the Welsh school effect', *Journal of Education Policy*, 13, 1: 115–24.

Hills, L. (1990) 'The Senga syndrome; reflections on 21 years in education', in F.M.S. Paterson and J. Fewell (eds) *Girls in their Prime: Scottish Education Revisited*, Edinburgh: Scottish Academic Press.

Maclean, C. (1994) 'The theory and practice of equal opportunities in Scotland', *Scottish Affairs* 6, Winter, 36–51.

Middleton, S. (1984) 'The sociology of women's education as a field of study', *Discourse* 5, 1: 43–62.

Paterson, F. and Fewell, J. (1990) (eds) *Girls in their Prime: Scottish Education Revisited*, Edinburgh: Scottish Academic Press.

Paterson, H. (1983) 'Incubus and ideology: the development of secondary schooling in Scotland, 1900–1939', in W.M. Humes and H.M. Paterson (eds) *Scottish Culture and Scottish Education 1800–1980*, Edinburgh: John Donald.

Phillips, A. (1997) 'From inequality to difference: a severe case of displacement', *New Left Review* 224: 143–53.

Scottish Consultative Council for the Curriculum (1993) *Curriculum and Assessment 5–14: Cross-Curricular Aspects*, Dundee: SCCC.

Scottish Education Department (1975) *Differences of Provision for Boys and Girls in Scottish Secondary Schools: A Report by HM Inspectors of Schools*, Edinburgh: HMSO.

—— (1976) *Sex Discrimination Act 1975*, SED Circular no. 974, 24 February 1976, Edinburgh: SED.

—— (1977a) *The Structure of the Curriculum in the Third and Fourth years of the Scottish Secondary School* (The Munn Report), Edinburgh: HMSO.

—— (1977b) *Assessment for All: Review of the Committee to Review the Third and Fourth years of Secondary Education* (The Dunning Report), Edinburgh: HMSO.

Scottish Office Audit Unit/HM Inspectors of Schools (1998) *Examination Results in Scottish Schools, 1996–98*, Edinburgh: HMSO.

Scottish Office Education Department (1992) *Curriculum and Assessment in Scotland: National Guidelines; Reporting 5–14; Promoting Partnership*, Edinburgh: HMSO.

Scottish Qualifications Authority (1997) *Examination Statistics 1997*, Edinburgh: SQA.

Strathclyde Regional Council (1988) *Sex Equality in the Education Service: The Report of a Regional Working Party*, Glasgow: Strathclyde Regional Council Department of Education.

Turner, E., Lloyd, J., Stronach, I. and Waterhouse, S. (1994) *Plotting Partnership: Education Business Links in Scotland*, Report for the Scottish Office Education Department, Stirling: University of Stirling.

Turner, E., Riddell, S. and Brown, S. (1995) *Gender Equality in Scottish Schools: The Impact of Recent Educational Reforms*, Manchester: Equal Opportunities Commission.

Weiner, G. (1994) *Feminisms in Education; An Introduction*, Buckingham: Open University Press.

Weir, A.D. (1988) *Education and Vocation: 14–18*, Edinburgh: Scottish Academic Press.

Willms, D.J. (1996) 'School choice and community segregation: findings from Scotland', in A.C. Kerckhoff (ed.) *Generating Social Stratification: Toward a New Research Agenda*, Boulder, CO: Westview Press. 131–51.

—— (1997) 'Parental choice and education policy', *Briefing 12*, Centre for Educational Sociology, Edinburgh: CES.

Young, I.M. (1990) *Justice and the Politics of Difference*, Princeton, NJ: Princeton University Press.

3   Beyond one border

Educational reforms and gender equality in Welsh schools

Jane Salisbury

Introduction

This chapter will present an analysis derived from a recently completed UK Equal Opportunities Commission funded research project *Educational Reforms and Gender Equality in Welsh Schools* (Salisbury 1996b). It reports on one of the first albeit small-scale, empirical studies of a decade (1984–94) of educational reforms and their impact upon gender equality. The chapter's focus on Wales renders more *visible* post-reform school life in a challenged deindustrialising European region. The aims of the research involved evaluating the impact of government reforms on gender equality mapping student performance over a decade and ascertaining any noticeable changes in school cultures and equal opportunities policy-making. The chapter reveals a mixed picture of beneficial policies and procedures arising from some of the reforms, pockets of knowledgeable and sensitive practice from committed groups and individuals but, overall, no infrastructure for the delivery of equal opportunities on a broader and systematic basis.[1]

Survey data from local education authorities (LEAs), primary and secondary schools will be used to examine the role played by Local Government Education Departments in supporting school initiatives for gender equality over the last decade. It will reveal a mixed picture for Wales. In-depth case study material is then used to explore the interconnection between central government policy and local context by considering the experiences of one local education authority in Wales. Data from a variety of local contexts and settings reveal the ways changing national policies and reforms are mediated. The qualitative case study undertaken in an urban LEA in South Wales enabled a detailed picture of how equality and gender issues were being tackled within schools and at LEA level.

Having given a brief background to the study, the descriptive section which follows highlights some distinctive features of the Welsh education system providing a policy context for the curricular and organisational reforms. Later sections go on to describe the perceived and actual impacts of major educational innovations on gender equality in schools in Wales.

A border makes a difference: the policy context in Wales

Education in Wales as in England and Scotland (see Arnot *et al.* 1996; David *et al.* this volume; Turner *et al.* 1995; Riddell, this volume) has experienced major policy changes in particular over the last decade (1984–94). Such changes have resulted in the main from central government policy specifically directed towards the reform of education or towards other parts of the public sector which have nevertheless impacted on education. The numerous reforms will not be rehearsed here in detail (readers needing specific details are referred to Salisbury 1996b). It is not intended to provide a comprehensive account of the policy context, but to identify some of the key factors and issues for education in Wales. Unlike Scotland, Wales has tended to be assimilated into the English education system and has been subject to largely the same reforms, though with variations and 'time lags' that take into account local structures and organisation. The educational reforms within the time frame of 1984–94 with which the gender equality research project was particularly concerned are difficult to characterise. They are not aimed at one particular policy objective or outcome though it can be argued that the key aim of central governments, behind the various reforms including education over the last fifteen years has been to improve standards in the delivery of public services as judged by consumers themselves. The framework of analysis adopted for the research project follows Whitty's (1989) perception of the reforms as having two policy thrusts in direct tension with each other: the first aiming to assert greater control over schools e.g. the National Curriculum and regular inspections and the second, encouraging choice competition and marketisation of schools through the introduction of self-managing schools and new types of school provision. The analysis here distinguishes between curricular and organisational reforms, and separate empirical sections discussing each type are provided in the second half of the chapter.

While the legal requirements of the various Education Acts apply equally to Wales and England, the distinctions between the two countries are not merely those of geographical boundaries, but rather extend to include issues of language, culture, heritage and demography. Each of these factors, along with the marked occupational segregation of men and women in labour markets, give Wales its own specific characteristics. Such factors demonstrate the need for the education system in Wales to be considered independently (Reynolds 1990, 1995; Delamont and Rees 1997). Any discussion of education in Wales needs to take account of a number of implications which have become explicit since the 1980s when there have been major policy changes and educational reforms. These include issues surrounding a culturally specific curriculum for pupils in Wales, the position of the Welsh language and the role of Welsh medium education and the continued support for the rural schools. In Wales there are deeply entrenched patriarchal values and attitudes (Betts 1994; T. Rees 1994, 1999) and these have particular implications for gendered experiences within education at both staff and pupil levels (Salisbury 1996b). Surveys by the Wales Assembly of Women (1995) on women and training, research on *Women in Post Compulsory Education and Training* (Istance and Rees 1994) along with edited collections of research on women and girls in Wales such as *Our Sisters' Land* (Aaron *et al.* 1994) and *Our Daughters' Land* (Betts 1996), combine to portray structural and cultural factors shaping experience and identities.

Girls in Wales continue to achieve better results in a wider range of subjects than boys in GCSE examinations – a situation reflecting the UK and Europe as a whole (Daniel 1994; Arnot *et al.* 1996; Startup and Dressel 1996; Gorard *et al.* 1998a). They are also more likely to participate in education beyond the age of 16 though boys' staying-on rates have increased in the last five years. Regional analyses (Istance and Rees 1994) reveal substantial variations from one county to another; the staying-on rate for girls is highest in the rural counties of Wales (Dyfed, Powys and Gwynedd) and it is these three counties which have the lowest percentage of female school leavers with no qualifications or graded results. *Un*qualified female school leavers, however, are found in greater concentration in Wales than in any other UK region (Central Statistics Office 1993: Table 5:7; Istance and Rees 1994; Welsh Office 1995b).

Data collected by the Careers Service in Wales indicate that girls' potential is not realised and that they leave school with limited horizons compared to boys (Daniel 1994: 165). Despite their continuing improved performance relative to boys in examinations, girls persistently demonstrate narrow aspirations when selecting subject options and careers as the majority of girls still enter sex-stereotyped female areas of employment. Much awareness work needs to be done to combat these patterns. It is argued that girls and boys in Wales need earlier careers education before gender stereotypes become too rigid (Pilcher *et al.* 1989a, 1989b; Delamont 1990; Salisbury 1996a). Along with preparation for work and insights into changing labour markets and employment patterns, young people in Wales need to understand the changes in family structure and be prepared for family life in which traditional domestic identities are no longer as central for contemporary women (Betts 1994: 27).

Analyses of women's position in the labour market in Wales (Rees and Willcox 1991; T. Rees 1994; EOC 1997b) reveal a low rate of female economic activity (although this has been rising recently). The Welsh workforce is highly segregated both horizontally and vertically with women working in a narrow range of industries and in the lower grades within these sectors, often in relatively low-paid, low-skilled part-time employment.

Women at work in Wales are less likely than those in England to be in highly paid professional or technical posts. A study commissioned by HTV Wales illustrated the paucity of women in top jobs in Wales (Rees and Fielder 1991, 1992). Both the public and private sectors in Wales have minute numbers of women in senior posts, an indication that the 'glass ceiling' (which women can feel but not see, and which prevents their route to the top), is double glazed. The proportion of women managers is much lower than in England and the proportion of women head teachers in Wales is actually declining (Rees and Fielder 1991, 1992). Women's current position in the labour market in Wales and the under-utilisation of their skills are a major contributory factor to the underperformance of the Welsh economy (see for example T. Rees, in press). Initiatives and strategies such as WISE, GIST, Chwarae Teg and Opportunity 2000 to improve girls' and women's involvement in education and training and economic participation rates have been implemented (EOC/Chwarae Teg[2] 1993; Istance and Rees 1994). It is increasingly recognised that the failure to develop women's skills and increase labour market participation will lock Wales into a low skill, low pay economy.

Institutional gaps: the reforms in Wales

People in Wales have demonstrated considerable loyalty to state education in schools governed by the Local Education Authorities. The market philosophy underpinning the 1988 and the 1993 Education Acts, which actively encourages schools to opt for Grant Maintained Status, does not have the same traditional base in Wales as it does in England. According to Loosemore (1981) and Self (1985), the 'conservative' nature of Welsh education extends to a belief in the state system which has always operated within an atmosphere of co-operation, rather than competition. Welsh Office records demonstrate the resistance to the adoption of Grant Maintained Status by schools in Wales, fewer than 1 per cent of schools in Wales have opted out compared to more than 4 per cent in England (Halpin *et al.* 1997). Despite concerted government pressures on schools to seek status, only eleven of Wales's 227 secondary schools and five of the 1,704 primary schools in the principality have 'opted out' and as yet, no date has been set to install a National Funding Council for Schools. Furthermore, the Assisted Places Scheme which allowed for competition between the independent and the state sectors was virtually unworkable in Wales since only 2.5 per cent of pupils in Wales attend independent schools, compared with 8.5 per cent in England (only eight of these schools have been able to offer assisted places). Since 1988 state-funded schools have become more popular with a declining proportion using the fee-paying sector (Gorard 1996). Wales has no City Technology Colleges and the Welsh Office has no proposals for their introduction. It appears that there has been no response among industries in Wales to the CTC initiatives. Thus many of the reforms instigated at the 'national' (i.e. England and Wales) level have exerted relatively little impact on the education system in Wales. Delamont and Rees (1997) have argued that a distinctive Welsh system comes to be conceptualised in terms of a 'series of institutional gaps'.

The 1988 Education Reform Act (ERA) installed a National Curriculum for all state schools in England and Wales. Scotland has its own education laws (see Riddell and Croxford chapters in this volume) and the Act does not apply to Northern Ireland (see Gallagher *et al.*, this volume). The Act provided Wales with the same attainment targets as England, even though pupils in Wales study Welsh language and literature as a compulsory part of the curriculum, without extra time, making ten foundation subjects at primary level and eleven in the lower age group at secondary school. In Wales in the mid-1980s, reactions to emerging policies for a national curriculum resulted in the unified chorus – '*which nation?*' (Elwyn Jones 1994). Critics argued that the educational framework passed down to Wales ensured that the Welsh language looked like 'an addition to a curriculum drawn up for England' (Bellin *et al.* 1994).

The Curriculum Council for Wales (CCW) increasingly took policy initiatives and developed an independent standpoint on a number of curriculum themes. Its 1993 advisory paper entitled 'Developing a Curriculum Cymreig' specified ways to permeate 'Welshness' throughout a range of subjects as a cross-curricula strategy. Wales has its own set of National Curriculum orders which are distinct from those of England for music, art, history, geography, religious education and Welsh as a first and second language. Dearing's 'slimmed down' 14–16 curriculum with a developed vocational strand and the reintroduction of curricular options at the end of Key Stage 3 may well encourage gender-stereotyped choices by pupils and undermine recent trends. The Welsh language as optional rather than compulsory subject has also undermined the earlier commitment to a bilingual Wales as enshrined in the earlier 1988 ERA provisions.

Equity issues surrounding the provision of education through the medium of Welsh (Baker 1990) parallel the concerns in Northern Ireland for equitable distribution of resources in its Catholic and Protestant schools (see Gallagher *et al.* this volume). Pressure groups in both Welsh-speaking and Anglicised regions of Wales have fought for the right to have children educated through the medium of Welsh. Demanding positive action and using the language of 'entitlements' Welsh-medium school campaigns can be seen as successful social movements (Rawkins 1979). Over the last three decades a dynamic system of Welsh medium education has, according to Morris Jones (1995: 105), originated from 'a grass roots enthusiasm allied to middle class expertise in skilful lobbying'. During this period the Welsh Office has provided considerable funding to assist in establishing Ysgolion Cymraeg (Welsh-medium schools) and to enable an increase in the levels of teaching through the medium of Welsh in existing schools in Wales.

The increased emphasis on parental choice and open enrolment in the 1988 and 1993 Education Acts sees parents as consumers free to choose a school assisted by published school performance tables or 'league' tables. Promoting competitive efficiency among education providers was the main objective with the intention that 'good' schools will expand to accommodate increased pupil numbers while the 'poor' schools will contract and possibly be forced to close. In Wales, however, the geographical distances between some schools dictates that for as many as 40 per cent of parents and pupils no real choice pertains. That school standards in Wales can be 'levelled up' by such competitive strategies is somewhat problematic. Recent reports (published since the EOC study) of ongoing research in 700 secondary schools in Wales (Gorard and Fitz 1998) has shown how schools have become less stratified since 1988 in terms of indicators of poverty and educational need. Research on the impacts of the quasi-market in different geographical regions inside the Wales border is much needed.

The construction of a market in education involved the creation of interlocking policy initiatives aimed at forcing competition between schools and increasing parental choice left social justice and equality issues largely absent. Several writers have noted how few of the educational reforms have directly focused on equality issues and pointed out that there is no single agreed definition of what is actually understood by equal opportunities. Recent strategies for change appear to have been premised on one of two interpretations of 'equality of opportunity' and 'equality of outcome' (Riley 1994: 13). The former liberal approach assumes that 'rigorous administrative controls and formalized systems will ensure that fair play takes place'.

The raising of standards and the levelling up discourse of achievement with attendant 'targets' can be likened to liberal concepts of equal opportunity in that they aim to improve performance for *all* students. Key stage testing in the National Curriculum is a clear example also and both GCSE and TVEI had a focus on improved curriculum access for all students. The current and ongoing rationalisation of vocational qualifications can also be seen in this light.

This liberal approach to equal opportunities is firmly embedded in a number of recent Welsh Office consultation documents: *People and Prosperity: An Agenda for Action in Wales* (1995c), *A Bright Future: Getting the Best for Every Pupil at School in Wales* (1995d) and *Building Excellent Schools Together* 'BEST' (1997). Each of these documents specifies whole Wales targets and urges schools and LEAs to work strategically towards their achievement. In a close reading of these 'policy texts' it is possible to trace a distinct shift from benchmark (five GCSE A* to C grades) targets to increasingly elaborated quantifiable measures embracing both the National Curriculum core subjects and vocational equivalents. At the time of the EOC research (1994–95) schools were only 'encouraged' to set targets, but congruent with central government's imperatives of performativity, it is now a statutory requirement for all schools to set specific targets and objectives and include these in their annual school development plans.

It is interesting to note that performance statistics and targets included no reference to gender until the Welsh Office's (1997) 'BEST' document. Failing to disaggregate achievement by gender, however, may have resulted in targets being set which will not raise expectations for some girls. Boys, however, are firmly in the frame.

> By 2002 . . . the extent to which boys underperform by comparison with girls should be *cut by half against* the 1996 results:
>
> - at ages 7, 11 and 14;
> - in the attainment of 5 GCSE grades A*–C or vocational equivalent;
> - and in the achievement of two or more A levels or vocational equivalent.
>   (Welsh Office 1997: 31, original emphasis)

It is increasingly well known that boys lag behind in English and Modern Foreign Languages with girls now catching up in Science and, as some media headlines describe, 'outperforming' boys at GCSE on aggregate measures (see Arnot *et al.* 1996; David *et al.* and Riddell and Gallagher *et al.*, this volume for a discussion of 'gender gaps' in examination achievements). The complexity of differential performance of boys and girls has been oversimplified in many research accounts and media representations, however. Further, the reporting of differences in boys' and girls' GCSE results in terms of the 'benchmark' of five A–C grades may mask other differences which are apparent when we examine what happens after compulsory schooling has finished, particularly at A level (Weiner *et al.* 1997; EOC 1998; Paechter 1998; Gorard *et al.* 1998a, 1998b).

In Wales the independent Office of Her Majesty's Chief Inspector of Schools (OHMCI) with its regular five-year cycle of inspection visits has a vital role to play here, though a content analysis of inspection reports in the early 1990s (Jones 1995) revealed few commentaries which addressed crucial gender issues. In Wales concern continues to be expressed on the need for a more rigorous monitoring and reporting on equal opportunities and gender issues, particularly with the reduced role of the LEA. More recently since the publication of the Wales EOC report, OHMCI's (1997) survey work on gender and achievement in Wales has been positively received by the teaching, research and policy communities.

The Local Government (Wales) Act 1994, which came into effect on 1 April 1996 marked a milestone in the legislative history of Wales. The Act created 22 new Unitary Authorities to replace the former 8 County Councils and 37 District Councils. Each Welsh unitary authority is a new council, inheriting responsibilities, rights and assets from the former county and district councils. Inevitable fragmentation and disruption occurred with some advisory services depleted (Butler *et al.* 1995). Equal opportunities and gender equality work in schools will depend upon the commitment of governing bodies and the ability of the reorganised education authorities to support it. Given what we know about subject choice and achievement, staying on rates and patterns of participation in post-16 courses for males and females in Wales it is important for such work to continue and develop. Subsequent sections of this chapter will show that in Wales, an infrastructure for gender equality and equal opportunities work is absent.

Impact of educational reforms on gender equality in schools in Wales

Various factors have affected the ways in which recent education policies have impacted upon equal opportunities practices in schools. Such factors include economic and geographic conditions, the history of individual school policy-making on equal opportunities, previous levels of support to schools, and the patterns of achievement already in place prior to the reforms. Survey data provided by the eight (original) LEAs and samples of primary and secondary schools revealed surprisingly that the majority of equal opportunities policies were developed relatively recently, after the ERA in 1989. Only one LEA had such a policy in 1987! Five of the LEAs had specific policies on gender, whereas schools tended to have more 'generalist' policies encompassing gender. The chief impetus for the development of equal opportunities policies in the Welsh LEAs was described as coming from LEA Officers and the TVEI. Schools reported that LEAs and head teachers were the main catalysts though Governors and OHMCI criteria were identified by primary schools and the National Curriculum by secondary schools.

   Primary schools were less enthusiastic about equal opportunities (EO) indicating that they were one of a number of issues, rather than a specific priority. Posts of EO responsibility and working groups were reported by a minority of schools. Over half of the secondary schools reported having working groups and a third had a general equal opportunities co-ordinator. The surveys sought to identify the range of ways in which institutions were putting their policies into practice; LEA data revealed that the majority of staff with responsibilities for equal opportunities were working within fragmented and multiple job descriptions (e.g. careers, cross-curricular concerns, curriculum Cymreig). The reduction of staff in LEAs had removed or substantially reformed the role of the specialist equal opportunities adviser or officer. 'This post of EO co-ordinator *was* full time in 1987 now it's only part of a post – it was made point three (0.3) of a post in 1993 which is a great shame!' (EO co-ordinator).

   Observation, interviews and documentary analysis undertaken as part of the 'fieldwork' revealed a variability in the knowledge of previous and current equal opportunities and gender work across the LEA. External factors, such as budget reductions, have also influenced the ways in which schools have been able to tackle educational inequalities for their staff or pupils.

   Noticeable features of the research were the terminology and vocabularies used by schools and LEAs to discuss gender and equal opportunities issues. Different 'meanings' resulted in specific approaches and also reflected current political and educational priorities. The language used to describe gender equality work included 'value added' and 'raising standards'; equal opportunities was defined under 'rights and responsibilities' and 'effective citizenship'. Themes of 'entitlement and inclusivity' and 'equal opportunities as integrated' permeated the data at all levels. The language used to 'construct' gender issues provides insights into current concerns, policies and practices and school cultures.

   The varying impact of particular curriculum, organisational and administrative reforms are considered in terms of their perceived positive and negative effects on gender equality. A complex picture of the impact of specific reforms on policies and practices emerges from the survey and qualitative case study of the LEA.

Curriculum, assessment and monitoring reforms

In the survey questionnaires to LEAs, primary and secondary schools, specific reforms were identified (i.e. TVEI, GCSE, National Curriculum, SATs, GNVQs, OHMCI Inspections, examination league tables) which had aimed either at changing curriculum and examinations or improving pupil performance and standards. The majority of LEAs saw most of the reforms in a more positive light, though three LEA respondents attributed negative effects to SATs and the publication of exam results.

   Enthusiasm for the reforms was not quite so evident in the school surveys, however. Respondents from Welsh primary schools were less positive than their English counterparts about testing, the National Curriculum and levels of attainment in terms of promoting gender equality. Respondents from Welsh secondary schools, though positive about GCSEs, National Curriculum and TVEI were much less enthusiastic than English respondents (Arnot *et al.* 1996). Case study material provides insights into the current concerns and strategies used for equal opportunities as well as revealing changes in school cultures, these contribute to an understanding of the impacts of some of the reforms which are now discussed.

The General Certificate of Secondary Education (GCSE)

GCSE was also seen positively in the LEA survey though with a minority having negative views. Welsh secondary school respondents were less positive with just a half of them seeing GCSEs as having a favourable effect on gender equality in schools. Interviews conducted as part of the case study generated data suggesting that the introduction of GCSEs has had mixed outcomes. 'The coursework elements in GCSE have boosted girls' grades' was a typical view of a number of secondary school staff who believed that girls' 'abilities to knuckle down to tasks and projects were an asset' giving them advantages over their male classmates. Girls continue to perform well in GCSE even in subjects where the coursework elements have been reduced. Gender and ethnicity, however, were seen to impact negatively upon the experiences of Asian girls, who often were unable to participate in GCSE coursework related activities. An equal opportunities co-ordinator identified some of the equality problems experienced by Muslim and Sikh girls in her co-educational inner city comprehensive:

> [They] are gravely disadvantaged in their coursework and syllabus coverage for subjects like geography and science when parents prevent them from attending field trips . . . because of cultural imperatives they unwittingly disadvantage their girls – staying overnight is totally out of the question and sometimes teachers have to cancel trips because over half the class is unable to go!

Careers teachers and work experience co-ordinators also expressed concern about the ways many Asian girls avoided 'unescorted' work experience and pointed out that their equal opportunities problems were greater than those of white girls.

LEA survey respondents were unanimously positive about GNVQ and its impact on gender equality though secondary school respondents failed to identify their views. Staff were optimistic about new GNVQ provision in the case study LEA and a number of schools had made 'bids' to be involved in a Welsh Office-funded 'GNVQ key stage 4 Development Scheme'.

National Curriculum

Over half of the Welsh LEAs and secondary school respondents considered the National Curriculum as having a positive effect on gender equality. Primary school respondents appeared neutral though over half of them felt that cross-curricular themes had impacted positively upon gender equality in their schools. Advantages listed included: 'It minimises stereotypical choices', 'all students encouraged to study technology and sciences', 'NC highlights the need for differentiated tasks and examinations.' Disadvantages mainly focused on the reduction in pupils' subject choices with some teachers bemoaning the 'loss of variety and non-academic courses e.g. Media studies and motor vehicle, etc.'

Staff in the urban area of South Wales revealed an optimism in the National Curriculum as a vehicle for extending gender equality. The frequency with which LEA and school staff used the term 'entitlement' was marked. Originally identified as a right within the promotional discourse of the NC, entitlement was increasingly used as a surrogate for equal opportunities. Stressing inclusivity, a head teacher of a multi-ethnic inner city primary school explained:

> the NC is a catalyst for much more solid work with special needs and ESL [English as a Second Language] . . . it reminds us that *all* children have an entitlement to a curriculum . . . all of us need to guard against merging in our minds ESL with SEN, they aren't synonymous!

Reflecting change over time and the initial stresses of implementation another primary head teacher summed up the overall feeling in the case study LEA: 'planning and delivering the National Curriculum was a headache in the early days – it was a constant worry for heads and teachers but it was a long overdue initiative!'

Standard Attainment Target or Task (SATs)

SATs drew mixed responses from the surveyed LEAs and schools with three-quarters of primary and secondary respondents adopting a relatively neutral position regarding the effects of SATs on gender equality. The teachers' boycott had meant that case study schools had not implemented the statutory testing and there were very mixed views about the practicality and feasibility of SATs:

> They tell us what we already know about our pupils!
>
> (Year 2 teacher)

> SATs could lead teachers, who are busy enough anyway, into an assessment-led pedagogy, you know, just teaching to the tests.
>
> (Primary advisor)

> If SATs can better inform educational decisions at the individual pupil level then the teaching profession must comply.
>
> (Secondary head teacher)

All primary schools in the case study LEA administered a 'base line schedule' test on all reception class rising 5 year olds and these data were used diagnostically in the first case then sent on to the Education department to establish a database in the county's new 'Value Added Unit'. LEA officers explained that when 'teachers eventually settle into SATs and things become routinised, valuable monitoring of gender and ethnicity would occur with a range of assessment data'.

The Technical Vocational Educational Initiative (TVEI)

TVEI was felt to have been beneficial in promoting gender equality for all LEA and secondary school respondents. This positive view of the initiative was reinforced in the LEA case study where TVEI had been a powerful catalyst in raising awareness of gender issues. The female advisory teacher with responsibility in the local scheme for Information Technology and equal opportunities had built up a supportive network of teachers and resource base at the local teachers' centre but she feared the future of this work when funding eventually stopped:

> At the moment each school can send its EO co-ordinator to the termly meetings because there's supply cover – I think that ongoing developmental work will be very difficult when the TVEI extension funding finishes . . . You might get one or two *really* committed people trying to collaborate but it will be tough.

A number of the teacher EO co-ordinators, observed at one of their termly work-shops, reported that 'TVEI had given them time, materials and contact with similarly positioned EO co-ordinators from other schools'. Speaking of the support he gained from this, one teacher confessed that 'everything I hear here . . . all the initiatives that are going on in other schools I take back to our Head. He *does* listen and we've "borrowed" a couple of ideas from other schools.'

A sense of camaraderie existed at the workshop when fifteen EO co-ordinators shared a number of outcomes of their work. Numerous gender-related achievements were reported, for example:

- Four schools had made requests for members of their Governing Bodies to train on the County's EO training module.
- Six schools were monitoring option choice in years 9 and scrutinising examination results by gender.
- Eight schools had sent middle management women staff on the County's 'Management Opportunities for Women' INSET Course.

(Case study fieldnotes)

Collectively, this group of equal opportunities co-ordinators (predominantly women) had written and produced an 'Equal Opportunities Induction Pack' which had been circulated to every secondary school in the county. It specified the role of the EO co-ordinator and lists of 'oughts' and 'shoulds' for school assemblies and classrooms. Some EO co-ordinators admitted, however, that their lack of status impeded progress:

> It's a low status role in my experience – nobody would do it so he [the head]
> gave it to me. There's no allowance paid for it so I suppose I do it for *love*!
>
> (Female teacher, mid-40s)

> I've got no pull with older senior colleagues and though in meetings they
> nod or agree, getting things done is quite slow!
>
> (Female teacher, 28 years)

A number of teachers agreed that the EO co-ordinator's role would carry more
weight if the person doing it was one of the senior management team 'who could
get people to attend meetings and get some money to help with EO work'.

Reforms to careers service and guidance

The impact of local careers services and teachers on raising the profile of issues of
gender equality in schools (often in conjunction with vocational education projects and schemes such as TVEI and work placements organised by the Education
and Business Partnerships (EBP), emerged as an important but an unexpected
finding of this research project. Careers officers, advisers and other involved staff
had welcomed the introduction of initiatives, charters and recent legislation covering the provision of careers services and information to pupils and parents. In
the case study LEA the careers service was providing all secondary schools with
flexible study units which incorporated non-stereotypical materials for teachers to
use in careers lessons and an 'itinerant team with a careers bus' visited all schools
regularly.

   The local Training and Enterprise Council (TEC) via its 'Stay Wide, Keep
Moving Women's strategy group' (consisting of women careers teachers, EBP
representatives, Opportunity 2000 Co-ordinators, LEA Officers and women
from local industries) had targeted four schools for the National 'Take Our
Daughters to Work Initiative' (TODTW). Teachers identified ongoing and
unresolved problems particularly for many working-class girls whom they felt
suffered from poverty of aspiration and low levels of self-esteem; this led to a
specific focus for the positive action:

> The chosen schools from across the county are large comprehensives where
> socio-economic data indicate high levels of unemployment . . . If your
> parents and family are out of work you can't tag along can you?
>
> (Careers teacher)

> It's important for working-class girls to see the possibilities for work that
> exist for women – usually middle-class parents know them anyway.
>
> (Careers Officer with responsibility for EO, case study notes)

The TODTW day has aims congruent with those of the Womens' National
Commission 'Women's Training Roadshow', a two-day event in which over

2,000 South Wales school girls attended an all-female careers fair (see Pilcher *et al.* 1988, 1989a, 1989b; T. Rees 1992) held in the case study LEA.

One of the case study schools welcomed the WISE (Women into Science and Engineering) (Whyte 1986) bus during the Spring term when all pupils are being asked to think about their 'options' for year ten. Female pupils in years nine, ten and eleven had opportunities to talk to the staff and study non-typical careers in science and engineering. The female deputy spoke of the value of such initiatives and the importance of 'work experience tasters' whereby both girls and boys experience non-traditional occupational settings. She argued enthusiastically that 'breadth and balance of the National Curriculum can be interpreted to include breadth in work experience placements'. Generally, senior managers and careers officers spoke favourably of improved careers materials but frustration was expressed about the marginal position of careers in most school timetables:

> Many teachers do their best to give kids careers information but in my experience 'Careers Education', 'Vocational Guidance' or whatever you call it will always be a CINDERELLA subject unless legislation forces schools to comply with a type of national curriculum for careers!
>
> (Female careers teacher)

The second Competitiveness White Paper published on 22 May 1995 stated that the government would seek an early opportunity to legislate on aspects of careers education and guidance in maintained schools and colleges in England and Wales. The typical 14 year old considering post-16 options is now able to choose from a variety of options including Modern Apprenticeships, Youth Training, GNVQs or GCE A levels, or a combination of these. Choice of institution is also wide. In view of these factors, one Chief Executive of a newly formed careers company emphasised the importance of 'high quality impartial advice aimed specifically at the individuals' needs'. Since the marketisation of education and the increased importance to schools and colleges of recruiting post-16 students to their own institutions, the necessity of impartial advice from the careers service for boys and girls will be crucial.

Data collection and monitoring

In terms of the effects on gender equality of introducing examination perform-ance tables, responses to the LEA survey were divided. Half of the respondents viewed this initiative negatively and an equal proportion positively, with one female respondent justifying her positive view with a scribbled note in the margin 'it has highlighted the *under*achievement of boys'. Data collection and its con-sequent emphasis on performance and competition appeared to have had a varied impact in the surveys and reactions and perceptions at case study level were mixed. 'League tables' were seen as potentially damaging to gender equality by several teachers including a Head of Modern Languages who was also an EO co-ordinator at his school:

> League tables, as we all know, reflect a tiny part of what schools *do* and with exam passes judged so crudely as performance indicators we have the dangerous situation of teachers and schools *competing* with each other . . . this market model is dangerous for all our pupils and has serious EO implications for boys and girls who are less able!
>
> (Case study interview)

A number of secondary school teachers while hostile to league tables – 'How does a school's position in a published league table help me with the realities of the classroom?' – felt that the close monitoring of girls' and boys' achievements at key stages and in public examinations was important. In a co-educational high school, gender monitoring of subject choices and attainment is stated in the school's EO policy and its annual school development plan. This school had promptly acted upon Value Added (VA) analysis of their 1994 GCSE results provided by the newly established Value Added Unit, and implemented 'mentoring schemes' and 'study wise' programmes to support pupils' quest for better results. As well as monitoring subject option take up and the distribution of gender in Mathematics and English sets, this school engaged in a close scrutiny of gender in its disciplinary procedures:

> *Withdrawal room*: The senior management team use a detailed proforma to monitor incidence of pupil withdrawals to a special room. Data are monitored and analysed termly by a male deputy head teacher. This year 'On 83 occasions a boy has been sent to the withdrawal room and on 25 occasions a girl has been sent. The referring teachers were male on 75 occasions and female on 33 occasions.'
>
> (Case study notes and written data from deputy head)

A member of the senior management team had also conducted a survey following O'Keefe and Stoll's (1991) work into truancy patterns and again this case study school provided detailed gendered analysis of post-registration truancy which they had shared with their staff during school based INSET. The gender equality and equal opportunities work was described as 'leading edge' by the Director of Education who saw this school as a 'flagship for the county'.

OHMCI inspections

OHMCI inspections were viewed favourably in the LEA survey with all respondents indicating their positive effects on gender equality in schools. In the same way that OFSTED attracted support across the English LEA case studies, in the South Wales urban case study the 1993 reform for OHMCI statutory inspections was generally viewed as potentially valuable in promoting gender equality.

The inclusion of criteria for equal opportunities in OHMCI's (1994) *Framework and Guidance for the Inspection of Schools* and *Technical Paper 7* was viewed as a 'vital catalyst for schools to develop rigorous EO policies and practices'. The primary advisor with responsibility for equal opportunities described how in his normal pastoral visits and more formal INSET sessions he had 'pushed' for staff to address equal opportunities. He explained that this official emphasis from the inspectorate allowed him to say, 'You *must* have an EO policy prepared for inspection.'

At the 'Developing Equal Opportunities' INSET day, this advisor stressed to the primary heads and deputies that OHMCI expected to see 'evidence of a school's equal opportunities work permeating across all aspects of the life of the school'. He circulated nine hefty policy guides, (including official OHMCI criteria and the county guidelines for tackling racial harassment) to facilitate discussion workshops and help the trainees write and revise policies and develop equal opportunities school action plans. Fieldwork across the LEA indicated that most schools had either generic, all-inclusive or gender-specific equal opportunities policies. On a less favourable note, a number of secondary school Equal Opportunities co-ordinators working within TVEI funding complained that 'inspectors' scrutiny of EO in their school was cursory – 'we had worked hard at our policy and had started monitoring but we got a lip service response which, quite frankly, was disheartening'. These teachers in the Welsh LEA case study felt that inspectors had approached their EO work superficially, reflecting perhaps its low priority? One female deputy in a co-educational high school with a well developed set of EO policies had re-read her school's inspection report, following an interview for this project to discover that 'EO wasn't given a specific mention'. Casting her mind back and talking to colleagues she could recall that 'They [OHMCI] mentioned our equal opportunities work in their oral report and feedback . . . they were pleased with the whole school policy and how it had been translated into action plans for all staff.' This deputy who had established a cross-curricular EO working group in 1991 and who had invested a lot of time into policy development, implementation and monitoring remarked, 'It was a pity that such important work remained invisible in the final inspectors' report.' There appear to be a marked variation in the importance attached by different inspection teams to issues beyond the formal curriculum. A content analysis of a sample OHMCI reports (Jones 1995) from inspections conducted in 1994, revealed a paucity of commentary on gender and equal opportunities issues generally. *Technical Paper 7* states that 'equal opportunities may be co-ordinated but should not be inspected by a single inspector as if it were a discrete area or task', reflecting the stance that equal opportunities principles should permeate the whole inspection process. Little evidence to support this outcome was identified in the content analysis.

Reforms concerning the administration and organisation of schools

This section discusses a cluster of the reforms which were aimed at redistributing the organisation and funding relationships between schools and LEAs. The community charge (poll tax) and council taxes attracted little comment across the study reflecting the perception that they were unconnected directly to education.

Parents and governing bodies

Whether the greater involvement of parents in the life of schools could impact positively was doubted by LEA respondents in Wales. Parent govenors nevertheless were perceived to have had a positive impact with at least half of them. Similarly, the impact of governing bodies on equal opportunities was felt to be positive in half of the LEAs, though two (one quarter) saw this reform as having a negative influence on gender equality work. These data contrast with those from the case study area where there was more enthusiasm for increased parental power and the *Parents' Charter*.

Evidence from the case study LEA revealed that parental involvement was sought and valued by schools. The head teacher of an urban multi-ethnic primary school explained how he consulted with community leaders and invited all parents into school every Friday morning for whole school assemblies followed by coffee. Observational fieldwork confirmed this head's claim that 'this is a school *of* the community working *for* the community'. For this head teacher, who was acutely aware of the local market, 'Failure to have an EO policy and multicultural mission statement could result in parents voting with their feet to another nearby school.' He had regularly provided EO training for all staff, voluntary classroom helpers and lunchtime supervisors using six differentiated whole school policies! The difficulties of involving women and minority ethnic parents in the work of governance (rather than only as lunchtime supervisors) worried him:

> My governors and I are sensitive to the needs of the community and in particular we try to have members from the various ethnic minority groups employed at the school . . . We have only two women governors at present and we would like to do something about it. That's in the future but they are often very reluctant.
>
> (Primary head teacher of multi-ethnic school)

A female deputy head teacher of a co-educational inner city comprehensive spoke of parents as 'not only clients to whom we provide a service but a *resource* for the school'. In these two schools visited for the case study, staff spoke of 'partnership with parents' and described a number of initiatives involving collaboration.

Both of these case study schools had extensive EO policies dealing separately with gender and ethnicty. In the co-educational comprehensive these were introduced to all pupils via the tutorial scheme for Personal and Social Education (PSE). The policy contained themes of social justice, inclusion and effective citizenship merged with elements from the 'levelling up and raising standards' emphasis of the post-reform context. Anti-bullying policies included anti-racist dimensions, reflecting the needs of the population served by the LEA which had developed a proforma for recording racial harassment. Parents in these schools (who were also included in EO policies) were involved as positive 'role models', in mentoring schemes, as informal careers experts, sports coaches and reading partners and at both schools parents were involved in reviewing and monitoring the effectiveness of the equal opportunities policies.

Open enrolment and Grant Maintained Schools

There was an equal division amongst Welsh LEAs about the value of open enrolment and its positive or negative effects on gender equality. It is interesting to note that seven of the eight LEAs respondents failed to indicate how they saw 'opting out'; the single respondent considered it as having very negative effects on gender equality. This lack of data or non-response from the Welsh survey is a little surprising since only eleven of Wales' 227 secondary schools and five of its 1,074 primary schools have 'opted out' to date suggesting considerable loyalty to LEA-supported state education.

The benefits of opted out status for gender equality remained unstudied in the LEA case study as access to its three co-educational GM schools was not available. The researcher did note their favourable examinations data in the Welsh Office published school performance tables along with the anxious comments of staff from neighbouring schools who, aware of the market and choice thrust of reforms, felt vulnerable about the likelihood of middle-class parents relocating their bright sons (and daughters) into the performing GM schools: 'We continue to recruit kids from families who cannot transport, the locals and the loyal socialists.'

Local Management of Schools (LMS)

The impact of LMS on gender equality was perceived negatively by half of LEA survey respondents and positively by two. LMS was generally seen as undermining ongoing policy and development work for equal opportunities in schools in the Welsh case study LEA. One deputy head of a primary school felt that in the 'long term LMS could have potentially damaging or eroding effects' on his school's equal opportunities and gender work 'because governing bodies give low priority to such work'. Survey data revealed a discrepancy between what LEAs claimed to provide in terms of Equal Opportunities monitoring and training and what provision primary and secondary schools reported. A key concern is whether LMS has encouraged governing bodies to take up monitoring and training responsibilities vacated or neglected by LEAs:

> The power of the governors is quite terrifying especially when you have groups who spend valuable time criticising the length of skirts worn by female staff! ... Appointment decisions rest totally with the governors and EO policies are forgotten.
>
> (Case study notes, male deputy)

Concern was also expressed by LEA officers about the uptake of equal opportunities training modules offered by the County's Governor Support Unit. One advisor pointed out that since LMS which was phased in during 1990, the LEA's training role had weakened considerably. He referred to the voluntarism and gift time given by people in these gubernatorial roles:

> the trouble with Governors' training is you can't impose it on them! Governors will *ask* you to lay on some training for them – to do the INSET they need. The Director of the Governor Support Unit has put on a number of initiatives but the take up varies.
>
> (Case study interview, advisor)

The Governor Support Unit established by this LEA in 1989 with Welsh Office funding had developed a compendium of eleven training modules, including: Governors and the Law, Equal Opportunities, National Curriculum and School Inspections. Numbers for governors who had undertaken Equal Opportunities training and other modules were unavailable and it was impossible to map out governors' patterns of participation across this training menu. The researcher was told, however, by a friendly secretarial assistant that 'LMS has been in great demand' and 'School Inspections is another popular choice'. Teacher governors at a co-educational comprehensive school expressed concern about levels of awareness and continuity among governing bodies. Frustrated by the lack of a mandatory minimum training one teacher described how the 'collective knowledge just bleeds away': 'Even if Governors *do* some of the training it gets lost when they go [leave the body]. There's no sort of apprenticeship or hand over period when governors change – it's all so *ad hoc*!' (Case study interview, teacher governor). The gendered distribution of these 'state volunteers' in Wales is discussed below briefly and this theme is explored in several other chapters in the volume.

The over-representation of men: a main concern

The continuing dominance of white male cultures in LEA hierarchies and schools was clearly evident in Wales. Progress towards a greater participation of women in senior management across the LEAs in Wales is slow. One illustration of this is that there are no women Directors of Education in any of the twenty-two new authorities. According to the 1994–5 Welsh Office figures there were 143 women and 954 men working as head teachers in primary schools. In the secondary sector there were 207 men compared to only twenty women and the number of women head teachers in secondary schools is reducing. The proportion of men to women on governing bodies of schools show a similar imbalance. Other studies have remarked on the paucity of women chairs of governing bodies (see Deem 1991; Deem and Brehony 1991; David 1993; Deem, this volume). In Wales over three quarters of the governing body chairs are male (Arnot *et al.* 1996; Salisbury 1996b: 31).

The urban South Wales LEA used for the in-depth case study was characterised by male over-representation at nearly every level of organisation within schools and the LEA itself. Even the county's EO advisor was a male though he recognised the incongruity somewhat candidly: 'I'm the token white male – the worst possible scenario isn't it?' At the time of the fieldwork for this study, governors of a co-educational comprehensive in an affluent middle-class 'catchment area' appointed a female head teacher – this was the first female secondary headship appointment in the LEA for *twenty years*, the last such appointment being in 1974!

In Wales the work of the teacher unions in relation to equal opportunities was seen as supportive and positive. Recent trade union activity on equality issues had dwindled in the case study LEA, though a group of former Senior Mistresses (now retired) had kept 'gender on the agenda' for well over twenty-five years in the NUT branch. Their continued voluntary work in the 'Women's Education Advisory Group' and in particular, their rigorous monitoring of senior positions and pressure on County Councillors had resulted in the LEA providing 'Management Courses for Women Teachers' in 1990. The male Director of Education, who was proud of this initiative planned to monitor the career trajectories of the forty women staff who had participated in it.

Snapshots and mixed and partial pictures of equal opportunities and gender equality work

The research project into Education Reform and Gender Equality revealed a mixed picture for Wales, where in the mid-1990s there appeared to be a commitment to equal opportunities from some individuals and groups. Equality issues were not viewed as a high priority in the majority of LEAs and schools. Welsh LEAs reported considerable post-LMS services, seven of the eight reported providing equal opportunities training for governors and six claimed to be monitoring gender equality for teachers, pupils and examination performance. Schools, however, reported a lack of equal opportunities training for senior managers and classroom teachers (Salisbury 1996b). From the limited data available for Wales, it was difficult to know to what extent the support and advice claimed to have been given by LEAs to schools was taken up by schools or matched their priorities.

The legislative changes have resulted in a considerable transfer of power away from local education authorities towards the governing bodies of individual schools and towards central government – specifically in Wales, the Welsh Office Education Department. This transfer of power poses serious questions for the future of LEAs and their coordinating functions and strategic planning.

In terms of equal opportunities and gender equality work, future progress in schools will depend upon the commitment of governors and the abilities of the newly reorganised education authorities to support it. A number of recent Welsh Office policy documents from both Conservative and more recently Labour administration (see Welsh Office 1995c, 1995d, 1997, 1998a) describe strategies which aim to improve the quality of experience and achievements of all young people in Wales. Educational achievement is now openly linked to economic development in the policy documents for Wales: 'Developing the talents of men and women is essential to prosperity: for themselves, their families, their communities and for Wales' (Welsh Office 1995c).

It might have been expected following the election of a Labour government in May 1997 that the use of assessment data as a mechanism for raising educational standards would be adapted to reflect a potentially different set of priorities in education policy (Daugherty and Freedman 1998). New Labour in Wales shows little sign of subverting the agenda of performativity; the parallel White Paper on education in England (DfEE 1997) and Wales (Welsh Office 1997) are laden with the familiar vocabularies and rhetoric about tests, targets and performance tables which typified the preoccupations of the previous Conservative administration.

All schools, colleges, Education and Business Partnerships, the Welsh TECs along with the newly established Careers Companies and education authorities are clearly identified in Welsh Office documents as having key roles and responsibilities in supporting a number of goals including valid work experience and post-16 routes of progression for students. ACCAC and OHMCI have crucial work to do in both advising and reporting on recent and ongoing educational initiatives such as the slimmed down National Curriculum for primary schools. Monitoring the Welsh schools' and colleges' progress against the national education and training targets (NTETs) set by NACETT (1995) has already led to the close scrutiny of differential performance and the identification of separate targets for schools in Wales (Welsh Office 1998a). Current and future trends in statutory assessments and subject choices and in the post-16 achievements of boys and girls in Wales are now recognised as vital data. In the context of different achievement levels it has been argued the setting of gender-based targets for each subject, (both for entry and performance) would help Wales to raise its present standards and perhaps lead to productive research which would identify different strategies to improve performance in some subjects for each sex (Salisbury 1996b).

Recently completed research on the comparative performance of boys and girls in schools in Wales (Gorard *et al.* 1998a) commissioned and funded by ACCAC, studied the 'gender gaps' in school outcomes at the ages of 7, 11, 14, 16 and 18 from 1992 to 1997. The analysis undertaken shows the trends in differential attainment by boys and girls over time in each subject area and at each level of attainment; most notably, it demonstrates that 'national' concerns over the so-called gender gaps (in performance) are justified in some subjects and some levels of attainment, but not in others. Briefly, then, the pattern of achievement gaps revealed in the study are underpinned by girls gaining more of the higher attainment levels at Key Stages 1 to 4 in English, Welsh, Languages and Humanities – no such achievement gaps are observed in other subjects such as Mathematics and Science. Moreover, for the years examined closely in the study, the only indication of any changes in the achievement gaps is confined to these higher levels of attainment. It remains a matter of concern for schools that in general terms, boys are performing less well than girls in most subjects and that many students of either gender appear to be underachieving. This research evidence, however, provides an important corrective to many previous accounts of boys' 'underachievement'.

Concluding remarks

The research reported here reflects imperatives set by policies initiated by British central government. What is of interest analytically, as Delamont and Rees (1997) point out, is the interaction between policies whose origins are outside of Wales and the specificities of their implementation within Wales. There is much research still to be done as some of the intriguing data from the EOC study on gender (along with other studies such as Reynolds 1995 and Gorard 1998) suggest that the differences between schools in Wales may be as interesting as those between Wales and other parts of the UK.

Without doubt sample sizes and poor response rates problematise the general-isability of the analysis for Wales provided in the EOC study. Nevertheless, quantitative and qualitative data enabled Welsh policy-makers and planners to gauge some of the perceived effects of multiple reforms on gender equality. Most importantly, it highlighted the need for systematic, rigorous and uniform data collection on achievement levels by gender and identified numerous policy implications and 'oughts and shoulds' for the key policy actors in Wales (Salisbury 1996b: 36–9). Though it would be foolhardy to make grand claims, the publication of the EOC's modest bilingual report for Wales has been an heuristic and generated a productive focus for both OHMCI and the newly formed Qualifications, Curriculum and Assessment Authority for Wales (ACCAC). Each of these responsible bodies has undertaken surveys or commissioned research which specifically explores the gender dimension (for example, WSSA/OHMCI 1996; OHMCI 1997; Gorard *et al.* 1998a).

It is clear from these recent publications that qualitative research, involving in-depth longitudinal case studies of a range of schools and classrooms across Wales is needed to develop a better understanding of how, where and why gender differences in statutory assessments and examination performance exists. The role that different types of school play, in particular Welsh-medium schools on which there are no ethnographic data – is needed especially given Reynold's (1995) claim that attainment levels in these schools are consistently higher than those in English-medium schools. Indeed, the influence of school organisation, setting, banding, tiered entry schemes along with classroom processes and assessment modes, needs to be investigated thoroughly over a longer time frame since all of these factors have been linked to the differential performance of boys and girls in recent research.

How far mandatory target setting (introduced in Autumn 1998 in Wales) will shape teachers' and schools' practices and reduce the apparent 'gender gaps' between boys' and girls' attainments is yet to be discovered. In Wales currently, an important set of research questions is emerging; the impacts of the local government reforms of 1996 are not yet apparent and whether or not administrative devolution to Wales will result in significantly different 'national' policies is a question for a future research agenda.

Notes

1   A fuller discussion of these themes and findings which compare both England and Wales is provided by Arnot *et al.* (1996) in a parallel report titled *Educational Reforms and Gender Equality in Schools*.
2   Chwarae Teg is Welsh for the expression 'fair play'.

References

Aaron, J., Rees, T., Betts, S. and Vincentelli, M. (eds) (1994) *Our Sisters' Land: The Changing Identities of Women in Wales*, Cardiff: University of Wales Press.

Arnot, M., David, M. and Weiner, G. (1996) *Educational Reforms and Gender Equality in Schools*, Manchester: EOC.

Awdurdod Cwricwlwm ac Asesu Cymru (ACAC) (1994) *The National Curriculum Proposals in Wales*, Cardiff: ACAC.

—— (1995) *Review of the National Curriculum Assessment Arrangements: First Phase*, Cardiff: ACAC

Baker, C. (1990) 'The growth of bilingual education in the secondary schools of Wales', in W.G. Evans (ed.) (1990) *Perspectives of a Century of Secondary Education in Wales*, Aberystwyth: CAA.

Ball, S.J. (1990) *Politics and Policy Making in Education: Explanations in Policy Sociology*, London: Routledge.

Bellin, W., Osmond, J. and Reynolds, D. (1994) *Towards an Education Policy For Wales*, Cardiff: Institute of Welsh Affairs.

Betts, S. (1994) 'The changing family in Wales', in J. Aaron, T. Rees, S. Betts and M. Vincentelli (eds) *Our Sister's Land: The Changing Identities of Women in Wales*, Cardiff: University of Wales Press.

—— (ed.) (1996) *Our Daughters' Land: Past and Present*, Cardiff: University of Wales Press.

Butler, I., Davies, M. and Noyes, P. (1995) *Planning For Children: The Effects Of Local Government Reorganisation*, Wales: NSPCC Cymru.

Careers Service in Wales (1994) *Pupil Destination Statistics in Wales 1993*, Cardiff: Careers Service in Wales.

Central Statistics Office (1993) *Regional Trends 28*, London: HMSO.

Curriculum Council for Wales (CCW) (1993) *Developing a Curriculum Cymreig*, Cardiff: CCW.

Daniel, P. (1994) 'Promoting gender equality in schools', in J. Aaron, T. Rees, S. Betts and M. Vincentelli (eds) *Our Sisters' Land: The Changing Identities of Women in Wales*, Cardiff: University of Wales Press.

Daugherty, R. (1997) 'National Curriculum assessment: the experience of England and Wales', *Educational Administration Quarterly* 33, 2: 198–218.

Daugherty, R. and Freedman, E.S. (1998) 'Tests, targets and tables: the use of Key Stage 2 assessment data in Wales', *The Welsh Journal of Education* 7, 1: 5–21.

David, M.D. (1993) *Parents, Gender and Education Reform*, Cambridge: Polity Press.

Deem, R. (1991) 'Governing by gender? School governing bodies after ERA', in P. Abbot and C. Wallace (eds) *Gender, Power and Sexuality*, London: Macmillan.

Deem, R. and Brehony, K. (1991) 'Governing bodies and Local Education Authorities: relationships, contradictions and tensions', in M. Golby (ed.) *Exeter Papers on School Governorship No. 3*, Exeter School of Education, Exeter University: Fairway Publications.

Delamont, S. (1990) *Sex Roles and the School*, London: Routledge.

Delamont, S. and Rees, G. (1997) *Understanding the Welsh Education System: Does Wales Need a Separate 'Policy Sociology'?* Working Paper 23, Cardiff: School of Education.

Department for Education, Welsh Office, Scottish Education Department, Department of Education for Northern Ireland and the University Funding Council (1993) *Education Statistics for the United Kingdom*, London: HMSO.

DfEE (1997) *Excellence in Schools*, London: DfEE.

Elwyn Jones, G. (1990) *Which Nation's Schools?* Avon: Bookcraft.

—— (1994) 'Which nation's curriculum? The case of Wales', *The Curriculum Journal* 5, 1: 5–16.

EOC/Chwarae Teg (1993) *Realising Potential: Increasing the Effectiveness of Education and Training Provision for Women*, Cardiff: EOC.

Equal Opportunities Commission (1997a) *Briefings on Women and Men in Britain: The Labour Market*, Manchester: EOC.

—— (1997b) *Facts about Women and Men in Wales 1997*, Cardiff: EOC.

—— (1998) *Gender and Differential Achievement in Education and Training: A Research Review*, Manchester: EOC.

Evans, G. (1997) 'Good governance', *The Welsh Journal of Education* 6, 2: 84–94.

Gerwitz, S., Ball, S. and Bowe, R. (1995) *Markets, Choice and Equity in Education*, Buckingham: OUP.

Gorard, S. (1996) 'Fee-paying schools in Britain: a particularly English phenomenon', *Educational Review* 48, 1: 89–93.

—— (1998) '"Schooled to fail?" Revisiting the Welsh school effect', *Journal of Education Policy* 13, 1: 115–24.

Gorard, S. and Fitz, J. (1998) 'The more things change ... the missing impact of marketization', *British Journal of Sociology of Education*, 19, 3: 365–76.

Gorard, S., Salisbury, J., Rees, G. and Fitz, J. (1998a) *The Comparative Performance of Boys and Girls in Schools in Wales*, Cardiff: ACCAC.

—— (1998b) 'The "politician's" error: a reanalysis of the gender gap in school performance', paper presented to the Educational Research in Wales Conference, Gregynog, 4 July 1998.

Halpin, D., Power, S. and Fitz, J. (1997) 'Opting into the past? Grant Maintained Schools and the reinvention of tradition', in R. Glatter, P. Woods and C. Bagley (eds) *Choice and Diversity in Schooling: Perspectives and Prospects*, London: Routledge.

Istance, D. and Rees, T. (1994) *Women in Post Compulsory Education and Training in Wales*, Manchester: EOC.

Istance, D., Rees, G. and Williamson, H. (1994) *Young People not in Education, Training or Unemployment in South Glamorgan*, Cardiff: South Glamorgan TEC.

Jones, A. (1995) *A Content Analysis of Recent OHMCI Reports on Schools in Wales*, London: Fawcett Society.

Le Grande, J. and Bartlett, W. (eds) (1993) *Quasi Markets and Social Policy*, London: Macmillan.

Loosemore Report (1981) *The Schools Council for Wales Curriculum Re-Appraisal*, Cardiff: Schools Council.

Morris Jones, B. (1995) 'Schools and speech communities in a bilingual setting', in B. Morris Jones and P.A. Singh Ghuman (eds) *Bilingualism, Education and Identity Essays in Honour of Jac L. Williams*, Cardiff: University of Wales Press.

National Advisory Council for Education and Training Targets (1995) *Developing Skills for a Successful Future*, London: NACETT.

OHMCI (1994) *Framework and Guidance for the Inspection of Schools*, Cardiff: Central Office of Information.

—— (1997) *The Relative Performance of Boys and Girls*, Cardiff: Office of Her Majesty's Chief Inspector in Wales.

O'Keefe, D. and Stoll, L. (1991) 'Unwillingly to lessons: curriculum, truancy and nationalised education', *Economic Affairs* 8: 20–8.

Paechter, C. (1998) *Educating the Other: Gender, Power and Schooling*, Lewes: Falmer Press.

Phillips, R. (1996) 'Education policy making in Wales: a research agenda', *Welsh Journal of Education* 5, 2: 26–42.

Pilcher, J., Delamont, S., Powell, G. and Rees, T. (1988) 'Women's training roadshows and the "Manipulation" of schoolgirls' career choices', *British Journal of Education and Work* 2, 2: 61–6.

—— (1989a) 'Evaluating a careers convention: methods, results and implications', *Research Papers in Education* 4, 1: 57–76.

Pilcher, J., Delamont, S., Powell, G., Rees, T. and Read, M. (1989b) 'Challenging occupational stereotypes: women's training roadshows and guidance at school level', *British Journal of Guidance and Counselling* 17, 1: 59–67.

Rawkins, P. (1979) 'The implementation of language policy in the schools of Wales', *Studies in Public Policy No. 40*, Glasgow: University of Strathclyde.

Rees, C. and Willcox, I. (1991) *Expanding the Role of Women in the South Wales Workforce*, Cardiff: Welsh Development Agency.

Rees, T. (1992) *Women and the Labour Market*, London: Routledge.

—— (1994) 'Women and paid work', in J. Aaron, T. Rees, S. Betts and M. Vincentelli (eds) *Our Sisters' Land: The Changing Identities of Women in Wales*, Cardiff: University of Wales Press.

—— (1999) *Women and Work: Twenty-five Years of Equality Legislation in Wales*, Cardiff: University of Wales Press.

Rees, T. and Fielder, S. (1991) *Women and Top Jobs in Wales*, Report for HTV Wales Cardiff, Social Research Unit, Cardiff: University of Wales College of Cardiff.

—— (1992) 'Smashing the dark glass ceiling: women at the top in Wales', *Contemporary Wales: An Annual Review of Economic and Social Research*, Cardiff: University of Wales Press, 5: 99–114.

Reynolds, D. (1990) 'The dragon sleeps: education in Wales 1979–1989', in W.G. Evans (ed.) *Perspectives of a Century of Secondary Education in Wales*, Aberystwyth: CAA.

—— (1995) 'Creating an educational system for Wales', *The Welsh Journal of Education* 4, 2: 4–21.

Riddell, S. (1992) *Gender and the Politics of the Curriculum*, London: Routledge.

Riley, K. (1994) *Quality and Equality: Promoting Opportunities in Schools*, London: Cassell.

Salisbury, J. (1996a) 'Take Our Daughters to Work: a positive action for some school girls in Wales', in S. Betts (ed.) *Our Daughters' Land*, Cardiff: University of Wales Press.

—— (1996b) *Educational Reforms and Gender Equality in Welsh Schools*, Cardiff: EOC.

Salisbury, J., Gorard, S., Rees, G. and Fitz, J. (1998) 'The comparative performance of boys and girls in Wales: an alternative view of the gender gap', paper presented to the ECER conference in Ljubljana, September 1998.

School Curriculum and Assessment Authority (1993) *The National Curriculum and its Assessment: Final Report* (The Dearing Report), London: SCAA.

School Curriculum and Assessment Authority/Curriculum and Assessment Authority for Wales (ACAC) (1994) *Report on Key Stage 2 Pilot*, ref. KS2/94/129, London: SCAA.

Self, D. (1985) 'And forgiveth our trespasses', *TES* 20 December 1985.

Startup, R. and Dressel, B.M. (1996) 'The culture and aspirations of Welsh secondary school pupils: a comparison between the sexes?', in S. Betts (ed.) *Our Daughters' Land*, Cardiff: University of Wales Press.

Turner, E, Riddell, S. and Brown, S. (1995) *Gender Equality in Scottish Schools: The Impact of Recent Reforms*, Manchester: Equal Opportunities Commission.

Wales Assembly of Women (1995) *Education and Training*, report for UN Fourth World Conference on the Status of Women in Beijing 1995, Cardiff: WAW.

Weiner, G., Arnot, M. and David, M. (1997) 'Is the future female? Female success, male disadvantage and changing patterns in education', in A.H. Halsey, P. Brown, H. Lauder and A. Stuart Wells (eds) *Education, Culture, Economy, Society*, Oxford: Oxford University Press.

Welsh Office (1995a) *Careers Education and Guidance, Proposed Legislation: A Consultation Paper*, Welsh Office: Cardiff.

—— (1995b) *Statistics of Education and Training in Wales: Schools*, Cardiff: Welsh Office.

—— (1995c) *People and Prosperity: An Agenda for Action in Wales*, (Redwood Report), Cardiff: Welsh Office.

—— (1995d) *A Bright Future: Getting The Best For Every Pupil At School in Wales*, Cardiff: Welsh Office.

—— (1997) *Building Excellent Schools Together*, Cardiff: Welsh Office.

—— (1998a) *Target Setting: Guidance for Headteachers and Governing Bodies*, Cardiff: Welsh Office Education Department.

—— (1998b) *Learning is for Everyone*, London: HMSO.

Whitty, G. (1989) 'Central control or market forces', in M. Flude and M. Hammer (eds) *The Education Reform Act 1988: Its Origins and Implications*, Basingstoke: Faber Press.

Whyte, J. (1986) *Girls into Science and Technology*, London: Routledge and Kegan Paul.

WSSA/OHMCI (1996) *Tackling the Underachievement of Boys*, Cardiff: OHMCI.

4 Gender, educational reform and equality in Northern Ireland

Anthony M. Gallagher,
Robert J. Cormack and
Robert D. Osborne

Introduction

Throughout the Thatcher and Major years in Britain, a low priority was attached to equity issues in education (Siraj-Blatchford and Troyna 1993). This was not so in Northern Ireland for reasons we will explore in this chapter. Due to the political conflict a great deal of attention has focused on the need to promote greater equity between the two main religious communities across a range of dimensions. Thus, for example, Northern Ireland has arguably the strongest legislation against discrimination in employment in any European jurisdiction, and has a policy environment within which equity issues are accorded more time and attention in comparison with Britain. Although the primary focus of this attention has been on religious divisions, there has been an impact on other social dimensions, including gender. In Britain there has been a heated debate in recent years on the apparent underachievement of boys (as discussed in other chapters in this volume and evident in a series of *TES* articles including: 'Male brain rattled by curriculum "oestrogen"', 15 March 1996; 'Coursework link to girls' success queried', 24 November 1995; 'Females do better on reflection', 20 October 1995; 'Why teenage boys think success is sad', 18 August 1995). By contrast, in Northern Ireland it has long been known that the lowest levels of educational achievement are found amongst boys leaving secondary schools, in particular, Catholic schools. As we will describe below, the government has instituted a number of significant policy changes on equity groups, both in terms of religious background and gender, and the expectations held of government in this area are higher in Northern Ireland than in Britain. Furthermore, employment legislation has led to the development of strong equal opportunities units within the two higher education institutions. What we find, then, is that despite the fact that the Conservative governments from 1979 to 1997 were largely antithetical to equity concerns, they were obliged, due to social pressure, to incorporate equity dimensions in legislation and policy in Northern Ireland. This had the consequence of creating a distinctive policy climate in Northern Ireland where equity concerns were more strongly rooted in debates and discussions, arguably extending beyond the specific arenas within which equity measures were introduced. This is not to say that Northern Ireland is a fully equitable society, nor is it to say that gender differences to the disadvantage of women do not exist. Rather, we would argue that the particular context created in Northern Ireland is one where the government has been obliged to take equity concerns more seriously and within which the expectations of and demands made on government are higher than is the case in Britain. In order to illustrate this theme we will examine policy and practice across a range of educational contexts. We begin by outlining briefly the education system in Northern Ireland.

Education in Northern Ireland

Education in Northern Ireland is administered by five Education and Library Boards (ELBs), which are roughly equivalent to LEAs in the rest of the United Kingdom. The ELBs deal largely with administrative functions and never had the degree of political authority accorded to LEAs in Britain. Central direction is provided by the Department of Education in Northern Ireland (DENI). In addition to a number of non-departmental public bodies covering a variety of areas including assessment and the curriculum, there exists a Council for Catholic Maintained Schools (CCMS) and a Northern Ireland Council for Integrated Education (NICIE).

The three main distinctive aspects of the schools system in Northern Ireland are the retention of selection at age 11, the existence of parallel religious school systems for Protestants and Catholics, and the relatively high extent of single-sex schools.

The structure of the education system in Northern Ireland has been largely shaped by the 1947 Education Act, the equivalent to the 1944 Education Act for England and Wales. As in Britain this established a selective system of grammar and secondary schools and a selection procedure to identify those pupils most able for the academic curriculum of the grammar. Unlike Britain, selection at age 11 remains the predominant form of transfer from primary to secondary education in Northern Ireland (Wilson 1986), although a system of delayed selection has operated in one part of Northern Ireland since 1969 (McKernan 1981) and about a dozen or so comprehensive schools exist.

The biggest change since 1947 has been provided by the Education Reform Order (ERO) (1989). The ERO introduced many of the education reforms established in England and Wales under the Education Reform Act (1988), in particular introducing elements of marketisation into education. The Northern Ireland legislation included a number of important features that were particular to the local context. Thus, while the reforms included a common curriculum, local management of schools, a higher degree of school choice for parents and, in order to inform choice, a larger amount of educational data in the public domain, they also included the option for parents in an existing school to vote to change its status to a religiously integrated school and the incorporation of two cross-curricular themes linked to community relations issues (Education for Mutual Understanding (EMU) and Cultural Heritage) into the common curriculum.

The second feature mentioned above lies in the extent of religious separation.

Currently there are about 460 Catholic primary schools and 490 Protestant primary schools. At the post-primary level there are 77 Catholic secondary and 31 Catholic grammar schools, and 75 Protestant secondary and 40 Protestant grammar schools. The religious nomenclature of the schools reflects a *de facto* rather than a *de jure* position and is based on the high degree of religious homogeneity of the pupils and teachers within the separate school systems. Since 1980 a number of integrated schools, catering for both Protestant and Catholic pupils, have developed: currently there are more than thirty primary and secondary integrated schools, with more opening each year, and in total they account for a little over 3 per cent of the total pupil enrolment in Northern Ireland. It is important to note also that most of the schools in Northern Ireland do not come under the authority of the ELBs: this is so for all Catholic schools, most of the integrated schools and about three-quarters of the Protestant grammar schools. These schools had always had a degree of administrative autonomy, although the reform measures also introduced financial autonomy through formula funding.

Table 4.1 summarises data on the numbers of boys and girls in grammar and secondary schools in Northern Ireland and illustrates the third feature in that there is a relatively high proportion of single-sex schools, particularly in the grammar sector.

Much of the research on achievement in Northern Ireland has tended to focus either on the outputs of the two religious school systems or on the consequences of the selective system. There has been very much less large-scale research on gender issues and much of this has happened because of funding support from the Equal Opportunities Commission in Northern Ireland (EOCNI). In the next part of the chapter we examine the broad patterns of the research evidence on attainment as mediated by gender. While we are interested in the broad patterns emerging from this evidence, we highlight the way in which some of this evidence was used by the EOCNI to challenge and change government policy in a key educational area. Despite this, however, it remains true that government has tended to pay closer attention to the policy implications of research on education attainment as mediated by religion, and we next include an example of a body of research which led to significant change in government practice to illustrate this

Table 4.1 Pupils in secondary schools by sex and school type, 1994–95

	Secondary Schools				Grammar Schools		
Schools	*Boys*	*Girls*	*Total*	*Schools*	*Boys*	*Girls*	*Total*
21	12,269	–	12,269	15	13,504	–	13,504
119	33,549	28,302	61,851	37	15,070	16,362	31,432
21	–	15,414	15,414	19	–	15,466	15,466
161	45,818	43,716	89,534	71	28,574	31,828	60,402

Source: Unpublished data supplied by the Department of Education, Northern Ireland.

point. We conclude the chapter with a broader discussion on the role of equity policy generally in Northern Ireland, and how this has been affected by the period since the education reforms of the later 1980s.

Gender and attainment

We now turn to research in Northern Ireland which has focused more specifically on gender patterns in education. Morgan (1995) provides the most comprehensive summary available on this work and notes the emergent pattern in Northern Ireland such that the attainment of girls is now higher than that of boys. Morgan was unable to identify the reasons for this change, although he did point to some of the explanations that have been offered in the literature. More particularly, Morgan (1995) highlighted a concern that attention on this emergent pattern of attainment may divert attention from the continuing curriculum differences between boys and girls in schools, and further reduce the already limited extent to which the results of research on gender have influenced the development of the Northern Ireland curriculum. In the remainder of this section of the chapter we will examine some of the broad patterns found in research on gender and attainment in Northern Ireland.

Wilson (1985) was the fourth in a series of reports charting the progress of a cohort of some 3,000 pupils who entered post-primary education in 1975. In a previous paper, Wilson had reported higher performance among the girls on a verbal reasoning ability test taken in their first year of post-primary school. Wilson (1985) also found an attainment advantage for girls in performance at 18 years. This attainment advantage was not apparent among the pupils in the cohort who sat for A level examinations, but was instead a consequence of more girls than boys staying in school at age 16 years and entering for A levels. The attainment advantage then related to the cohort as a whole. Johnston and Rooney (1987) offered an overview of gender patterns in education in Northern Ireland using DENI data. They identified a greater tendency for girls to stay beyond compulsory schooling than boys. On the basis of examinations entered they found a pattern such that girls were more likely to study humanities subjects while boys were more likely to study science subjects. However, they noted that throughout the 1980s the examination entry pattern for boys had changed little, while that for girls had moved towards a science only, or science and arts mix. Using school leavers data for 1983–4 Johnston and Rooney showed that girls achieved higher attainments than boys. Thus, for example, while 24 per cent of girls leaving school had passed one or more A level, this was so for only 20 per cent of boys; and while 50 per cent of boys left school with less than one O level pass, this was so for only 41 per cent of girls.

As indicated above, the EOCNI has funded a number of research studies over the years on gender issues in education. One issue which has been addressed on a number of occasions relates to the under-representation of women in senior positions in schools, despite their over-representation among the teacher workforce (INTO 1993): see also the chapter by Rees *et al.* in the present volume.

The EOCNI also maintained a close interest in a research programme carried out in the 1980s by the Northern Ireland Council for Educational Research (NICER) on the 11+ selective system. The NICER research on the transfer system resulted in six separate publications focusing on such issues as the opinions of primary teachers, curriculum allocation in primary schools, the statistics of transfer between primary and post-primary schools, the experience of border-band pupils and an examination of the predictive efficiency of the transfer tests. Our interest here lies in the gender issues raised by the research.

At the time of the NICER research, the pupils in the transfer age group were placed into three categories on the basis of their performance on verbal-reasoning type tests. The top 20 per cent were placed in grade A, the next 10 per cent were placed in grade M and the rest of the pupils taking the test were placed in grade G. Any pupils who opted not to take the tests was treated as if they were grade G pupils. Grade A pupils were entitled to a non-fee-paying place in a grammar school, grade M pupils were entitled to a non-fee-paying place if they could find a school willing to admit them, and grade G pupils could only obtain grammar school places as fee-paying pupils.

For the purposes of grade categorisation, boys and girls were treated as two separate cohorts. The official justification offered for this practice was that, as girls matured earlier than boys, they tended to perform better on verbal-reasoning-type tests at age 11 years. However, when both sexes had gone through puberty to achieve maturity, the academic performance of boys 'caught up' with that of girls. On these grounds it was felt that to treat boys and girls as a single population at age 11 years would unfairly disadvantage boys, despite claims by the EOCNI that this practice might be illegal under article 24 of the Sex Discrimination (Northern Ireland) Order 1976.

Data collected by Sutherland and Gallagher (1987) suggested that the premise used to justify this practice may not have been valid. Their study of border-band pupils found that of the fifth form pupils, girls achieved, on average, nearly one O level pass more than the boys. They also gained slightly higher average and total points scores than the boys, although not significantly so. While almost 74 per cent of the girls achieved four or more O level (or equivalent) passes, this was so for 58 per cent of the boys: this cut-off point was chosen as it represented the minimum level of attainment required to retain or obtain a place in the sixth form of a grammar school. Gallagher (1988) used a larger sample of pupils of some 1,500 pupils randomly drawn from the transfer cohort of 1981. The information collected on the pupils included their transfer grades, sex, type of post-primary school attended, social background and performance in public examinations. Gallagher found that on average and total points attainment scores, and the four O level criterion, girls achieved higher attainment than boys. In addition, Gallagher found this to hold also for boys and girls with the same transfer grades.

Following the publication of these two research reports the EOCNI supported a test case alleging that the policy of treating boys and girls as separate populations for the determination of qualified status amounted to sex discrimination. The legal challenge was successful and resulted in an additional 305 girls being given qualified status. Since no boys were displaced from the qualified group, the EOCNI returned to the court to argue that any girls with marks at or above the lowest 'qualified' boy should receive a grammar place. The judge agreed and a further 555 girls were given qualified status.

A further feature of Gallagher's (1988) analysis is of relevance to the broader issue of gender differences in attainment. Of the total sample of pupils, 292 (19 per cent) had completed five years of post-primary education without obtaining a qualification in public examinations of any kind. Of these pupils, 279 had left school. These leavers were more likely to be boys than girls (62 per cent vs. 38 per cent), 96 per cent had obtained a grade G or not entered the transfer tests, 97 per cent had attended secondary schools, and they were slightly more likely to have attended Catholic than Protestant schools (54 per cent vs. 46 per cent). The majority of these pupils had not entered for any public examinations: only 31 had entered for any examinations, and only 10 had entered for four or more subjects. In other words, the high level of unqualified leaving was related more to non-entry to, rather than failure in, public examinations (see also Gallagher 1997).

As part of the education reforms there had been much discussion on how the transfer tests might be linked into assessment procedures. After a variety of options were considered, the DENI decided to cease using the verbal-reasoning-type tests in favour of a composite test of English, maths and science questions. On these tests pupils are assigned to one of four grades, with the top 25 per cent being assigned a grade A. If the ability of the EOCNI to use the NICER research evidence to change DENI policy demonstrated the efficacy of arguments based on equity considerations, the shift to attainment tests helped to illustrate their limits.

Table 4.2 shows the relative proportions of boys and girls achieving the top grades on the 11+ tests for three years in each of three distinct periods. Between

Table 4.2 Proportion of boys and girls achieving the top grade in the 11+ selection tests (selected years)

Year	Boys	Girls
1982/83	51.9	48.1
1983/84	51.7	48.3
1984/85	52.0	48.0
1990/91	46.5	53.5
1991/92	46.4	53.6
1992/93	45.8	54.2
1993/94	49.8	50.2
1994/95	46.1	53.9
1995/96	51.2	48.8

Source: These data are calculated from data in Wilson (1986), DENI (1996) and a press release from the Northern Ireland council for the Curriculum, Examinations and Assessment (CCEA).

1982–3 and 1984–5 boys and girls were treated as separate populations in the assignment of grades, with the result that a slightly higher proportion of boys received the top grade. For the second period shown on the table, 1990–1 to 1992–3, boys and girls were treated as a single population, but now a higher proportion of girls were assigned the top grade. In the most recent period, when attainment tests rather than verbal-reasoning tests are used for the selective procedure, there is variability in the comparative rate at which boys and girls are assigned the top grade.

Interestingly, for the 1994–5 tests many teachers complained that the tests were too difficult for pupils because they required an excessive amount of reading. Defending the tests, the minister with responsibility for education in Northern Ireland accepted that they had had a high reading content, but suggested that the 'levels at which some of the questions were pitched in mathematics and science was lower than [the previous] year' (Northern Ireland Information Service, 21 October 1994). The balance of questions referred to by the minister might be expected to enhance the performance of girls and, as we can see from Table 4.2, girls did, in fact, comprise a higher proportion of the top grade pupils that year. In the following year, however, boys comprised a higher proportion of the top grade group which has led some commentators to suspect that the type of questions used in the tests may have shifted to favour boys. Some media commentators have even gone so far as to suspect that this shift was deliberate in order to 'balance' the sex intakes to grammar schools, although there is no evidence to support this claim and the fault, in all probability, lies in the use of an unreliable selective test. Patricia Murphy's chapter (this volume) further explores issues around bias in assessment.

Returning now to research on attainment further up the schools system, two EOCNI-funded studies had provided comparative data over time on the GCSE/O level attainment and A level subject choice of pupils in a sample of grammar schools. McEwen *et al.* (1985) had collected data on 694 boys and 732 girls in the sixth forms of 21 grammar schools. The data included details of the A levels they were following, their O level and other public examination results and a variety of attitudinal items. Ten years later Gallagher *et al.* (1997) returned, as far as possible, to the same schools and collected similar data on 728 boys and 872 girls. On the curriculum patterns Gallagher *et al.* (1997) found that a little over a third of the pupils in the sample schools were taking no Science A levels, and this proportion was similar for boys and girls. They also found that, for those pupils who were taking Science A levels, boys were more likely than girls to be taking two or more Science subjects (40 per cent versus 31 per cent). Despite this general pattern, the extent of the difference in the average number of Science A levels taken by boys and girls had narrowed between 1985 and 1995. There was some continuing evidence of gendered A level subjects but they argued that it was no longer accurate to suggest that girls taking Science A levels were confined to a narrow range of subjects only taken by girls. In this vein, a comparison of overall A level entries in schools for 1978 and 1994 showed that while the proportion of girls taking Physics in both years has hardly changed, there had been a marked increase in the proportion of girls taking Biology and, perhaps more significantly, Chemistry.

Analysis of the GCSE attainments of the pupils in the sample schools showed that girls in 1995 passed a higher average number of GCSE examinations than boys and achieved a higher average grade score. In addition, while boys entered for a slightly higher average number of science GCSE subjects, girls had a higher average grade score on these subjects. The 1995 figures were compared with O level data from the 1985 study. Over the period the average number of examinations passed and the average grade score had increased for all pupils. For the present purposes, however, the main interest lies in the comparative pattern over time for boys and girls. Here it was found that an attainment advantage did not exist for girls in 1985, but did in 1995. In other words, the attainment of the girls had increased at a higher rate over the ten-year period. The evidence in this study did not suggest that attainment differences were explained by curriculum differences in that that boys achieved higher levels of attainment in only three GCSE subjects, Mathematics, Physics and Computer Studies, and apart from the first of these the attainment gap in favour of boys was quite narrow. Indeed, they pointed to an interesting feature of their data in regard to the relative performance of boys and girls in some of the traditionally 'male' subjects: only a very small number of girls, for example, were taking GCSE CDT or Technology, but their attainment levels were markedly above those of the boys taking these subjects.

A key explanation for the change in attainment patterns appeared to be linked to pupils' expectations. Gallagher *et al.* (1997) had extended the original study to include focus group interviews in ten of the participating schools. This qualitative evidence suggested that the changes identified in the study were attributable less to the girls' perceptions of the academic subjects themselves, and more to their perceptions of the occupational opportunities they believed to be open to them in the future. If an important reason for choosing to study Science A levels lies in their direct relevance to particular occupations and more girls now believe those occupations are open to them, then more girls than in the past will choose to study those Science A levels.

The role of expectations was also examined using a variety of approaches on the questionnaire completed by pupils in the sample schools. The pupils were asked what they expected to do after they had left grammar school. In practice the majority of grammar school pupils enter higher education and this was the emergent pattern from the survey. However, there was an interesting difference when the responses to this question in the 1985 and 1995 studies were compared. In both studies about 92 per cent of boys said that they expected to go to university after leaving grammar school. However, for girls the pattern had changed somewhat: in 1985, 72 per cent said they expected to go to university, but in 1995 this figure had increased to 87 per cent.

As a simple attempt to measure stereotypes the pupils were asked to indicate whether they thought a series of domestic tasks were more appropriate for boys, for girls or were appropriate for both groups. The same questions had been asked in the 1985 study. As might be expected, on most of the items offered in the questionnaire, most of the respondents felt that the tasks were appropriate for boys and girls. However, there were some interesting differences. In general, girls tended to display a less stereotyped set of judgements. Also, while both groups showed some evidence of a move away from stereotyped judgements in 1995, as compared with 1985, this move seemed to be more marked for the girls. In other words, changes in educational choices for girls appeared to be best explained by changes in their perceptions of the opportunities available to them in the wider society.

Above we have highlighted some of the main themes in the research on education and gender in Northern Ireland. One aspect of this evidence which we mentioned in the opening section of the chapter is that the higher attainment of girls over boys has been known for a considerable period of time. This is so because of the close interest that was paid to the comparative performance of pupils in the Protestant and Catholic school systems and because of research carried out on the consequences of the selective system. We have seen above also the way in which the EOCNI was able to draw on some of this evidence to promote change in government policy. It remains true, however, that government action on equity concerns in education has been more marked in regard to the religious school systems. This is illustrated particularly when we examine the relationship between research on educational attainment and labour market opportunity.

Research on gender and the curriculum is a little more limited. As a precursor to the introduction of the common curriculum the DENI carried out a survey of the timetable followed by a sample of pupils across all secondary and grammar schools in Northern Ireland. The purpose of the survey was to measure the level of change that would be needed in order to introduce the common curriculum. Although the DENI did not publish any results from the survey, secondary analysis of the data was carried out by Cormack *et al.* (1992e). The main purpose of the secondary analysis was to compare the curriculum followed by pupils in Protestant and Catholic schools. Some differences were found on this social dimension, although Cormack *et al.* also found that differences due to school type, grammar and secondary, and gender were greater than the differences due to religion. In particular, boys spent more time than girls on Science and Technology subjects, particularly once the subjects ceased to be compulsory. This difference interacted with religion to the extent that pupils in Catholic schools spent less time, on average, on Science and Technology than pupils in Protestant schools, although this too was linked to the relatively large number of single-sex schools. The religious difference prompted significant capital expenditure to build science and technology facilities in schools where these resources were lacking: this expenditure tended to be concentrated in Catholic schools and single-sex girls' schools.

Attainment and religion

Research on education and religion in Northern Ireland has tended to focus either on the impact of separate schools on social stability/instability, or on the relative outputs from the two parallel religious school systems and the impact of this on labour market opportunity. We will focus on the latter theme here. Boyle (1976) found that educational attainment and occupational achievement were linked and that Protestants did better on both compared with Catholics. However, when mediating factors were taken into account the educational advantage enjoyed by Protestants was only marginal. A later series of studies (Osborne and Murray 1978; Osborne 1985, 1986; Osborne *et al.* 1989) examined O and A level passes and school leaver statistics in order to assess differences between the two religious school systems. Considering qualifications first, the broad pattern revealed was that prior to the mid-1970s proportionately fewer pupils in Catholic schools were obtaining O and A level passes than might have been expected. From the mid-1970s to the early 1980s the gap between the school systems declined and, over the last part of the 1980s had remained fairly stable (see Osborne *et al.* 1989: 142; see also Cormack *et al.* 1992c). It seemed possible that much of the gap in attainment could be explained by the smaller proportion of pupils in the Catholic school system attending grammar schools (Livingstone 1987; Gallagher 1989; Osborne *et al.* 1989).

This, and a number of other possibilities, were examined in a series of research studies carried out for the Standing Advisory Commission on Human Rights (SACHR) in Northern Ireland, a body established, under statute in 1973, to advise the Secretary of State on the human rights aspects of legislation and policy in Northern Ireland. In 1987 the SACHR published a critical analysis of the effectiveness of the 1976 Fair Employment Act (SACHR 1987), highlighting the continuing significance of the 'unemployment gap' between Protestants and Catholics such that the latter were about twice as likely as the former to be unemployed. The SACHR report was one of the factors leading to the passage of strengthened fair employment legislation, including a statutory requirement on employers to monitor the religious composition of their workforces annually, in 1989. The SACHR report had examined a number of possible contributory factors to the unemployment gap between Protestants and Catholics including the role of separate education systems which it decided to investigate further.

In an echo of the Swann/Rampton Committee in Britain, the SACHR investigation focused on possible explanations for differential levels of qualifications among leavers from Protestant and Catholic schools. This included research on the link between social class and attainment, funding arrangements for schools, curriculum differences between Protestant and Catholic schools and access to grammar schools. A number of additional research papers on statistical, structural, attitudinal and historical issues were commissioned. Cormack *et al.* (1991) examined evidence on the level and implications of capital and recurrent funding of schools in Northern Ireland, including an assessment of comparative evidence on the funding of Catholic schools in Scotland and Ontario, Canada. They concluded that the arrangements for capital funding, whereby voluntary schools received up to 85 per cent grant towards capital costs, resulted in a financial and administrative burden on the authorities of Catholic schools in Northern Ireland, and probably impacted on the educational delivery of the schools. In addition, a consistent pattern of per capita differential was found across primary, secondary and voluntary grammar schools. They argued that both factors were likely to impact on the educational delivery of Catholic schools and hence contribute to the attainment gap between leavers from Protestant and Catholic schools.

Another aspect of this research focused on grammar school provision. Previous research in Northern Ireland had pointed to the 'added value' in attainment terms of a grammar school education (Gallagher 1988), but it was unclear whether the proportionately smaller size of the Catholic grammar sector was explained by an actual shortage of places in Catholic grammar schools (a structural explanation) or by choice on the part of some parents of pupils attending Catholic schools (a choice explanation). Cormack *et al.* (1992d) examined this issue using data provided by the DENI on actual enrolments in post-primary schools in 1990, the physical capacities of schools and pupil projections for 1995. The physical capacity of schools has become important because of the new policy of open enrolment whereby grammar schools may admit pupils up to their physical capacity, on the basis of published criteria. The analysis showed that, in 1990, 34 per cent of pupils in Catholic schools were in grammar schools, while 41.5 per cent of pupils in Protestant schools were in grammar schools, thus illustrating the basic differential in the relative sizes of the grammar sectors. If, in 1990, grammar schools were operating at full capacity, the grammar enrolment of the Catholic sector would have risen to 35.8 per cent, while that for the Protestant sector would have risen to 45.6 per cent. Thus, while both grammar sectors would have increased in size, the level of increase would have been greater in the Protestant sector. Finally, based on the DENI projections for pupil enrolments in 1995 and on the assumption that the present capacity of grammar schools did not increase, the potential grammar enrolment of the Catholic sector would be 33.4 per cent, while that for the Protestant sector would be 45.8 per cent.

Government's community relations policy in Northern Ireland comprised three main elements: the promotion of cultural tolerance, the promotion of Protestant–Catholic contact, and a commitment to equality. Education policy had tended to focus on the first two of these, mainly through a variety of programmes designed to work towards reconciliation. The government's response to the SACHR investigation, however, provided a demonstration of its commitment to equity in education. Following discussions with Catholic authorities, in November 1992, it was announced that a new category of voluntary school would be created which would receive 100 per cent capital grants. The DENI agreed to monitor the impact of educational policy on the Protestant and Catholic school systems, and in July 1992 the DENI announced plans to spend £7 million to provide extra places in Catholic grammar schools. Thus, while the Northern Ireland version of the Education Reform Act (Education Reform Order, Northern Ireland, 1989) committed government, for the first time, to support initiatives towards the development of new integrated schools for both Protestants and Catholics, the Order acknowledged that, for the foreseeable future, most pupils will continue to be educated in religiously segregated schools and the response to the SACHR research demonstrates a commitment to equitable treatment of these separate schools.

Current evidence on attainment

One further consequence of the education reforms, and some of the measures discussed above, has been the greater provision of attainment data from the DENI. Here we present the most recent evidence. Table 4.3 shows the comparative pattern of attainment of school leavers from Catholic and 'other' schools: this is based on the DENI definition which differentiates between schools under Catholic management arrangements and all other schools. These data show the increased levels of qualifications achieved by school leavers overall, and suggest a continuing decline in the difference between leavers from Catholic and other schools. This difference is, however, highest when we consider the data for all schools, as the new catholic grammar places will not have an impact on the data for another year or two. Table 4.4 shows the attainment data for boys and girls, showing the continued pattern of higher achievement achieved by girls.

Equity policy

To this point we have focused on evidence on educational achievement and how this is mediated by gender. The main point to emphasise is that debates and discussions on these issues have extended over a considerable period of time and have been closely linked to wider social debates on issues such as employment

Table 4.3 Highest qualifications of school leavers in 1989–90 and 1994–95 by management type (Catholic/Other) and school type (grammar/secondary/all schools) (%)

	1989–90		1994–95	
	Catholic	*Other*	*Catholic*	*Other*
Grammar				
3 A Levels or more (or equivalent)	49	51	57	57
5+ GCSE A*–C (or equivalent)	12	15	17	22
5+ GCSE A*–G (or equivalent)	22	25	23	27
No GCSEs	1	1	1	–
Secondary				
3 A Levels or more (or equivalent)	4	1	5	3
5+ GCSE A*–C (or equivalent)	10	10	19	20
5+ GCSE A*–G (or equivalent)	45	55	61	69
No GCSEs	24	22	10	8
All schools				
3 A Levels or more (or equivalent)	18	21	23	25
5+ GCSE A*–C (or equivalent)	11	12	18	21
5+ GCSE A*–G (or equivalent)	38	43	48	51
No GCSEs	17	14	7	4

Source: Calculated from data published in the Department of Education, Northern Ireland Statistical Press Release, 17 December 1997, 'Qualifications and Destinations of Northern Ireland School Leavers 1993–94 and 1994–95'.

Table 4.4 Highest qualifications of school leavers by gender and school type, 1994–95 (%)

	Boys	Girls
Grammar		
3 A Levels or more (or equivalent)	54	60
5+ GCSE A*–C (or equivalent)	20	19
5+ GCSE A*–G (or equivalent)	28	23
No GCSEs	1	1
Secondary		
3 A Levels or more (or equivalent)	3	6
5+ GCSE A*–C (or equivalent)	15	24
5+ GCSE A*–G (or equivalent)	62	69
No GCSEs	11	6
All schools		
3 A Levels or more (or equivalent)	21	28
5+ GCSE A*–C (or equivalent)	17	22
5+ GCSE A*–G (or equivalent)	50	50
No GCSEs	8	3

Source: Calculated from data published in the Department of Education, Northern Ireland Statistical Press Release, 17 December 1997, 'Qualifications and Destinations of Northern Ireland School Leavers 1993–94 and 1994–95'.

equality. As we indicated at the start of the chapter, the primary focus has been on religious divisions, but the climate created by these discussions has consequences for policy and practice on other social dimensions such as gender. We have seen that the educational underachievement of particular groups of boys has been known for a considerable time, and the fact of this pattern has not generally led to the 'moral panic' that appears sometimes to be evident in Britain. However, this is not only the emergent pattern from research evidence, but is also found in policy practice. We can see a further example of the gains, and the limits, of this situation if we look at equity measures on gender within the two universities in Northern Ireland.

Equal opportunities in the universities

In 1986 the Fair Employment Agency (FEA as it was then) decided to conduct a formal investigation into the provision of equality of opportunity in Queen's University and the University of Ulster. This intervention was not widely welcomed in either university. There was something of a sense that the universities were above the sordid discriminations pertaining elsewhere in the Province. A part of the conclusion of the FEA's investigation into Queen's University is worth quoting since it set off what has been a continuous external and internal debate since its publication almost a decade ago:

Overall the Agency found that there were major areas of under-representation of Roman Catholics of Northern Ireland origin relative to Protestants of Northern Ireland origin. The agency would expect the primary research and educational institution in the Province to take a leading role in matters of such importance as the promotion of equality of opportunity. However, until the time of this investigation, the University had not monitored its own employment pattern, it had not reviewed the effectiveness of its recruitment procedures nor had it assessed the impact of its actions on the relative opportunities for employment offered to Protestants and Roman Catholics.

(FEA 1989: 43–5)

The University of Ulster began monitoring recruitment during 1986 and this, together with an improving profile, seems to have led the Fair Employment Commission (FEC, as it had then become at the time of the University of Ulster (UU) report) to be more favourably disposed to the UU than to Queen's.

However, neither institution introduced extensive monitoring until there was external pressure to do so. While fair employment legislation focuses on religion clearly little if anything useful can be delivered in terms of the provision of equal opportunity without accurate monitoring information. The universities were galvanised into action as the result of the FEA/FEC reports. While gender equality issues coat-tailed on issues of religion it might be observed that both universities found it easier to deal with gender issues than with the more sensitive and, in some quarters, contentious issue of the religious profile of the institution.

The University of Ulster appointed a professor for 'women's opportunities' in 1987. This was an innovative move intended to promote research in the area but also to offer the University advice on the development of courses and issues of concern to female staff and students. This was followed in 1988 by the establishment of the Centre for Research on Women which, over the years, has become a highly productive centre. Queen's established a Centre for Women's Studies in the 1990s. Its focus is on co-ordinating modules making up degree pathways in women's studies.

High profile cases taken to both the Fair Employment Tribunal and the Equal Opportunities Tribunal have kept the pressure on the universities to continually improve and refine their provisions for the enhancement of equality of opportunity. Both universities now have in place the following measures:

- mandatory courses in recruitment and selection for those staff involved on recruitment panels;
- recruitment panels and other committees are expected to have a reasonable representation by gender and religion;
- mandatory equal opportunities workshops for all staff;
- sexual harassment policies together with trained sexual harassment counsellors/advisers;
- an increasing range of family friendly policies and procedures, e.g. career breaks, adoptive leave, enhanced paid maternity leave.

However, despite ten years of development, equal opportunities policies and procedures do not appear to have shattered the 'glass ceiling'. At present one of three
pro-vice-chancellors in both universities is a woman. But less than 10 per cent of
the professoriat in both institutions are female. Northern Ireland still retains a
patriarchal family culture and, to some extent, this continues to colour and inhibit
a full-blown commitment to gender equality.

Equality, education and the future

Returning to our main theme, we can see how most of the trends we have focused
on above pre-dated the education reforms of the late 1980s and did not appear to
be unduly affected by them. In part this may be explained by the fact that the
reforms were designed with the education system in England and Wales in mind,
and reflected debates in that jurisdiction which were largely absent from discussions in Northern Ireland (Gallagher 1997). To take just one point mentioned at
the start of the chapter: the marketisation of education had a significant impact
across the UK, but in Northern Ireland its impact was somewhat different as over
half the schools were outside the jurisdiction of local education authorities in any
case. These schools were affected by open enrolment, but, as we have seen above,
the main impact of this was to lead to an increase in the proportion of pupils
going to grammar schools.

We have seen how various initiatives were taken to address gender issues in
education, although most of the main impetus of debates and discussion did
centre on issues linked to religion. Thus, from the mid-1980s onwards, from
which time the renewed emphasis on equity was evident, the key focus of equity
concerns was the relative position of Catholics and Protestants. *Inter alia* this led
to the provision of additional social information, some of which could be
deployed by groups such as the EOCNI to pursue gender objectives.

One final example will be examined to illustrate another aspect of the
situation in Northern Ireland. In the latter part of the 1980s an approach to
equity, based on 'mainstreaming' was being developed in Whitehall: the basic
idea was to introduce procedures for 'equality proofing'. The approach was
taken up by the Northern Ireland Office and developed as a policy for
Northern Ireland departments, but such was the climate of discussion here that
the original equality proofing proposals were criticised for being overly negative,
insufficiently proactive and for not being based on consultation with interested
organisations in Northern Ireland. The equality proofing guidelines were with-
drawn for review, during which time widespread consultation took place. The
measure was reintroduced as the Policy Appraisal and Fair Treatment (PAFT)
Guidelines.

The PAFT Guidelines were launched in 1994 as a means of seeking to ensure
that issues of equality and equity were fully integrated into 'policy making and
action in all spheres and at all levels of Government activity whether in regulatory
and administrative functions or in the delivery of services to the public' (CCRU
1995). The Guidelines aim to ensure that people in named social categories do

not suffer arbitrary disadvantage due to government action, and aim to promote equality for people in the same categories: the social categories include people who differ on the basis of their religion, gender, age, ethnic group, disability status, marital status, sexual orientation and whether or not they have dependants. The Guidelines are supposed to be applied in most spheres of government activity and also to non-departmental public bodies. The PAFT initiative had its origins in the work of the Ministerial Group on Women's Interests (MGWI) under the Conservative government, but it had far greater prominence in Belfast than in Whitehall. As we have seen, in Northern Ireland the Guidelines were subjected to far stiffer critical tests on performance in this area than was the case in Britain.

An evaluation of the PAFT initiative conducted in 1995–6 in Northern Ireland revealed a very patchy picture (Osborne *et al.* 1996). Major questions were unresolved including the status of the guidelines of PAFT considerations *vis-à-vis* other policy priorities, the methodology for conducting PAFT appraisals and the method being used to ensure implementation across the public sector. This evaluation was part of a broader evaluation of fair employment policy generally and the impact of the 1989 Fair Employment Act in particular. Following the critical evaluation the SACHR recommended that PAFT should be put on a statutory basis.

The Conservative government fell before it produced its response to the SACHR recommendations, and the somewhat delayed proposals from the current Labour government were issued for consultation in March 1998, and formed part of the political agreement arrived at between the British and Irish governments, and most of the political parties in Northern Ireland in April 1998.

The Labour government proposed significant changes to the PAFT initiative. This included the idea of making the promotion of equality a statutory obligation for government departments and public bodies, but in a way somewhat different from that proposed by SACHR. The proposal was to be given effect by requiring government departments and public bodies to publish equality statements outlining how they would pursue their statutory obligation. The standards for these equality statements would be set by a new Equality Commission which would result from a merger of the existing commissions dealing with religion (FEC), gender (EOCNI) and race (Commission for Racial Equality in Northern Ireland, formed in 1998, CRENI) and the Northern Ireland Disability Council. The Equality Commission would also be responsible for validating specific equality statements and monitoring their implementation.

The Conservative government was a reluctant recruit to equality policy in Northern Ireland. This is not to say that they were opposed to equality, but in education, as in other areas, the Conservatives preferred to rely on market forces to achieve policy objectives. Thus, even when, as in Northern Ireland, the government was obliged to give active consideration to equity issues, this was typically on the basis of a minimalist approach which involved setting a basic framework and then allowing market forces to operate. The circumstances in Northern Ireland meant that the extent of direct government action was somewhat greater than in the rest of the UK due to the different policy environment, but this action was always limited. The examples we considered above illustrate this: educational initiatives addressed equity concerns largely on the basis of religion, and the gender benefits that were derived from this were largely spin-off benefits that occurred despite government action rather than because of this action. The critics of the previous government, as in the debate on PAFT, tended to prefer a more statist approach which required government to deliver set goals and targets. The current Labour government appears to be adopting a 'third way' between the 'hidden hand' of the market and the 'heavy hand' of the state. Certainly, this is the approach which informs the new approach to the PAFT guidelines. A similar approach is evident in education policy: in England and Wales a policy direction based on raising standards through pressure and support for schools has been in place since the election. In Northern Ireland the School Improvement Programme, only announced in March 1998, adopts a broadly similar framework even if there appears to be a somewhat different balance between the pressure and support sides of the policy. The lesson from the PAFT proposals is that Labour will attach a higher proactive priority to equity concerns than the previous government, but not an absolute priority. As with previous governments the main focus of attention has been on the issue of religion, possibly to the cost of other concerns – the EOCNI may take the view that the PAFT proposals were framed with religion firmly in mind, and gender firmly out of mind – but an entirely new range of political possibilities have been opened up because a political agreement has been achieved. A key part of the agreement focuses on an equality agenda, and while this may concentrate on religion, we have seen above how other issues can benefit from this context.

References

Boyle, J.F. (1976) 'Educational attainment, occupational achievement and religion in Northern Ireland', *Economic and Social Review*, 8, 2: 79–100.

CCRU (1995) *Policy Appraisal and Fair Treatment: Annual Report 1994*, CCRU: Belfast.

Cormack, R.J., Gallagher, A.M. and Osborne, R.D. (1991) 'Educational affiliation and educational attainment in Northern Ireland': the financing of schools in Northern Ireland', Annex E, *Sixteenth Report of the Standing Advisory Commission on Human Rights*, House of Commons Paper 488, London: HMSO.

Cormack, R.J., Gallagher, A.M., Murray, D. and Osborne, R.D. (1992a) 'Curriculum, access to grammar schools and the financing of education: an overview paper', Annex H, *Seventeenth Report of the Standing Advisory Commission on Human Rights*, House of Commons Paper 54, London: HMSO.

—— (1992b) 'Report on school size', Annex B, *Seventeenth Report of the Standing Advisory Commission on Human Rights*, House of Commons Paper 54, London: HMSO.

—— (1992c) 'Secondary analysis of the DENI's teachers' survey (1989)', Annex C, *Seventeenth Report of the Standing Advisory Commission on Human Rights*, House of Commons Paper 54, London: HMSO.

—— (1992d) 'Access to grammar schools', Annex E, *Seventeenth Report of the Standing Advisory Commission on Human Rights*, House of Commons Paper 54, London: HMSO.

—— (1993) *Fair Enough? Religion and the 1991 Population Census*, Belfast: Fair Employment Commission.

Cormack, R.J., Gallagher, A.M., Osborne, R.D. and Fisher, N. (1992e) 'Secondary analysis of the school leavers survey 1989', Annex D, *Seventeenth Report of the Standing Advisory Commission on Human Rights*, House of Commons Paper 54, London: HMSO.

Cormack, R.J., Gallagher, A.M., Osborne, R.D. and Fisher, N. (1992f) 'Secondary Analysis of the DENI Curriculum Survey', Annex F, *Seventeenth Report of the Standing Advisory Commission on Human Rights*, House of Commons Paper 54, London: HMSO.

Cormack, R.J. and Osborne, R.D. (eds) (1983) *Religion, Education and Employment*, Belfast: Appletree Press.

—— (eds) (1991) *Discrimination and Public Policy in Northern Ireland*, Oxford: Clarendon.

DENI (1996) *Transfer Procedure Test Results 1989–90 to 1995–96*, Statistical Bulletin 1/1996, Bangor: Department of Education in Northern Ireland.

FEA (1989) *Report of an Investigation into Queen's University*, Belfast: Fair Employment Agency.

FEC (1990) *Report of an Investigation into University of Ulster*, Belfast: Fair Employment Commission.

Gallagher, A.M. (1988) *Transfer Pupils at 16*, Belfast: Northern Ireland Council for Educational Research.

—— (1989) 'The relationship between research and policy: an example from Northern Ireland', *The Psychologist: Bulletin of the British Psychological Society*, 2, 2: 62–3.

—— (1997) 'Attitudes to education in Britain and Northern Ireland,' in L. Dowds, P. Devine and R. Breen (eds) *Social Attitudes in Northern Ireland, The Sixth Report 1996–97*, Belfast: Appletree Press.

Gallagher, A.M., Cormack, R.J. and Osborne, R.D. (1994) 'Religion, equity and education in Northern Ireland', *British Educational Research Journal* 20, 5: 507–18.

Gallagher, A.M., McEwen, A. and Knipe, D. (1997) 'Science education policy: a survey of the participation of sixth-form pupils in science and other subjects over a ten year period, 1985–1995', *Research Papers in Education* 12, 2: 121–42.

INTO (1993) *A Report on Equality of Opportunity in Educational Management*, Belfast: Irish National Teachers' Organisation.

Johnston, J. and Rooney, E. (1987) 'Gender differences in education', in R.J. Cormack, R.L. Miller and R.D. Osborne (eds) *Education and Policy in Northern Ireland*, Belfast: Policy Research Institute.

Livingstone, J. (1987) 'Equality of opportunity in education in Northern Ireland', in R.D. Osborne, R.J. Cormack, and R.L. Miller (eds) *Education and Policy in Northern Ireland*, Belfast: Policy Research Institute.

McEwan, A., Curry, C.A. and Watson, J. (1985) *Science and Arts Subject Choices: A Sample Survey of Lower 6th Form Students in Northern Ireland*, Belfast: Equal Opportunities Commission.

McKernan, J. (1981) *Transfer at 14: A Study of the Craigavon Two-tier System as an Organisational Innovation in Education*, Belfast: Northern Ireland Council for Educational Research.

Morgan, V. (1995) *Gender, Assessment and the New Northern Ireland Curriculum*, Belfast: Equal Opportunities Commission for Northern Ireland.

Murray, D. (1992) 'Science and funding in Northern Ireland grammar schools: a case study approach', Annex G, *Seventeenth Report of the Standing Advisory Commission on Human Rights*, House of Commons Paper 54, London: HMSO.

Osborne, R.D. (1985) *Religion and Educational Qualifications in Northern Ireland*, Research Paper 8, Belfast: Fair Employment Agency.

—— (1986) 'Segregated schools and examination results in Northern Ireland: some preliminary research', *Educational Research* 28, 1: 43–50.

Osborne, R.D. and Cormack, R.J. (1987) *Religion, Occupations and Employment, 1971–81*, Belfast: Fair Employment Agency.

Osborne, R.D. and Murray, R.C. (1978) *Educational Qualifications and Religious Affiliation in Northern Ireland: An Examination of GCE 'O' and 'A' Levels*, Research Paper 3, Belfast: Fair Employment Agency.

Osborne, R.D., Gallagher, A.M. and Cormack, R.J. (1989) 'Review of aspects of education in Northern Ireland', Annex H, *Fourteenth Annual Report of the Standing Advisory Commission on Human Rights*, London: HMSO.

—— (1996) 'The implementation of the PAFT guidelines in Northern Ireland', in E. McLaughlin and P. Quirk (eds) *Policy Aspects of Employment Equality in Northern Ireland*, Belfast: Standing Advisory Commission on Human Rights.

SACHR (1987) *Religious and Political Discrimination and Equality of Opportunity in Northern Ireland: Report on Fair Employment*, London: HMSO.

Siraj-Blatchford, I. and Troyna, B. (1993) 'Equal opportunities, research and educational reform: some introductory notes', *British Educational Research Journal* 19, 3: 223–6.

Sutherland, A.E. and Gallagher, A.M. (1987) *Pupils in the Border Band*, Belfast: Northern Ireland Council for Educational Research.

Wilson, J.A. (1985) *Secondary School Organisation and Pupil Progress*, Belfast: Northern Ireland Council for Educational Research.

—— (1986) *Transfer and the Structure of Secondary Education*, Belfast: Northern Ireland Council for Educational Research.

5 Mainstreaming European 'equal opportunities'

Marginalising UK training for women

Jacky Brine

Introduction

The education and training policies of the European Union (EU) are related to its central concerns of economic growth and peace, and to the construction of the regionalised bloc itself (Brine 1995a). Within the European Union there has been a long-standing relationship between training policy, the European Social Fund (ESF) and the European labour market. The founding Treaty of Rome (EC 1957) provided the legal basis for the European Commission's (EC) activities in each of the three interlinked concerns of this chapter: vocational training, the European Social Fund, and equal opportunities. This initial equality legislation, based on the demand for equal pay between women and men, was driven by the concerns of economic growth: it was to prevent member states gaining 'unfair' advantage by undercutting wages by paying women less. Importantly, this legislation provided the route for all subsequent equality policies and actions (Meehan 1992; Prechal and Senden 1993; Brine 1998). Of significance to this chapter is the fact that European equal opportunities was, until the mid-1990s, defined solely as gender equality, and this remained the remit of the Equal Opportunities Unit referred to below. This meant that throughout the EC's training policy, the inequality experienced by women was addressed solely as gender inequality, and the solution to this was equally gender based: women were to be given access to that which men had. There was a general failure within the EU to understand that women also experienced discrimination because of their ethnicity, social class, age and geographical location as well as their gender. The move in the 1990s to 'mainstream' equal opportunities programmes implied a more sophisticated view of the complex nature of discrimination and an appropriate strategy for positive action. However, because women continued to be defined solely in relation to their gender the net effect of mainstreaming was a reduction in and dilution of training programmes for women.

Immediately following the European devastation of the Second World War, it was believed that economic growth would lead to cohesion between the previously warring member states, and would also protect the embryonic Community from the new Eastern European Communist states. Peace between the member states, and with neighbouring states, was seen as dependent on economic growth, and from the late 1960s to the late 1970s, this discourse of economic growth determined training and employment policy. As the effects of the 1973 oil crisis affected nation–state economies, the late 1980s became a period of transition and struggle between the demands of economic growth and peaceful unity. By the mid-1990s the hitherto implicit relationship between training policy and peace within and across the member states was found in the Commission's repeated references to the fear of social unrest, to the concern with long-term unemployment, social exclusion and the rise of neo-fascism (EC 1993a, 1994, 1995). The Treaty of Amsterdam (EC 1997) recognised the increased pressure placed on the intricate relationship between economic growth, peace and the construction of the EU by its enlargement to include Cyprus and the Central and Eastern European Countries of Estonia, Poland, Czech Republic and Slovenia.

The construction of the European Union is a long-term project, but this does not mean that it has been part of a determined modernist progression to a federal state, nor that it is within the control of one director or group. The construction of the EU has been (and is) a site of contest, struggle and compromise, not only between the member states themselves, but between individual politicians and bureaucrats; between administrative departments and of course between different individual interests and interest groups. Within this chapter, the European Union is defined as the constructed regionalised 'state' – that is, a political grouping of member states within a geographically defined area. This is distinct from the European Commission which is used here to refer to the entire EU policy-making body, that is, all those involved in the process through which European policy is finally adopted by the Council of Ministers. This includes the civil service of the EU, the European Parliament, the Economic and Social Committee, the European Court of Justice, the Committee of the Regions and the Council of Ministers.

Since the Maastricht Treaty of the Union (EC 1992), the concept of subsidiarity has meant that member state governments have had greater powers of interpretation and implementation of European policy. Nevertheless, the relationship between the European Commission and the member state government has not been easy. It signals a complex struggle between the nation–state and the regionalised state which has increased as the EU has moved into the areas of social policy that previously were the domain of the nation–state. Yet, the tension is exacerbated because, within the context of globalisation, nation–states are increasingly reliant (yet also vulnerable to) the strength and size of the regionalised state.

The tension at the interface of economic and social policy between the EC and the UK government forms the background to this chapter. I explore the discursive drift that occurs as European equality policy works its way through subsequent layers of interpretation within the member state. From its original concern with equal pay, by the late 1990s gender-based equality was to be 'mainstreamed' across all EC policies and activities, including education and training (*Official Journal* 1993). Mainstreaming within this context implies that equal opportunities concerns were to inform all initiatives, rather than being focused on a small number of targeted programmes. The European Social Fund was one of the main policy arena to be affected by 'mainstreaming'.

The next section of this chapter provides a brief introduction to the EC's Equal Opportunities Action Programmes for Women and Men, and the European Social Fund. It then focuses on the European and British involvement with this policy during 1996, that is towards the end of the British Conservative government's long relationship with the Commission. The following central section considers the extent of 'mainstreaming' within ESF funded training for long-term unemployed women within Scotland, Wales and England. Finally, the 1997 change in government is considered in relation to the future UK involvement with European policy.

European equal opportunities policy

The European Social Fund (ESF) is one of the European Commission's key Structural Funds. It has defined training policy and provided funds for training long-term unemployed people. It began in the early 1960s, and, as I have discussed elsewhere (Brine 1995b), significant shifts in European training policy were reflected in its major Reforms: 1971, 1977, 1987 and 1993. Women have been a 'targeted group' since the 1971 Reform. The ESF's Objective 3, (ESF/3), has been the largest funder of training programmes in the UK: 60 per cent of the UK's ESF/3 allocation from the EC match-funds all of the UK government's own Youth Training and Employment Training programmes. Within the 1994–99 programme, ESF/3 was divided into four priorities which the UK government refers to as 'pathways': first, pathways to employment; second, pathways to a good start in working life; third, pathways to integration; and fourth, pathways for equal opportunities for men and women. In theory, long-term unemployed women, according to age, are 'eligible beneficiaries' under all the pathways of ESF/3.

A key policy document on European training policy was the Commission Regulation on the Structural Funds for 1994–99 (*Official Journal* 1993). This stressed the need for a strategy to mainstream equal opportunities and tackle unemployment (ibid.: 39). Along with its emphasis on mainstreaming, the Regulation also provided for specific provision aimed at tackling ongoing inequalities between women and men:

> The promotion of equal opportunities for men and women on the labour market especially in areas of work in which women are under-represented and particularly for women not possessing vocational qualifications or returning to the labour market after a period of absence.
>
> (ibid.: 40)

Whilst promoting 'equal opportunities for men and women', the Commission clearly intended that the Equal Opportunities pathway should address the under-representation and under-qualification of *women*, targeting those women 'not possessing vocational qualifications, or returning to the labour market after a period of absence'. Furthermore, priority was to be given to training women for occupations in which they were under-represented (ibid.: 40). Finally, despite its reference to 'women', the discourse of ESF provision shows that funds were clearly targeted on a *particular* group of women: low and under-educated women, women most at risk of unemployment and social exclusion (Council of Europe 1992; OECD 1992; Brine 1995b).

The EC's Equal Opportunities Unit was established in 1976 and began its first Action Programme in 1982. Following its introduction in the Third Action Programme (1991–95), mainstreaming equal opportunities became a major theme of the Fourth Action Programme (1996–2000). It would be reasonable to assume that this would be reflected in UK policy by 1996. However, recent research (Brine 1996), shows that this was not the case, and that moreover, the immediate trend was towards the marginalisation of training for women rather than towards increased provision through the permeation of all programmes by gender equality concerns.

UK interpretation of European equal opportunities policy

In order to understand the UK government's interpretation of EC Equal Opportunities policy, it is helpful to look at the annual guidelines produced by the Department for Education and Employment (DfEE) for training providers and managers wishing to apply to the European Social Fund (ESF/3). An analysis of the annual Guidelines has shown that, year by year, there have been significant discursive shifts in UK policy, first, in relation to European ESF/3 policy, and second, in the former Conservative government's explicit understanding of unemployed people. Significantly, from 1991, despite the Third Action Programme's introduction of the concept of 'mainstreaming' equal opportunities policy, the UK Guidelines for 1991 to 1993 made no mention whatsoever of equal opportunities (DE 1990, 1991, 1992). The 1994 Guidelines, despite reminding applicants that they must show 'good practice in equality of access and equal opportunities', including an equal opportunities policy in place for their own staff, removed the general possibility for single sex training, leaving only the Equal Opportunities (EO) pathway with this explicit possibility. The EO pathway was now concerned with 'single sex' provision for either women *or men* returners, and with providing training for women *or men* in sectors or occupations where they have been traditionally under-represented. The importance of this was further strengthened by the apparent neutrality of the other pathways. Other than in the few references to 'ethnic minorities', the language of the other pathways was gender and race 'neutral'. While this 'neutrality' did not explicitly prohibit access to any of the pathways, the explicit references within the EO pathway led, as I will show, to a marginalisation and reduction of provision for unemployed women. By way of contrast, documents intended for EC consumption (e.g. the Single Programming Document of 1994; DE 1993a), were replete with references to gender and the position of women in the labour market. Thus from 1993 to 1996 the UK government used a chameleonic discourse. The EC was reassured of its concern with women's issues, while trainers and managers within the UK were led to believe that gender equality issues required only minimal attention and certainly did not need to be at the forefront of all training programmes (DE 1993b, 1994; DfEE 1995).

Since 1996, the marginalisation of women's issues has become more marked in documents produced for the EC by the UK government. The Single Programming Document (SPD) for 1997–99 (DfEE 1996a) refers increasingly to the 'special needs' of men, particularly within the EO pathway. It is noted, for instance, that 'men find it difficult to break into employment areas which have been predominantly female' (ibid.: 36). While 'the vital and growing contribution of women in the labour force' (ibid.: 36) is recognised, there is a consistent concern for the position of men:

> Men are disproportionately affected by long term unemployment as the industries in which they were traditionally employed are declining, and those sectors which are increasing are taking on part-time employees, an area of employment which is dominated by women.
>
> (ibid.: 36)

Equal opportunities itself was also redefined. It was no longer gender specific but concerned with race, disability, age and religion as well as gender and 'women's rights more generally' (ibid.: 25), however, the meaning of 'women's rights' was not clarified. Whereas the European discourse of equal opportunities has been exclusively related to gender, the UK discourse of equal opportunities has been more generally inclusive. This redefinition highlighted the discursive shift between the European and the UK concepts of equal opportunities. At the same time it diluted the EU attempt to mainstream gendered equal opportunities in order to give unemployed women access to the full range of funded training opportunities within ESF/3.

To summarise, although in the SPD for 1997–99 while the UK continued to declare its compliance with the principle of equal opportunities for men and women, there was a discursive shift from the original *Single Programming Document for 1994–1999* (DE 1993a). This shift continued and strengthened the process of marginalisation and evaporation which occurred throughout the annual Guidelines of 1994–96. First, there were explicit statements that equal opportunities should relate to race, religion and disability as well as gender. Second, there were no explicit 'equal opportunities' statements attached to the other pathways, and, in contrast to the first SPD, neither were there any direct references to the possibility of single-sex training. Third, the concept of gender-based equal opportunities relating to gender was confined to the EO pathway. Finally, while it might, just, be possible to argue that there was some evidence of mainstreaming the UK's broadly defined conception of equal opportunities (i.e. embracing ethnicity, age, disability), there was no evidence of mainstreaming the

EC-defined *gender-based* equal opportunities for women and men, as defined in the Fourth Equal Opportunities Action Programme and included and required within the Regulation of 1993.

Interpretation of UK policy by training managers and providers

The focus of this section of the chapter is on the interpretation of ESF/3 policy *within* the administrative sectors of the UK. My research into the implementation of ESF/3 within the UK was a multi-sited study which was based on discursive analysis of policy and guidance documents and semi-structured interviews with 'key people' from five ESF administrative sectors (Brine 1996).[1] The term 'key people' is interpreted as those who were, nationally or locally, the person in charge of their sector's ESF or ESF/3 provision.

On one level the research explored sectoral differences. Along with the DfEE the sectors were the voluntary sector represented nationally by the National Council for Voluntary Organisations (NCVO), the Training and Enterprise Council/Local Enterprise Council (TEC/LEC), the Further Education (FE) sector and the Women's Training Network (WTN). On another level it explored the differing contexts of England, Wales and Scotland. And finally, at the third level it both added to the national interpretation, and explored tensions *within* each of the sectors, by including, within England, Wales and Scotland, a regional case study. Altogether twenty-one semi-structured interviews were conducted within the sectors at both national and regional level. In addition to the DfEE documents, these other sectors also produced, at the national level, their own supplementary interpretations of the ESF/3 Annual Guidelines. Although this section concentrates primarily on the data relating to the sectoral interpretation of policy and mainstreamed equal opportunities I shall highlight some significant national differences.

Understandings of the training needs of women and equal opportunities

The interviews began with a discussion of organisational structure, relationship of organisation to government policy-makers, internal decision-making procedures and their own understanding of ESF/3 policy. The interviewees were then asked for their opinion of the training needs of women. Despite having responded easily and knowingly to all the preceding 'general' policy questions the interviewees from the DfEE, the Training and Enterprise Council and the further education sector were unable to offer a satisfactory response to this question, as these responses indicate:

> The training needs of women? I was just thinking of who would be the best person for you to speak to – that would be more our training side.
>
> (TEC interviewee)

Joanne would probably have been the best one to answer that! She deals with – has responsibility for *women's* training.

(TEC interviewee)

I probably wouldn't be able to answer that question, that is not my job; that is the college's job to decide what the training needs of unemployed women are.

(FE interviewee, national level)

Those from the voluntary sector and the Women's Training Network, however, responded relatively easily to this question concerning the specific needs of women:

I need to think about this. Well, I think for anyone who is unemployed, they want training in skills where they have a chance of getting work – that applies to anyone.

Of unemployed women, the training needs? That's a question! I think ideally they need to have vocational guidance and counselling built in, confidence building built into the schemes. I think that they do need to just be for women.

Despite their key positions within the organisation, and their clear policy roles in relation to the ESF/3, this general initial response of 'I'm not the right person to talk to' was closely linked with a second statement of the following kind: 'this is a training question and I'm to do with policy'. In order to protect the anonymity of interviewees within easily identifiable national organisations, I shall not be disclosing their gender, their job title or other distinguishing features. While, at another time, it may be fruitful to question the extent to which the 'culture' of these institutional settings encouraged such responses, this was not the aim of this research. Nevertheless, the fact remains that all the interviewees were 'key people'. Their response implied that training for women was first, not a policy issue, and second, not an issue of concern to the 'top' personnel, but at best a delegated responsibility.

Responding to a question regarding their understanding of equal opportunities within ESF/3, the majority of interviewees referred to the DfEE's 'equal opportunities' funding criteria. The general feeling across the TEC/LEC, further education and voluntary sectors was that the equal opportunities criteria were concerned with the general policy of the provider and not the actual training provision. Sometimes this feeling was expressed critically, but more often uncritically. In selecting projects for funding, little attention was paid to whether they appeared to offer equal opportunities within that particular training programme.

With the exception of the Women's Training Network, there were varying degrees of confusion regarding the concept of 'equal opportunities'. For example, one national FE interviewee thought equal opportunities actually prohibited single-sex training; another understood equal opportunities to refer to men as well as women, and another was not even sure that it was an essential selection criterion in the first place. A number of assumptions were made by respondents about the nature of women's and men's training needs and equal opportunities. Outlined below, these combined to dilute the training aimed explicitly at women.

The Equal Opportunities pathway is the pathway for women

Responses to a question concerning the training needs of women were instruct-ive, with most interviewees assuming that this related to the EO pathway. There was, with the exception of the voluntary sector, an overwhelming belief that the EO pathway was in fact the pathway for women. The DfEE used a national database to assign ESF funds to training projects. A DfEE interviewee stated that by using a shifting definition of under-representation they could include all the provision for women under the EO pathway. This interview revealed a disregard for the spirit of the pathway and the Commission's explicit demand that gender-based equal opportunities be mainstreamed across ESF/3.

Within the TEC/LEC sector there was confusion and contradiction in their understanding of both specific and mainstreamed provision. One interviewee argued at first that the whole of ESF/3 should be available for training women, but later linked women exclusively with the EO pathway, and men with the other three pathways: 'If there is high male unemployment then, basically, you can do projects for them under the pathway to employment, the long-term unemployed, or the pathway to integration, under inner cities or something like that.'

The Further Education Funding Council constructed an apparent 'neutrality' within ESF/3 and did not link women's training specifically with any one path-way. However, this lack of direction tended to lead either to the marginalisation of women into the EO pathway or to the absence of training for women. An English regional interviewee thought that individual colleges would decide for themselves whether 'they might identify that particular niche market [i.e. women] as an area where there was a demand'.

The majority of interviewees responded to the question concerning the train-ing needs of women either by interpreting it to mean single-sex provision for women (seen as only available under the EO pathway), or by interpreting it to mean the EO pathway (therefore single-sex provision). Either way, there was an automatic relationship between women, single-sex provision and the EO pathway. This effectively marginalised training for women into this particular pathway, and as I will show, restricted access to the funded provision available through the other three pathways.

The Equal Opportunities pathway is for men as well as women

At the same time as generally locating the training of women within the EO pathway, there was, within the TEC/LEC and Further Education sector, a belief that the EO pathway was for men as well as women. This TEC interviewee explained:

> There are not actually that many 'women-only' projects for women returning to the labour market. It also includes men returning or men going into sectors where they're traditionally under-represented, because the equal opportunities pathway isn't just about women returning to the labour markets, it's also about men returning and the promotion of men and women into sectors where they are traditionally under-represented.

Similarly, in Wales a national FE interviewee pointed out that 'returners' programmes within the EO pathway were open to men as well as women:

> They are obviously women-oriented courses, but they couldn't prevent a man from going on it – and neither could they prevent that man from getting funding. And quite often there are a couple of men on these courses.

In Scotland, a college was, in 1996, running, under the EO pathway, a 'men-only' training course in child care. Ironically, the perceived 'market need' for this course came as a result of other ESF/3 provision for women. The colleges in the region had insisted on using registered childminders and had subsequently discovered both a general shortage in the region and a gender (male), under-representation. Although the 'official' rationale was that it was safer to use registered childminders, the interviewee added, 'It is really to avoid students benefiting members of their family, by using ESF funds.' In the explicit interest of 'safety', regardless of mothers' fears of child-abuse, and in the covert interest of fund allocation, men were being trained under the EO pathway to become registered childminders. In yet another example of an 'enabling' policy effectively disabling women, the interviewee added that this 'equal opportunities' action, preventing women from using family or friends, actually presented 'a problem for a lot of students – finding a registered childminder'. This concern with the traditional under-representation of men, and with 'men-only' training, contributed to the 'mainstreaming' of the EO pathway.

The other pathways are for men

Within the DfEE and TEC/LEC sectors, a consequence of the EO pathway being seen as the pathway for women has been the ghettoisation of women within this pathway and their simultaneous exclusion from the other pathways. The pathways to employment and integration were seen as being for unemployed *men*, not women. This Welsh TEC interviewee explained: 'The other three pathways are open competition for both male and female – but the number of females, looking at the statistics, that are actually fit to go on the schemes is limited.' Reflecting on why this might be so, the interviewee suggested it might be because of: 'the structure of the courses and things like that. It might be full-time and they need to go to college and this might not fit in with their domestic circumstances and so on.'

This interviewee assumed that women should *fit in* with standard 'male' provision and implied that their lack of involvement across the pathways was a direct result of their 'domestic circumstances'. Within this regional Welsh TEC the provision under the other three pathways, while apparently 'gender-free', was nevertheless designed for men, and women were expected to 'fit in' with it. Similarly, an English DfEE interviewee suggested that in some of the ESF/3 training programmes operated by the Training and Enterprise Council, there would be nothing under the EO pathway because, in that particular TEC: 'there's no need – there's no real need for that equality'.

Mainstreaming equal opportunities provision

In practice, the funding criterion of demonstrating compliance with equal opportunities policies was interpreted in a minimal way, with training providers merely having to show that they had an EO policy in place for their own staff. They were not called upon to monitor the inclusion of women in their programmes across the board. The exception to this was the voluntary sector, which made the greatest effort to mainstream gendered equal opportunities across the whole of their provision under ESF/3. The National Council for Voluntary Organisations stressed, in their supplementary Guidance documents, that it was a requirement of the ESF and the European Parliament that, *across all pathways*, women should be monitored – that is, women should be included in all pathways. Therefore, uniquely, the NCVO wanted to know how many women were trained under each pathway, not just the EO pathway (NCVO 1995). A national voluntary sector interviewee stated that as a sector, they prioritised, and the interviewee believed, they achieved, 'a high preponderance of female participation rates' across all courses as well as 'women-only' courses.

One Scottish FE interviewee referred specifically to 'one project for women under the pathway for young people [good start in working life], and there is one under the long term [pathway to employment]'. This interviewee displayed an unusual understanding of European policy, and this understanding enabled the college to find the spaces within the DfEE Guidelines in which to manoeuvre. The provision was not officially 'women-only' but, nevertheless, this interviewee believed that they would in practice 'attract women only, but because of the Sex Discrimination and the equal opportunities ruling we can't advertise it as such'.

Further research is needed in this area, but findings so far show that there are individuals, primarily in the FE and voluntary sectors, and more often in Scotland, and to a lesser extent (particularly in relation to women) Wales, who find the spaces and gaps within the UK's interpretation of ESF policy to use the funds in the interests of social justice. This appears to be linked to a knowledge of the underlying European policy, for example, a consortium of Scottish colleges, Local Authorities, LECs and the voluntary sector support a Brussels-based office, and, until recently, the NCVO themselves had a European Officer.

Based on the above analysis, the following general points can be made about the process of interpretation of ESF/3 in the UK. Although the WTN interviewee believed that, in theory, provision for women was possible across the whole of ESF/3, in practice the Women's Training Network continued to focus on under-representation and single-sex training for 'returners', the exclusive concerns of the EO pathway. With the exception of the voluntary sector, the perceptions of interviewees from all the other sectors were that training for women was almost always equated with the EO pathway. Similarly, with rare individual exceptions, the interviewees from all sectors, in all three countries, commonly believed that single-sex training was only possible under the EO pathway, and that, furthermore, 'equal opportunities' meant this particular pathway and no other.

Interviewees from the voluntary sector tended, along with one Scottish FE interviewee, to be concerned with mainstreaming equal opportunities across ESF/3. Nevertheless, in terms of informing future policy and influencing change, these particular 'rare individuals' appear, within the context of ESF/3, to have minimal influence. Crucially, however, in implementing their interpretation of the policy at a regional or local level, they indicate the importance of the agency of individuals and social groups within policy-imposed structures.

There is an identifiable sequence in the assumptions made by the interviewees. First, provision for women equalled the EO pathway. Second, single-sex provision equalled the EO pathway. Third, the EO pathway equalled ESF/3's 'equal opportunities' provision. Fourth, equal opportunities provision equalled single-sex training for men as well as women. In this way, there was a continual discursive drift away from European ESF and equal opportunities policy. This drift began in the UK government's SPD/94 and was immediately pushed significantly further in the 1994 ESF/3 Guidelines. There was a strong tendency for the key personnel within the sectors to define the mainstreaming of equal opportunities as the mainstreaming of the EO pathway. The consequence of this was the marginalisation of women, or more accurately, their exclusion from the remaining 'gender-neutral' ESF/3.

Future policy directions

The Commission's policy intentions of the 1990s were to mainstream gender-based equal opportunities, while at the same time, maintaining some specific provision for women. Throughout the 1990s, the Conservative government showed scant regard for the spirit of these intentions. There is strong evidence of the marginalisation of training for women into the EO pathway rather than across the whole of ESF/3. Many projects targeted at the unemployed or minority ethnic groups simply reached men, ignoring the needs of women. This unidimensional view of women was of course in line with the EC's original conceptualisation of equal opportunities as pertaining mainly to inequalities between women and men. The policy of mainstreaming implied positive action across all programmes for a range of disadvantaged groups including women, but because training providers and managers tended to see women exclusively in gender terms, training provision for women decreased rather than becoming more diverse. The extent to which the Labour government's response will differ from this, remains to be seen.

Throughout the first year of the new Labour government, the future of ESF/3 funded training in the UK was in a state of flux. First, there was the change of government; second, the EC approval of SPD/97 was considerably delayed; third, the ESF/3 management structure was in the middle of the Conservative's restructuring; and fourth, there were the rumblings of unease as the ESF funding implications of European expansion to include Cyprus and the Central and Eastern European Countries began to sweep through the UK system. Following its Conservative predecessor, the Labour government has continued to link state benefits with training provision. The Conservative's Job Seeker Allowance remains untouched, and Project Work has been replaced by Welfare to Work and the New Deal for young people under 25 and for lone mothers. The government has announced its intention to extend it to include all long-term unemployed adults. The changes in the SPD for 1997–9 will be as beneficial to these Labour programmes as they would have been to the Conservatives, not only in their direct ability to match-fund this provision but also through the explicit provision for work experience which is as intricately linked into Labour's policies as they were into the Conservative's. The Labour discourse on lone mothers suggests that although women's training will continue to focus on confidence gaining, the more general support of childcare for lone mothers may actually increase the range of training opportunities available – at least, for these particular women. This *may* lead away from marginalisation and more towards the mainstreaming envisaged by the EO Unit. However, the government's announced increased funding of childcare for lone mothers will only be available to registered childminders and therefore will cut out many women who were already undertaking this work.

It is too early within the Labour administration to discuss the pathologisation of 'the unemployed', and such a discussion would itself be the subject of a separate paper. However, an initial reading suggests that, whereas the Labour discourse has remained focused on the efforts and abilities of the unemployed person to find employment, and not on the structure of capitalism or the effects of globalisation, there is a slight shift in that the unemployed person is not so readily portrayed as such a 'scrounger' on the state, but more as someone who needs 'help' back into the labour market. It is also evident that groups such as single mothers and disabled people are being seen as an integral rather than a semi-detached part of the labour force. Hence, the Labour's government's discursive investment in education and training. This discourse appears more readily to echo and even reinforce that of the European Commission, and will, undoubtedly, change the future UK involvement with, and interpretation of ESF/3 policy. The government's submission of future Programming Documents to the Commission will provide the clearest indication of change and of their intentions regarding mainstreamed equal opportunities. The complex relationship between the nation–state and the regionalized state referred to at the beginning of this chapter, has then, with the Labour government, shifted but not disappeared. The arena of social policy within which the ESF is increasingly located remains a contested site, as the UK continues to be reliant on the strength and size of the EU for protection against the forces of globalisation, and on EU funds with which to implement its domestic policy.

Note

1 These interviews were carried out by Sue Kilminster, the research assistant on this project.

References

Brine, J. (1995a) 'Educational and vocational policy and the construction of the European Union', *International Studies in Sociology of Education* 5, 2: 145–63.

—— (1995b) 'Equal opportunities and the European Social Fund: discourse and practice', *Gender and Education* 7, 1: 9–22.

—— (1996) *Integration of women into the labour market within the framework of ESF objective 3 in the United Kingdom: Full Report*, Submitted to the European Commission, August 1996.

—— (1998) 'The European Union's discourse of "equality" and its education and training policy within the post-compulsory sector', *Journal of Education Policy* 13, 1: 137–52.

—— (1999) (*Under*)Educating women: Globalizing Inequality, Buckingham: Open University Press.

Council of Europe (1992) *The Employment Trap: Long-Term Unemployment and Low Educational Attainment in Six Countries*, Strasbourg: Council of Europe Press.

Department of Employment (1990) *European Social Fund: Guidance on Applications for 1991*, London: DE/ESF Unit.

—— (1991) *European Social Fund: Guidance for 1992 Applications*, London: DE/ESF Unit.

—— (1992) *European Social Fund: Guidance for 1993 Applications*, London: DE/ESF Unit.

—— (1993a) *The European Social Fund: A Plan for Objective 3 in Great Britain: 1994–1999*, London: DE/ESFU.

—— (1993b) *European Social Fund: Guidance for 1994 Applications: Objective 3*, London: DE/ESFU.

—— (1994) *European Social Fund: Guidance for 1995 Applications: Objective 3*, London: DE/ESFU.

Department for Education and Employment (1995) *European Social Fund Guidance for 1996 Applications (Objective 3)*, London: DfEE/ESFU.

—— (1996a) *Objective 3 – United Kingdom Single Programming Document for the period 1997–1999*, London: DfEE/ESFU.

—— (1996b) *European Social Fund Objective 3: 1997 Applications Guidance*, London: DfEE/ESFU.

European Commission (1957) *Treaty of Rome*, Brussels: Commission of the European Communities.

—— (1992) *Treaty of the Union*, Brussels: Commission of the European Communities.

—— (1993a) *White Paper: Growth, Competitiveness, Employment: The Challenges and Ways Forward into the 21st Century*, Luxembourg: OOPEC.

—— (1993b) *Community Structural Funds 1994–1999: Regulations and Commentary*, Luxembourg: OOPEC.

—— (1994) *European Social Policy: A Way Forward for the Union – A White Paper*, Luxembourg: OOPEC.

—— (1995) *White Paper on Education and Training: Teaching and Learning: Towards the Learning Society*, Luxembourg: OOPEC.

—— (1997) *Treaty of Amsterdam*, Brussels: Commission of the European Communities.

FFORWM (1995) *FE Sector Wales European Social Fund (Objective 3): Description of the 1996 Selection Process*, Cardiff: FFORWM.

Foucault, M. (1977) *Discipline and Punish*, New York: Pantheon.

—— (1980) *History of Sexuality, vol. 1*, New York: Vintage.

Further Education College Scottish Sector (1995) *1996 Objective 3 – ESF: Selection Process – Summary and Deadlines*, Edinburgh: FECSS.

Further Education Funding Council (1995) *Circular 95/31: European Social Fund Objective 3 Applications for 1996 (+ Supplement)*. London: FEFC.

Hirst, P. and Thompson, G. (1995) 'Globalization and the future of the nation state', *Economy and Society* 24, 3: 408–42.

Meehan, E. (1992) 'Researching women in Europe: European Community policies on sex equality', *Women's Studies International Forum* 15, 1: 57–64.

National Council for Voluntary Organisations (1995) *NCVO European Social Fund Guidance: A Guide to ESF Applicants in 1996*, London: NCVO.

Official Journal (1993) *OJL 193, Council Regulation (EEC) No 2084/93 of 20 July 1993*, Brussels: European Commission.

Ohame, K. (1990) *The Borderless World*, London: Collins.

Organisation for Economic Co-operation and Development (1992) *Adult Illiteracy and Economic Performance*, Paris: OECD.

Prechal, S. and Senden, L. (1993) *Equal Treatment after Maastricht: Special Report of 1993 of the Network of Experts on the Implementation of the Equality Directives*, Brussels: European Commission, DG V, Equal Opportunities Unit.

Women's Training Network (1996) *Membership Information Pack*, Leeds: WTN.

Part 2

Structures and processes in schools and classrooms

6 Gender and national curricula

Linda Croxford

Introduction

In the 1990s, as in earlier decades, the subjects and courses chosen for study by young women in schools, colleges and at university tend to be different from those chosen by young men. Differences in curriculum at school lead to gender differences in the qualifications obtained by young women and young men and unequal opportunities to pursue subsequent careers. National curricula have a potential role in reducing inequality by providing all pupils with entitlement to a common core curriculum. In principle, a national curriculum should ensure that pupils of both sexes experience all modes of study and areas of knowledge, so that gross differences in experience of curriculum are prevented.

However, national curricula also provide a means for the government to exert central control over the curriculum taught in schools. It is unfortunate that the national curriculum introduced in England and Wales as part of the Education Reform Act 1988 (ERA) was influenced more by the conservative political agenda than educational or egalitarian principles. It provoked such intense opposition that the potential benefits of a common core curriculum for promoting gender equality may have been obscured. The compulsory part of the national curriculum was reduced in 1994, opening possibilities for greater flexibility and choice but also reintroducing possibilities of gender inequality. It is useful to consider the different approach taken to curriculum reform in Scotland, where there has been a long tradition of consensus rather than conflict in the relationship between schools and the Scottish Education Department (SED).[1] A nationally recommended curriculum framework for the secondary stages in Scotland had been developed in 1977. The political pressure for central control of the curriculum emanating from the 1988 Conservative government was mediated in Scotland by the existing structures for educational policy-making. Thus, the definition of a common core curriculum for the 5–14 age group was worked out through discussion between policy-makers and practitioners, and achieved widespread support among the educational community.

In this chapter, some of the purposes of a national curriculum are outlined, and the different national curricula that are currently in place in the UK are described. I will suggest that there is still considerable scope for gendered subject choice in all UK education systems, and empirical data for Scotland are used to illustrate this.

What are the purposes of a national curriculum?

In principle, a national curriculum can serve a number of purposes:

1   *Entitlement and equality:* to provide an entitlement for every child to be taught what is in the national curriculum; ensure that every pupil experiences the different modes of study included in the national curriculum; introduce all pupils to the common culture of society.
2   *Promote priority areas:* to ensure that all pupils study priority areas of the curriculum, such as science and technology, in which there is a perceived need to increase participation.
3   *Accountability:* to increase accountability of schools; to provide a framework for monitoring school provision and pupils' attainment; to provide continuity and progression between stages of schooling and between different schools.

These purposes have appealed to UK policy-makers at different times over the past three decades, and have consequences for the ways in which the different curricula of the UK have been implemented. The first two of these purposes have particular importance for promoting gender equality.

Entitlement and equality

In the 1960s the idea of a common core curriculum was perhaps an extension of the comprehensive ideal. The introduction of comprehensive schooling in 1965 had a number of purposes, including the reduction of social inequality. But within comprehensive schools the curriculum experienced by pupils was differentiated on the basis of streaming and the distinction between certificate and non-certificate pupils. This led a number of curriculum theorists to put forward ideas about a common core curriculum that should be the entitlement of all pupils. In particular, Hirst identified seven or eight distinctive forms of knowledge in which all pupils should have experience, and argued:

> If the objectives of our education differ for sections of our society so as to ignore any of these elements for some of our pupils, either because they are considered too difficult, or for some reason they are thought less important for these pupils, then we are denying to them basic ways of rational development and we have indeed got inequality of educational opportunity of the most far reaching kind.
>
> (Hirst 1969: 150)

In Scotland, where comprehensive reorganisation was more universal than elsewhere in the UK (McPherson and Willms 1987), the need for a comprehensive curriculum for the 14–16 age-group led to the development in 1977 of the first common core curriculum in the UK (Croxford 1994).

There was overt discrimination in the provision of courses for girls and boys prior to the Sex Discrimination Act (SDA) 1975 (SED 1975). The SDA made this unlawful, and thereafter schools were required 'to ensure that any differential provision for boys and girls . . . is based on genuine differences of need or interest' (SED 1976). However, some feminists put forward the ideas of a common core curriculum as a way to ensure that girls experienced the same curriculum as boys and thus avoid the effects of underlying prejudices and assumptions which could be interpreted as 'genuine differences of need or interest' (Byrne 1978).

Part of the rationale for the national curriculum for England and Wales described in a consultation document was to ensure that: 'all pupils study a broad and balanced range of subjects throughout their compulsory schooling and do not drop too early studies which may stand them in good stead later' and 'all pupils regardless of sex, ethnic origin and geographical location, have access to broadly the same good and relevant curriculum and programmes of study' (Department of Education and Science 1987: 3–4).

Priority areas of the curriculum

The view that priority should be given to teaching more science and technology in schools, in order to create a labour force that can compete in world markets, has been repeated frequently by policy-makers. This theme was part of the influential speech at Ruskin College in 1976 by the then Prime Minister James Callaghan, who advocated a common core curriculum as a means of ensuring this priority. A similar theme is expressed by the government White Paper *Realising Our Potential* (HM Government 1993). The priority given to science and technology in the curriculum has had the effect of increasing female participation in these areas, and thus reducing gender inequality; this will be discussed more fully later in the chapter.

Accountability

The decision to introduce a national curriculum in England and Wales was made by a government which emphasised the purpose of ensuring public accountability of schools. Prior to ERA 1988, the curriculum taught in England and Wales varied greatly between schools. By means of the ERA, all schools were required to teach the specified subjects, and to test pupils' attainments in these subjects. The political emphasis on accountability thus triggered the introduction of the national curriculum at the end of the 1980s, even though the other purposes of providing a common entitlement, and promoting science and technology had been under discussion for a longer period of time. Subsequently, the Northern Ireland curriculum and the 5–14 programme in Scotland were developed in a more gradual manner, encouraged by the same political imperative.

National curricula in the UK: what are the differences?

Within the UK there are four different 'national curricula', in England, Wales, Northern Ireland and Scotland, respectively (Table 6.1). Some of the differences of definition arise from differences in education systems and national culture between the four territories, including the different structure of education in Scotland compared to elsewhere in the UK, and the position of the Welsh language in Wales.

The basic design of the national curriculum for England and Wales, and Northern Ireland, introduced through the Education Reform Act 1988 and the Education Reform (Northern Ireland) Order 1989, and subsequently modified in 1993, includes the division of schooling into Key Stages, and the definition in terms of subjects. Table 6.1 shows the 'core' compulsory subjects. For each subject and Key Stage programmes of study set out what pupils should be taught and attainment targets set out the expected standards of performance. The basic model of the national curriculum has been adapted to the special circumstances of Wales and Northern Ireland. In Wales an important place is given to the Welsh language, which is an additional subject, either core or non-core depending upon the cultural and linguistic orientation of the school. In addition, four non-core subjects, history, geography, art and music have subject orders that are distinctive to Wales and contribute to the 'Curriculum Cwmreig' (Cox 1997). In Northern Ireland the Irish language is accommodated in a few schools, and greater prominence is given to cross-curricular themes such as 'Education for mutual understanding', which are expected to permeate all areas of study.

The national curriculum in Scotland does not bear the title 'National Curriculum', and is not defined by legislation. It has been developed in two development programmes through consultation with practitioners: the curriculum for the 5–14 age-group is defined by the 5–14 National Guidelines; the curriculum for the 14–16 age group is defined by the Curriculum Framework. The compulsory elements of the curriculum are defined in terms of five curricular areas for the 5–14 age group, and eight modes of study for the 14–16 age group. Within each curricular area there are programmes of study, and attainment targets set for broad age-groups and stages of schooling. Arrangements for assessment of attainment are much more flexible than in England and Wales, and are not conducted at specific time points; teachers have discretion to use national tests for confirmatory purposes, when they consider their pupils have reached a particular level of attainment. At the 14–16 stage there is choice of subject courses within each mode. The syllabus of each course is defined by the Scottish Qualifications Authority. In addition, there are a number of elements of personal and social development, including 'Equal opportunities, understanding and tolerance', which are expected to permeate all modes, courses and activities.

Overall, despite differences in detail and terminology, the four national curricula appear to be providing a broadly similar curriculum to pupils in each part of the UK. Each national curriculum covers the same subjects or subject areas. The content of subject courses is likely to be broadly similar since the content of

Table 6.1 The UK 'national' curricula

Definition	England The National Curriculum	Wales The National Curriculum	NI The Northern Ireland Curriculum	Scotland 5–14 Programme
Age/stage 1	5–7/KS1	5–7/KS1	5–8/KS1	5–7/P1–P3
Curriculum content	English Mathematics Science Technology History Geography Art Music PE	English (except in Welsh-speaking classes) Welsh Mathematics Science Technology History Geography Art Music PE	English Irish (in Irish-speaking schools) Mathematics Science Technology History and Geography Art and design Music PE	Curricular areas: Language Mathematics Environmental studies Expressive arts Religious, social and moral education
Age/stage 2 Curriculum content	7–11/KS2 as stage 1	7–11/KS2 as stage 1	9–11/KS2 as stage 1	8–12/P4–P7 as stage 1
Age/stage 3 Curriculum content	11–14/KS3 as stages 1 and 2 plus foreign language	11–14/KS3 as stages 1 and 2 plus foreign language	12–14/KS3 as stages 1 and 2 plus foreign language and six cross-curricular themes	13–14/S1—S2 as stage 1

Table 6.1 Continued

Definition	England The National Curriculum	Wales The National Curriculum	NI The Northern Ireland Curriculum	Scotland Curriculum Framework
Age/stage 4	14–16/KS4	14–16/KS4	15–16/KS4	15–16/S3–S4
Compulsory curriculum	English Mathematics Science PE Technology Modern foreign language	English Welsh (except in non-Welsh-speaking schools) Mathematics Science PE	English Mathematics Science History or Geography PE Modern foreign language 6 cross-curricular themes	Modes: Language and communication Mathematical studies Scientific studies Social and environmental studies Technological activities Creative and aesthetic activities Physical education Religious, social and moral education
Choice	additional subjects	additional subjects	additional subjects	choice of subjects within modes

academic subjects is determined by subject specialists in the teaching professions and university departments who form a UK-wide, and indeed international, constituency. As a consequence, the four UK national curricula have similar implications for gender equality. There may be differences of emphasis and content within particular subject courses in parts of the UK which promote gender equality, but the detailed content analysis needed to identify these is beyond the scope of the present study. Issues concerning equal opportunities are expected to be addressed as cross-curricular themes in Scotland and Northern Ireland; however, the position of cross-curricular themes is less secure, and more easily ignored, than the position of compulsory subjects and modes in the curriculum.

Two aspects in which the differences in national curricula may have an impact on gender relate to the position of Welsh language, and different structures of subject choice. The definition of the national curriculum for Wales, to include both Welsh and English language at all stages, has enhanced the position of language in Wales compared to elsewhere. Language is an area of the curriculum in which females have been more successful than males, so this aspect of the definition of the national curriculum has gender implications. Potential divergence arises also from different opportunities for subject choice at the 14–16 stages. In Scotland pupils are not required to study all three sciences, as do pupils elsewhere in the UK, and consequently have the opportunity to drop individual science subjects which may reduce their career options. On the other hand, pupils in Scotland are required to study at least one subject in each mode, and pupils in Northern Ireland are required to study one subject in each area of study, whereas pupils in England and Wales can drop history, geography, art and music. Gender implications of subject choice are discussed in the next section.

The dramatic introduction of the national curriculum in England and Wales through the Education Reform Act in 1988 was characterised by a degree of conflict between the politicians and teaching profession. This can be contrasted with the different experience of curricular reform in Scotland, in which there was a more consultative consensual approach. In consequence, the definition of the national curriculum in terms of 'subjects' reflects the approach of politicians, whereas the definition of curriculum in Scotland, in terms of curricular areas and modes of study, is more in tune with the approaches of educational theorists. Although the method of introduction, and style of definition of the curriculum have aroused less criticism and opposition in Scotland than in England and Wales, these differences do not have obvious implications for gender equality in schools. However, a recent study has found that the more consensual change strategy in Scotland can be more conservative and less challenging to conventional hierarchies or divisions (Howieson *et al.* 1997).

Changes to the national curricula

The national curricula for England and Wales were reviewed, streamlined and simplified in 1994, following widespread protest, and evidence that the national curriculum and assessment requirements were unmanageable, and were detracting from the teaching of basic skills (Dearing 1994; Cox 1997). In Scotland, some modifications to the recommendations for the curriculum framework and 5–14 guidelines were made in response to government priorities, such as the requirement for modern foreign languages. The national curriculum for Northern Ireland was developed at a later stage than those for England, Wales and Scotland, with the consequence that it avoided some of the problems experienced elsewhere.

The 'New Labour' government has indicated that there will be 'a thorough review of the National Curriculum in due course' (HM Government 1997: 22). The policy document for England, *Excellence in Schools*, reiterates the role of the national curriculum in ensuring entitlement, but hedges this view with possible variation to allow specialisation by some schools:

> The curriculum for the next century – and its associated assessment – will be guided by
>
> - our vision of curriculum reflecting a common framework and a common entitlement;
> - the needs of children at different ages and different stages of their development; and
> - the needs, character and ethos of the individual school.
>
> (HM Government 1997: 22)

The document requires greater priority to be given to literacy and numeracy in the primary curriculum: 'To help support the new strategies for literacy and numeracy, the existing National Curriculum needs to be more sharply focused on giving all children a proper grounding in the basics within a broad and balanced curriculum' (ibid.). The emphasis on literacy and numeracy is reflected in policy statements for Wales and Scotland also, and seems to suggest a possible narrowing of the curriculum in primary schools.

Anxiety about disaffection and social exclusion, particularly in respect of low-attaining boys, may have an effect on the national curriculum at KS3 and KS4. There are suggestions that there should be more vocational options leading to GNVQ level 1, as a means of motivating low attaining pupils. The introduction of vocational courses will inevitably lead to increasing gender differences in curriculum on the lines of current labour market segregation.

The distinctiveness of the Scottish and Welsh curricula may be reinforced by the introduction of a new Scottish Parliament and Welsh Assembly. Future developments in Scotland and Wales are hard to predict as new political forces may develop. The new political fora will create opportunities for more public debate about the priorities for education, and give more scope for developing areas of the curriculum relating to national and cultural identities.

Implications of national curricula for gender equality

A common feature of each national curriculum is that between the ages of 5–14 all pupils,[2] regardless of gender, must study the required subjects or curricular areas. All pupils are entitled to develop the same learning skills, and experience the same areas of knowledge. This is an important means of ensuring that girls and boys have equal opportunities to learn. In theory, it removes the possibility that schools might make different provision for girls or boys. In practice, however, the reality of classroom experiences of different areas of the curriculum may still differ for girls and boys, because of the attitudes and behaviours of children and teachers, and the influences of society. Research has shown the existence of a 'hidden curriculum'. For example, textbooks may use sex-biased examples and illustrations (Centre for Mathematics Education 1986). There may be differences in the way that teachers respond to verbal participation by female and male students, and the way they assist female and male students (Stanworth 1983; Holly 1985; LaFrance 1991). Teachers' attitudes and expectations may feed sex-stereotyped attitudes to certain subjects (Riddell 1992).

A further common feature of each national curriculum is the element of choice of subjects to be studied for external examinations, especially GCSE and Standard Grade, during the last two years of compulsory schooling. The extent of choice in each system is somewhat limited; all pupils must continue to study English, mathematics, a science and a language but, for example, in Scotland pupils choose a subject within each mode, and similarly elsewhere pupils can choose to study additional subjects. By allowing choice of subjects at the 14–16 stages, the national curricula provide the opportunity for pupils to make gender-biased subject choices.

Gender differences in subject choice

'Choice' is a concept which tends to be regarded highly in our democratic society. Allowing pupils to choose the subjects they study at the 14–16 stage gives them more 'ownership' of their curriculum, and reduces the likelihood that they will be alienated by an over-prescriptive curriculum. However, 'choice' can be a problem when the individuals responsible for making choices are overly influenced by the traditional attitudes and unequal opportunity structures of society. 'Choosing or channelling?' (Kelly 1981) describes the double-edged process of subject choice which leads to so many girls choosing to study 'girls' subjects' and thereby limiting their choices for future careers.

The reasons why girls and boys choose to study different subjects may be influenced by a complex interaction of factors (Whyld 1983; Pratt *et al.* 1984). The attitudes and expectations of parents, families and peer groups reinforce stereotypes of appropriate subjects for girls and boys. For example, in early childhood aspects of play, such as the encouragement of boys to play with cars, Meccano and Lego are thought to reinforce male interest in science and technology. Families which, because of their own traditional upbringing, find it 'normal' for a girl to find maths difficult, or consider it 'cissy' for a boy to learn to sew, may inadvertently encourage girls and boys to take more interest in some subjects than others. Peer-group pressure further influences children's attitudes to what are 'boys' subjects' and 'girls' subjects', and creates situations in which it is very difficult for individuals not to conform to the norm for their gender. The stage at which national curricula allow choice of subjects for public examinations including GCSE, is when children are aged 13–14, and most susceptible to peer-group pressure. Gender differences in subjects chosen are more pronounced among working-class pupils than among middle-class pupils (Croxford 1994, 1997). Subsequent choice of subjects for post-compulsory and higher education may be critically dependent on the choices pupils make for GCSE (or Standard Grade in Scotland).

Teachers' attitudes and behaviours affect pupils' subject choices in different ways. Some pupils will choose a subject just because they enjoy the subject or like the teacher and this may, or may not, have significance for gender differences. However, a popular female teacher may provide a positive role model which encourages girls to take a particular subject, but have an opposite or neutral effect for the boys. Some teachers may have their own attitudes about the suitability of their subject for boys and girls, which they express in a range of overt and covert ways. For example, a study of option choice in one school demonstrated the use of sexist jokes and body language by a male teacher of technology designed to discourage female students from choosing that option (Riddell 1992).

A common reason for a pupil to choose a particular subject is because s/he believes s/he is good at it, and has a good chance of passing the examination (Ryrie *et al.* 1979). This perception is derived from views expressed by teachers, as well as the pupil's estimation of her/his own ability and the relative difficulty of the subject. Some subjects, such as physics and foreign languages, are considered to be more difficult than others. It has been argued that a reason why so few girls study physics is that girls tend to be less confident than boys of their own ability, and less likely to choose difficult subjects (Kelly 1987). However, this explanation is less convincing with respect to foreign languages, which are difficult subjects studied more by females than by males. It seems likely that decisions to attempt difficult subjects are influenced by interacting influences of what pupils enjoy, what they find difficult, and what they consider to be appropriate and useful for their future careers. Both male and female pupils perceive that science subjects are more useful for the careers of men than of women (Assessment of Performance Unit 1989).

Most pupils making their subject choices at age 13–14 have vague and unrealistic career ideas (Howieson and Semple 1996). Young people have very low levels of awareness of post-16 opportunities for employment and training (Foskett and Hemsley-Brown 1997). An increasing proportion of young people perceive the need to stay on in full-time education post-16, and possibly go on to university; their subject choices may be influenced by advice concerning entrance requirements. However, there are many pitfalls in this process, and pupils can make decisions to drop subjects at age 13–14 which they subsequently find are necessary for entry to the course of their choice.

The curriculum for the post-compulsory stages in all parts of the UK is increasingly characterised by choice rather than prescription (Raffe 1997). The trend of the *Higher Still* reforms in Scotland, the proposed *Scottish Qualifications Framework*, and unified *Welsh Framework* are towards seamless but flexible qualifications frameworks. To a lesser extent the trend towards flexibility is evident in England also (Howieson *et al.* 1997). Young people making their course and career choices will be faced with a bewildering array of options, and need to be very well informed in order to make choices that will benefit their career prospects.

For the majority of pupils, parents are the primary source of advice about careers. The extent to which parents have relevant knowledge and experience to advise their children on relevant course choices and careers varies considerably and is particularly influenced by which segment of the labour market they occupy, with middle-class parents having knowledge of a wider range of careers (Howieson *et al.* 1993). Advice from parents may reinforce existing gender stereotypes about what are considered appropriate male and female careers.

A very welcome three-year initiative 'to improve the quality and coverage of careers guidance for pupils from age 13' was heralded by the 1994 White Paper, *Competitiveness: Helping Business to Win* (HMSO 1994). One of the aims of what became known as the Year 9 and 10 initiative was to help secure informed choices of Key Stage 4 subjects and courses for students in Year 9. There is, however, a need for a more comprehensive approach, which should include:

- careers education and guidance on a continual basis from early stages of schooling, to help young people as they develop and their ideas form;
- recognition of the importance of subject teachers in providing advice to the more academic pupils, and the need to keep them informed about new developments in courses and career opportunities;
- improved information for schools;
- independent advice from the careers service.

Young people have the responsibility for making course choices which will affect their future career opportunities, and they need a range of good quality information, rather than mis-information, in order to do this. In the next section, some empirical evidence of the extent to which young people's choices of subjects are clearly differentiated by gender is discussed.

Choice within the national curriculum: some empirical evidence with respect to participation in science in Scotland

Each of the national curricula in the UK ensures coverage of core curricular areas up to the age of 14, and thereafter each allows an element of choice of subjects for public examinations. To illustrate the consequences of such choice empirical data from Scotland is used, but a similar picture could be gained from all parts of the UK.

In Scotland all pupils have been required to study science since the introduction of the curriculum framework in 1983. However, pupils in Scotland are free to choose between physics, chemistry, biology and general science, whereas pupils elsewhere are required to study all three science subjects. The effects of this choice on gender differences in participation can be seen using data from a national survey of young people in Scotland.

These data are used for a number of reasons. First, a great deal of priority has been given to increasing participation in science subjects since the 'Great Debate', and this priority continues to be emphasised in government publications. Second, science is a curricular area which was formerly regarded as less important for girls than for boys (Ministry of Education 1963). Third, data for Scotland are used because the curriculum framework influenced participation in science in Scotland at an earlier period than elsewhere, and, finally, data for Scotland cover a longer time-period than is available elsewhere in the UK. The analyses illustrate the stability of gender-stereotyping of subject choices.

Figure 6.1 provides an overall picture of the trends in the proportion of girls and boys who studied any science at the age of 14–16; it shows the effect of the Sex Discrimination Act (1975) and the introduction of the curriculum framework.[3] Prior to the Sex Discrimination Act, less than 50 per cent of girls studied any science, compared to 70 per cent of boys.[4] Participation in science by working-class girls was particularly low at around 25 per cent (table not shown). There was a gradual increase in the proportion of girls studying science following the Act, but gender equality had not been achieved by 1984. Pupils aged 16 in 1986 were the first to be affected by the curriculum framework; following its introduction there was a rapid increase in the proportion of all pupils studying science, and a corresponding reduction in gender differences. This illustrates the effectiveness in reducing gender differences of making a core curricular area a universal requirement.

Figure 6.2 moves away from the overall picture of the science mode to look at the detail of individual science subjects. It shows significant and continuing gender differences in participation in science subjects. More girls than boys study biology, and fewer girls than boys study physics and chemistry. There has been considerable increase in the proportion of all pupils studying biology over the two decades, and the increase has been greater among girls than among boys. The proportion of girls studying physics has more than doubled over the period, but is still only half the level of participation by boys. The proportion of girls studying chemistry has risen and has almost caught up with levels of participation by boys. The status of general science is somewhat different from that of the three separate science subjects, because it is studied mainly by pupils of lower attainment who do not intend to carry on with science after the age of 16. The introduction of the curriculum framework had the effect of increasing participation in general science quite dramatically, and this affected boys and girls more or less equally.

Does it matter if girls and boys study different science subjects? From the

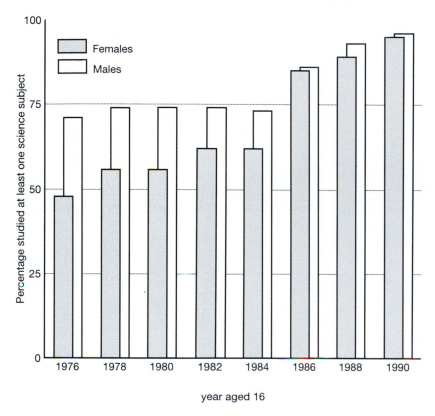

Figure 6.1 Percentage of pupils who studied any science at age 14–16 in Scotland, 1976–90

Source: Calculated from Scottish Young People's Survey Leavers Series 1977–83 and Cohort Series 1985–91 in Lamb (1997)

point of view of a common core curriculum any science subject can introduce pupils to scientific principles and methods of study, and thus provide for the pupils' education in science. However, we need also to consider the role of curriculum and public examinations in providing the credentials for entry to jobs, higher education and subsequent careers. From this perspective, gender differences in science subject participation leads to inequality of credentials; physics has a high status as a credential which brings subsequent benefits for entry to higher education and future careers. The status hierarchy of subjects is an unofficial but generally recognised aspect of competition for entry to higher education and careers. By allowing choice of subjects for Standard Grade the Scottish curriculum framework provides scope for young people to make choices which may create differences in subsequent opportunities.

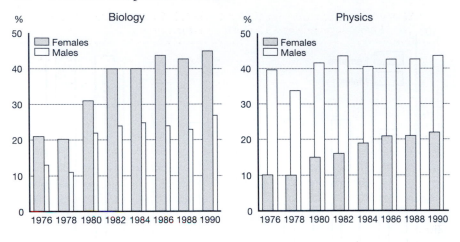

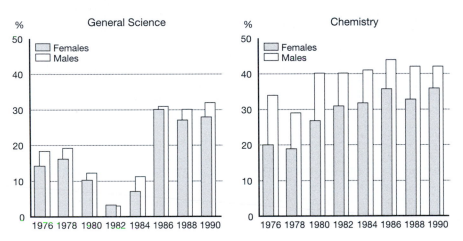

Figure 6.2 Gender differences in science subjects studied at age 14–16 in Scotland, 1976–90

Source: Calculated from Scottish Young People's Survey Leavers Series 1977–83 and Cohort Series 1985–91 in Lamb (1997)

Gender differences in post-compulsory education

The cumulative effect of subject choices is revealed by gender bias in subjects studied in post-compulsory and higher education throughout the UK (see Tables 6.2 and 6.3). At GCE A level (or SCE Higher Grade in Scotland) the subjects in which female students were a clear majority were home economics, religious studies, modern languages, English literature and social studies (more than two-thirds of students taking these subjects were female). Conversely, the subjects in which female students were a small minority were craft design and technology (CDT), computer studies, and physics, (less than one-third of

Table 6.2 Subject course entries for GCE A level/SCE Higher Grade in Great Britain, 1994–95: percentage of entrants who were female

	Female %	Number of entries (= 100%) thousands
Craft, Design, Technology	18	14.2
Computer studies	19	13.4
Physics	24	44.6
Economics	35	27.5
Physical education	37	10.9
Mathematics	38	81.9
Geography	45	48.3
Chemistry	45	51.6
Other science	49	8.7
Business studies	49	33.2
History	56	49.6
Classical studies	58	7.7
Art and design	61	39.4
English	62	59.3
Biological sciences	62	61.8
Social studies	66	77.9
English literature	69	58.2
Modern languages	69	54.5
Religious studies	76	8.6
Home economics	97	2.9

Source: DfEE (1996), Table 31.

Table 6.3 Full-time first degree courses started by UK students in 1995–96: percentage of students who were female

	Female %	Number of entries (= 100%) thousands
Engineering and technology	15	68.5
Architecture	21	22.1
Mathematical science	24	48.7
Physical sciences	36	47.6
Business and financial	49	80.6
Medicine and dentistry	51	23.7
Humanities	53	31.4
Social Sciences	56	91.8
Creative arts	57	57.8
Biological sciences	60	48.3
Languages	70	56.0
Allied medicine	75	35.7
Education and teacher training	77	53.3
All subjects	51	794.8

Source: DfEE (1996), Table 22b.

students taking these subjects were female). These patterns of subject choice are shown even more strongly at entry to degree courses in higher education (see Table 6.3); young women are concentrated in education (teacher training), subjects allied to medicine and languages, young men in engineering and technology, architecture and mathematical sciences. Differences in courses followed at A level and degree level lead on to differences in career opportunities and continuing wage differences.

Conclusion

National curricula provide an entitlement so that all children are taught the key areas of knowledge and skills which are considered important within each education system. This entitlement has potentially important implications for gender equality because in the past there has been considerable gender discrimination in the provision of courses. Although discrimination was made unlawful by the Sex Discrimination Act there are still deep-seated attitudes that some subjects are more appropriate for girls or boys. These attitudes need to be changed. A national curriculum goes some way towards this by ensuring that all children are required to study the common curriculum between the ages of 5–14. Nevertheless there is still a long way to go in changing deep-seated gender bias in attitudes to the curriculum.

Such attitudes are revealed by the continuing gender differences in subject choice amongst the 14–16 age group. The choice of subjects at the 14–16 stage has further implications for course and career choices later in life. There is therefore a need for young people, their teachers and parents to be given effective information and advice about the implications of their choices for their future equality of opportunity. Such information and advice is particularly important in view of the increasingly flexible frameworks for courses and qualifications post-16 as a result of Higher Still reforms in Scotland and comparable changes elsewhere in the UK.

I would argue that the part of the curriculum studied by young people in their last two years of compulsory schooling which is common and compulsory is relatively small, and might indeed be too small. For this stage of schooling it might be more appropriate for the majority of pupils to continue to study a larger common element of courses, in order to keep their options open. The large amount of subject choice allowed by the final two years of national curricula in the UK has been formed on the assumption that high proportions of young people leave school at the age of 16, and should choose the subjects they study for school-leaving examinations. However, it is becoming the norm for young people to stay on to post-compulsory education, and the public examinations at age 16 are less important than subsequent qualifications for their future career opportunities. Some 57 per cent of all 16–18 year olds in the UK were in full-time education in 1995–96 compared to just 29 per cent in 1980–81 (DfEE 1996). Gender differences in post-compulsory courses and careers would be reduced if there were a larger common entitlement and less choice of subjects for the final two years of each national curriculum.

However, there are a number of conflicts inherent in the national curricula of the UK. First, there is a conflict between the objective of providing a broad and balanced core curriculum, and the need to ensure there is sufficient emphasis on basic skills such as literacy and numeracy. Policy statements by the 'New Labour' government suggest that there should be a sharper focus on basic skills, but this may lead to a narrowing of the common core curriculum.

Second, there is a conflict between the need to ensure that young people have a common curriculum entitlement, and the danger of alienating students through an overly prescriptive curriculum. This tension is most evident in providing for the needs of less academic pupils, particularly low-attaining boys. The moves by the 'New Labour' government to reintroduce more vocational courses for these pupils echo the advice of the Brunton Committee in 1963 that the 'vocational impulse' should be the motivating force for the less able child (SED 1963). However, the problems of alienation are seen to refer more to males than females. There are dangers foreshadowed earlier that a reduction in the core of the curriculum, and reintroduction of more vocational options, may increase gender inequality in participation, entry and qualifications outcomes.

Third, there is conflict between common curricular provision by schools, and the emphasis by governments on educational markets and parental choice of schools (Adler 1997).

Finally, there is a conflict between the potential use of a national curriculum by the government to exert central control over what is taught in schools, and the views of teachers and other educational professionals. The experience in Scotland of developing a curriculum framework through consultation and consensus demonstrates the value of a partnership approach to policy-making. It is encouraging to find that the 'New Labour' government endorses such an approach, and promises that the coming review of the national curriculum will be 'a genuinely collaborative exercise in which all our partners in education will have a chance to participate' (HM Government 1997: 22).

Inequality should be a matter for continuing concern among the educational community, and must not be obscured by the competing problems of the twenty-first century. Inequality in curriculum can be reduced by a national curriculum which provides a common entitlement to all pupils. We need to ensure that future debate about the national curricula is informed by principles of equity.

Acknowledgements

This chapter is the result of a research project funded by the Economic and Social Research Council entitled 'A "Home International" Comparison of 14–19 Education and Training Systems in the UK' (Grant no R 000 23 6840).

Notes

1   The department is now called the Scottish Executive Education Department.

2 The national curricula apply only to schools in the public sector, not the independent sector.
3 Pupils aged 16 in 1986 were the first to be affected by the Curriculum Framework.
4 Data are shown for school sessions 1973–76, from a survey of school leavers in 1977.

References

Adler, M. (1997) 'Looking backwards to the future: parental choice and educational policy', *British Educational Research Journal* 23, 3: 297–313.

Assessment of Performance Unit (1989) *Science at Age 13: A Review of APU Survey Findings 1980–1984*, London: HMSO.

Byrne, E. (1978) *Women and Education*, London: Tavistock.

Callaghan, J. (1977) Speech at Ruskin College, Oxford.

Centre for Mathematics Education at the Open University, in association with Inner London Education Authority (1986) *Girls into Mathematics*, Cambridge: Cambridge University Press.

Cox, T. (1997) 'The impact of the National Curriculum on primary education in Wales', paper presented to the seminar Culture, Curriculum and Community, at the University of Wales Swansea, November 1997.

Croxford, L. (1994) 'Equal opportunities in the secondary school curriculum in Scotland, 1977–91', *British Educational Research Journal* 20, 4: 371–91.

—— (1997) 'Participation in science subjects: the effect of the Scottish Curriculum Framework', *Research Papers in Education* 12, 1: 69–89.

Dearing, R. (1994) *The National Curriculum and its Assessment*, London: SCAA.

Department of Education and Science (1987) *The National Curriculum 5–16: A Consultation Document*, London: HMSO.

DfEE (1996) *Education Statistics for the UK*, London: HMSO.

Foskett, N. and Hemsley-Brown, J. V. (1997) *Career Perception and Decision Making among Young People in Schools and Colleges*, Leeds: HEIST.

Hirst, P. (1969) 'The logic of the curriculum', *Journal of Curriculum Studies* 1, 2: 142–58.

HM Government (1993) *Realising Our Potential: A Strategy for Science, Engineering and Technology*, London: HMSO.

—— (1997) *Excellence in Schools*, Cm 3681, London: HMSO.

HMSO (1994) *Competitiveness: Helping Business to Win*, London: HMSO.

Holly, L. (1985) 'Mary, Jane and Virginia Woolf: ten-year-old girls talking', in G. Weiner (ed.) *Just a Bunch of Girls*, Milton Keynes: Open University Press.

Howieson, C. and Semple, S. (1996) *Guidance in Secondary Schools*, Edinburgh: Centre for Educational Sociology.

Howieson, C., Croxford, L. and Semple, S. (1993) *Choices in a Changing World*, a report to Scottish Enterprise, Edinburgh: Centre for Educational Sociology.

Howieson, C., Raffe, D., Spours, K. and Young, M. (1997) 'Unifying academic and vocational learning: the state of the debate in England and Scotland', *Journal of Education and Work* 10, 1: 5–35.

Kelly, A. (1981) 'Choosing or channelling?', in A. Kelly (ed.) *The Missing Half*, Manchester: Manchester University Press.

—— (ed.) (1987) *Science for Girls*, Milton Keynes: Open University Press.

LaFrance, M. (1991) 'School for scandal: different educational experiences for females and males', *Gender and Education* 3, 1: 3–14.

Lamb, J.M. (1997) 'Surveys and data', in Centre for Education Sociology *Brochure*, Edinburgh: University of Edinburgh.

McPherson, A. and Willms, J. D. (1987) 'Equalisation and improvement: some effects of comprehensive reorganisation in Scotland', *Sociology* 21, 4: 509–39.

Ministry of Education (1963) *Half Our Future* (The Newsom Report), London: HMSO.

National Commission on Education (1993) *Learning to Succeed: A Radical Look at Education Today and a Strategy for the Future*, London: Heinemann.

Pratt, J., Bloomfield, J. and Seale, C. (1984) *Option Choice: A Question of Equal Opportunity*, Slough: NFER/Nelson.

Raffe, D. (1997) 'Higher Still in a European perspective', *Scottish Educational Review* 29, 2: 121–33.

Riddell, S. (1992) *Gender and the Politics of the Curriculum*, London: Routledge.

Ryrie, A. C., Furst, A. and Lauder, M. (1979) *Choices and Chances: A Study of Pupils' Subject Choices and Future Career Intentions*, Sevenoaks: Hodder and Stoughton for SCRE.

Scottish Consultative Council on the Curriculum (1989) *Curriculum Design for the Secondary Stages: Guidelines for Headteachers*, Dundee: SCCC.

Scottish Education Department (1963) *From School to Further Education* (The Brunton Report), Edinburgh: HMSO.

—— (1975) *Differences in Provision for Boys and Girls in Scottish Secondary Schools*, Edinburgh: HMSO.

—— (1976) 'Sex Discrimination Act 1975', SED Circular no. 947, 26 February 1976, Edinburgh: SED.

Scottish Office Education Department (1993) *Curriculum and Assessment in Scotland, National Guidelines: The Structure and Balance of the Curriculum 5–14*, Edinburgh: SOED.

Stanworth, M. (1983) *Gender and Schooling*, London: Hutchinson.

Whyld, J. (1983) *Sexism in the Secondary Curriculum*, London: Harper and Row.

7 Equity, assessment and gender

Patricia Murphy

Introduction

Innovations in assessment practice represent some of the most significant reforms in education in the UK in the last twenty years. Broadfoot (1996: 168) argues that 'prevailing social pressures, both ideological and practical may be analysed in terms of their manifestation in one of the defining characteristics of education systems – namely assessment'. In her view, assessment techniques provide one of the central mechanisms by which the changing base for social control within the broader society are translated into the educational process. Nevertheless, debates about policy related to equal opportunities rarely consider the role assessment plays in enabling or inhibiting equality in educational opportunities or outcomes. Typically the outcomes of assessment are used to establish the 'gender gap' in achievement without making problematic the role that assessment practices play in determining the gap.

Some of the assessment reforms considered in the chapter represent new conceptualisations of the purposes and practices of education and offer the potential for greater equality of educational provision and outcome. However, as with all assessment procedures, they can serve both a liberating and controlling role. To examine this paradox it is necessary to explore the way differing views and beliefs about teaching, learning and the nature of knowledge influence assessments. The critique offered in the chapter reflects a socio-cultural perspective on these issues. This perspective assumes that the settings that contextualise and frame assessment activities influence students' participation in assessments and determine the tasks they perceive and the solutions they judge appropriate (Murphy 1995). In this chapter the impact of changes in assessment on the performance of males and females in national assessments and external examinations of academic rather than vocational achievements is explored and related to research evidence about the nature of gendered learning. In so doing, some of the conflicts inherent in current assessment practices are identified and the implications for future policy and practice considered.

Changes in assessment policy

National assessment

Through the 1970s there was growing concern in England and Wales that with the demise of the 11+, and the proliferation of exam syllabi, particularly through the introduction of the Certificate of Secondary Education (CSE), educational standards were no longer known and furthermore, were declining. The Labour Prime Minister of the time urged teachers to 'satisfy the parents and industry that what you are doing meets their requirements'. He argued for 'a basic curriculum with universal standards' (Callaghan 1976). One outcome of the debate on educational standards, initiated by Callaghan's speech, was the establishment of the Assessment of Performance Unit (APU). This was funded by the Department of Education and Science (DES) to monitor the performance of populations of primary and secondary pupils aged 11, 13 and 15 in England, Wales and Northern Ireland. Monitoring commenced in 1978 and ended in 1989. Mathematics, language (English) and Science were monitored over time and across age and single monitorings occurred in Modern Languages and Design and Technology. One of the main aims of the Unit was to provide evidence about standards of performance. Participation of schools in the monitoring was voluntary and sampling of pupils and of tests meant that individual pupils could not be identified and were assessed only on aspects of subject achievement (for discussion see Johnson 1989; Foxman *et al.* 1991). Consequently while the APU played a major role in promoting assessment at local authority and school level and influenced educational practices, it did not fulfil its role as a mechanism for accountability. It did provide an operational basis for the development of such a mechanism. As Broadfoot argues:

> It only required the advent of the powerful New right political movement to translate a general belief in the benefits of competition into the concept of market accountability and for APU technology to be transformed into the basis of a national assessment programme.
>
> (1996: 208)

The English and Welsh national assessment programme introduced in the TGAT report (DES 1987) replaced the APU and was the central mechanism for the introduction of the National Curriculum. The programme had two aims – to promote effective learning and teaching in schools, and to improve the accountability of the educational system. The programme was predicated on the belief that comparison and competition informed by systematic assessment at individual pupil level would lead to increased efficiency in relation to the inputs and outputs of the education system. To achieve its aims the programme, like the APU, tested at fixed ages seen to be of educational significance, i.e. 7, 11, 14 and 16 years of age. Performance on tasks was referenced against statements of attainment mapped against a ten-level scale that in part defined the National Curriculum, and in addition functioned as criteria for assessment. The programme combined continuous assessment by teachers and externally developed standard assessment tasks and tests. The Task Group's report (DES 1987) made little reference to views of learning. Within the guidance there were recommendations that a wide range of modes of presentation, operation, and response be used in assessment tasks 'to widen the range of pupils' abilities that they reflect and so to enhance educational validity' (DES 1987 VII: 49). The first national assessment standard tasks for primary children were generally written tasks with short and extended response formats, well illustrated and there was a practical performance element in the science tasks. Multiple choice format was not used, reinforcing the view that assessment methods were to 'fit' the achievements being assessed. Nevertheless, it was assumed that a narrow written test of achievement could provide a reliable and valid measure of individual achievement, an assumption challenged by APU evidence (Johnson 1989). Initially the tests were seen as supplements to teachers' continuous assessment but increasingly they came to be seen as the only valued form of assessment, particularly by politicians (Daugherty 1996).

The information provided by the programme was to enable policy-makers to judge the effectiveness of schools within the whole system and at local authority level. The information was made public in school league tables for use by schools for the purpose of professional accountability and by parents to facilitate freedom of choice and to provide them with the means to challenge teacher competence. In some respects therefore the programme could be seen as liberating, in that it increased parental choice, though only for some, and schools' ability to respond to market forces. On the other hand, the imposition of a crude input–output model where school effectiveness is judged by narrowly defined outcomes simultaneously allowed for greater control of teachers and pupils and the system as a whole.

Examination at 16+

In 1965 the General Certificate of Education (GCE) and Certificate for Secondary Education (CSE) dual system of examination was in place which in theory provided access to certification to 60 per cent of the school population. Calls for reforms of the system grew out of disparate concerns to extend access to certification and to reduce the diversity in provision so that universal standards applied in awarding grades. In 1978 the Waddell Committee proposed a single examination system based on a seven-point grading scale linked to existing GCE/CSE grades (later amended to an eight-point scale). The Committee also recommended a reduction in the examination centres to a few regional consortia and the introduction of national subject criteria. These proposals provided the means for greater government intervention and control of the examination process and consequently the education system as a whole. GCSE was to later (1994) act as the 'measure' of performance at age 16 for the national assessment programme. This meant that the initial purposes of the examination were changed to encompass the wider demands of accountability of the national programme.

The General Certificate of Secondary Education (GCSE) was introduced in 1988. The examination was to be appropriate for the majority of pupils. This was achieved through differentiated papers which required teachers to identify in advance the potential achievements of their pupils. This was justified in terms of positive achievement, as it was argued that the exam had to indicate what pupils could do rather than presenting pupils with assessments beyond their capabilities. This emphasis on demonstrating what pupils 'know and can do' was reinforced by the requirement for a single system of grade-related criteria against which grades would be awarded. This, it was argued, increased comparability between Boards, provided the information needed by the public, and was motivating for pupils, which in turn would lead to an increase in standards. The GCSE exams assessed broader definitions of subject achievement than prior systems. This was justified on a number of grounds. One, that human abilities were no longer understood to be normally distributed rather than that all pupils were capable of a wide range of achievements. Another that the focus on narrow academic definitions of achievement were inadequate to prepare and select pupils for employment. Consequently there was a need for a wider range of assessment techniques.

The examination included a significant performance component that was compulsory. This marked a radical shift from traditional practice and increased teachers' and students' involvement in the assessment process. The new methods included teacher-assessed coursework, orals, portfolios and investigations. The new system, while being more centrally controlled, provided access to certification to a greater proportion of pupils. Reliance continued to be placed on written examinations but these were to be supplemented by more informal and authentic performance assessments. In other words, there were inherent conflicts embodied in the system from its inception.

Assessment and learning

Objective tests that developed within the psychometric tradition were considered to be just forms of assessment for all. The tests were based on the assumptions that intelligence was represented in the population normally and that individuals possess a fixed, measurable level of intelligence that determines intellectual development. That is, if a student performs well on an item measuring a specific skill, etc., he or she will perform well on all items measuring that same skill. These assumptions determine which items are accepted and which are rejected in the process of test construction. In this way beliefs about learners and knowledge predetermine test outcomes. Roth (1997: 15) argues that current views of assessment continue to assume an information processing model of cognition. In such a view, the task of assessment is 'how to read out the stored knowledge [of the individual] in the most accurate and reliable way'. This model is assumed in examinations and national assessment tasks and tests. No attempts are made, for example, to establish the tasks pupils perceive and the solutions they consider appropriate and to judge performance in relation to these. Furthermore, a narrow test is assumed to represent and predict achievement within subjects.

The assessment reforms described represented in part a shift away from psychometric approaches towards an educational assessment culture (Gipps 1994). Educational assessment is based on a quite different conception of intellectual development. It presumes that many achievements are attainable by all pupils, but how and when they attain them will vary. The use of differentiated papers in GCSE tiered tests and extension materials in national assessments are reflections of this view of achievement. Thus, within national assessments and examinations there are conflicting models of 'mind'.

Challenges to the view of cognition assumed by traditional forms of assessment come from socio-cultural and situated theories of cognition. Wertsch (1991: 6) describes a socio-cultural approach in the following way: 'The basic goal of a socio-cultural approach to mind is to create an account of human mental processes that recognises the essential relationship between these processes and their cultural, historical and institutional settings.'

Socio-culturalists assume human agency in the process of coming to know. It is the pupils who construct meaning in tasks and that meaning is partly determined by the ideas and experiences they bring to situations. In other words, assessors do not give tasks to pupils. Roth explains that differences in human reasoning are to be expected:

> with changes in the social and material resources they have available for tasks and with the ways they interpret their tasks in relation to goals precisely because the structure of the world arises from the interpretative horizon of individuals, the structured patterns in their experience and affordances of the present context as they perceive them.
>
> (Roth 1997: 16)

One of the main findings of the APU monitoring in Science was the heterogeneity in students' responses on items judged to be measuring the same construct. Murphy examined APU findings and noted that students' perceptions of tasks were often very different given the same circumstance. A gender dimension was established which revealed that:

> girls more than boys tend to value the circumstances in which assessment tasks are set and take account of them when constructing meaning in the task. They do not abstract issues from their context. Conversely, as a group, boys tend to consider issues in isolation and judge the content and context to be irrelevant.
>
> (Murphy 1996: 111)

Gender patterns in students' responses have been established in numerous assessments nationally and internationally (Gipps and Murphy 1994). Research shows that their sources either as measures of real differences in achievement or as assessment artefacts can only be determined by examination of sub-effects within items.

Equity and bias

In assessment, equality of opportunity is typically understood as an absence of bias in instruments. A test instrument is said to be biased if the assessment disadvantages one group over another. Typically it is facial bias that informs the test construction process for national assessments and examinations. Facial bias is defined as particular words, item formats, or representations which disadvantage a group within the population tested, irrespective of whether the disadvantage is realised in assessment outcomes. There have been attempts within national assessment and GCSE to enhance access to items by the use of diagrams and illustrations, careful attention to the level of language used and the avoidance of stereotypes, all of which are aspects of facial bias. Other changes in test construction have been informed by research into gender effects. For example, the reduction in use of multiple-choice items is based on the grounds of lack of fitness for purpose and on the grounds that females, as a group, are disadvantaged by such items (Gipps and Murphy 1994).

Authenticity in relation to what is being assessed and in the meaning tasks have for pupils has been improved by increased use of real-world contexts. As noted earlier, girls, more than boys, engage with real-world contexts and their performance is enhanced on such items. Nevertheless, the factors that influence pupils' participation in assessments are not well understood by those who construct exams and national assessment tests. For example, GCSE syllabuses in English pay attention to the balance between male- and female-authored texts but items in exams do not take account of gender differences in pupils' preferred choices of text content and style.

The national assessment outcomes for pupils aged 10 to 11 were examined for gender bias in terms of girls' and boys' equal performance on the tests as a whole, on sub-groups of items and individual items (Nelson and Boyes 1996). A lack of significant difference in girls' and boys' performance was interpreted as an absence of bias in the tests. The belief that unequal performance between groups is indicative of bias in tests is predicated on the assumption that groups are equally able and importantly that score distributions on the construct(s) being measured are equivalent for groups. This reflects a psychometric view of achievement. Both assumptions indicate an impoverished understanding of the way pupils acquire and deploy their understanding.

Goldstein (1993, 1996) challenges the assumption that unequal outcomes indicate bias as group differences arise, not just from the type of instrument used, but from the construction of the assessment itself and the interaction of those being tested with it. It is in the interpretation of scores, rather than the score itself that the problem of test invalidity lies: that is, if the inferences drawn from scores has different meanings for sub-groups than for the rest of the test population. In this perspective differential outcomes are considered to reflect real differences in the social and curricular experiences of different groups which may influence the actual achievement of individuals and how they interact with particular assessments. Cole (1997) reported on a major review of data from 400 tests and measures that were undertaken by nationally representative samples across the ages in the USA. She concluded that a 'primary result from this large amount of data we examined was that some of the differences between the genders are real differences – found in many measures by many different approaches and in many samples' (ibid.: 23). It follows that assessors have therefore to face the 'difficult task . . . to determine how much of the problem [of differential performance] resides in pupils' perceptions of the subject and outside experience and how much in the structure and assessment of the subjects' (Stobart *et al.* 1992a: 262).

Impact of changes in assessment on girls' and boys' performance

Early evidence from national assessments in England and Wales in English, Maths, and Science and Technology found that 7 year-old girls out-performed boys across the subjects tested. Girls' higher performance was particularly noticeable in English. These findings have been reported in the public domain as evidence of boys' underachievement, particularly in English. This has been attributed to teaching methods: 'Boys are left behind by modern teaching' (*Daily Telegraph*, 5 January 1998); lack of an appropriate curriculum: 'Male brain rattled by curriculum oestrogen' (*Times Educational Supplement*, 15 March 1996) and the lack of appropriate role models which has led to a recruitment drive for male primary teachers and exhortation for male carers to take a greater role in home literacy activities. Belief in these factors have led to radical changes in some school structures and approaches to pedagogy, some of which are reported uncritically in the media, for example, 'Team spirit, discipline and a motivating young master puts boys on par with the girls' (*The Guardian*, 14 January 1998).

Many of the explanations cited in the media for performance differences between boys and girls are not based on research evidence. What evidence we have is typically ignored or unknown. For example, there is evidence that girls come to school better equipped than boys to deal with school-type activities. The skills that girls appear to be more proficient at reflect the pre-school gendered activities that children engage with. The activities which girls choose to do have been labelled as 'creative'. Boys, on the other hand, opt for 'constructional activities' (Browne and Ross 1991). In a more recent study pre-school teachers commented on the way girls' predispositions were more congruent with typical nursery activities:

> Girls are much more interested in drawing and as a result quite often are more forward than boys when it comes to using pencils and scissors.
>
> Girls seem to enjoy the colours and the process of drawing. Boys just aren't interested.
>
> (Murphy 1997: 122)

Getting them [the boys] to settle down to a story is really quite a task. What I resort to is any book that has a tractor, a dumper in it, any sort of machinery. I don't have a problem settling the girls.

(ibid.: 121)

One teacher observed about boys' interests 'I think it inclines them more to the sort of mathematical side of things, science.'

Evidence from baseline assessment conducted with reception class pupils at around age 5, found that the largest gaps in favour of girls were in the areas of social skills, letter identification, writing and drawing (see Arnot *et al.* 1996). There appears to be a close correspondence between these achievements and girls' preferred activities.

The distribution of national assessment results differed for boys and girls. More boys than girls were located at the extreme ends of the grading scheme and girls were clustered in the medium range (Gipps and Murphy 1994). Some boys therefore excel in their performance across the subjects and proportionately more boys than girls achieve the highest grades in Mathematics and Science, findings which have not caused public or political concern about girls' possible underachievement.

National assessment tasks for primary pupils have changed over the years. In general, there has been an erosion of the Task Group on Attainment Targets (TGAT) model to reduce those assessments that reflect a view of 'mind' consonant with current research into learning and to value traditional forms of written assessment over and above teachers' continuous assessment. Items remain short, or extended response types. These changes have not affected the trend for girls' to out-perform boys in English.

At secondary level the tests for pupils aged 13–14 years are tiered. Teachers decide what tier to enter pupils for. There is no analysis by gender of entry patterns to tiers to help interpret overall performance by gender. At secondary level the tests revealed similar patterns to those at the earlier ages with girls scoring higher than boys in English and Mathematics, and more boys than girls scoring at the extremes. The findings in English and Mathematics were consistent with the earlier findings of the APU.

International surveys, however, show similar performance for girls and boys in mathematics at ages 13–14 across countries and an overall difference on tests in favour of boys at age 13 in England. This difference has been attributed to the item format as 80 per cent of the questions were presented in multiple-choice form (Keys *et al.* 1996). National assessments in Science, even without a performance element, showed no significant difference between girls' and boys' results. International surveys in contrast using multiple choice items, found the gender gap in favour of boys in England and Scotland to be amongst the highest of the countries surveyed (ibid.).

Sources of invalidity

The outcomes of statutory assessments at various key stages and public examinations are used to establish the so-called 'gender gap' in achievement without making problematic the role that assessment practices play in determining the gap.

Assessments to serve accountability at system and school level have to be seen to be providing valid measures of individual outcomes. Furthermore, they assume that lack of attainment given similar curriculum experiences reflect either, first, a lack of competence/ability at the individual pupil level and/or, second, a lack of competence in the system in relation to teaching, its organisation, management and resourcing. However, this assumes equal access to tests which is hidden by tiered entry. It also assumes that what is measured is acquired within the system rather than without. Gender is a significant influence on pupils' learning outside of school and learning outside of school has a significant impact on learning in school.

National assessments provide few insights into gender differences in performance. This is because of the limited number and type of tasks used and the lack of error analyses to illuminate children's alternative understandings. The tests themselves are judged to be invalid measures of individual achievement because they fail to recognise, first, the nature of human achievement and, second, how people acquire and use their understanding. Evidence of this has been established by research into assessment. Three issues are described here to exemplify potential sources of invalidity in such assessments.

Gendered interests and achievements

Pre-school children's interests corresponded closely with their attainments as measured by baseline assessments. The same relationship between interest and attainment has been found over a wide range of tests, test situations, and ages of students. For example, parallels in patterns of interests and performance were found for USA students from grade 4 through to graduate students. 'In interest areas most related to school course work and activities, females score higher on scales that involve the arts, writing and social service where males score higher on mechanical areas, athletics and science' (Cole 1997: 16). Very similar performance patterns were reported for pupils in Scottish, English and Welsh schools.

Prior experience positions pupils differently in relation to assessments. Where prior experience corresponds to the experience being assessed, pupils approach tasks with confidence. In the APU surveys boys were reported as having more experience of certain measuring instruments and science equipment than girls. Boys outperformed girls on precisely those instruments they had access to outside of school (Johnson and Murphy 1986). Davies and Brember's (1995) study in six primary schools in England found that one of the three topics where boys reported more interest than girls in infant school was 'weighing and measuring' and this interest continued through school. In using instruments in their hobbies and pastimes outside of school boys are also learning about measurement more generally, i.e. when to use it and how to do it. Hence 'real' differences in pupils' attainments arise. Boys' superior performance on measurement was also found in the early APU mathematics surveys.

Girls across the ages in the APU science surveys were found to consistently outperform boys on the practical tests of making and interpreting observations (DES 1988, 1989). Girls more than boys took note of colours, sounds, smells and texture. Boys, on the other hand, took note of structural details. When asked to observe phenomena or objects and events without any cues as to what was salient, girls as a group and boys as a group paid attention to different details given the *same* circumstances. The details correspond closely to their gendered interests and activities. The APU Design and Technology survey of 15 year olds showed that on tasks of a quite different nature girls again focused on 'aesthetic variables' and 'empathised with users' needs'. Boys more than girls focused on 'manufacturing issues' and were more competent than girls in their application of knowledge of structures (Kimbell *et al.* 1991). From an assessment perspective it is important to note that girls' and boys' observations indicate real differences in their views of relevance rather than competence. These two examples of gender effects indicate that simplistic links between national assessment, ability and teaching lead to misrepresentations of pupils' and teachers' competence and misunderstandings of the nature of learning and hence what constitutes effective teaching.

Gendered territories

The content of a task, i.e. what it is about rather than what has to be done is an essential part of a task's structure and meaning. Pupils' perceptions of content can lead to constructs being assessed unrelated to those assumed by an assessor. Girls and boys come to school with clear views about what constitute girls' territories and boys' territories which Browne and Ross (1991) refer to as gendered domains. Children's early years experiences are crucial in forming these views. APU science items which involved content related to health, reproduction, nutrition, and domestic situations were generally found to show girls performing at a higher level than boys across the ages. Findings corroborated in more recent studies (Chilisa 1997). More girls than boys attempted these questions. The gender gap in performance arose because of the increased confidence of girls combined with the lower response rate of boys. In questions where the content was 'masculine' the converse occurred. Typical 'masculine' contents included cars, building sites, submarines, machinery, etc. Alienation from particular content areas is a source of differential performance affecting both boys and girls. Current assessment policy which relies on narrow written tests takes no account of this.

Gendered learning influences what Roth refers to as the 'interpretative horizons of individuals' and determines what pupils come to understand as salient in situations. The way assessment tasks are situated is referred to here as the *context* of the task. The task might, for example, be embedded in a shopping trip, a sporting activity, a domestic dilemma or a school event, etc. Pupils determine what in a context is salient to the task (Boaler 1994; Murphy 1995; Cooper 1996). Typically context is treated superficially in assessments and is used to enhance authenticity without consideration of its impact on pupils' perceptions of tasks. Examples of this litter the national assessments. There are planks of wood that have to be sawn into equal parts without any loss due to the cutting effect and the sawdust, puddles that miraculously dry up in a regular pattern and car-parks which you can enter but not leave. All examples which conflict with pupils' everyday understanding of the world and hence make 'answers' problematic. In maths and science assessments it has been found that girls more than boys attempt to integrate features of the context in their reformulation of the task and its goal or solution. As a consequence, many girls achieve lower scores because the task they reformulate is complex or because there is no apparent solution available. Boys are more likely to reject the context as irrelevant, their approach correspond-ing to the assessors'. Cooper's (1996) research raises another issue. He found that working-class children, boys and girls alike, unlike middle-class children have a general tendency to give value to contextual variables which leads them to respond within an everyday frame of reference and hence achieve lower scores on national assessment tasks than other groups. He comments on the 'possibility that such items may systematically underestimate the . . . capabilities of children from certain social backgrounds' (ibid.: 2).

If baseline and national assessment policy is to take account of gender effects, scores need to be interpreted in terms of, first, children's opportunities to learn and, second, children's views of tasks. Similarly, attention needs to be given to the types of tasks used, given the well-established gender differences in pupils' inter-ests. For example, the APU findings showed that in primary schools girls enjoy reading fiction but boys are interested in hobby-type magazines. Consequently, different tasks might reflect different achievements for sub-groups. Furthermore, any attempts to close the gap between girls' and boys' achievements would have to address existing teaching strategies which actively exploit children's differing interests, thus compounding the potential for gendered learning.

Performance in GCSE examinations

In any review of overall population performance it is important to note that within regions and boards results will not reflect the overall trend. Table 7.1 shows the 1996 entry and grades A*–C figures for all GCSE groups in 1996. The trend has been for girls as a group to out-perform boys across a range of subjects (Arnot *et al.* 1996). The large difference in performance in English in favour of girls has been maintained and the gap in performance in maths in favour of boys has continued to reduce. These trends are reflected in examination results in Scotland as well (Turner *et al.* 1995).

It is worth noting that the entry populations are often not comparable in some subjects. For example, in Science more girls than boys are entered for the single science award (not in table) and more boys than girls are entered for the

Table 7.1 Percentage of male/female entry and male/female achieved grades A*–C for main GCSE subjects, 1996

Subject	% Entry M	% Entry F	% A*–C M	% A*–C F	Diff % A*–C (M–F)
Art/Design	48.5	51.5	50.0	68.1	−18.1
Biology	52.0	48.0	79.4	71.6	7.8
Chemistry	60.7	39.3	86.0	86.4	−0.4
Combined Science	49.8	50.2	50.2	50.9	−0.7
English	50.1	49.9	48.9	65.8	−16.9
English Lit.	47.4	52.6	56.2	70.4	−14.2
French	46.4	53.6	43.5	57.3	−13.8
Geography	55.5	44.5	51.1	57.3	−6.2
History	49.0	51.0	53.2	60.8	−7.6
Maths	49.3	50.7	47.0	46.5	0.5
Technology	61.8	38.2	40.1	55.2	−15.1
Physics	63.3	36.7	85.7	85.0	0.7
All subjects	49.3	50.7	49.9	58.3	−8.4

Source: 1996 Inter-Group Statistics i.e. all GSE groups, SEG, Surrey

Note: M = Male, F = Female

single sciences e.g. Physics, Chemistry and Biology. The population of girls and boys entering the combined science award may therefore reflect different ability spreads. In technology where there is a large difference in favour of girls this reflects quite different option choices within the subject. Females continue to dominate entry and performance in Home Economics. Similar trends occur in entry in Standard Grade in Scotland (Turner *et al.* 1995).

Formal examinations and sources of invalidity

Let us now turn to the role of examinations and consider such factors as 'content and style effects', 'modes of response' and other issues which contribute to the differential outcomes of boys and girls.

Content and style effects and modes of response

Girls' performance advantage in English has been related to the construction of examinations. Stobart *et al.* (1992b) examined girls' and boys' achievement in GCSE English. At the time of the study girls were achieving 14 per cent more grades A to C than boys. It was found that examination questions focused upon characters, their feelings and motivations. In the review of pupils' coursework folders only a limited number of types of writing were offered for examination – stories, descriptions, pieces of writing about personal life plus a form of argument based on an issue of public concern and something in response to reading fiction. High marks tended to be awarded for descriptive, narrative writing. It was common to find girls' folders containing a majority of imaginatively based work and boys' containing more discursive pieces, or pieces which had some clear basis in fact.

Teachers in their marking seemed to reward and encourage narrative and descriptive writing, in which girls excelled, over and above factual and analytical work; the type of piece boys preferred to submit. The APU surveys of English (Gorman *et al.* 1988) described girls' preferred style of written response as 'extended, reflective composition'. Boys' style of response was more often episodic, factual and focusing on commentative detail. There was a link between the imbalance in girls' and boys' exposure to different types of reading material outside of school and their preferences and skills in writing in school (Gorman 1987). Overall, writing which drew on the field of personal affection and emotions was more highly valued than that based in a public or political domain. When boys' personal writing was less intimate than that of girls, there was a perceived undervaluing of their work by teachers. In reviews of pre-college students' writing performance, content that corresponded to students' out of school interests and socialisation was associated with higher performance. Females' performance was increased on contents that were concerned with aesthetics and human relations whereas male enhanced performance was associated with contents concerning science, technical matters and politics (Carlton 1997).

Numerous studies have identified a tendency for girls to perform better when responses involve extended writing whereas boys do better when responses are short or right/wrong (Stobart *et al.* 1992b; Carlton 1997; Sutherland 1997). Response format act as important cues to pupils to 'see' what type of response is required. Often structured responses create barriers to pupils whose preferred responses do not 'fit' the frame supplied. Typically more females than males find difficulties with a tightly structured response. Males, on the other hand, find a lack of structure problematic (Gipps and Murphy 1994).

Assessments always represent a selection from a diverse domain. It is the selection and marking which reveal the assessor's construct of the subject and where inequity can reside. The content and style effects reported here again reflect gendered learning which in this case leads to an underestimation of boys' literary skills. However, the reverse effect occurs in examinations at post-16 (Murphy and Elwood 1998).

Coursework and sources of invalidity

Coursework was introduced into GCSE examinations to improve the 'fitness for purpose' of the assessment, not because of any concern with gender. The 'official' view of what constitutes coursework is that offered by the Schools Curriculum and Assessment Authority (SCAA) in their document *GCSE Regulations and Criteria*:

> Coursework consists of in-course tasks set and undertaken according to conditions prescribed by an awarding body. Coursework activities are integral to,

rather than incidental to, the course of study. Coursework is normally marked by a candidate's own teacher according to criteria provided and exemplified by the answering body, taking national requirements into account. It is moderated by the awarding body.

(SCAA 1995: 13)

Initially, the amount of coursework in the GCSE varied between subjects and between syllabuses. This reflected the profession's views of 'achievement'. For example, two-thirds of entries in English were for 100 per cent coursework syllabuses. Coursework in mathematics was not introduced until 1991 and then syllabuses with at least 20 per cent coursework were the most popular.

Perceptions and tensions about coursework

Coursework allows quite different achievements to be assessed compared with exams. It allows opportunities for pupil autonomy and removes the time constraints of exam situations. It also allows teachers to assess their pupils' achievements. In both these respects this form of assessment is more congruent with current understanding about the nature of learning and of knowledge. Nevertheless, there remains a deep mistrust of such assessments which is believed to be 'non-standard, in fact, sub-standard' (Baker and O'Neil 1994: 14). Consequently, groups seen to be doing well on such assessment are held in low esteem. Studies have shown that girls' average coursework marks are higher than boys' and more 'bunched'. Stobart *et al.* (1992b) found that girls do better on coursework relative to exams. Despite these beliefs, coursework scores were found to make a greater contribution to the grade distributions of boys than girls. In a more detailed study Elwood (1998) compared the intended weighting of assessment components with the achieved weighting and also established that coursework functions differently for girls and boys. Examinations playing a more important role in final grades than intended for girls than for boys.

Prior to the publication of this research in 1991, John Major, the Conservative Prime Minister, spoke out in favour of traditional testing, and against teachers' assessments in both national assessment and GCSE. This paved the way for the devaluing of the continuous assessment element in national assessment and the reduction in 1994 of GCSE coursework. It must be remembered that in 1994 GCSE was used to test the final phase of the National Curriculum. The diversity in syllabuses, particularly in the amount of coursework, was seen as a threat to establishing standards. Consequently coursework was limited to 20 per cent in most syllabuses. Syllabuses with no coursework were accepted in Mathematics and a 40 per cent limit was allowed in English with 20 per cent given over to oral assessment. Ironically, as research evidence from assessment increasingly provides support for the social nature of learning, assessment practice increasingly represents a model of mind which denies this.

Differentiation

Teachers' interpretations and constructs of pupil ability are implicated in the differential performance of boys and girls and their entry to levels and tiers. Evidence about the links between teachers' beliefs, students' attributions and performance was also forthcoming from the Stobart *et al.* (1992b) study. The research found that more girls than boys were entering for the GCSE Mathematics lower foundation level and intermediate level exams, and more boys than girls (21 per cent versus 12 per cent) were not entered for any exam. The reasons for this differentiated-entry policy were explained in interviews with teachers and pupils alike in terms of the teachers' beliefs about the affective not the cognitive, characteristics of pupils. Boys rate their mathematical ability more highly than girls – this is also the case in other subjects. Teachers believed boys would be demotivated and hence disruptive if placed in a low exam tier. Both teachers and girls believed that girls lacked confidence in their mathematical ability and were more fearful of failure than boys. Consequently teachers tended to place girls in the intermediate rather than higher exam tier to protect them from such anxiety. The research and later evidence suggests that both males and females underachieved because of teachers' beliefs.

Differentiated exam papers were introduced to cover the range of achievements for a population and to ensure positive achievement for all pupils. In spite of the evidence that entry patterns are limiting the access to certification of some boys and girls, differentiation continues. There are also different practices between subjects which may mean that gendered access also varies between subjects. The findings also raise concerns about potential gender effects in teachers' allocation of pupils to national assessment tests at ages 13 to 14.

Implications, priorities and future research

Selections of assessment tasks and methods provide overt messages to students about what is valued knowledge and which approaches to learning are valued. What Wiliam describes as the way that forms of assessment 'canonise certain aspects of knowledge' (1996: 132). Understanding of student-task interactions in assessment is both informed by and informative of understanding of learning and teaching. Research evidence points to the limitations of assessment practice which relies on written operation and narrow objective response modes. The power of assessment to determine students' future opportunities means that we can no longer accept what current forms of assessment purport to represent, i.e. valid generalisable measures of human achievement. National assessment levels and examination grades are likely to have different meanings for *sub-groups* within the population, i.e. what is being assessed is not the same (for the reasons discussed in earlier sections of this chapter). This limits their function as mechanisms for accountability and as tools to inform teaching. Teacher assessment has been limited and devalued over the years. It is reported separately in national assessment indicating its different status. This may be appropriate as research evidence makes it clear that what is assessed by these very different forms is not equivalent. There is a need to reintroduce the notion of the complementarity of these two modes of assessment. Taken together, they provide different insights into achievements and needs. However what needs to alter is the perceived difference in quality of the two measures, both in national assessment and in GCSE. Black and Wiliam's (1998) extensive review has established that formative, continuous assessment with effective feedback to pupils significantly enhances teaching and learning. Policy-makers continue to reject these findings. Consequently, assessment policy aimed at raising standards is implicated in their potential decline.

If equity in assessment is to be achieved, higher priority needs to be given to continuous forms of assessment that allow pupils to determine what is problematic and how to frame responses and provides both pupils and teachers with information about progress and needs. Teacher assessment, its nature and role, needs to be reconceptualised and resources made available to develop teachers' practice and systems to maintain the quality of its outcomes and its reporting. There is no indication that current or future policy will give any priority to this.

Attention also needs to be directed to the assumptions that underlie test and examination construction. There is an urgent need to move away from assessment practice that relies on general criteria and which presumes that assessment tasks can engender the 'same' response from a population. Nor can we continue to adopt a normative approach to the grading and levelling of performance which presumes that half of the population are achieving below average. Far from introducing a culture of positive achievement, national assessment has reinforced the normalising process of education through the labelling of children by single gross levels. Assessment, like pedagogy, needs to be understood as an art that is in the process of evolution. As such, we need to be both more creative and more cautious in our practice of it. The limitations of assessment methods need to be explicit in the interpretation of responses to them.

Funded research into assessment is essential, given its role in determining individual life chances and views of teachers' and schools' effectiveness. Research such as Elwood's (1998) looking at the differential contribution of exam components needs to be extended. The consequences of differentiated national tests and GCSE exam papers on the access and subsequent achievement levels of sub-groups of pupils need to be examined across and within subjects. National assessment level data need to be accompanied by error analyses which make problematic how tasks and solutions are understood by pupils. The need to reconceptualise teacher assessment in national assessments has been argued for and there is an associated need to examine the nature of coursework across and within subjects and syllabuses. The evidence from this array of research would illuminate just what is being assessed and for whom and help uncover the myth of educational standards that currently determines so much of teaching and assessment practice in schools. Current policy under New Labour does not indicate that such a research agenda will be implemented. To do so would be to accept the challenges that research has raised about the validity of school league tables and the purposes they can serve. Rather, we have seen greater emphasis on narrow educational outcomes and the retreat in assessment practice extended to teaching. The irony is that the gap between policy rhetoric and practice is growing even larger. Without a review of school assessment we limit the possibilities of pupils attaining those achievements that are increasingly claimed to be of value in society and recognised as essential attributes of workplace practices.

References

Arnot, M., David, M. and Weiner, G. (1996) *Educational Reforms and Gender Equality in Schools*, Manchester: EOC.

Baker, E. and O'Neil, H. (1994) 'Performance assessment and equity: a view from the USA', *Assessment in Education* 1, 1: 11–26.

Black, P. and Wiliam, D. (1998) 'Assessment and classroom learning', *Assessment in Education* 5 (1): 7–75.

Boaler, J. (1994) 'When do girls prefer football to fashion? An analysis of female underachievement in relation to "realistic" mathematics contexts', *British Journal of Educational Research* 20, 5: 551–5.

Broadfoot, P.M. (1996) *Education Assessment and Society*, Buckingham: Open University Press.

Browne, N. and Ross, C. (1991) 'Girls' stuff, boys' stuff: young children talking and playing', in N. Browne (ed.) *Science and Technology in the Early Years*, Milton Keynes: Open University Press.

Callaghan, J. (1976) 'Towards a national debate', *Education*, 22 October 1994: 332–3.

Carlton, S. (1997) 'Equity in assessment: an empirical approach for identifying unexpected differences between groups in test performance', paper presented at the 23rd International Association for Educational Assessment Conference 'Equity Issues in Education and Assessment', Durban, South Africa, June.

Chilisa, B. (1997) 'Ecological and gender bias in science achievement', paper presented at the 23rd International Association for Educational Assessment Conference 'Equity Issues in Education and Assessment', Durban, South Africa, June.

Cole, N.S. (1997) *The ETS Gender Study: How Females and Males Perform in Educational Settings*, Princeton, NJ: Educational Testing Service.

Cooper, B. (1996) 'Using data from clinical interviews to explore students' understanding of mathematics test items: relating Bernstein and Bourdieu or culture to questions of fairness in testing', paper presented at the American Educational Research Association Conference, New York, April 1996.

Daugherty, R. (1996) 'In search of teacher assessment – its place in the National Assessment system of England and Wales', *The Curriculum Journal* 7, 2: 137–52.

Davies, J. and Brember, I. (1995) 'Attitudes to school and the curriculum in Year 2, Year 4 and Year 6: changes over four years', paper presented at the European Conference on Educational Research, Bath, 14–17 September 1995.

De Luca, C. (1997) 'Gender issues in fair assessment question', paper presented at the 24th International Association for Educational Assessment Conference 'Equity Issues in Education and Assessment', Barbados, West Indies, 10–15 May 1995.

Department for Education and Science (DES) (1987) *Task Group on Assessment and Testing: A Report*, London: DES.

—— (1988) *Science in Schools Age 11: Review Report*, London: HMSO.

—— (1989) *Science in Schools Age 13: Review Report*, London: HMSO.

Elwood, J. (1998) 'Equity issues in performance assessment: the contribution of teacher-assessed coursework to gender related differences in examination performances', paper presented at the 24th Annual IAEE Conference, Barbados, West Indies, 10–15 May 1998.

Foxman, D., Ruddock, G. and McCallum, L. (1991) *Assessment Matters: No. 2 APU Mathematics Monitoring 1984–1988 (Phase 2)*, London: Schools Examinations and Assessment Council.

Gipps, C. (1994) *Beyond Testing: Towards a Theory of Educational Assessment*, London: Falmer Press.

Gipps, C. and Murphy, P. (1994) *A Fair Test? Assessment, Achievement and Equity*, Buckinghamshire: Open University Press.

Goldstein, H. (1993) 'Assessing group differences', *Oxford Review* 19, 2: 141–50.

—— (1996) 'Group differences and bias in assessment', in H. Goldstein and T. Lewis (eds) *Assessment: Problems, Developments and Statistical Issues*, Chichester: Wiley.

Gorman, T. (1987) *Pupils' Attitudes to Reading*, Windsor: NFER-Nelson.

Gorman, T.P., White, J., Brook, G., Maclure, M. and Kispal, A. (1988) *Language Performance in Schools: Review of APU Language Monitoring 1979–1983*, London: HMSO.

Harris, S., Keys, W. and Fernandes, C. (1997) *Third International Mathematics and Science Study Second National Report Part 1*, Slough: NFER.

Johnson, S. (1989) *National Assessment: The APU Science Approach*, London: HMSO.

—— (1996) 'The contribution of large-scale assessment programmes to research on gender differences,' *Educational Research and Evaluation* 2, 1: 25–49.

Johnson, S. and Murphy, P. (1986) 'Girls and physics: reflections on APU survey findings,' *Occasional Paper 4*, London: DES.

Keys, W., Harris, S. and Fernandes, C. (1996) *Third International Mathematics and Science Study First National Report Part 1*, Slough: NFER.

Kimbell, R., Stables, K., Wheeler, T., Wosniak, A. and Kelly, V. (1991) *The Assessment of Performance in Design and Technology*, London: School Examinations and Assessment Authority.

Lightfoot, L. (1998) 'Boys who are left behind by modern teaching', *Daily Telegraph*, 5 January 1998, p. 4.

Murphy, P. (1995) 'Sources of inequity: understanding students' responses to assessment,' *Assessment in Education* 3: 249–69.

—— (1996) 'Integrating learning and assessment', in P. Woods (ed.) *Contemporary Issues in Teaching and Learning*, London: Routledge.

—— (1997) 'Gender differences: messages for science education', in K. Harnquist and A. Burgen (eds) *Growing up with Science*, London: Jessica Kingsley.

Murphy, P. and Elwood, J. (1998) 'Gendered experiences, choices and achievement – exploring the links', *International Journal of Inclusive Education* 2, 2: 95–118.

Murphy, P. and Gipps, C. (eds) (1996) *Equity in the Classroom: Towards Effective Pedagogy for girls and boys*, London: Falmer Press, UNESCO Publishing.

Nelson, N.W. and Boyes, E. (1996) 'Bias in standardised tests: some observations on the 1996 KS2 National Curriculum Assessments', paper presented to the European Educational Research Association, Seville, Spain, September.

Redwood, F. (1998) 'Top marks to the lads', *Daily Telegraph*, 14 January 1998, p. 19.

Roth, W.M. (1997) 'Situated cognition and assessment of competence in science'. paper presented at the 7th Conference of the European Association for Research in Learning and Instruction, Athens, August.

Roth, W.M., McRobbie, C., Lucas, K.B. and Boutonne, S. (1997) 'Why do students fail to learn from demonstrations? A social practice perspective on learning in physics,' *Journal of Research in Science Teaching*, 77, 34: 509–33.

Schools Curriculum and Assessment Authority (SCAA) (1995) *GCSE Regulations and Criteria*, London: SCAA.

Southern Examining Group (SEG) (1996) *Inter-group Statistics*, Guildford: Southern Examining Group.

Stobart, G., Elwood, J. and Quinlan, M. (1992a) 'Gender bias in examinations: how equal are the opportunities?', *British Education Research Journal* 18, 3: 261–76.

Stobart, G., White, J., Elwood, J., Hayden, M. and Mason, K. (1992b) *Differential Performance at 16+: English and Mathematics*, London: Schools Examination and Assessment Council.

Sutherland, G. (1997) 'Gender and patterns of achievement in higher education', paper presented at ESRC Seminar series 'Gender and education: are boys now underachieving?', London Institute of Education.

Turner, E., Riddell, S. and Brown, S. (1995) *Gender Equality in Scottish Schools: The Impact of Recent Reforms*, Manchester: EOC.

Wertsch, J.V. (1991) *Voices of the Mind: A Socio-cultural Approach to Mediated Action*, Cambridge, MA: Harvard University Press.

Wiliam, D. (1996) 'National Curriculum assessments and programmes of study: validity and impact,' *British Educational Research Journal* 22, 1: 129–41.

Williams, E. (1996) 'Male brain rattled by curriculum oestrogen', *The Times Educational Supplement*, 15 March 1996, p. 8.

Woodhead, C. (1996) 'Boys who learn to be losers', *The Times*, 6 March 1996, p. 18.

8 Gender in the classrooms of more and less 'effective' schools

Jill Duffield

Introduction

Much school effectiveness literature does not address gender directly. The implication is that there is a generic 'effectiveness' which applies to male and female pupils alike and in which staff gender is also irrelevant. Lists of correlates of school effectiveness extrapolated from large-scale studies do not include explicit commitment to gender (or other) equality policies, and analysis of examination outcomes does not identify greater 'added value' for girls. However, to the extent that effectiveness and improvement have been recruited to march under the policy banner of 'standards', gender has become highly relevant. The Labour government has embraced the notion of raising the 'performance' of schools in all settings, and established demanding achievement goals under which 80 per cent of pupils in England and Wales will have reached Key Stage 2 literacy and numeracy levels at age 11 (DfEE 1997: 2.21). Targets in Scotland are expressed more generally but the thrust of policy also highlights raising individual outcomes. Girls' achievements across the UK have been rising faster than those of boys, so that, in principle, factors underpinning girls' success might be of interest to policy-makers and the public. However, girls' increased success in public examinations had scarcely been established before anxieties began to be expressed about the 'failure' of boys, particularly in working-class settings (Wragg 1997; *The Observer* 1998). A BBC *Panorama* programme, 'The future is female' (October 1994) clearly shaped its story in terms of panic about boys.

This chapter is a contribution to the research on the importance of gender dynamics in classrooms and schools. It is concerned with gender from three perspectives:

- teachers' thinking about gender in categorising and assessing pupils' capabilities and achievements;
- researchers' observations of target pupils' participation in lessons and support from teachers;
- pupils' own descriptions of classroom support and themselves as learners.

The empirical work reported here is associated with studies of effective schools, part of the larger research agenda related to current government policy. Of the four schools from which the data were collected, two had been identified as 'more effective' and two as 'less effective'. The selected findings here illustrate classroom processes in which the matter of any relationship between such effectiveness and gender is explored in a preliminary way. However, an additional variable associated with social class is seen as crucial in work of this kind, and so the socio-economic status of the schools is a further consideration.

The work reported here was one feature of a larger study and its findings, though interesting, have to be treated as opening up questions which could be taken further in a research design tailored towards the links between gender and school effectiveness.

Research into gender in the classroom in recent years has suggested that, to simplify, boys dominate but girls make more progress. Earlier investigations (for instance, French and French 1984) cited boys' predominance in classroom inter-actions as an explanatory factor in girls' underachievement. However, the 'equal-isation and improvement' of public examination results has shown more rapid progress by girls both in Scotland and England (McPherson and Willms 1987; Ganson and De Luca 1995; Powney 1996; Furlong and Cartmel 1997), and girls' performance in most curriculum areas now surpasses that of boys of similar social background. Furlong and Cartmel's analysis of Scottish examination results by class and gender (1997) points to a striking continuation of trends revealed ten years ago by McPherson and Willms. Pupils passing three or more subjects at Scottish Higher Grade in 1991 form a social hierarchy, with 43 to 53 per cent of those from professional and managerial backgrounds reaching this attainment level, 17 to 25 per cent of those from skilled clerical and manual groups, and only 10 to 15 per cent of semi-skilled and unskilled groups. For each group, the trend since 1979 represents an increase for males and females which is faster for females, sharply so in both the professional and the unskilled categories. Males from classes 4 and 5 show relatively small increases over the period 1979 to 1991 (Furlong and Cartmel 1997). Recent research on gender and classroom interaction sug-gests, however, that girls' increased success has neither arisen from, nor resulted in, changed classroom patterns. Christine Howe's review (1997) supports earlier findings of boys' physical and verbal predominance and greater experience of having their contributions evaluated; key findings on girls were that they requested help more frequently than boys, and were more supportive of conversational partners (Howe 1997: 44).

School effectiveness research, emerging during the 1980s, set out to demon-strate that schools make a difference to pupils' progress and to measure such a difference. 'Effective' schools were those which 'added more value' to whatever attainments the incoming pupils presented. Multi-level statistical techniques isol-ated various factors to see if the effectiveness of a school operated similarly for all groups. Gender, along with ethnicity, was shown to fit in with the total school effectiveness picture. Mortimore and colleagues, for instance, found that the effectiveness of a school operated similarly for boys' and girls' progress especially in mathematics (Mortimore *et al.* 1988: 209–11) although Sammons reports (in

Gray *et al.* 1996: 20) that some studies have found slight differential school effects by gender. In Scotland, Linda Croxford's extensive research on school effectiveness measures indicates that: 'all schools are more effective for girls than for boys, but there are no significant differences between schools and therefore this never gets reported or discussed' (Croxford 1998, personal communication).

An important aspect of school effectiveness research has been to identify characteristics of schools associated with high effectiveness. Lists of these correlates of school effectiveness emerging from large-scale studies do not include explicit commitment to gender or other equality policies (for example, in Stoll and Mortimore 1985: 5). The role of the head teacher, 'firm and purposeful' but also 'participatory', is presented as the most important common factor associated with effectiveness, followed by 'shared vision and goals' and 'collegiality'. Gender equality goals are compatible with such features, but are by no means necessarily included. Pupil rights and responsibilities, and high pupil self-esteem are further elements of Stoll and Mortimore's effectiveness correlates within which gender-inclusiveness might, or might not, be found.

Efforts have been made in recent years to bring together school effectiveness research, identifying school success, and school improvement work with its focus on intervention and change (Gray *et al.* 1996). The Scottish Office Education and Industry Department (SOEID) has pursued an official interest in applications of the findings of school effectiveness research over a number of years, arguing that earlier school effectiveness research 'largely failed to generate knowledge useful for the school improvement enterprise' and pointing out that the SOEID's key interest was to improve the effectiveness of Scottish schools: that is, 'the extent to which they raise attainment' (Tibbitt *et al.* 1994: 153). It appears that 'a clear achievement of the research on school effectiveness is that it has captured the attention of policy-makers and engaged them in dialogue about the meaning of research findings' (Brown *et al.* 1997: 145). The SOEID has commissioned a major research project, the Improving School Effectiveness Project (MacBeath and Boyd 1996; MacBeath 1999), aiming to apply the outcomes of both the improvement and the effectiveness paradigms. However, Sally Brown has argued that the attempt to use school effectiveness research as 'the policy-makers' tool for school improvement' by attempting to 'back-map' the features of effective schools on to ineffective schools is doomed to disappointment, especially if such attempts are confined to organisational variables rather than reaching processes within the classroom (Brown *et al.* 1997: 139–40). One such process area is the role of gender in teachers' and pupils' thinking and in classroom interactions.

Gender findings of a school effectiveness study

A research project examining school support for lower achieving boys and girls in the early secondary years presents an opportunity for investigation of gender in the classroom, in the context of a small-scale school effectiveness study which also considered social class (Brown *et al.* 1996; Duffield 1998). The four project schools within one Scottish local authority were identified (in a study previously carried out for the local authority by the Centre for Educational Sociology, University of Edinburgh) as 'more' and 'less' effective. The school intake populations also differed by socio-economic status (SES).[1] The four schools were:

School A   high effectiveness, high-SES
School B   low effectiveness, high-SES
School C   high effectiveness, low-SES
School D   low effectiveness, low-SES.

In each school, we followed two classes through the first two secondary years (S1 and S2 in Scotland), tracking four target pupils in each class and observing lessons (204 in all) in English, Mathematics and Science. Post-lesson interviews with teachers were carried out in order to gain insight into teachers' thinking about the lessons, advocated in earlier work by Sally Brown (Brown and McIntyre 1993). Target pupils' progress was estimated by means of S2 school assessment, and pupil perspectives gathered by interview.

Teachers' thinking about gender in the classroom

Teachers' thinking was traced by means of initial discussions with subject teachers on which the selection of target pupils was based; from the progress made by the pupils by the end of S2, and from teachers' own accounts of each observed lesson.

Gender and teachers' categorisations of attainment

Selection of the target pupils revealed gender variations in teachers' initial thinking about pupil attainment. We asked subject teachers (6 per school, 24 in all) to describe each class in four broad categories of attainment in their subject over the first months of S1. We selected a boy and a girl from the 'well below average' (VL) and 'just below average' (L) categories across subjects, so that the target pupils, all seen as lower achievers, formed two distinct bands. Teachers' ratings were the main selection criteria; we also knew the pupils' scores on Edinburgh Reading Test at entry to secondary school.

Teachers' placement of boys in the broad categories was more stable across subjects in all four schools than the placement of girls. All the target classes contained boys rated as well below average in the three subjects, English, Maths and Science, whose reading scores were in the range 70 to 84; and boys rated 'just below average' with scores in the range 85 to 100. Two classes (at schools A and D) did not have any girl clearly in the VL category; the girl most nearly fitting the model was selected. The 'L' girls as a group varied by subject; half of them were seen by teachers of English as of average or above attainment, although lower ratings by Maths and Science teachers placed them within our target population. Favourable teacher perceptions in English were not necessarily accompanied by higher reading scores than the boys chosen as 'L'. This made us suspect that we were faced, not with a sampling problem, but with an indicator of gendered categorisation relating to interaction of perceived attainment and motivation.

Across all schools the majority of categorisations supplied by teachers displayed some degree of gender pattern, with more girls in higher and more boys in lower attaining sections. This included every class at School D. At School B only the Maths classes and at School C only the English classes' categories displayed this pattern. Most teachers used a mix of more or less explicit attainment criteria and approaches to work in categorising the classes for our research and several made generalised comments such as:

> Group 1 is all girls, they have the edge in language, their ideas are more formed; at this stage boys are inarticulate, respond to the pressures of the herd.
>
> (School D, English)

> Only one girl in the two lower groups, I'm not going to say it is not typical, girls are less bogged down over behaviour, organisation, attitude.
>
> (School A, Maths)

A minority of teachers (at Schools B, C and A) rejected the notion of gendered response to schooling and said that they found no consistent patterns. Teachers' thinking about gender and categories of attainment did not produce any evidence of a relationship with school effectiveness.

Gender and progress

Assessment at the end of S2 in the sample curriculum subjects was used as a progress measure for the target pupils. We compared the target pupils' results in school assessments with the teachers' initial categorisations, to see whether there were gender patterns among pupils exceeding, fulfilling or falling short of expectations, and whether any relationship emerged with more and less effective schools. The just below average ('L') boys were a mobile group whose progress was the most likely to have changed above or below teachers' original perceptions. More 'L' girls exceeded than fell short of expectations; as initial ratings had been higher than the boys, they were clearly the highest attaining group. The well below average (VL) girls remained closest to teachers' early estimation. There were six instances of upward mobility for the VL boys but only two for the girls. These comparisons were markedly affected by the volatility of measures at school D (low-SES, less effective). There was little difference in the progress changes at schools C and B, so that no conclusions can be drawn as to whether either the low effectiveness or the socio-economic profile of school D prompted the apparent tendency to make high assessments, or whether it was an idiosyncrasy of the classrooms in the research. Nevertheless, twelve S2 results (for the eight target pupils across three subjects) were in a higher assessment band than the 'discussion category' for the pupil in our S1 conversations: more than for the other three schools put together. School A assessments were the most consistent with S1 discussions overall.

Expectations about achievement and gender were explicitly mentioned just once, by a guidance teacher describing family expectations of a 'just below average' target girl making better progress than her brother:

> it comes back to academic expectations of boys and girls; she is expected to do well. The elder brother was always going to work with [self-employed builder] dad anyway . . . The family expect her to be the clever one.
>
> (Male guidance teacher of LG in school D)

This comment stood alone; we cannot say whether it indicates any general shift in working-class parents' expectations in line with girls' public examination progress.

Gender and teachers' thinking about classroom processes

We analysed teachers' spontaneous statements (about all pupils in the target classes) in the post-lesson interviews into a framework of pupil characteristics, progress and support. Across all four schools, teacher talk about pupil progress and support included more reference to boys, including negative comments about boys' lack of progress in organising their work or carrying out desired procedures. Discussion of progress and cognitive grasp of ideas was particularly centred upon boys at the two high-SES schools, especially school A (more effective, high-SES) where comments on support for boys outnumbered those for girls by 6:1 in Maths, 8:1 in English and 18:1 in Science.

SES linkage also appeared in the domain of pupil characteristics: boys' ability or attainments loomed larger in teachers' thinking at the high-SES schools. Comments on attainments at the low-SES schools less frequently specified boys or girls, although references to boys being badly behaved but able occurred, more positively expressed at 'effective' school C. Gendered 'effectiveness' patterns emerged for pupil characteristics only in that the 'less effective' schools (B, D), included more talk of girls' lack of confidence.

Teachers' thinking about lessons appeared to focus more on boys, especially in the high-SES schools. Boys were more visible to them in lessons, and they perceived boys' progress as more volatile. School effectiveness was not apparently salient in these patterns. Did classroom observation tell the same story?

Gender in the observed lessons

A small number of the observed lessons showed some gender bias in content and presentation. An English class listening to pupils' solo talks (School C) was very 'boy-centred', in contrast with several solo talk lessons seen. The male teacher apparently accepted that sport and armies were interesting topics, and reacted with resignation to two almost inaudible talks on animals by girls. The only confidently presented contribution from a girl was on Mohammed Ali, the boxer. However, more inclusive examples were seen in both of the 'less effective' schools. A play about a nineteenth-century mining village had a domestic setting (school D), and there was a 'home front' focus in a class novel about the Second World War (school B), both with female teachers, although neither of these drew out gender themes explicitly during the observation.

There were, however, observed instances of boys and girls at these schools responding equally positively to topics that might be thought stereotypically biased: for example, group work on fairy tales (school B, female teacher) or a male maths teacher filling in a few minutes at the end of a lesson with quiz questions on darts and snooker (school D).

Gender roles were explicitly addressed in S2 English lessons in schools A and C (the two 'more effective' schools), in the latter by the same male teacher who took the boy-centred talks lesson in S1. A video recording of a play about a girl going with her lorry-driver step-father on a working trip addressed family conflict, self-confidence and empathy as well as gender roles. Chairs from the usual paired rows of seating were drawn forward into the aisles and the entire class, often restless, watched the video with rapt concentration. The teacher's method was to show the whole play for pupils to feel their own response before he gave any input:

> I've done a lot of this . . . [children's] attention span is quite short nowadays and they get it more immediately than reading a novel over a term. There are underlying themes you can pick up, I have discussed film technique and the question of 'don't talk to strange men' versus confidence about speaking to people.
>
> (male teacher of English in school C)

The teacher planned to set written work including a diary for the central character, Rose, and a script for a conversation with her mother exploring tensions around helping at home. The subsequent discussion and writing lessons fell outside the observation, so that no direct data could be collected on boys' and girls' responses. The teacher did not explicitly refer to gender roles in his discussion of the planned work, although the boys were evidently expected to undertake writing tasks with a female persona.

At school A, the class read and discussed a story, 'The Topiary Garden', about the memories of an old woman who had become a gardener rather than a housemaid, at first by cross-dressing. In the post-lesson interview, the female teacher expressed personal interest in exploring the theme of gender roles through the story, but suggested that this would be an aspect accessible to 'the more able ones'. The lesson started with oral review of homework questions. Twelve boys and seven girls were called on to answer, six of the boys before any girl was asked: a possible inference could be that the teacher intended to include boys in a largely female scenario, although it could have been habitual behaviour. The questions drew out the symbolic use of the constraint of the 'natural' bushes into 'corseted figures of women' and the constraint upon the roles available to the central character. Pupils prepared further written work on their chosen story from the book, all with a cross-generation theme. 'The Topiary Garden' was by far the favourite amongst the girls; boys' choices varied but a Second World War story was the most popular.

In the two 'less effective' schools (B, D) occasional classes were seen with distinct boys' and girls' sides of the room, with teacher talk (one man, one woman) strongly directed towards the boys' side in both instances. Discussion in groups was used extensively in the high-SES schools; in school B, this was in self-chosen groups which tended to be single sex. School A English, however, included successful discussion tasks in groups structured for a mix of gender, attainment and personality. Same sex paired seating was also commonly seen at all schools; but boy/girl seating as a control measure was used in certain classes at C and D (the two low-SES schools).

Gender and participation in whole class question and answer

We found that within our lower-achieving target pupil sample, boys did not dominate whole class oral work. This fits other research where boys' predominance depended on very high participation by a few individuals (French and French 1984; Howe 1997). The split we found was between the girls at different attainment levels. Taking all 204 observed lessons across schools and subjects, Figure 8.1 shows the percentage of lessons where target pupils participated in whole class oral work by answering when offering (P answers), putting their hands up to answer but not chosen (hand up), or giving an answer when picked by the teacher but not offering (T asks P). The low (L, or just below average) target girls were marginally the highest contributors of volunteer answers, slightly ahead of the boys; while the very low (VL, the least able) girls were markedly less likely to answer. In only 6 per cent of all lessons was there more than a single public answer volunteered by a VL girl; and yet these girls were almost as likely to put up their hands to answer as the boys. In other words, their offers to answer were less likely

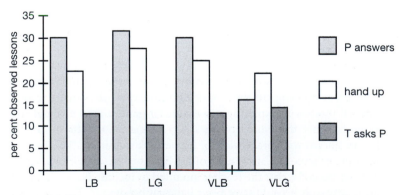

Figure 8.1 Target pupils' participation in whole class question and answers

to be taken up by teachers; yet they were called upon when not offering to answer slightly more than boys, and more than 'L' girls who were possibly perceived as not needing encouragement to participate. Where the teacher was female, the pattern was still more marked, with more participation by 'L' and even less by 'VL' girls.

Field notes indicate that class discussion, as opposed to problem-solving or memory questions, elicited more answers from 'just below average' target girls (and other more able girls) than from boys; this was not confined to 'more effective' or to high-SES schools. At school D, two girls evoked the mingled excitement and anxiety of starting primary school; the target LG described being scared of teddy bear pictures on the toilet doors. Discussion of writing dialect also emerged from a target LG's work, with other girls participating. The pupil, newly promoted to a differentiated upper section of the English class, had attempted to convey a Cornish accent in the dialogue she had written for homework. The female teacher persuaded her to read it out, and used it to question others and elicit ideas about Scots and other speech (school C, female teacher, LG). At school A, however, a male science teacher followed up boys' answers about bones without involving any girls. One boy who took part in this discussion was a target VLB who introduced the topic of the soft spot on babies' skulls. He had been previously noted as 'consistently ignored' and 'treated as invisible' by the teacher (school A, male teacher, VLB).

All schools had instances of more boys (in the class as a whole) being chosen to answer questions, or to come out and demonstrate a point. The pupils who displayed eagerness to do these activities tended to be boys; and boys were also seen to be more competitive in, for example, a class game of dot to dot co-ordinates (school B). Boys with their hands up to answer a male teacher, referred to in field notes as having a warm, positive, interactive style, were urged, 'Let's give the girls a chance'; the remark located the teacher and the male pupils as 'us' and the girls as 'other' (school D).

Individual support to target pupils

Turning to individual support to pupils by class teachers (the dominant teacher activity), we found that target boys received this support in more lessons than target girls, and received it more frequently within lessons. This gender gap appeared in all four schools but was least marked in school D. There was no clear linkage between pairs of schools either on the effectiveness or the SES dimensions. The VL girls were given class teacher support in 77 per cent of lessons, and the L girls were seen as the most independent of this group, with individual help in under three-quarters of lessons. The lowest attaining boys (VL) were almost always given some individual attention (91 per cent of lessons overall), and the just below average boys nearly as frequently (87 per cent). One 'L' boy and his partner were so delighted when they successfully connected a circuit board to control a powered Lego truck that they attracted the attention of a male teacher with another class in an adjacent part of the open plan lab. This teacher came over to see the two boys, and remained for ten minutes, discussing and playing with the truck (school C).

Women teachers' support to individuals was still more biased towards boys; similar high rates of support to boys were found, but girls, especially 'L' girls, received less class teacher support from female teachers. However, one very low achieving girl was seen to write very carefully, but discard several sheets and begin again repeatedly. Finally she gave in work covering about half a sheet of A4 paper in three widely spaced paragraphs. The teacher gave positive praise, describing the work as 'perfect, with no technical mistakes at all' (school C, female teacher responding to VLG).

There was no gender gap for target pupils seeking help. The lessons where pupils gained (male or female) class teacher support were evenly spread between target groups. There appeared to be some tendency for female teachers, in particular, to resist demands for attention by girls, especially the least able. L boys were the target group least likely to be rebuffed when they asked for attention.

In one school D maths class, teacher support was entirely directed towards boys for the first ten minutes of individual work (following a 'boy-directed' introduction); a girl had her hand up but by the time the male teacher moved to her part of the room, she had obtained help from a friend. At school C, an L girl and a VL boy were the only ones to put up their hands to the female teacher's invitation, 'who needs help?' The teacher helped the VLB then several other boys before turning to the L girl. In English, also at school C, a VL girl waited in vain for her folder while the teacher was drawn into advising those who had made an early start; minutes later, another girl urged the low achieving pupil to go forward and claim her folder.

Gender dynamics emerged as important in the curriculum, especially in English classrooms, in pupil participation and teacher response in oral work, and in teacher support to target lower-achieving pupils. School effectiveness, however, did not appear to be salient in shaping the operation of gender interactions in the sample of observed lessons. We now turn to the pupils' own accounts of their experiences in school.

Pupil perceptions and gender

Findings from our thirty-one target pupil interviews showed that more boys expressed unqualified confidence in their school progress. However, PE, liked by nine boys and one girl, was the only subject with a clear gender difference in perceptions of doing well or badly (cf. Cooper 1995). Personal subject preferences were explained by one boy:

> I like all the ones you talk in, to your teachers. I like PE because you run about and keep fit. In geography I'm no very good at countries, I know the capitals but I don't ken where they are.
>
> (LB, school D, less effective low-SES)

Gender-linked perception of differences between primary and secondary school included boys (especially at 'effective' school C) commenting on increased teacher pressure and rules: 'harder work, less talking and more punishment' (LB, C); 'at the primary you got to wear any clothes that you wanted to' (VLB, C). The novelty of a variety of teachers was appreciated by several pupils including a boy at the more effective high-SES school A:

> They're all different: you get some funny teachers and some that are really dull. I like a funny teacher, . . . they joke and laugh along with you . . . I think you get more done because you listen more to the nicer teachers.
>
> (LB, school A)

One L girl expressed anxieties about the start of secondary, and recognised adaptation to a larger community:

> You were a bit shaky about going to each class because you didn't know what the teacher would be like . . . you heard things about them in primary . . . but I survived . . . We all grew up together from nursery, all really close. I wouldn't say we are so close in this school . . . but we all still really care for one another. If someone gets bullied we all stick up for them.
>
> (LG, school B, less effective high-SES)

In common with other research, teacher explanation was the most emphasised form of classroom support, valued by girls and by boys almost as much. The only forms of classroom support for which more preferences were expressed by boys, were question and answer (four boys, one girl) and working alone (five boys, two girls). A girl compared the benefits of class or individual explanation:

> The teacher I've got is a good teacher, she explains it to you, not like the teacher in S1, she just kind of raced through it and I didn't catch on, nor did a lot of people. She spent a lot of time going round the class explaining to individual people . . . you want to understand it from the start, and [S2 teacher] makes it clear.
>
> (LG, school C, more effective low-SES)

One girl ascribed her slow progress to a lack of enough or the right sort of teacher explanation: 'if she doesnae explain it right I have to ask the person sitting next to me' but emphasised individual support: 'I like it better when she comes round . . . I can ask because I don't like saying it in front of everybody' (VLG, school B).

Individual help was limited by time and the teacher's priorities:

> Sometimes [the science teacher] doesn't come round . . . he is always on at the intelligent people, they are always ahead, ken, a couple of pages, and we

find it harder but he doesn't come, he says he will mark your jotter but he doesn't come up.

(LG, school D)

Pupils at the high-SES schools (A and B) were more positive than those in the low-SES schools about individual teacher help; the second LG at low-SES school D valued her independence:

When you are at the high school you'll no have somebody coming up to you asking 'are you all right? are you sure you can do this?' . . . in primary school the teacher would come about every five minutes. Here you can just get on with it and if you need help stick your hand up and ask . . . So in other words, you ken, you are depending on yourself, no one else.

(LG, school D)

Discussion in groups was more frequently used in the high-SES schools, but there were no differences by gender or school among pupils mentioning it favourably. One girl's awareness of discussion management skills stood out:

aye, everybody's got different opinions, it is better to put them all together . . . if they are thinking of something stupid, I say 'mm, maybe we will do that but I dinnae think it would really work, maybe Lisa's idea is better'.

(LG, school D)

This comment from the 'less effective low-SES' school recalls the finding of Griffiths (Griffiths and Davies 1993) that working-class girls incorporated a difficult member into discussion groups most skilfully, although in Griffiths' sample middle-class girls achieved the most effective completion of group tasks.

There were no clear findings suggesting that gender patterns of pupils' responses to school experiences differed in more and less effective schools. Across the schools in this research, the low achieving target boys were somewhat more confident of their progress than equivalent girls, and expressed more preferences for oral questioning and for working alone. Pupils in the high-SES schools were more positive about individual help from teachers.

We now draw together the three areas selected in this chapter, and look at the salience of gender in the classrooms of more and less effective schools as revealed in teacher thinking, observed lessons, and pupils' accounts.

Conclusion

The research drawn upon here kept an open mind about the effectiveness of any particular practices encountered in sample schools already identified as more or less 'effective'. It was an exploratory study, investigating processes, including gender, that might influence the learning progress of lower achieving pupils and looking also at the usefulness of school effectiveness as a basis for understanding what goes on in schools in different circumstances. Much of the gender data from the Brown, Riddell and Duffield (1996) study supports the standard current picture of boys dominating the classroom but girls achieving more. The distinct bias towards boys of classroom support and the selection of a pupil with hand up to answer, and the still more striking predominance of boys in teachers' accounts of lessons bears this out.

However, within the lower-achieving pupil sample, girls' classroom role was strongly influenced by levels of attainment. Just below average girls were favourably perceived, especially by teachers of English, and were as a group higher public contributors in lessons than the target boys, still more so with women teachers. If they were not called upon for answers and received less individual support, this could convey messages of independence. Their motivation and confidence were a feature of teacher thinking, and their assessed attainments on entering Standard Grade courses were higher than those of equivalent boys: they were poised to join the achieving girls identified in examination result analysis (Ganson and De Luca1995; Powney 1996; Furlong and Cartmel 1997). A small number of very low achieving girls, on the other hand, appeared to be in a singularly disadvantaged position. Often overlooked when they were ready to answer, less likely to be targeted for learning support, lacking in confidence, but with teachers, especially women, relatively ready to resist such demands for attention as they managed to make, they seemed to have the worst of both worlds.

These findings do not present any consistent relationship between gender issues and school effectiveness. At 'more effective' schools A and C, lesson materials challenging gender roles were seen. Self-chosen seating on male/female sides of the room with the boys' side disproportionately addressed in certain classrooms could have indicated a real factor at 'less effective' B and D. However, there is no basis here on which to over-ride the findings of quantitative research and demand the insertion of gender awareness among the characteristics of effective schools. The point is to reject any idea that the characteristics of a school like School A can be applied as a recipe to overcome the 'ineffectiveness' of schools in quite different circumstances. It was at school C, measured as effective but in a low income area of collapsed industry, where a gender difference emerged in pupil perceptions, with boys experiencing school as more pressurising, less supportive than girls did. In interviews at school management level, aiming to illuminate the wider culture of the school, school C reported efforts to challenge the macho culture of the surrounding area, but acknowledged that this was difficult; the pupils' accounts did not provide any evidence of these management goals being perceived by pupils.

Gender bias in the classroom may, perhaps, lie even more with teacher thinking than with the undoubted differences in pupil behaviour. The even gender balance of pupil-initiated support and offers to answer in class in our study, and the fact that teachers' recollected accounts of lessons were more boy-centred than their actual behaviour, point in this direction. Quantitative school effectiveness research has been chiefly concerned with value added attainment. Measures of attitude and behaviour have sometimes been included, but on the basis of correlating with effectiveness of attainment gains. With the important exception of the marginalised group of lowest achieving girls (similarly placed in the more and less effective schools in our study), girls' attainment progress was not shown to be disadvantaged by a lower profile in the classroom.

School improvement work could be a more appropriate arena than school effectiveness research in which to pursue the kind of scrutiny of the gender–learning interface reported here. A pilot school improvement study was initiated by a school (in a low-SES setting in England) concerned that boys' examination passes were much lower than those of girls (Wikeley and Jamieson 1996). The staff set an agenda for change and researchers acted as critical friends supporting open investigation into how current school processes operated unequally by gender. This kind of 'bottom-up' approach to improvement can take account of the gender culture experienced by pupils as well as comparing outcomes. Notions of improvement and effectiveness are bound up with those of quality. Aspin *et al.* (1994: 38–42) discuss 'dimensions of quality' comprising 'equity, excellence, democracy and justice'; to seek to improve a school involves these equity dimensions, even if the spur to change has been a defensive response to gender differentials in published attainments. Equity goals for their own sake have disappeared from the school policy agendas of recent years.

It is not enough to collect evidence of girls' average success and conclude that there is no need to consider gender when studying the effectiveness of schools or strategies for their improvement. Women still face pervasive disadvantages in society, exacerbated in socially deprived settings where particular features of gender identification can also exclude young males from educational success. The work reported here, illustrating gender processes in the classrooms of more and less effective schools, underlines the importance of gender as a factor in classroom interaction. To that extent, it reveals a limitation of school effectiveness as a framework for investigating school success, given that effectiveness research obliterates gender as a salient aspect. Gender issues in schools must not remain invisible, neither should they be examined in isolation. Further investigation of the interplay of gender and socio-economic background would be valuable. If effectiveness is a quality dimension, rather than simply a measure of attainment progress, then attention to gender equity should be built in as a feature of the learning school.

Note

1 Effectiveness and SES measures were by Lindsay Paterson *et al.*, Centre for Educational Sociology, Edinburgh. Value-added effectiveness was based on a statistical regression analysis of attainments for all S4 pupils in the authority in 1991, comparing Edinburgh Reading Test scores at entry to secondary school with S4 Standard Grade awards, overall and within seven curricular modes defined by the Scottish Consultative Council on the Curriculum. The two 'high effectiveness' schools had significantly positive figures in at least three modes and no significantly negative fiture. The other two schools had no significantly positive figure and at least

three significantly negative ones. SES measures were based on mothers' and fathers' occupations, employment and education.

References

Aspin, D., Chapman, J. and Wilkinson, V. (1994) *Quality Schooling: A Pragmatic Approach to Some Current Problems, Topics and Issues*, London: Cassell.

Brown, S. and McIntyre, D. (1993) *Making Sense of Teaching*, Buckingham: Open University Press,

Brown, S., Riddell, S. and Duffield, J. (1996) 'Possibilities and problems of using small-scale research to complement large-scale school effectiveness studies', in J. Gray, D. Reynolds, C. Fitz-Gibbon and D. Jesson (eds) *Merging Traditions: School Effectiveness and School Improvement*, London: Cassell.

—— (1997) 'School effectiveness research: the policy-makers' tool for school improvement?', in A. Harris, N. Bennett and M. Preedy (eds) *Organisational Effectiveness and Improvement in Education*, Buckingham: Open University Press, 138–46.

Cooper, J. (1995) 'Why are girls under-represented in Standard Grade physical education in Scottish schools?', *Scottish Journal of Physical Education* 23, 2: 28–38.

Department for Education and Employment (DfEE) (1997) *Excellence in Schools* White Paper, Cm 3681, London: HMSO.

Duffield, J. (1998) 'Learning experiences, effective schools and social context', *Support for Learning* 13, 1: 3–8.

French, J. and French, P. (1984) 'Gender imbalances in the primary classroom: an interactional account', *Educational Research* 26, 2: 127–36.

Furlong, A. and Cartmel, F. (1997) *Young People and Social Change*, Buckingham: Open University Press.

Ganson, H. and De Luca, C. (1995) 'Gender and the SCE examinations', paper presented to Scottish Educational Research Association (SERA) conference, Dundee 1995.

Gray, J., Reynolds, D., Fitz-Gibbon, C. and Jesson, D. (1996) *Merging Traditions: The Future of Research on School Effectiveness and School Improvement*, London: Cassell.

Griffiths, M. and Davies, C. (1993) 'Learning to learn: action research from an equal opportunities perspective in a junior school', *British Educational Research Journal* 10, 1: 43–58.

Howe, C. (1997) *Gender and Classroom Interaction: A Research Review*, Edinburgh: Scottish Council for Research in Education (SCRE).

MacBeath, J. (1999) 'School effectiveness and school improvement', in T. G. K. Bryce and W. Humes (eds) *Scottish Education*, Edinburgh: Edinburgh University Press 782–92.

MacBeath, J. and Boyd, B. (1996) 'Improving schools: the change profile', in M. Kirkwood, A. Roger and P. Rideout (eds) *SERA 1996: A Report of the Proceedings of the Annual Conference of the Scottish Educational Research Association*, Glasgow: University of Strathclyde, pp. 96–104.

McPherson, A. and Willms, D. (1987) 'Equalisation and improvement: some effects of comprehensive re-organisation in Scotland,' *Sociology* 21, 4: 509–39.

Mortimore, P., Sammons, P., Ecob, R. and Stoll, L. (1988) *School Matters: The Junior Years*, Wells: Open Books.

The Observer (1998) 'Caught in the gender gap: the trouble with boys', 4 January, p. 13.

Powney, J. (1996) *Gender and Achievement: A Review*, Edinburgh: Scottish Council for Research in Education (SCRE).

Stoll, L. and Mortimore, P. (1985) *Viewpoint: School Effectiveness and School Improvement*, London: Institute of Education.

Tibbett, J., Spencer, E. and Hutchinson, C. (1994) 'Improving school effectiveness: policy and research in Scotland', *Scottish Educational Review* 26, 2: 151–7.

Wikeley, F. and Jamieson, I. (1996) 'The gender puzzle: a pilot project', paper presented to the European Conference on Educational Research (ECER), University of Seville, September 1996.

Wragg, E. (1997) *Times Educational Supplement Greenwich Memorial Lecture*, May, London: TES.

9 All change, no change
Gendered regimes in the post-sixteen setting

Sheila Macrae and Meg Maguire

Girls and attainment: behind the rhetoric

'The evidence is in and the conclusion is clear: women can and do achieve academically as well as men' (Arlin Mickelson 1992: 149). Women in northern industrialised nations are moving into higher education in unprecedented numbers and are staying on to enrol on higher degree programmes. In the USA women now outnumber men on master's degree programmes although they are overwhelmingly located in 'traditional' female subject areas (ibid.). The picture for women's educational achievement in the West has never been brighter or better.

In schools too, the picture is equally rosy. In a recent UK report from the Office of Her Majesty's Chief Inspector of Schools and the Equal Opportunities Commission (1996: 6) it was unequivocally stated that, 'Girls out-perform boys at ages seven, eleven, and fourteen in National Curriculum assessments in English. Achievements in mathematics and science are broadly similar.' More importantly for this chapter, the report went on to state, 'girls are more successful than boys at every level in the GCSE'. Evidence for this claim has been gradually accumulated over time and clearly indicates that girls out-perform boys consistently at GCSE (NCER 1992; Harris *et al.* 1993) as well as at all stages of compulsory schooling (Sammons 1995).

Research has shifted to ask why these differences occur. It has been argued that gender cannot stand on its own as a factor for success; issues of ethnicity and class are deeply implicated in outcomes (Sammons 1995). Other studies examining factors which have influenced this 'gender divide' in formal examinations have considered issues such as bias in assessment, differential access to the curriculum as well as attitudinal predisposition, peer group pressure and family socialisation patterns (Stobbart *et al.* 1992; Riddell 1992; Gipps and Murphy 1994; Warrington and Younger 1996; Millard 1997). While these variables go some way towards 'explaining' the superior performance of females in relation to males, the issue of gender difference in examination attainment is by no means as clear-cut as all this suggests.

One of the frequently cited 'reasons' for the success of girls is that GCSE coursework favours female students. This is because of their superiority in reading and language activities (Millard 1997) as well as the somewhat stereotyped assumption that females 'may be more likely to work diligently' (Sammons 1995: 482). However, reality is never quite so straightforward. The evidence suggests that females have been out-performing males long before the introduction of GCSE (Murphy 1980). Indeed, girls were consistently achieving better grades than boys in the days of the eleven plus examination when boys' marks were adjusted to ensure comparable numbers of girls and boys entered grammar schools (Weiner 1985). Additionally, Elwood (1994) has demonstrated that coursework is only one factor in success and that the achievements of females are more complex.

Although females' academic success is not the main concern of this chapter, we do want to point out that the attainment of females and the myths about their earlier underachievement as well as their current success have contributed to what has become a 'moral panic' over boys' under-performance; a state so perilous that (Wragg 1997: 54) alleges this is 'the gravest social problem we're facing'. This state of panic may well result in even more attention being paid to males at the expense of females (Weiner *et al.* 1997). Thus, it is important to dispel any simplistic notion that females are doing exceptionally well and males are falling behind. The position is not as simple as this, as many experts in the assessment field have demonstrated (Gipps and Murphy 1994). Although females are doing better, on average, than males, there is a 'complex and changing pattern of measured performance in examinations between males and females from sixteen plus through to degree level' (ibid.: 256).

It is important to examine which subjects are chosen by females and males at GCSE as well as at A level. For while pass rates may be similar, differences occur in 'choice' of subjects which will have implications for life chances in the labour market. More specifically, in relation to post-16 vocational qualifications in the UK, females are more likely to be over-represented on 'traditional' caring-based courses and under-represented on higher status courses (Felstead 1996). Thus, the notion of 'change' and 'success' for females is, at the very least, problematic.

We are directly concerned in this chapter, through a consideration of some of our research work, with highlighting the ways in which patriarchal relations have persisted and continue to play a part in the social relations of young people. Through an exploration of some key themes which have emerged from our research we want to argue that the culture of 'heterosexualized femininity' (Thorne 1993) continues to shape the landscape of schooling, education and training in mid to late adolescence. However, before we approach this argument directly, it is important to sketch out the details of our research.

The study

Between September 1995 and August 1997[1] we tracked a group of young people during their final year of compulsory schooling, through their 'choice-making' and into their first year of post-16 education and training (Macrae *et al.* 1997a). The research focused on post-16 transitions within one inner-city education and training market.

The particular labour market is characterised by shifts away from small engineering plants and light manufacturing towards service work and high levels of local unemployment. As in other parts of the city, females are more likely than males to find employment and minority ethnic males are over-represented in the unemployment statistics (TUC 1996).

We started with a Year eleven cohort in a mixed, multi-racial urban comprehensive school, Northwark Park, and the local Pupil Referral Unit (PRU). Northwark Park is one of only two local authority schools in the borough and has approximately 700 pupils. It has gained a reputation as a 'caring' school and has a high number of students with Special Educational Needs. Perhaps for this reason, it does not attract many high flying students but does a sound job in meeting a wide range of complex social and educational needs. It is located in an area adjacent to many selective and more traditionally 'academic' schools, most of which are Grant Maintained. Our sample included students from a diverse range of backgrounds; students from many different minority ethnic communities as well as a small number of refugees. The PRU caters for a wide range of students from across the borough. The majority (in our sample) had had negative experiences of education and had either been excluded or had absented themselves from mainstream schools.

Our original sample comprised a total of 110 students: 81 from Northwark Park, and 29 from the PRU. From this cohort a smaller group was selected for in-depth study. This sub-sample was constructed to represent the range of students in terms of sex, social class, academic attainment, 'ethnicity' as well as the variety of post-16 destinations and routes. It also included some young people who had already opted out of formal education. The sub-sample consisted of 59 young people: 42 from the school and 17 from the PRU.

We are currently (September 1997–August 1999)[2] continuing with a smaller group from the above sub-sample: forty young people, selected, as before, to ensure that issues of 'race', class and gender can be addressed. Each student has been interviewed four times at the time of writing this chapter and by the completion of this second study (August 1999) we will have spoken with each participant on six occasions. Essentially our research seeks to 'capture and analyse the educational, work and domestic lives of these young people as they try to engage with one education, training and labour market setting in South London' (Ball *et al.* 1998: 1).

In this chapter we first examine the GCSE achievements of the original sub-sample. Drawing on our data we want to illustrate some of the gendered differences in attitude, motivation and behaviours which typified the group. We want to highlight the manner in which in-school relations and perhaps even more powerfully, out-of-school relations, typify the culture of 'heterosexualised femininity'. Thus our main focus is on gendered relationships. These are interwoven with issues of class and 'race' but it is not possible to discuss the effects of these at length in this short chapter. Through a necessarily limited use of our data set we hope to demonstrate that, while some things have changed, other older, patriarchal discourses have remained.

Girls and boys and GCSE results

First, it is important to record that the female students in our studies clearly out-performed the male students at GCSE. It is evident from the data (see Tables 9.1 and 9.2) that not only did the female students gain more passes overall, those in Northwark Park also significantly out-performed the male students in the key area of grades achieved between A* to C. In the local PRU, eleven of our sample of the eighteen students were female. (The reason for this is, at the time of the study there were more Year Eleven female students on the roll than males.) While none of these students scored well (that is, A* to C grades) the females still (just) out-performed the males overall.

Attitudes and motivations

These results certainly support the contention that females are doing better than males. It became evident from our in-depth interviews that there were other significant differences between the sexes in, for example, attitudes and motivations. As in other studies (Siann *et al.* 1996; Warrington and Younger 1996), the female students in our cohort generally had clearer goals and firmer ideas about their futures, regardless of 'race', class or academic attainment. Overall, the males in our study were less coherent, more vague and gave the impression of being less

Table 9.1 Northwark Park GCSE results, 1996

GCSE results	Female n = 21	Male n = 21	Female %	Male %	Percentage difference
Number achieving 5 A*–C passes	7	3	33.3	14.28	+19.05
Total A*–C passes	87	42	67.44	32.56	+34.9
Total D–G passes	74	89	45.4	54.6	−9.2
Total passes	161	131	55.32	45.01	+10.31
Average number of passes	7.66	6.23			+1.42

Table 9.2 Pupil referral unit GCSE results, 1996

GCSE Results	Female n = 11	Male n = 7
Number achieving 5 A*–C passes	0	0
Total A*–C passes	4	2
Total D–G passes	20	10
Total passes	24	12
Average number of passes	2.2	1.7

concerned about their future plans than the female students. The males certainly had considerably less to say than the females about their post-16 choice-making. The contrast between Gillian, whose mother (a lone parent) works as a caretaker and Dean, whose mother works as a cashier and whose father is a carpenter, illustrates this difference:

> I want to be in the RAF. I have always wanted to be in the RAF. I am in the Air Cadets at the moment. I am doing well at the moment because I have just got my Corporal's stripes . . . I went up to the RAF Careers Office myself and told them all about what I wanted to do. I don't want to be a low person, I want to be an officer so I get more money . . . I could get a sponsorship to go to university but I don't need to do that. It is five GCSEs, C and above and two A levels, E and above. And if I get them, they [the RAF] will pay for me to do my A levels, so I have decided to stay here [Northwark Park] to do them.
>
> (Gillian, white, eight GCSEs, four grade A*–C)

> I would like to be a doctor but I haven't really chased up any colleges or anything . . . I would like to be an engineer. If I wanted to do that I think it would be better to do the mechanics first, then go on to engineering . . . I am not sort of devoting all my attention to staying on. Really, I would rather do an apprenticeship where I am getting paid.
>
> (Dean, white, seven GCSEs, one grade A* – C)

Not only were the females more focused, they also tended to work collaboratively and to support one another in the 'choice-making' process. They regularly discussed their progress, their ambitions and their future plans among themselves. This was not the case for most of the males in our study. They would sometimes tell one another where they were thinking of going but this was more of an information exchange rather than a discussion. Even this did not always happen, as evidenced in the following exchange with Patrick who is talking about his friends. Patrick, a white student, gained two D–G grades at GCSE and came from a home where neither his mother nor step-father worked:

Int: Just give me an idea of who is staying on. John, what is he doing?
Patrick: I don't know.
Int: Mary?
Patrick: I don't know.
Int: Do you talk to them about what they are doing next year?
Patrick: No. I just play football. There's no time for that.

This contrasts powerfully with the behaviour of one group of females who spent a great deal of time considering their options and encouraging each other:

> Yes, my friends because, I mean, I don't know, once a week, at least once a week it comes up, what A levels have you decided upon finally and, what

do you want to be, and all of this. And that is quite useful because you can find out what everybody else is doing and you think, that doesn't sound too bad.

(Anne, Chinese, nine GCSEs, all A*–C grades)

The female students discussed their ambitions with their friends and their friends' parents. They debated their options, giving one another praise and support:

I watched some films about lawyers and then I thought, I can't really get a full picture because that is all movies, isn't it. It isn't really like that. So I asked my friend's dad, he is a lawyer, and he told me what you had to do and how long you were at university, and he answered some questions for me. And my mum is a teacher so I asked her some things about that. And then I, well, I just ask my friends' mums if they like their jobs and stuff and, in their opinion, what I should do, because they all thought I should be a teacher, but I don't want to be a teacher.

(Lucy, white, nine GCSEs, six grade A*–C)

Agesh, we keep telling Agesh. She wants to be a doctor and we want her to be a doctor. So we encourage her and that, and tell her, yes, go for it. You can do it.

(Anne, Chinese, nine GCSEs, all A*–C grades)

Here it is important to note that all these young women, some of whom come from minority ethnic backgrounds, are middle-class and the expectation is that they will proceed to higher education. Thus, it could be argued that their success-ful networking is a reflection of *class*, not gender or 'race'.

However, the fact that, in the majority of the interviews, the young women's choice-making conversations were both qualitatively and quantitatively different from those of the young men is not surprising. Females, according to Lees (1993), come to know themselves through their relationships with others; their 'female gender identity' is strengthened through their interpersonal transactions. On the other hand, it is argued, 'male gender identity' is threatened by intimacy, while 'female gender identity' is threatened by separation (Gilligan *et al*. 1990). Similarly, Tannen (1992) illustrates how women use language primarily to make connections and reinforce intimacy, while men's main aim is to preserve their independence and negotiate status. Having information can be a form of hier-archy for some males and, therefore, those with more information can be seen as having higher status. Males, therefore, may be reluctant to ask for information as this may suggest they are in some way inferior (Connell 1996). This (potentially essentialist argument) may go some way towards explaining why some of the young men in our studies appeared to make their post-16 choices on only the barest of information:

Int: Can you tell me if you have been to any Open Nights?
James: No. I didn't receive the information quick enough. I was too late.

Int: So why have you chosen St Faith's?

James: The application forms, I couldn't understand them, they weren't set up very well. The only one that was set up well was St Faith's, so I just filled it in.

Int: What do your parents think about your choice?

James: My dad is happy and my mum is quite happy.

Int: Quite happy with your decision in general. Were they in any way helpful to you in your decision? Did you talk to them? Did you discuss it?

James: I told them what I was going to do. I didn't discuss it. I just told them what I wanted. They accepted it.

James (white, eight GCSEs, six grade A*–C) came from a similar home background to Anne, Lucy and Agesh. His parents were ambitious for him and had hopes that he would be the first in the family to progress to Higher Education. However, unlike the young women, James did not appear to discuss his future plans with school friends:

Int: Just a few questions about your friends. What are their choices? What are they doing, your close friends?

James: My closest friend, he is going to College as well; A level course, Riverway College. My other friend is going to St Faith's as well, but I am not sure whether they got in or not.

Int: Have you ever discussed these things together, like how they make their choices?

James: No, I didn't find out until after, that they went to St Faith's.

Int: Why was that?

James: We don't really socialise outside school and when we are in school there is school work to think about and at break time we play games.

Int: Do you know how your friends have come to their decisions, what has influenced their decisions?

James: No, not really. We don't speak about that.

The differences between the young women and men were not confined to the ways they spoke about their 'choice-making'. Again, it is only possible to include small extracts from the data to illustrate another significant difference, this time concerning attitudes towards studying and revising for GCSEs. It was evident from the data that, in general, the female students were better organised, had started early and were more concerned (perhaps too concerned) than the male students:

Rena (Keynan-Asian, nine GCSEs, six grade A*–C): I don't know about you but I feel like a great weight on me. I have got to do something now. Don't you forget to do little things because you have got so much? I keep forgetting to fill in my college application form.

Int: You must!

Rena: I know.

Lucy: To think about the college you want to go to. Thinking means taking time and you have to work, work, work so hard. I don't know.

Rena: I just fall behind with the course work. You think you are working and working and teachers give you a deadline and you think, 'Oh, my God'. We have got all these deadlines and I am thinking, I am not going to do it.

Wayne's (white, five GCSEs, all grades D–G) post-16 'choosing' behaviour was fairly typical of the (predominantly working-class) males who appeared to experience little more than the odd twinge of concern:

Int: Do you feel, Wayne, as if you are under any pressure to get on and make decisions, or not?

Wayne: Yes, sometimes but I try not to think about it that much, not during school anyway. No, just like now and again I think I get worried.

Int: What do you do then?

Wayne: After a little while I just forget about it.

In common with other studies (notably the survey of 30,000 students in 1994 by Keele University), the males in our study, regardless of 'race' or class, were less committed to learning than the females. They were less well prepared, expressed less interest and were badly organised in terms of revision and post-16 choosing. Two middle-class males, from supportive homes, expressed difficulty in starting their GCSE revision:

> *Luke* (white, nine GCSEs, seven grade A*–C): Well I started revising, well I started in the Easter but not hard.

> *Aaron* (white, four GCSEs, no grades A*–C): I keep meaning to but then something else comes up or my mates come round or something. Usually I'm too busy.

Good girls, wives and mothers: in-school relations

During the course of interviewing the student cohort and the subsequent coding of data, it became strikingly evident that the females took responsibility for the males in their school. They frequently made reference to the additional difficulties which, in their opinion, males had to overcome. For some of the female students this was reinforced by experiences which their older brothers had gone through. For others, it was in consequence of seeing their male peers disengaging from school work. In many ways, the females were taking on an extra burden; they were adopting a nurturing and caring role for the male students in their friendship groups. Perhaps too, they were being socialised into and rehearsing their future roles as wives and mothers.

A wide range of research has pointed out the way in which young females come to occupy positions which 'inscribe their subordination on the basis of gender' (Thorne 1993: 170). Indeed, Connell (1987) has argued that the most socially valued form of femininity is that which is centred on attending to male demands and requirements. That males come first is the message most females learn, not necessarily explicitly but by example. This received 'wisdom' is caught from an early age and endorsed through education, training and employment. Women also learn that to transgress established modalities of femininity may incur the disapproval of other females as well as the wrath of males, sometimes violently expressed (Rich 1980). Females, therefore, look after the feelings of males and work at making them feel good, by encouraging, smiling, admiring and generally perpetuating their primacy. Indeed, this is the basis of the relationship between the sexes (Cline and Spender 1987). As Woolf (1928: 35) so perspicaciously pointed out: 'Women have served all these centuries as looking-glasses, possessing the magic and delicious power of reflecting the figure of a man at twice its natural size.' In these ways, 'young women and men learn to constitute and reconstitute themselves in a constantly evolving process and . . . this process is gendered. Girls and boys learn what behaviour is expected of them' (Cline and Spender 1987: 5). Therefore, it is perhaps not surprising to observe that the process of gender performativity or 'heterosexualised femininity' was and is enacted by the young females in our study. It was apparent that their in-school social relations conformed to this requirement. The females in some ways acted as surrogate 'mothers' to the male students; their caring and nurturing work shoring up a reworked version of 'hegemonic masculinity' (Connell 1983):

> I think it is probably easier for girls. I think there is more boys that get into trouble . . . but boys do find it a bit harder because they have to play the tough image.
>
> (Sinead, white, nine GCSEs, three grade A–C)

Other female students identified what they regarded as a gender difference which almost 'couldn't be helped': a stage to be gone through:

> Loads of people have dropped out of their courses and stuff, mostly boys, I think, because, I don't know about on the whole, but in this school I think girls try harder and boys are going through a stage at the moment where, 'I don't want to do this any more, I want to do this and I want to play football or whatever'.
>
> (Lucy, white, nine GCSEs, six grade A–C)

However, while some of the attitudes of the female students towards their male peers seemed to be suggesting that 'they can't help it' there was, at the same time, a stronger maternal tone evident in their responses particularly towards the end of the following extract:

Kirsty   (white, ten GCSEs, all grade A*–C):I think it has been quite a few boys
not doing a lot of work and there is a few of the boys that have been hard
working who stopped doing that and became more lazy. Like one of the
boys I am friendly with, John, he has become more lazy . . . he was doing
lots of work and now he has started bunking and giving in his course
work late and it is not as if he has got anything else to do. Like, I mean, it
is such a waste because he is clever and he has just got to do just such a
little amount of work and he can get away with it. But I think he has just
realised that he can get away with it. Because, like, he would occasionally
bunk a lesson and he realised that he didn't need to go and, like, everything will be all right. 'Don't worry about it. Don't worry about it'. That
is what they all say, and I say 'I'm not worried about you but you should
be, because you are going to fail and then what will you do? So don't
waste it'. His personality hasn't changed, he is just too lazy.

Int: Well maybe he'll come to his senses.

Kirsty: He better. We've [female peers] been trying to make him see sense for
ages now.

Help and support, both emotional and practical, ran like refrains through many
female conversations. This 'servicing' of males in the classroom was also found in
Lees' (1993) study. Interestingly, none of the male students spoke about supporting anyone in the terms described by the young women. Neither did they suggest
that they needed or received any support. Rather, in their conversations, they
created an image of 'lone rangers' making their own decisions, often on extremely
limited and shaky evidence with little or no reference to anyone (witness James
above).

What this suggests is that while the females are doing well at school (as to an
extent they always have done), the discourses of caring and nurturing, as well as a
propensity to take on responsibility for the male students, attending to their needs
and demands, have persisted (Lees 1993). This is even more evident when we
consider the social relations of the young women in our study as they progressed
beyond compulsory schooling.

The more things change, the more they are the same

In many ways in this chapter we are struggling with a number of paradoxes; our
central point is that, while some changes have impacted on the lives of girls and
young women, other aspects of their social, cultural and material worlds have
almost remained untouched. For example, one of the most profound changes to
the lives of Western women in the twentieth century has been in relation to paid
work and the labour market. Many more women now work for longer periods of
their lives. At the same time, participation rates for men have slowly declined and
changes in many local labour markets in the UK have reduced the number of
'traditional' and frequently 'masculinised' manual waged jobs in manufacturing
(Haywood and Mac An Ghaill 1996). One consequence of this change in

employment patterns is that it is sometimes argued that traditional constructions of femininity and masculinity are being challenged. However, although there have been changes, it is important to state that while women may well be more employable than men, it is often the case that 'the work they do is poorly paid and women tend to occupy part-time, subordinate positions' (Maguire 1995: 561).

More importantly for this chapter, we now want to examine the *continuity* and *persistence* of formations of 'heterosexualized femininity' (Thorne 1993) which have consequences for the lives of the young people in our studies. Our point is that, 'while the language, expectation and appearance of relationships may change, the underlying patterns of heterosexual relationships are striking in their resilience' (Holland *et al.* 1998: 193). With this in mind, it is our intention to explore some of the social and cultural relationships that have emerged from our interviews with the young people in our studies.

Heterosexuality is both complex and pervasive. '[It] . . . is not, as it appears to be, masculinity-and-femininity in opposition: it *is* masculinity' (Holland *et al.* 1998:11) and both women and men must live by its conventions or risk the consequences. Holland *et al.* (1998) present a convincing argument to show that heterosexuality is more than a pattern of sexual practices; it includes both sexual and gender relations.

Sexual and gender relations

While it was not part of our study to investigate the young people's understanding of their sexuality or their sexual practices, it became evident from our interviews that boyfriends in particular (and girlfriends to a lesser extent) were an important part of the lives of the cohort by the age of 17. Indeed, a taken-for-grantedness that the young people would have partners, was a motif in many interviews:

Int: Do you find that there is pressure on young women to have boyfriends?
Amma   (African, eight GCSEs, three Grade A*–C): I think it is not so much of a pressure but kind of like a surprise if you don't have one, you know. I think a lot of my friends automatically expect me to have one, so when they were speaking to me for the first time in College, when we were all getting to know each other so, do you and your man want to come, that kind of thing. I don't have a boyfriend. Oh. It is more a surprise than a pressure . . . You are just expected to, everyone is expected to be with somebody these days you know, so it is just more of a surprise.
Int: Do you think that there is social pressure on young women of your age to have a bloke?
Kirsty (white, ten GCSEs, all grade A*–C): Yes, definitely because when I first started at St Faith's like, people would come and chat to you and say, what do you do and all that, and have you got a boyfriend? And it was like, no I haven't. Really? This girl was saying to me. Really? No I haven't. Oh God, you're quite pretty. Why haven't you got a boyfriend?

> I was like, there is no one I like at the moment. So it was, like, have you been looking? You have been looking, haven't you? I couldn't believe it.

This notion of 'prettiness' was a depressingly common theme in the interviews with female respondents. A focus on physical appearance and a 'need' for a male partner characterised many of the responses. This perhaps should be of no surprise as Thorne (1993: 170) demonstrated:

> Girls are pressured to make themselves 'attractive' to get a boyfriend, to define themselves and other girls in terms of their positions in the hetero-sexual market . . . Active efforts to get and keep a boyfriend lead many young women to lower their ambitions, and the culture of romance perpetuates male privilege.

The following two students are discussing their move from Northwark Park to a Sixth Form College:

Agesh (Indo-Caribbean, nine GCSEs, all grade A*–C): There are lots of people coming from the single sex schools, so they were so excited. Like, we are used to having mixed classes, and you don't think anything of it if you have got a boy sitting next to you. They were so excited, the girls had all their make up on and all their hair was done.
Int: This is 1997.
Kirsty (white, ten GCSEs, all grade A*–C): Yes, you wouldn't think it. It is brilliant, there is this girl . . . she is unbelievable. She is this black girl and she has got this big wig and hair all the way up there.
Agesh: She wears these big enormous white boots with heels and wears these tiny dresses and it must take her hours to get ready. And it's all so the boys take notice of her.

This power of the male gaze to determine and regulate the behaviour of many women is recognised by others (for example, Bartky 1990; Wittig 1992; Attwood 1993) and is captured in the notion of women's lives being overseen by an imaginary male who regulates their thoughts and actions. Kirsty and Agesh recognise this but distance themselves from this position. However, it is claimed that we all (women and men) see the world through male eyes and, if we are to avoid personal and social censure, we learn to live by the conventions of heterosexuality which privilege masculine meanings and desires (Rich 1980). This concept is succinctly expressed by Holland *et al.* (1998) who talk about the 'male-in-the-head'. Through such an idea it is possible to understand why young women are prepared to put themselves at risk in their sexual relations.

Questions on their sex lives did not form part of the interview, but several young women raised the subject and were quite prepared to talk about this area of their lives:

My friend, Kayleigh, I met her last week and she said she was going out with Jason. Well we got to talking about sex and I said, do you come, do you come? No, she said. So I said, well, I'll give you a few hints but she wasn't interested. She said she didn't like sex. So I said, I don't understand that. Why are you having it, then? And do you know what she said? She said, I don't like to say no. She's having sex and she doesn't like it but she doesn't like to say no. I don't understand that.

(Kirsty, white, ten GCSEs, all grade A*–C)

It also transpired that Kayleigh was taking no precautions because the subject was too embarrassing to broach:

I mean, you can't get any more intimate than having sex, can you, but she's too embarrassed to bring it up. She doesn't want to upset them. But it was the same with Ruth. She said she couldn't, she just couldn't ask them. She was having sex with all these blokes and she actually thought she was infertile because she never used condoms or nothing and then about a month after she told me, she was pregnant. The father never comes near her.

(Kirsty, white, ten GCSEs, all grade A*–C)

This reluctance or inability to use contraceptives or be assertive in sexual relations is widely recognised and well documented. Rich (1980) for example, outlined the problems of sexual expression within a patriarchal/heterosexual system where girls and women are not on an equal footing with men and sexual expression takes place on male terms. Similarly, Lees (1993: 200) points out some of the risks involved for women when they try to take responsibility for their sexual behaviour:

It [condom use] involves talking about the sexual encounter rather than 'letting it happen', which is not only far more embarrassing to negotiate but also involves carrying condoms around with all the risks of exposure . . . for a woman to carry condoms can be seen as challenging the patriarchal definition of her as innately responsive to male initiative, as reactive rather than pro-active. Such a challenge demands more than assertiveness training for women. It demands shifting the meaning of sexuality and of sexual identity.

A small minority of our young people are now parents and several females have had terminations. Gillian, who briefly contemplated a termination, soon decided to have the baby and has recently been given council accommodation along with her partner. She had been an ambitious 16-year-old with well-articulated future plans. She regarded her pregnancy as a mere 'blip' in her ambitions and spoke positively about her situation:

I have actually lived a lot of my life, I have been in the cadets; I learned everything going; I have done disco dancing, majorettes, the brownies, guides. I have done a lot with my life for how old I actually am . . . When she is about six months I will stop breast feeding I will go back to College and I want to study to be a teacher. I love kids and I want to be a nursery school teacher so when she is on holiday basically I will be on holidays.

(Gillian, white, eight GCSEs, four grade A*–C)

Jamie, her partner, who had been a school truant, had learning difficulties and a poor work record. According to Gillian's mother, he did not see the point in working unless he really enjoyed it and, therefore, he left most jobs after a week or so. During her pregnancy Gillian had worked in a bakery while Jamie (who had moved in with Gillian, her mother and younger brother) languished at home. She was quick to point out Jamie's parenting skills and proudly recounted the ways in which he was caring for their four-month-old daughter:

When I actually express the milk he will feed her, he has fed her twice in the night . . . He found it tiring the next day . . . He does actually change her, he baths her, if I need a bit of sleep in the morning. She likes to talk in the morning, at nine o'clock she is very active and he will like play with her, and let me put my head down.

(Gillian, white, eight GCSEs, four grade A–C)

The use of the word 'let' is interesting. Gillian does not appear to be describing a relationship in which both (unemployed) parents are equally involved in the raising of their child. Rather, she talks with pride and gratitude of his limited efforts. That women give men 'prizes' for behaving in a decent, responsible and reasonable way and are grateful when they are not tyrants, is an important and basic premise on which many female–male relations are built. Cline and Spender summed it up thus:

Daily, almost hourly, women's efforts and achievements go unacknowledged while those of men are held up for all the world to admire . . . The reason we remain unaware is that this practice is so deeply entrenched in our value system that we simply accept it as part of the way the world works.

(1987: 14)

Despite what appear to be glaring inequalities in many female–male relationships there was enormous social pressure on a small minority of our cohort to settle down and reproduce. This was a trend which patterned the social lives of the educationally disaffected (Macrae *et al.* 1997b). Tina, a chronic truant, who appeared much older than her sixteen years, spoke at length about her boyfriend, Mark:

His parents accept me and I go up there [Mark's home] when I have got the money and he comes down here [Tina's home] when he has got the money. And they let Mark sleep down here. I am not allowed to sleep up there because Mark has got younger brothers and sisters in the house, so that is understandable. But Mark is allowed to sleep down here, and Mark's mum really, really wants me to have a baby. She keeps going, 'it is about time you had a baby, isn't it'. Things like that. She shouldn't really. Mark's oldest brother, his girlfriend Tracy is saying that she shouldn't really be pushing me and Mark to have a baby. But she isn't, I don't think she is, because I have always wanted children. I see Mark as a person to have them with.

(Tina, white, no GCSEs)

Tina seldom left the house during the day, preferring to read and listen to music. In the evenings she sometimes accompanied Mark to the pub. Lees (1986) showed how girls must attach themselves to men and men's interests in order, safely, to access public spaces. Men's social and recreational activities frame the space in which women move. Furthermore, it is not uncommon for men to ignore their girlfriends and spend the evening in the pub talking to their friends, and about women in sexist ways within female earshot (Lees 1986).

Sometimes we go out but not very often because we are saving up to go to Florida in October next year. Now and then we do go out, but I would rather stay in than go out because, if we go out to the pub, it is with his work mates. But they don't bring their wives or their girl friends and I feel like a goose-berry because there is just me and all his work mates. I would rather that he went out with his mates, then me go out with him, than be bored stiff sitting there and nobody speaking to me. But if somebody starts chatting me up he doesn't like it. So I say to him, what do you want me to do, just sit there and be bored. He doesn't speak to me but I'm not supposed to speak to anyone else.

(Tina, white, no GCSEs)

It was with pride that Tina displayed her engagement ring and explained why Mark had given it to her. The proprietorial tone was evident in her voice:

I think he wants me to wear his ring on my finger to like ward off any other guys, because I am not allowed to go out anywhere because I keep getting chatted up by other people. If I go to like the pub with my friends, I am always getting chatted up and he doesn't like it. He is very jealous. So he likes me to wear the ring but I'm quite popular down the pub and that.

(Tina, white, no GCSEs)

The engagement ring was a clear message to all other males and, although Mark had not found it necessary to defend 'his property', Tina realised that she was playing a risky game by 'chatting to other blokes'. The threat of male vio-lence, although not expressed in so many words, was a fact of life recognised by some of the young women in our study and they had their own ways of trying to avert it:

Like, if I am coming home and it is dark, I always have my keys in my hand. They are like a weapon, just in case, you know. I don't even think about it now, I just do it. I put my finger through the key ring and I'm ready for anyone. My dad says anything can be used as a weapon and I've always been like that. You just never know.

(Kirsty, white, ten GCSEs, all grade A*–C)

Similarly, Agesh (Indo-Caribbean, nine GCSEs, all grade A*–C) is aware of the need not to provoke; not to challenge but to stay 'sweet' and thus, hopefully, avoid trouble:

Agesh: There is just men that come up my road. I have never seen them before. They are weird. They just come up and start talking.
Int: Does that bother you?
Agesh: Yes.
Int: What do you do?
Agesh: I just sort of smile and chat and keep walking and hope I get to my house before anything happens.

What we want to illustrate is the manner in which aspects of 'heterosexualised femininity' (Thorne 1993) have worked to shape the sexual and gender relations of our cohort. While some of the young women (mainly middle-class and more traditionally 'successful') were aware of the limiting effects of what Holland *et al.* (1998) have called the 'male-in-the-head', others were caught up in a world where their sex has meant an 'everyday lived experience . . . of gender domination' (Lees 1993: 5).

Conclusion

In this chapter we have argued that in general terms, the young women in our study, regardless of class or 'race' have gained more qualifications at 16 than their male peers. However, although in this chapter, we have not been able to pay enough attention to differences *between* the young women, we do want to point out that factors of class in particular, as well as 'race' do impact upon female attainment. Thus, while we celebrate the achievements of the females in our studies we want to sound a note of caution. They are gaining more GCSEs at 16 in terms of numbers of examinations but their post-16 'choices' are still gendered in a 'traditional' manner. Females are still more likely than males to be pursuing arts and humanities at 'A' level and following 'feminised' vocational courses such as child development or hair and beauty GNVQs/NVQs.

In relation to sexual and gender relations, our data reflect an equally complex picture. While some of our cohort are clearly assertive and confident in their relationships and speak of their capacity to resist some of the more overt versions of 'heterosexualised femininity' which are on offer in contemporary society, others are caught up in these practices which frequently work to position them in subordinate relationships to males. For all sorts of reasons then, our data suggest that 'all change, no change' aptly describes the gendered regimes operating in our post-16 setting.

Acknowledgements

Both studies, from which the data in this chapter are drawn, have been funded by the ESRC to whom we extend our thanks.

Notes

1 'Education Markets in the Post-sixteen Sector of One Urban Locale' L123251006.
2 'Choice, Pathways and Transitions: 16–19 Education, Training and (Un)employment in One Urban Locale' R 000237261.

References

Arlin Mickelson, R. (1992) 'Why does Jane read and write so well? The anomaly of women's achievement', in J. Wrigley (ed.) *Education and Gender Equality*, London and Washington: Falmer Press.
Attwood, M. (1993) *The Robber Bride*, London: Bloomsbury.
Ball, S.J., Macrae, S. and Maguire, M. (1998) 'Young lives at risk in the "futures" market: some policy concerns from on-going research', in '*The Learning Society Programme: Research and Policy*', seminar at Bristol University, 27–28 January.
Bartky, S.J. (1990) *Femininity and Domination: Studies in the Phenomenology of Oppression*, London: Routledge.
Centre for Successful Schools (1994) *Gender Differences and GCSE Results*, Keele: University of Keele.
Cline, S. and Spender, D. (1987) *Reflecting Men: At Twice their Natural Size*, London: Andre Deutsch Ltd.
Connell, R.W. (1983) *Which Way is Up? Essays on Class, Sex and Culture*, London: Allen and Unwin.
—— (1987) *Gender and Power*, Stanford, CA: Stanford University Press.
—— (1996) *Masculinities*, Cambridge: Polity Press.
Elwood, J. (1994) 'Equity issues in performance assessment. Undermining gender stereotypes: examination performance in the UK at 16', paper presented at the American Research Association Conference, New Orleans, 4–8 April.
Felstead, A. (1996) 'Identifying gender inequalities in the distribution of vocational qualifications in the UK', *Gender, Work and Organization* 3, 1: 38–50.
Gilligan, C., Lyons, N. and Hammer, T. (1990) *Making Connections: The Relational Worlds of Adolescent Girls at Emma Willard School*, Cambridge, MA.: Harvard University Press.
Gipps, C. and Murphy, P. (1994) *A Fair Test? Assessment, Achievement and Equity*, Buckingham: Open University Press.
Harris, S., Nixon, J. and Ruddock, J. (1993) 'School work, homework and gender', *Gender and Education* 5, 1: 3–15.
Haywood, C. and Mac An Ghaill, M. (1996), 'What about the boys? Regendered local

labour markets and the recomposition of working class masculinities', *British Journal Of Education And Work* 9, 1: 19–30.

Holland, J., Ramazanoglu, C., Sharpe, S. and Thomson, R. (1998) *The Male in the Head: Young People, Heterosexuality and Power*, London: The Tufnell Press.

Lees, S. (1986) *Losing out: Sexuality and Adolescent Girls*, London: Hutchinson.

—— (1993) *Sugar and Spice: Sexuality and Adolescent Girls*, London: Penguin Books.

Macrae, S., Maguire, M. and Ball, S.J. (1997a) 'Competition, choice and hierarchy in a post-sixteen education and training market', in S. Tomlinson (ed.) *Education 14 – 19: Critical Perspectives*, London: Athlone Press.

—— (1997b) 'Whose "learning" society? A tentative deconstruction', *Journal of Education Policy* 12, 6: 499–509.

Maguire, M. (1995) 'Women, age and education in the United Kingdom', *Women's Studies International Forum* 18, 5–6: 559–71.

Millard, E. (1997) 'Differently literate: gender identity and the construction of the developing reader', *Gender and Education* 9, 1: 31–48.

Murphy, P. (1980) 'Sex differences in GCE exam entry statistics and success rates', *Education Studies* 6, 2: 169–78.

National Consortium for Examination Results (NCER) (1992) *Examination Results Summer 1992: Data All Authorities*, Bath: National Consortium for Examination Results.

Office of Her Majesty's Chief Inspector of Schools and Equal Opportunities Commission (1996) *The Gender Divide: Performance Differences between Boys and Girls at School*, London: HMSO.

Rich, A. (1980) 'Compulsory heterosexuality and lesbian existence', *Signs* 5, 4: 641–60.

Riddell, S. (1992) *Gender and the Politics of the Curriculum*, London: Routledge.

Sammons, P. (1995) 'Gender, ethnic and socio-economic differences in attainment and progress: a longitudinal analysis of student achievement over nine years', *British Educational Research Journal* 21, 4: 465–85.

Siann, G., Lightbody, P., Stocks, R. and Walsh, D. (1996) 'Motivation and attribution at secondary school: the role of ethnic group and gender', *Gender and Education* 8, 3: 261–74.

Stobbart, G., Elwood, J. and Quinlan, M. (1992) 'Gender bias in examinations: how equal are the opportunities?', *British Education Research Journal* 18, 3: 261–76.

Tannen, D. (1992) *You Just Don't Understand: Women and Men in Conversation*, London: Virago.

Thorne, B. (1993) *Gender Play: Girls and Boys in School*, Buckingham: Open University Press.

Trades Union Congress (1996) *Talking 'Bout My (Lost) Generation*, London: TUC.

Warrington, M. and Younger, M. (1996) 'Goals, expectations and motivation: gender differences in achievement at GCSE', *Curriculum* 17, 2: 80–93.

Weiner, G. (ed.) (1985) *Just a Bunch of Girls: Feminist Approaches to Schooling*, Milton Keynes: Open University Press.

Weiner, G., Arnot, M. and David, M. (1997) 'Is the future female? Female success, male disadvantage and changing gender patterns in education', in A.H. Halsey, H. Lauder, B. Brown, and A.S. Wells (eds) *Education, Culture, Economy, Society*, Oxford and New York: Oxford University Press.

Wittig, M. (1992) 'The straight mind', in M. Wittig (ed.) *Feminist Issues*, Hemel Hempstead: Harvester Wheatsheaf.

Woolf, V. (1928) *A Room of One's Own* (reprinted 1991), London: Hogarth Press.

Wragg, E.C. (1997) *The Cubic Curriculum*, London: Routledge.

Part 3

Delegation and the new managerialism

10 Gendered governance

Education reform and lay involvement in the local management of schools[1]

Rosemary Deem

Introduction

In this chapter I want to examine some ways in which gender may be relevant to an understanding of the processes and organisational cultures arising from recent changes to the composition of and responsibilities attached to the governance of state maintained schools in England. By governance, I mean the practice of bringing together lay people, whether they are parents, politicians, business people or community activists, as members of formally constituted bodies which have responsibility for overseeing the administration and broad strategic direction of individual schools. Though the composition and responsibilities of governing bodies vary considerably, lay school governance is a feature of educational systems in many countries (Deem 1994a). This chapter concentrates on processes and cultures of reformed governance in England and it is not assumed that the issues raised here necessarily take the same form in the rest of the UK (Deem 1996). Indeed, there are considerable cultural, political and economic differences between England, Scotland, Northern Ireland and Wales, as well as variations in the kinds of educational reforms which have occurred (Arnot *et al.* 1996; Brown 1996; McKeown *et al.* 1996). However, to the extent that the research reported here analyses features of processes and cultures of school governance and raises wider issues about citizenship and participation in public life, there is no reason to assume that those concerns are irrelevant to governance of schools in Scotland, Wales and Northern Ireland.

Gender, along with ethnicity, 'race' and class, played an important role in our plans to discover how volunteer school governors were going to enact and cope with a range of new and demanding responsibilities given to them via education reform legislation passed in England between 1986 and 1989. Using theoretical sampling, we chose ten governing bodies of primary and secondary Local Education Authority (LEA) maintained co-educational schools in two different areas, all of whose members were newly appointed or elected in the autumn of 1988. The schools included ranged from those situated in suburban or semi-rural areas and with mainly white and usually at least partly middle-class pupils on roll, to inner city schools which had either or both of extensive working-class pupil intakes and a high proportion of students from black or Asian households. We then commenced four years of intensive observation of the meetings of those governing bodies. We made extensive and near-verbatim notes about what was said, who spoke, the length and content of discussion items and individual interventions, noted decisions taken and also observed seating arrangements for each meeting. We collected extensive documentation connected with the meetings, including agendas, minutes and briefing papers. We used two questionnaires to survey all the governors in the study, one in the early stages of the project with regard to governor motivations and backgrounds and a second at the end of the project, in order to gain some sense of their reflections on their term of office. We also conducted semi-structured interviews with head teachers, chairs of governing bodies and sub-committees, co-opted business governors, and teacher governors.

Though school governance is a widely studied feature of educational systems, very little contemporary research has focused on the gender issues involved (Evans 1988; Dehli 1996; see Rees *et al.*, this volume). In so far as gender has been considered, it has been mainly in respect of the relative balance of membership of governing bodies, though survey evidence from England at the time of our research did not suggest that women were under-represented nationally on governing bodies (Keys and Fernandes 1990). However, membership of an organisation does not guarantee full participation and this was one of the issues we wished to research.

The ways in which gender relations and identities appear to be relevant to enactment of governance, in the context in which we researched it, include the extent to which gender identities and relations figure in the motivations of women and men to become governors and the kinds of experiences which they regard as appropriate to draw upon in their gubernatorial activities. These concerns do not rest on an essentialist assumption that all women are the same – certainly, in our study, women governors differed considerably in their membership of ethnic groups, their social class and occupational status, as well as in political allegiance. However, what we did observe, in that specific context, were that some underlying cultural assumptions of governors in general grouped women together for certain purposes as though they were the same (for example, in the making of decisions about who joined what sub-committee, it was often assumed that women had no financial knowledge). Further dimensions are the gender dynamics of governing body meetings and the extent to which discourses about schools and education markets may exclude women, or position them in particular gender specific relationships to what Gerwirtz *et al.* (1995) call 'lived markets'. Additional gender issues are raised by an exploration of the organisational cultures of school governing bodies and the ways in which organisational enactment of school governance may rest partly (though by no means exclusively) on gendered assumptions about knowledge and expertise. This enactment also rests on sets of bureaucratic practices which, partly because of gendered patterning of labour market experiences and involvement in political activities, may be less familiar to many women than they are to men.

Under the provisions of reforms to schooling in England undertaken since the mid-1980s, there have been a number of changes directly affecting school governance. These include the delegation of responsibility for budgets, including staffing, to state-funded schools from local education authorities. Governors, alongside head teachers, are charged with ensuring that budgets are properly drawn up and that deficits are not incurred. Other significant changes include the introduction of National Curricula and testing, both of which have to be implemented and monitored at school level but which also bring with them a diminution in the curricular and assessment autonomy of teachers. A final but crucial change affecting governance is constituted by attempts to reconceptualise the state-maintained school system as a quasi-market system in which schools compete for pupils and the funds which go with them. Thus governors and head teachers must find ways of ensuring that their schools are effectively marketed to potential pupils and their parents and also ensure that the externally available performance indicators (e.g. exam and standard assessment test league tables) are as favourable as possible. In little over a decade between 1986 and the present, school governors in England have moved from being genuine volunteers who participated in the ritual celebrations of school life, supported their head teacher when necessary and showed an interest in the welfare of pupils and teachers, to something much closer to a board of directors, with a wide range of responsibilities ranging from finance to site-maintenance. Furthermore, governor performance, like that of teachers and head teachers, is now monitored by school inspectors.

Educational policy analysis and gendered perspectives

Governance is, as the contributors to this book show, one of many aspects of education reform where gendered and feminist perspectives are both relevant and important. Yet despite a wide range of feminist critiques and explorations of current educational reforms from gendered standpoints, gender analyses have largely failed to permeate the malestream analysis of educational policy (Deem and Brehony 1998). This is so whether one looks at the 'policy turn' (Deem 1996) which has almost completely subsumed the sociology of education in the UK (Shilling 1993; Ball 1994; Halpin and Troyna 1994; Brehony forthcoming), or at the mass of more descriptive policy writing which has appeared in areas like school management. Thus Ranson, reviewing recent trends in theorising educational policy, makes no mention of any feminist work at all, despite the apparent similarities between his project of educating for citizenship in a democratic learning society (Ranson 1995), and the emphasis in my own, Brehony and Heath's work on school governance as a form of gendered, racialised and classed citizenship (Deem *et al.* 1995). He also fails to notice other significant work on education policy by feminists (Arnot and Barton 1992; David 1993; Weiner 1994), and does not acknowledge the debt which educational policy in general owes to feminist analyses. Finally, Ranson does not take account of feminist scholars whose approach to educational policy issues encompasses wide-ranging new themes, such as Kenway's work on marketisation or new technologies (Kenway 1994; Kenway 1995; Kenway 1996).

The failure of malestream educational policy analysts to take feminist scholars seriously is paralleled by the apparent inability of many educational policy researchers to examine educational policy reforms in the wider context of changes in social policy and welfare provision in highly industrialised countries. Educational policy is often seen as a special sub-set of public policy which cannot be understood outside its own policy parameters. Feminist policy researchers in the UK have, in general, been more willing to acknowledge the connections between educational and social policy, both from a social policy perspective (Hallett 1996) and from an educational policy standpoint (David 1993) than have their male counterparts. Feminist scholars have also been quick to grasp the significance of tracing similar developments in reformed social welfare organisations and their cultures across a wide range of public institutions (Itzin and Newman 1995). Perhaps it is the case that feminist researchers focusing on women are the most likely to perceive the different ways in which social and public policy come together. As Dehli (1996) observes, processes like marketisation are dynamic and constantly produced and reproduced and are contextualised and recontextualised in the lived experiences of both those for whom public services are provided and those who provide them. In many instances, the providers and the consumers will be the same people, namely women.

Why be a governor? Some gendered parameters

Lay school governance remains a voluntary activity in England, though it is worth noting the relatively recent change from a notion of a governor as a volunteer in the purely amateur sense of someone who has no particular expertise in the processes or activities of that which they govern, to 'state volunteers' who are still unpaid but who are regarded almost as agents of the central state for the purposes of implementing educational policies and therefore subject to inspection and regulation alongside teachers and heads, as well as being held accountable for school 'failures' (Deem *et al.* 1995). With this change in mind, we were therefore interested in the reasons people gave for becoming governors. While the data did not indicate strong gender differences in motivations, with many women and men indicating that they saw being a governor as an important form of community or voluntary involvement in education in general and children's schooling in particular, there were some sharp divisions between those who saw the task as essentially one of public service and those who had more managerial, political or business-oriented motives (Deem 1994c). The latter were more likely to be men but also more likely to be co-opted governors rather than parents or local authority nominated governors. There was also a considerable gender difference between those who saw school governing, especially in primary schools, as a logical extension of helping teachers and pupils in the classroom (this group were almost exclusively women) and those (mainly men) who saw lay governance as a way of achieving cultural change in education by exposing schools to business practices and processes. The latter group had views and values not inconsistent with late 1980s, and early to mid-1990s, government policy, on the perceived need to move state schools and teachers away from public sector values and practices towards private sector values and organisational forms, thereby injecting elements of business and enterprise cultures. These divisions between those with a business-oriented perspective and a child- or school-oriented view of school governance are illustrated in the following two extracts from interviews:

Male governor (co-opted business person)

I: What arguments do you think you'd like to make, or could be made for the presence of representatives of business and commerce on school governing bodies?

C: I think that what we bring to it is a knowledge and understanding of how this works as a business, because at the end of the day, you can think about this school as a business, and particularly in this Local Management of Schools, when you've got budgeting and you've got to think about where the money goes and what happens to it, you need people with some experience of actually doing that.

Woman parent governor:

I: Were you involved at the school before, were your children at the school before you became a Governor?

D: Yes because my eldest is now coming up 16 and I got onto the Friends of Knighton and then that overlapped with becoming a Governor, so it goes back a way.

I: And, before you were a Governor, did you come into school at all as a helper or anything like that?

D: Yes, reading, art and craft and that sort of thing.

I: So you knew the school pretty well because you've had how many children through altogether?

D: This will be my third.

Though there were a tiny number of women governors who expressed views similar to those of the male businessman, we encountered no men whose involvement in school governance had arisen through helping out in school. A few men drew on their parental status to emphasise the need for schools to be business-like in their approach to pupils whose future depended on high educational standards but this draws on fathering very indirectly. Mothers, by contrast, tended to draw directly on that mothering experience in becoming and serving as school governors.

Though gendered identities as mothers were an important aspect of some women's interests in school governance, there was little evidence that either gender or social class alone were the sole basis for sustained alliances between governors over particular issues, though political affiliation often was so utilised. Indeed, alliances between women governors based on gender were not very apparent in any of our observations of governing bodies at work, though on occasion women governors did back each other up if they suspected that male governors were trying to score gender-related points against them. There was certainly no evidence to suggest that there were secret caucuses of feminist governors meeting in dark smoke-filled rooms and concocting plans to overthrow head teachers. However, so far as male governors were concerned, personal friendships, shared cultural capital and business contacts were all invoked at different times in alliances based, at least implicitly, on masculine gender solidarity and homosociability. This was often apparent when male-dominated sub-committees such as finance or buildings reported their discussions.

In analysing our research data with regard to other ways in which governance might be gendered, we also considered the extent to which women actually participated in governing (effectively the transformation of formal citizenship into substantive citizenship), in which activities they were involved, the compatibility of their own values with those of their governing body and school, and the gendered cultures of governance as form of organised activity. We concluded that in the context of school governance in England, while women, along with a number of other marginalised social groups, have achieved greater formal citizenship through the extension of categories of governors such as greater parental membership, many of them have not so far achieved substantive citizenship on the same terms as men (Deem *et al.* 1995). Thus, at the end of 1992, just over 50 per cent of the governors we studied were women, which was an increase of some 10 per cent from when we began the research in 1988. This is close to the national percentage of female governors and suggests that women are equal with men in relation to the formal exercise of citizenship through school governance. But when we looked at the average participation rates of male and female governors in formal governing body meetings (for more detail on this analysis see Deem *et al.* 1995: 146–8), men intervened much more often than women. In itself this might not be significant, except that important decisions also seemed to be more often brought about by male contributions to debates. Furthermore, in every governing body we researched, there was at least one silent governor, that is one that never spoke in the meetings we observed. The majority of silent governors were women, though it was difficult to discover the reasons for their silences, other than lack of confidence and feelings of exclusion. Nor did many women hold significant office in the governing bodies we studied (only two out of ten were chairs, for example), though we recognise that this is not necessarily typical of all governing bodies.

Gender and markets

Much of the activity of school governors in the restructured educational system in England is now related to the operation of schools in a quasi-market. Though the features of these markets are much debated by theoreticians (Le Grand and Bartlett 1993; Gewirtz *et al.* 1995; Woods and Bagley 1996), the effects of them are felt intensely by school governors over many issues such as exam and test result league tables, school uniform, the state of school buildings, pupil truancy, and recruitment of pupils and staff, all of which form a major part of discussions in governing body meetings (Deem *et al.* 1994). Markets are extensively discussed in the educational and social policy literature but this literature is not without its problems. First, as Kenway and her colleagues have noted, the concept of marketisation includes rather more than parental choice of schools or the restructuring of a particular schooling system (Kenway *et al.* 1993). It involves processes of privatisation (that is, the movement of publicly funded services, staff and resources to private organisations), commercialisation (the introduction of exchange relations into publicly funded organisations), commodification (turning public services like education into commodities) and residualisation (dealing with the effects of choice in public services). Furthermore, as Dehli (1996) notes, a simple binary opposition between markets and state (or, one might add, between public and private) does not encompass the complexities of marketisation.

Markets are not a new phenomenon in industrialised societies – the whole process of industrialisation was predicated on new forms of exchange – but what is relatively new is their extension to public services, in the complex ways indicated by Kenway *et al.* (1993). This means that people respond to social or quasi-market ideas at least partly on the basis of what they already know about markets. They are likely to have extensive experience of them, whether as children consuming snacks, clothing and music (Kenway *et al.* 1996), teenagers entering labour markets or adults purchasing food and housing. In many respects this experience is a gendered one, just as it is also affected by ethnicity, class and disability. Thus, in the UK, women are less likely than men to have significant economic capital (even in full-time employment, they are likely to receive up to 30 per cent less pay than men), and are frequently employed in gender-segregated parts of the labour market. Thus women are often differently positioned in relation to market discourses and practices as compared with men. In addition, men's experience of markets, particularly those men in professional and executive jobs, is often to do with their employment, both in connection with the sale of their labour power and the buying and selling of commodities and services at work, or with their leisure time where consumption is a major facet of male sport and leisure. Conversely, women are more likely to have experience of household consumption, both on their own behalf and on behalf of others. Thus women and men may come to school governance and educational markets with very different prior experiences of markets, consumption and production.

In our research we found some indication that concepts of social or quasi-markets and running schools as quasi-businesses sat more uneasily (and differently) within women's experiences as compared with men's experiences. Women governors tended to feel more unhappy than men governors when staff were made redundant, seeing the human side of things rather than the economic rationale for job losses: 'I find it really difficult to come to decisions which affect staff's and children's lives; it cannot be right to make staff redundant who are competent and contributing to school' (female parent governor after redundancies were discussed in her governing body meeting). Some women governors also did not see women as having the necessary expertise to make 'hard' decisions:

> when you're faced with things like difficult budgetary situations, potential
> redundancies, staff handling issues, to expect … that the honourable

> housewife, if it's a housewife who hasn't had a career before . . . whether they can actually cope with that without a lot of guidance and support. And it's so easy to make the wrong decision.
>
> (Female LEA governor, primary school)

Men also tended to parade their experiences in the workplace at governing body meetings and in interviews, stressing their heavy management responsibilities, the size of the budgets they handled or the number of staff for whom they were responsible, in a way not usually evident amongst women, even those who had such experiences.

While there is no more general evidence outside the confines of this study about whether there is a gender dimension to those who express scepticism about market and business discourses, it is worth noting that in the UK, many women in part- or full-time semi-skilled work are employed in the retail sector, from which have come many of the models of business culture which public sector institutions are supposed to emulate (Maidment and Thompson 1993). Thus more women than men may have direct experience of such practices in their everyday work, including some of the negative consequences of things like extended opening hours. The endeavours to normalise business cultures and values may please some head teachers of schools (Gewirtz *et al.* 1995) but may well make many mothers very uneasy, especially if they value their children's well-being and development as much as their future capacity to become exam-passing commodities in the schooling system.

Furthermore, so far as many of the women governors we studied were concerned, the normalising of business and market discourses was something which exerted gendered powers of social inclusion and exclusion. Thus women were less often members of finance committees than male governors as illustrated in Figure 10.1.

Though some of our case study governing bodies had a dazzling array of sub-committees, in practice, finance sub-committees were usually the key committee, examining monthly budget projections and out-turns and making recommendations to the main governing body about financial decisions (on which other decisions like staffing or books often rested). Thus the increased emphasis on money and markets in schooling may have served to marginalise precisely some of the new constituencies of governors, like mothers, that the education reforms have brought into governing bodies.

Governors: chief executives or volunteers?

In their study of markets, choice and schools, Gewirtz and her colleagues note that school managers experience a form of bilingualism in adopting new managerial discourses while still remaining positioned in other discourses (Gewirtz *et al.* 1995). Research on women managers suggests that trilingualism rather than bilingualism is more common (Ozga 1993; Tanton 1994; Deem and Ozga 1997), as women with managerial positions in education come to terms with

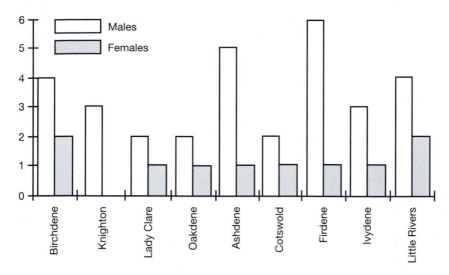

Figure 10.1 Gender composition of finance sub-committees

discourses of managerialism, gender relations and markets, as well as those discourses linked more centrally to schooling. Itzin and Newman's book on cultural change in public sector organisations indicates some of the ways in which such organisations in the UK are changing. Women may interpret and experience those changes in many different ways (Itzin and Newman 1995).

Of course, governors are not usually acting as managers in the accepted sense of someone with day-to-day responsibilities for managing other workers. In our study it was clear that they did not really manage teaching and learning; this was an area which all of our governors shied away from (Brehony and Deem 1995). One of the most hard-fought struggles which we witnessed in our research was that of boundary maintenance between head teachers and governors, where head teachers expected and wanted to keep day-to-day control over their school, with governors being responsible only for setting the policy parameters. In practice this division was difficult to police and there is a very clear sense in which lay governors are engaged in surveillance or regulation of those who work in schools. We found many male governors, especially those with professional and managerial jobs, whether ostensibly political representatives, fathers of current pupils or business people, actively wanted to exercise this surveillance and were often very enthusiastic about overseeing building maintenance, helping organise the school's finances or suggesting new ways of marketing the school to prospective pupils and parents. This was sometimes regardless of whether they actually had specific relevant expertise. Women governors, on the other hand, unless they had specific expertise in a field like accountancy or personnel management, often exercised their governance responsibilities in other ways, through participating in school trips, assisting in classes, through sub-committees for pupil welfare and behaviour, or curriculum. Indeed, the membership of sub-committees and working groups of our ten governing bodies revealed some very interesting gender patterns, with more men than women in membership of such sub-groups even on governing bodies where more than half the members were women (see Figure 10.2).

The 1988 Education Reform Act transferred considerable financial

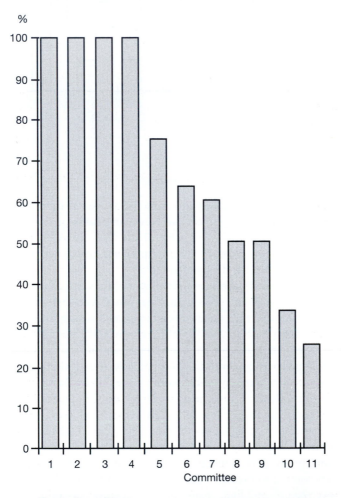

Key to Committees
1: Co-ordinating committee
2: Finance
3: Marketing
4: Sex education
5: Sites and Buildings
6: Staffing

7: Admissions Appeals and Complaints
8: Appointments and recruitment
9: Suspensions and exclusions
10: Curriculum
11: School visits

Figure 10.2 Percentage of governor sub-committees with a male majority

responsibilities (including *de facto* hiring and firing powers over teachers) to schools and placed heavy emphasis on parent power, governor and head teacher-led local management, and parental choice of schools. It was the aftermath of the 1988 Act which gave rise to the often complex and bureaucratic webs of sub-committees and working groups established by many governing bodies (Baginsky *et al.* 1991) and which sent schools and heads searching for business expertise on their governing bodies, something suggested by the 1986 Education Act when widening the composition of school governing bodies.

Thus while the 1986 Education Act opened up governance to a wider social group, the requirements of market discourses and financial management consequent on the 1988 Reform Act effectively reduced the scope available to those without business or political/trade union expertise. It is not being suggested here that women governors are necessarily less competent than men at financial management. Pahl's work shows that many women living with male partners already have extensive experience of running household budgets (Pahl 1983, 1989, 1990). Rather, it is argued that the actual financial skills and knowledge of women governors were sometimes under-valued, both by male governors and by women themselves, as we saw in the earlier quotation about housewives and financial decisions.

Furthermore, it was clear that mothers often saw the task of governance as one in which they got involved with improving individual educational experiences, not an activity in which they helped schools and head teachers to manage their budgets, 'sell' their school to prospective pupils and their parents or engage in hiring and firing of staff. While this view was not exclusive to women, the following extracts illustrate some typical male/female polarisations around this issue:

> I think one of the great problems with people in schools . . . they're in a local world and believe that that's the most important thing in the world is teaching. It may be, but I happen not to agree with them, but there you are. Do you see what I mean? They have a little world in which they live and in which they believe very firmly that the rest of the world should fit in with as little interference as necessary . . . You can't sack teachers readily, they know that, and they feel that they are in a cloistered community anyway . . . Well this, at the end of the day, is a business.
>
> (Male, Chair of Finance sub-committee, secondary school)

> I was thinking about the Curriculum meeting last week. Somebody like [Marianne Shepherd] does such a superb job with working out this scheme that there was nothing else that we can do than to say, 'That is wonderful. Go ahead with it.' If the school was not running efficiently, I feel we'd be a lot more effective in actually doing something, and I would feel I would have to shout, if I was not happy with things, I would feel I had to say, 'Now look here, this will not do. This is not doing the best for the children in the community.' But because I feel it is in fact running extremely well, under

difficult circumstances, I'm very happy just to go along with what's put forward, and I usually agree with what's been put forward.

(Female, Chair of Curriculum sub-committee, secondary school)

Gendered organisational cultures and 'new managerialism'

Recent contributions to debates about gender and organisational cultures have focused either on feminist alternatives to bureaucracies or on the intricate ways in which gender and sexuality inform organisational practices (Ferguson 1984; Ramsay and Parker 1992; Savage and Witz 1992; Adkins 1995). Two important issues in examining notions of gendered governance are the extent to which governing bodies adopt bureaucratic organisational practices and whether they make use of what Clarke and others have called the 'new managerialism', where emphasis is placed on efficiency, effectiveness, value for money, and performance and target-oriented working styles (Clarke *et al.* 1994). 'New managerialism' is an ideology that appeals, albeit in different ways, to both Left and Right (Taylor-Gooby and Lawson 1993a, 1993b). It is characterised by an emphasis on markets, a mixture of public and private welfare provision and funding, decentralisation, the deregulation of employment relationships, and new forms of accountability. Its vocabulary is rich with reference to customers, producers, consumers, empowerment, charters, excellence and performance indicators.

School governing bodies are a particularly interesting form of organising. They are neither a completely independent organisational form, being more or less loosely coupled to the school for which they are responsible (Orton and Weick 1990), nor are they an organisation that has a permanent existence. Indeed, their evanescence is one of the characteristics which makes them distinctive in organisational terms. Given these features, it might be expected that governing bodies would take on some of the cultural characteristics of post-modern rather than modern organisations, with an absence of hierarchies, a strong emphasis on facilitation rather than management, networks rather than tiers of authority, a flexible and non-rule bound approach, and a decentred structure.

Nothing could be further from the actual situation we found in our research. Governing bodies in England have surrounded themselves with all the trappings of classic trade union, local government and private corporation bureaucracies, including hierarchies, a saturation of rituals about formal procedures, and little or no flexibility. Though some women have extensive experience of such organisational forms, many do not and hence it is quite easy for governing bodies to by-pass or marginalise the skills and experiences of mothers, women teachers, women with experience of voluntary organisations and so on, in favour of those (usually but not invariably, men) who have experience of local politics, business organisations or trade union activity. This tendency is manifested in the allocations of women and men governors to sub-committees and working groups. It is also apparent in the differential concerns of mothers (but not fathers) for the emotional and affective aspects of education as compared to the abstraction of academic standards or the marketing and finances of schooling. There is also the likelihood that mothers will be more involved than fathers in getting to know the staff and children in their school. Finally, these differences are evident in the participation of male and female governors in formal meetings and in the marginalisation of some female governing body clerks as little more than domestic servants. It was not accidental that women were prominent amongst the minority of governors we identified in our research as 'silent', who played no verbal part in formal meetings. Yet some of those 'silent' women governors, especially in primary schools, were amongst those who came into school frequently and who were very important to the welfare of the institution on a daily basis (Deem 1994b).

Newman, in a paper which develops some very exciting ideas about cultural change, gender and public sector organisations, suggests that there are three different types of cultural forms currently in existence in this sector (Newman 1995). There is what she calls the traditional form, with specialised divisions of labour and formal hierarchies and gendered/sexualised sets of meanings and values, and then the competitive organisation, which emphasises 'macho management', cost-cutting, fast decision-making, informal hierarchies and a hetero-sexual culture. Finally, there is the transformational organisation, where team-work, communication skills, empowerment and 'feminine' management skills are utilised and valued. School governing bodies, as we observed them, seemed to have most of the elements of the traditional model, interspersed with elements of the competitive but few elements, if any, of the transformational form. I disagree with Newman (1995) about the links between 'new managerialism' and the transformational form, since education in England is a model *par excellence* of the 'new managerialism' in action, yet has almost no signs of the transformational form, despite the arguments of some writers on total quality management (Murgatroyd and Morgan 1993). However, the collection in which Newman's article appears (Itzin and Newman 1995) does not deal at all with educational institutions and it is possible that the different dynamics of education as a service have affected the interplay of 'new managerialism' with forms of organisational culture, in ways which are distinct from those of other spheres of local government or the health service. From what we have seen in our research, there seems little scope in the English system of school governance for many women's distinctive values, ways of doing things and values to emerge or to shape what happens. It is hard to escape the view that while ideas about markets and individual and organisational competitiveness are part of the dominant discourses about education, this will remain the case.

Conclusion

In this chapter I have suggested some ways in which the governance of reformed schools in England displays evidence of engendered processes. This evidence relates not simply to the gender composition of governing bodies but to the discourses, ideologies, governing and organisational practices which make up the business of governing schools. Gender is as frequently used as a basis for exclusion as it is for inclusion. Though school governance as an organisational mode is an unusual one because of its evanescent qualities, and though the activities of governors are not management as conventionally described, nevertheless examining the organisational cultures of school governing bodies involved in management of schools is a useful and important exercise which allows us to see the extent to which gendered practices and ideas have permeated those cultures. The symbol of the education quasi-market has created a variety of different responses both from school governors as individuals and whole governing bodies (Deem *et al.* 1994; Gewirtz *et al.* 1995), and some of those responses are undoubtedly gendered. Similarly finance, both as a symbol and as a sphere of organisational practice, does not seem to have been something (in our research sites at least) which has been as attractive to women governors as to male governors.

This analysis also extends to values. Values about markets, business, enterprise, efficient management, individualism and competition sit uneasily with those which emphasise public service on the basis of need, social justice, collective ideas, human development of the aesthetic and the emotional as well as the cognitive. Though resistance to the former kinds of values have certainly not been confined to one gender, there is some indication that mothers, and women teachers, are amongst those who resist them most strongly, though we should not ignore the differences that class, cultural capital, political affiliation and ethnicity make to such positioning. In respect of organisational practices, our research data show that school governors have become involved in activities which are allocated at least partially on the basis of gender and which limit the extent of women's participation in active citizenship as manifested in the governing of schools.

Despite the positioning of governing bodies in conditions of late or post-modernity, there is not much indication that the organisational practices of those bodies we studied have changed very much from those which have a closer fit with modernity. The bureaucratic, formal, hierarchical organisational structures, which are a legacy of local authorities, have remained in place. However, a shift to different organisational practices more in keeping with the conditions of post-modernity (for example, the dominance of information structures over other kinds of structures, time–space compression, the heightened significance of culture and so on) would benefit and widen the participation of women governors and those from minority groups. Ironically such organisational changes are taking place in those very businesses and other private sector organisations (Peters and Austin 1985; Peters 1989; Sentell 1989; Handy 1995a, 1995b) which schools and governing bodies are supposed to emulate. The models of business which governing bodies in England are following are those more suited to modernity than post-modernity and do not have the advantages for women that alternative organisational practices and models might have (Ferguson 1984; Ramsay and Parker 1992; Itzin and Newman 1995). If future phases of educational reform genuinely want to widen the basis of lay involvement in the administration and management of schooling, then the gendering of organisational symbols, values and practices will need to be taken much more seriously than hitherto or the discourses of governance will remain heavily gendered, itself an important cultural message to school students. At the same time women governors themselves will need to use the ambiguities and contradictions of discourses about markets, education reform and school governance, to open up new spaces for themselves and for the protection of girls' varied interests in schools, as the interests of boys seem once more about to take centre stage.

Note

1 The chapter is based on a paper first presented at the American Educational Research Association Conference, New York, April 1996

References

Adkins, L. (1995) *Gendered Work: Sexuality, Family and the Labour Market*, Buckingham: Open University Press.

Arnot, M. and Barton, L. (eds) (1992) *Voicing Concerns*, Wallingford, Triangle.

Arnot, M., Raab, C. and Munn, P. (1996) 'Devolved management: variations of response in Scottish school boards', in C. Pole and R. Chawla-Duggan (eds) *Reshaping Education in the 1990s: Perspectives on Secondary Schooling*, London: Falmer Press, pp. 89–104.

Baginsky, M. *et al.* (1991) *Towards Effective Partnerships in School Governance*, Slough: National Foundation for Educational Research.

Ball, S. J. (1994) 'Some reflections on policy theory: a brief response to Hatcher and Troyna', *Journal of Education Policy* 9, 2: 171–82.

Brehony, K. J. (forthcoming) 'Developments in the sociology of education 1950–1993: from structural functionalism to policy sociology', in R. Burgess (ed.) *Developments in Sociology*, London: UCL Press.

Brehony, K. J. and Deem, R. (1995) 'School governing bodies: reshaping education in their own image', *Sociological Review* 43, 1: 79–99.

Brown, S. (1996) 'Educational change in the United Kingdom: a North South divide', in C. Pole and R. Chawla-Duggan (eds) *Reshaping Education in the 1990s: Perspectives on Secondary Schooling*, London: Falmer Press. 149–63.

Clarke, J., Cochrane, A. and McLaughlin, E. (eds) (1994) *Managing Social Policy*, London: Sage.

David, M.E. (1993) *Parents, Gender and Education Reform*, Cambridge: Polity Press.

Deem, R. (1994a) 'Free marketeers or good citizens? Education policy and lay participation in the administration of schools', *British Journal of Educational Studies* 42, 1: 23–37.

—— (1994b) 'Researching the locally powerful; a study of school governance', in G. Walford (ed.) *Researching the Powerful in Education*, London: University College London Press, pp. 151–73.

—— (1994c) 'School governing bodies – public concerns or private interests?', in D. Scott (ed.) *Accountability and Control in Educational Settings*, London: Cassell, pp. 58–72.

—— (1996) 'Border territories: a journey through sociology, education and women's studies', *British Journal of Sociology of Education* 17, 1: 5–19.

Deem, R. and Brehony, K.J. (forthcoming) 'Educational policy making and analysis', in S. Brown, B. Moon and M. Ben-Peretz (eds) *International Encyclopaedic Dictionary of Education*, London: Routledge.

Deem, R. and Ozga, J. (1997) 'Women managing for diversity in a post modern world', in C. Marshall (ed.) *Feminist Critical Policy Analysis: A Perspective from Post Secondary Education*, London and New York: Falmer, pp. 25–40.

Deem, R., Brehony, K.J. and Heath, S. (1994) 'Governors, schools and the miasma of the market', *British Educational Research Journal* 20, 5: 535–49.

—— (1995) *Active Citizenship and the Governing of Schools*, Buckingham: Open University Press.

Dehli, K. (1996) 'Between market and state? Modalities of power and difference in the marketization of education', paper presented to the American Educational Research Association annual conference, New York, April.

Evans, T. (1988) *A Gender Agenda: A Sociological Study of Teachers, Parents and Pupils in their Primary Schools*, Sydney: Allen and Unwin.

Ferguson, K. (1984) *The Feminist Case Against Bureaucracy*, Philadelphia: Temple University Press.

Gewirtz, S., Ball, S. and Bowe, R. (1995) *Markets, Choice and Equity in Education*, Buckingham: Open University Press.

Hallett, C. (ed.) (1996) *Women and Social Policy*, Hemel Hempstead: Harvester Wheatsheaf.

Halpin, D. and Troyna, B. (eds) (1994) *Researching Education Policy*, London: Falmer.

Handy, C. (1995a) *Beyond Certainty: The Changing Worlds of Organisations*, London: Hutchinson.

—— (1995b) *The Empty Raincoat: Making Sense of the Future*, London: Arrow Books.

Itzin, C. and Newman, J. (eds) (1995) *Gender, Culture and Organisational Change*, London: Routledge.

Kenway, J. (ed.) (1994) *Economising Education: The Post-Fordist Directions*, Victoria: Deakin University Press.

—— (ed.) (1995) *Marketing Education: Some Critical Issues*, Geelong: Deakin University Press.

—— (1996). 'The Information Superhighway and post modernity: the social promise and the social price', *Comparative Education* 32, 2: 217–31.

Kenway, J., Bigum, C. and Fitzclarence, L. (1993) 'Marketing education in the post modern age', *Journal of Education Policy* 8, 2: 105–22.

Kenway, J. *et al.* (1996) 'Changing education: consumer contexts, cultures and kids', paper presented to the American Educational Research Association annual conference, New York, April.

Keys, W. and Fernandes, C. (1990) *A Survey of School Governing Bodies*, Slough: National Foundation for Educational Research.

Le Grand, J. and Bartlett, W. (eds) (1993) *Quasi-Markets and Social Policy*, London: Macmillan.

McKeown, P., Donnelly, C. and Osborne, R. (1996) 'School governing bodies in Northern Ireland: responses to local management of schools', in C. Pole and R. Chawla-Duggan (eds) *Reshaping Education in the 1990s: Perspectives on Secondary Schooling*, London: Falmer Press, pp. 71–88.

Maidment, R. and Thompson, G. (eds) (1993) *Managing the United Kingdom*, London: Sage.

Murgatroyd, S. and Morgan C. (1993) *Total Quality Management and the School*, Milton Keynes: Open University Press.

Newman, J. (1995) 'Gender, and cultural change', in C. Itzin and J. Newman, (eds) *Gender, Culture and Organisational Change*, London: Routledge, pp. 11–29.

Orton, J.D. and Weick, K.E. (1990) 'Loosely coupled systems: a reconceptualization', *Academy of Management Review* 15, 2: 203–23.

Ozga, J. (1993) *Women in Educational Management*, Milton Keynes: Open University Press.

Pahl, J. (1983) 'The control and allocation of money and the structuring of inequality in marriage', *Sociological Review* 31, 2: 237–62.

—— (1989) *Money and Marriage*, London: Macmillan.

—— (1990) 'Household spending, personal spending and the control of money in marriage', *Sociology* 24, 1: 119–38.

Peters, T. (1989) *Thriving on Chaos*, London: Pan Books.

Peters, T. and Austin, N. (1985) *A Passion for Excellence*, Glasgow: Collins.

Ramsay, K. and Parker, M. (1992) 'Gender, bureaucracy and organisational culture', in M. Savage and A. Witz (eds) *Gender and Bureaucracy*, Oxford: Blackwell.

Ranson, S. (1995) 'Theorising educational policy', *Journal of Educational Policy* 10, 4: 427–48.

Savage, M. and Witz, A. (eds) (1992) *Gender and Bureaucracy*, Sociological Review Monographs, Oxford: Blackwell.

Sentell, G. D. (1989) 'Creating the quality management system: change and organizational culture', *Tappi Journal* 72: 275–86.

Shilling, C. (1993) 'The demise of sociology of education in Britain?', *British Journal of Sociology of Education* 14, 1: 105–12.

Tanton, M. (ed.) (1994) *Women in Management: A Developing Presence*, London: Routledge.

Taylor-Gooby, P. and Lawson, R. (eds) (1993a) *Markets and Managers*, Milton Keynes: Open University Press.

—— (1993b) 'Where we go from here: the new order in welfare', in P. Taylor-Gooby and R. Lawson (eds) *Markets and Managers*, Buckingham: Open University Press, pp. 132–49.

Weiner, G. (1994) *Feminisms in Education*, Milton Keynes, Open University Press.

Woods, P.A. and Bagley, C. (1996) 'Market elements in a public service: an analytical model for studying educational policy', *Journal of Education Policy* 11, 6: 641–53.

11 Women head teachers in Northern Ireland

Teresa Rees, Philip Heaton and
Lyn McBriar

Introduction

The new managerialism introduced into schools in the UK in the 1980s and 1990s impacted significantly upon the everyday lives of those who work in schools and members of governing bodies. The shift towards the Local Management of Schools (LMS) enshrined in the 1988 *Education Reform Act*[1] altered in particular the roles of both head teachers and those who chair governing boards. Head teachers are now expected to have more responsibility for financial management and for marketing their school in their local communities, to attract pupils, governors and sponsorship. Team-leading experience and new technology skills are increasingly an advantage for an aspiring head teacher. Chairs of governing bodies now play a more significant role in staff selection processes. What effect are these changes likely to have on the gender balance of head teachers?

It is particularly pertinent to pose this question in the context of Northern Ireland. Here, while many educational reforms that have been introduced in Britain also pertain, including LMS and changes in the role of governing bodies (see McKeown *et al.* 1996), others do not. Parental choice for secondary schooling operates within the context of a selective system organised by the 11+ examination. A range of employing authorities are responsible for the provision of schools, many of which are of specific religious denominations. Spatial configurations of political and religious affiliation impact upon school choice. One of the consequences of these patterns of provision is the survival of some single-sex grammar and 'secondary' schools. This is a major contributor to the fact that the proportion of female heads and deputy heads of schools for 11–18 year olds in Northern Ireland is higher than that in Scotland, or England and Wales (see below).

The concepts of equal opportunity and fair employment have of course a special resonance in Northern Ireland (see McLaughlin and Quirk 1996). The 1975 and 1989 Fair Employment Acts set the framework which made discrimination on the grounds of religion illegal. This is monitored by the Fair Employment Commission in the same way that the Equal Opportunities Commission in Northern Ireland reviews sex discrimination. The Standing Advisory Commission on Human Rights (SACHR) was set up to advise the Secretary of State on the adequacy and effectiveness of the law preventing discrimination. Revised government guidelines on Policy Appraisal and Fair Treatment (PAFT) came into effect in Northern Ireland in January 1994.[2] They address the consideration which should be given to equality dimensions of gender, ethnicity, disability, age and sexual orientation in the design and delivery of policies. Although similar guidelines also exist in the rest of the UK, PAFT has a higher profile in Northern Ireland than elsewhere and this means the issue of fair treatment is more likely to be a live one in policy debates (see Osborne *et al.* 1996).

While awareness of the issue of discrimination on the grounds of religion is clearly finely tuned in Northern Ireland, that on the grounds of gender is less developed. Female economic activity rates have traditionally been low compared with Britain and the pay gap between women and men is wider. Despite a high staying-on rate of both males and females in education and an enviable record on educational attainment, there are relatively few women in top managerial positions. The number of women head teachers therefore is something of an exception to the more general pattern of gender segregation in the labour market.

The 1990s have been characterised by a series of special initiatives in Northern Ireland aimed at enhancing the role of women in the labour market. These include Opportunity 2000, led by Business in the Community and backed by the government which invites employers to set themselves targets on women in management positions to achieve by the millennium (see Business in the Community 1996). More recently, the Fair Play initiative has been launched: this consists of a consortia of public and private sector employers committed to enhancing the role of women in work both qualitatively and quantitatively.[3] The Equal Opportunities Commission for Northern Ireland is consulting with a range of organisations with a view to making proposals to amend the sex discrimination legislation: this would include the imposition of a statutory obligation on employers and educational and training bodies to take positive action measures to address equality of opportunity. In response to Opportunity 2000, the Department of Education Northern Ireland (DENI) launched an Action Plan on Women's Issues in 1993 which is updated annually. One of its priorities is to reduce the under-representation of women at head teacher and deputy head teacher level – posts known in Northern Ireland as Principal and Vice Principal.

As part of its commitment to Opportunity 2000, DENI identified as a priority for action the reduction of the under-representation of women at Principal and Vice Principal level in Northern Ireland schools of all ages. In 1995, the Department commissioned a study to identify the barriers – actual or perceived – to women's progression to higher posts so that the employing authorities could devise appropriate action plans for change.[4]

This chapter gives an account of some of the findings of that study and discusses the feasibility of policy changes that might enhance the number of women in Principal posts. It begins with a 'political arithmetic' of school Principals across the education sectors in Northern Ireland. It then goes on to describe the results of study, derived *inter alia* from interviews and focus groups with Principals and questionnaire surveys of teachers and school governors. In essence the chapter argues that gender remains a crucially significant determinant of who is deemed to be appropriate to be Principal of which kind of school. Moreover, the effects of LMS may well act as a deterrent for many women seeking promotion, not because of the demands of the job but because some of the ways in which the nature of the job has changed make it less acceptable for women to undertake it within the context of Northern Ireland society. This includes the additional time commitment for management and the more public role. It will be necessary to counteract some of the effects of the educational reforms on the role of the Principal and alter the procedures by which Principals are selected to reduce the impact of gender on who is appointed in future.

School Principals in Northern Ireland: a political arithmetic

In 1998, women constituted 71.0 per cent of all teachers (of nursery, primary, secondary, special and grammar schools) but held only 41.9 per cent of Principal positions and 57.5 per cent of Vice Principal posts (figures from DENI). The proportion of primary school Principals who are women in Northern Ireland is similar to that in the rest of the UK (see Table 11.1). However, the proportion of female Principals and Vice Principals of schools for 11–18 year olds (secondary

Table 11.1 School Principals and Vice Principals in N. Ireland, Scotland, England and Wales, 1996–97

Type	Female (%)	
	Principals	Deputy Principals
Primary		
N. Ireland	45.5	68.3
Scotland	72.6	88.6
England and Wales	53.4	70.4
(Wales)	(47.3)	(69.1)
Secondary		
N.Ireland	29.3	41.0
Scotland	7.0	13.0
England and Wales	24.1	34.4
(Wales)	(11.8)	(30.5)

Sources: Calculated from figures supplied by Department of Education, Northern Ireland, Department for Education and Employment (1997) *Statistics of Education: Teachers, England and Wales, 1997 Edition* London: Stationery Office (Table 12.20); Scottish Office (1997) *Summary Results of the 1996 School Census* Edn/B1/1997/3 Edinburgh: Scottish Office Education and Industry Division (Tables 8 and 16); Welsh Office (1998) *Statistics of Education and Training: Schools,* Cardiff: Welsh Office (Table 12.6.1).

Note: Figures for primary include nursery schools. Figures for secondary include special schools and grammar combined), although less than a third, is much higher than in the rest of the UK. This is in part a result of the preponderance of single sex schools in the Province. The introduction of the co-educational comprehensive system in Britain led to a decline in the single sex school and with it, a drop in the number of female heads.

The employing authorities for teachers in Northern Ireland comprise the five Education and Library Boards, the Council for Catholic Maintained Schools (CCMS), the Northern Ireland Council for Integrated Education (NICIE) and the voluntary grammar school sector, all of whom have taken steps to improve the efficiency of promotion and selection procedures in recent years (see DENI 1999: 29–30). These include introducing clear definitions of appointment scheme guidelines and accompanying guidance notes, providing appropriate sample job specifications for various levels of post and using advisers, assessors and Personnel Department staff to supply professional, technical and procedural advice. In addition, the need to offer equal opportunities training to governors and for governors to take up that training has been recognised by the employing authorities: greater in-house resources have been made available to address this issue. Finally and crucially, the 'continuous service' short-listing criterion for senior level posts, which operated in CCMS, and which clearly discriminated against teachers who took a career break, has been revised.

Table 11.2 shows a gender breakdown of teaching staff in N. Ireland by type and denomination of school at May 1996. Women constitute well over two-thirds of all teachers and make up the majority in every sector. The division between the age groups of pupils is particularly stark, with no male nursery teachers and relatively few in the primary sector.

The proportion of women Principals and deputies by type of school in 1998 is shown in Table 11.3. This indicates how there are no male Principals in nursery

Table 11.2 Teaching staff in Northern Ireland, by sex and school type, 1996

	Nursery		Special		Primary		Secondary		Grammar		Total
	F	M	F	M	F	M	F	M	F	M	
Controlled	119	0	519	115	3642	652	1684	1167	526	388	8812
Voluntary	0	0	0	0	0	0	0	0	1556	1443	2999
RC Maintained	52	0	27	11	3345	980	1792	1431	0	0	7638
Other Maintained	0	0	25	5	54	7	0	0	0	0	91
Controlled Integrated	0	0	0	0	23	0	13	10	0	0	46
Grant Maintained Integrated	0	0	0	0	98	23	129	70	0	0	320
Totals	171	0	571	131	7162	1662	3618	2678	2082	1831	19906

Source: DENI (1999)

Table 11.3 School Principals and Vice Principals in N. Ireland by sex, 1998

Type	Male	Female	Total	% Female
Nursery				
Principal	0	90	90	100.0
Vice Principal	–		–	–
Primary				
Principal	538	359	897	40.0
Vice Principal	229	493	722	68.3
Secondary				
Principal	125	34	159	21.4
Vice Principal	157	100	257	38.9
Special				
Principal	20	29	49	59.2
Vice Principal	16	43	59	72.9
Grammar				
Principal	53	19	72	26.4
Vice Principal	103	49	152	32.2
Total				
Principal	736	531	1,267	41.9
Vice Principal	505	685	1,190	57.6

Source: Calculated from figures supplied by Department of Education, Northern Ireland.

schools (unsurprisingly, given the picture in Table 11.2). In primary schools, where there are considerably more female than male teachers employed, three out of five Principals are male. Moreover, men are 2.5 to 3 times more likely than women to be the Principal of a secondary or grammar school. Women constitute 21.4 per cent of secondary school Principals and 26.4 per cent of grammar school heads (23 per cent altogether).

Data from the employing authorities show that men are substantially more likely than women to apply for the post of Principal. However, when women do apply, they enjoy a higher success rate (DENI 1999: 11). The number of appointments at Principal and Vice Principal level in the 1992–4 period for Area Board and CCMS schools of all types is shown in Table 11.4. A particular point of interest here is the fact that women are more likely to apply if a post is re-advertised. This relates to data presented later in the chapter on women's atti-tudes to promotion. The table also shows that women are far more likely to reach Vice Principal than Principal level in both primary and secondary level schools: this, it appears, is the 'glass ceiling' (Hall 1996) for women in teaching in Northern Ireland.

The post-11 schools which have a woman Principal are marginally more likely to be grammar than secondary, to be girls-only, to be in a rural area and to be small. Very large schools, (of 1,100 pupils plus) are almost six times more likely to have a male than a female Principal.

Table 11.4 Appointments at Principal and Vice Principal level, 1992–94, by sex (Area Boards and CCMS)

Year	Principals				Vice Principals			
	Female		Male		Female		Male	
	No.	%	No.	%	No.	%	No.	%
1992	42	30	62	60	54	62*	33	38
1993	37	42*	51	58	52	59*	36	41
1994	35	43*	47	57	47	58*	34	42

Source: DENI (1999)

Notes:
a.   Data unavailable for North Eastern Library Board.
b.   * denotes appointments include re-advertisements.

The study

The study of barriers to women's progression conducted for DENI used a variety of methods and generated a considerable volume of data, only some of which are reported on here (see DENI 1999 for an account of the whole project). The methods included a questionnaire survey of a statistically representative sample of 1,739 teachers at all levels (male and female) (a response rate of 51 per cent); eleven focus group interviews comprising Principals, Vice Principals, and Assistant Teachers (seven all-female, four all-male); twelve work diaries completed by male and female Principals and Vice Principals over a period of four weeks giving an account of their work and non-work activities; and in-depth interviews with a theoretically sampled group of ten women Principals in different sectors (four primary, three grammar and three secondary), with various levels of experience, to explore their work and non-work histories and their perceptions of gender imbalance in senior positions. We also conducted a survey of 585 school governors (a response rate of 41 per cent) who had been involved in at least one prescribed post appointment during the previous three years. Some of them were also invited to take part in scenario-writing exercises designed to elicit constructs germane to decision-making on appointments. Finally, we consulted with a wide range of individuals in the crowded playing field of actors involved in the provision of education in Northern Ireland, such as representatives of the employing authorities and the recognised trade unions.

The results reported on here focus on two broad and important sets of questions. What is the perceived impact of LMS on the role of the Principal, and how might this affect the future gender balance of incumbents of this role? Second, how has LMS affected the role of governor in the selection process, and what are the implications of this for the impact of gender on who is appointed to Principal posts? These are considered in turn.

The role of Principal

The role of the Principal has changed considerably since the advent of LMS, in the view of our respondents (see also Hall *et al.* 1986; Hall 1993). It is viewed now as being much more akin to that of a manager than a teacher. While the Principals themselves, teachers and governors shared some common views about the changing role, there were also some misconceptions held by teachers as to what governors look for in an aspiring head to fill the posts.

Principals' views

The ten women Principals interviewed in-depth were asked to describe the characteristics of a successful Principal post-LMS. Their responses included traditional characteristics for a head teacher such as integrity, empathy with children, staff and parents, good record keeping, delegation skills, self-belief and 'an ability to switch off when things go wrong'. However, those reported by the Principals which reflect the changing role in particular included the following:

- ability to promote the school in the local community, by entering competitions, inviting local people/past pupils to prize giving, and seeking positive publicity wherever possible;
- ability to look outside the education sector for role models, through networking with the business community and establishing education/business partnerships;
- team-working and motivation skills – being able to maximise the resources of everyone in the school (pupils, teachers and non-teaching staff).

In other words, there is now more of an emphasis on external relations and on human resource management, including delegation of some of the additional responsibilities. Daily responsibilities have become more diverse and include additional emphasis on activities such as: administration; financial management (including budgets); marketing and promotion; staff management, including handling staff cuts where necessary; an understanding of information technologies (IT); health and safety; and maintenance and managing sub-contracts (for example, for the school canteen).

In order to fulfil the role of Principal, there was a general view that a candidate should be someone who has been responsible for a 'whole school policy' in their previous post: either through school committee work, performing well at staff meetings or being in career development posts. They spoke too of the need to be 'highly visible'.

The Principal's role was experienced as 'difficult' because:

- one has to be totally committed and be fully involved in everything;
- it can be lonely;

- one needs to manage parents carefully;
- one is constantly on call (usually for parents).

These responsibilities have implications for the time needed to fulfil the role adequately. Long hours are seen as unavoidable. The majority of the Principals we interviewed echoed the words of one who described herself as being 'on call 24 hours a day – literally'. They, along with the majority of Principals who completed diaries for us, reported that they always work in the evenings and most also work at weekends. Much of this 'out-of-school hours' work comprises administrative tasks which they have been unable to complete during normal working hours.

The changes brought about as a result of LMS appear to have added to the Principals' workload in three ways. There were more information requirements: this led to Principals seeking to manage new IT themselves as well as having to develop an IT strategy for the school. For many this involved developing new understanding as well as skills. Second, there were new financial management responsibilities. Some managed to delegate these at a day-to-day level. Finally, the role had become more public as a result of the need to develop closer links with employers and to market the school to parents. It was more necessary to attend functions and meetings, and to network within the local community.

The Principals described how it was the increased volume and diversity of work, rather than its complexity which caused them concern. This impacted upon the amount of time they needed to spend on work and work-related tasks. The issue of time is of crucial importance given that, as the work diaries showed, women Principals spend far more hours on domestic responsibilities than their male peers (see also Cunnison, 1994 on women teachers and family constraints).

Several female diary keepers referred to their husbands 'helping' them with cooking and shopping, but only if they were ill, at a meeting or otherwise engaged. This fairly traditional domestic division of labour is similar to that in the Province as a whole as shown in the Northern Ireland Attitudes Survey, where only 8 per cent of women and 10 per cent of men stated that domestic responsibilities were shared (Montgomery and Davies 1991). Moreover as Table 11.5

Table 11.5 Average weekly hours spent by teachers on domestic responsibilities, by sex, 1996

Item	Average time spent, %	
	Female	*Male*
Less than 5 hours	11.2	18.6
6–10 hours	23.7	41.9
11–20 hours	30.4	27.8
21–30 hours	19.8	6.9
More than 30 hours	14.8	4.8

Source: DENI (1999)

Note: Teachers' survey, N = 1,739.

shows, over a third of the women teachers stated that they spent over twenty-one hours a week on domestic responsibilities, compared with just 12 per cent of men.

In summary, the responses from the Principals suggest that the post-LMS changes in role make it a more public one, one where more staff management, financial management and IT skills are required, and one that is more time-consuming. All three of these dimensions have gender implications. The next sections of this chapter examine the perceptions of teachers and governors.

Teachers' views

The Principals' perceptions of changes in their role post-LMS are shared to an extent by other teachers. Participants in our focus groups said that the new requirements which deterred them from seeking a Principal post were the finance and marketing responsibilities. There is also a view that the Principal's role is extremely stressful: 65 per cent of female respondents to our teachers' survey and 62 per cent of males considered the job 'very stressful'. By contrast, the Vice Principal's role (which is far more likely to be occupied by a woman) is seen as much less stressful. This image of the level of stress attached to the two roles affects individuals' decisions as to whether to apply for these posts themselves.

The women teachers said that they did not apply for promotion for a variety of reasons including being deterred by the selection process, enjoying teaching too much, facing hostility from others and becoming too visible in the community. Women also reported that they lacked faith in their own abilities and felt this was true of other women teachers more generally:

> women generally try to compromise and find it difficult to make potentially unpopular management decisions;
> women take set-backs too personally;
> some women at Assistant Teacher level are fearful of new technology and computerisation.

More women (39.9 per cent) than men (22.7 per cent) said they were happy to stay at their current job level for the rest of their career. Over twice as many men (27.1 per cent) as women (12.5 per cent) aspired to becoming a Principal, although the differential between the genders was less marked at Vice Principal level (men 28.1 per cent; women 18.5 per cent). One third of the men agreed that promotion was an incentive for them to perform well, compared to just over a quarter of the women.

Governors' views

The 585 respondents to our governors' survey had all participated in the appointment of teachers. For some this included a Principal or Vice Principal post. They were asked to rate the qualities they regarded as of most value in a Principal. The responses are shown in Table 11.6.

Table 11.6 Qualities rated by school governors in their Principal, 1996 (%)

	Very important	Fairly important	Fairly unimportant	Very unimportant	NA
Being a personnel manager	66	25	1	0.5	7.5
Motivating teachers	85	7	1	0.5	6.5
High level of academic qualification	16	63	13	1	7.0
Participating in the community	24	50	17	1	8.0
Maintaining discipline	80	11	1.5	0	7.5
Being active in the church	11	31.5	35	15	7.5
Being a finance manager	37	53	3	1	6.0
Ability to 'market' the school	50	40	3	0.5	6.5

Source: DENI (1999)

Note: School Governors' Survey, n = 585.

From Table 11.6 it is evident that not only do governors value the 'traditional' competencies of a Principal, such as ability to motivate teachers and impose discipline, but they also want someone who can be a strong finance manager (90 per cent believe that this is either very or fairly important) and who can market the school (again, 90 per cent place great emphasis on this attribute). These are the functions which the Principals themselves said were not difficult but were time-consuming.

If the characteristics and qualities required of a school Principal in the late 1990s are changing, this must impact upon the process of appointment and the kinds of skills that appointing panels seek. The next section examines the changing role of the governor in this process.

The role of governor

Since LMS, governors have had a more important role to play in the running of schools including the appointment of Principals and Vice Principals. Members of the Board are now expected to assume more of a managerial role, to have responsibility for handling budgets and finance, and to manifest greater ownership of how the school is run. The time commitment of the role has inevitably increased as a consequence of these changes. The skill level, experience, networks and other forms of 'cultural capital' of governors can be crucial in the work of supporting schools.

Deem (1989, 1991) has examined the extent to which gender and race are on the agenda for the post-LMS governing bodies in England. More particularly, one study of school governors in England found that the extent to which the socio-economic and demographic characteristics of governors reflected those of the catchment area for the school was highly variable (Deem *et al*. 1995: 37). While in some schools, there was a tendency for the governors to have quite different characteristics (especially where the pupils were from less privileged backgrounds or from ethnic minority groups), in others, characteristics were broadly similar. Deem *et al*. (ibid.: 73) report that some 20 per cent of the lay governors in their study were reported as working in further, higher or adult education. Given the highly traditional gender segregation patterns in N. Ireland, how has this impacted on who becomes a school governor?

The characteristics of the governors in our survey were as follows. Over two-thirds were between 35 and 54 years old. Two-thirds were male, and of them, two-thirds were in full-time employment compared with only one-third of the females. Men outnumbered women by around three to one in primary, secondary and grammar schools. The women governors tended to be representatives of either the teachers or the parents. A fifth of the sample – and here there will undoubtedly be quite a contrast with the rest of the UK – were clergy.

Governors provide their services, which can be onerous, in a voluntary capacity. It can be difficult to find people willing to make this contribution. This has led in some sectors to a resistance to limiting terms of office to four years and hence a tendency to re-appoint willing candidates. As a consequence, some governors in our survey had served in that capacity for many years. The average period of tenure was found to be nine years, with a range from one to twenty-nine years. Women were more likely than men (51 per cent compared with 22 per cent) to have served as a governor for three years or less and more men (30 per cent) than women (11 per cent) had been a governor for fourteen years or more.

The picture, then, is one where women governors are outnumbered and have less experience of being a governor than their male colleagues. They are also more likely to have a connection with the school as a teacher or a parent.

One of the most important responsibilities for governors is the appointment of teachers, including of course Principals and Vice Principals. However, in our governors' survey, well over a third of women (38.8 per cent) and men (35.5 per cent) stated that they did not believe that 'the school's selection processes allowed each candidate's abilities to be assessed properly'. These reservations were shared by two-thirds of the respondents to our teachers' survey: 62 per cent of the women and 69 per cent of the men agreed or strongly agreed with the statement that 'the selection process does not properly assess applicants' capabilities'. This concern was echoed in the views expressed by the Principals in the interviews, as follows:

> many governors still rely on gut feel despite all the procedures set out for them;

governors will often say they need someone for a senior job who has already been Principal or Vice Principal in a large school – this is often a man;

there is a minority view amongst governors that the less documentation there is, the less chance of being caught out;

governors are sometimes tempted to put a woman on to the shortlist just to make up the numbers;

sometimes governors want a man for the job because there are already too many women on the teaching staff of a school.

These comments suggest that to a greater or lesser extent, governors, teachers and Principals have reservations about the selection procedures. Some governors believe the process is too restrictive and should be expanded to include presentations, and group assessments or psychometric testing. This would involve selection panels in further training. However, for the employing authorities, there is a tension between a desire for professionalism in appointing and a need to avoid extending the time commitment required of governors. Some 43 per cent of the governors believe that they have very little influence in revising the existing procedures or setting new guidelines. The interviews with Principals identified financial management, marketing, and personnel and discipline matters *inter alia* as crucial features of the role post-LMS. As Table 11.6 showed, some of these aspects were also reflected in the qualities rated by governors in Principals. But how gendered are these qualities in the minds of governors? To address this question, governors were asked for their views on various gender stereotypes on teaching. The results are set out in Table 11.7.

Table 11.7 shows that the governors on the whole said that they rejected the notion that gender is associated with skills such as managing finance, marketing, personnel and maintaining discipline. Despite the reservations they expressed about the systems within which they have to operate for the appointment of teachers, this clearly bodes well for equal opportunities. Moreover, just half the governors (49 per cent of women and 55 per cent of men) had received equal opportunities training and most of those reported that it was helpful or very helpful.

The image of governors being resistant to gender-stereotyping did not accord, however, with teachers' views of them. Table 11.8 shows how teachers' perceptions of governors' views are far more traditional. Nearly half (49 per cent) of both male and female teachers agree or strongly agree with the statement that governors think men are better than women at ensuring discipline in schools. Women teachers are more likely than men teachers to think also that governors associate women with pastoral roles and see men as breadwinners and women's careers as secondary.

This image of governors held by teachers may well influence the extent to which they will put themselves forward for promotion. In particular it may be a partial explanation for the pattern observed in Table 11.4 whereby women appeared to be more likely to put themselves forward and be appointed to a Principal post when it had been re-advertised.

Table 11.7 Governors' attitudes to gender stereotypes, 1996

It is merit not gender that determines promotion

Strongly Agree (%)		Agree (%)		Neither (%)		Disagree (%)		Strongly Disagree (%)	
F	M	F	M	F	M	F	M	F	M
42.5	47.0	37.5	49.2	6.1	1.6	11.3	1.6	1.3	–

Women are not as effective as men in 'marketing' schools

Strongly Agree (%)		Agree (%)		Neither (%)		Disagree (%)		Strongly Disagree (%)	
F	M	F	M	F	M	F	M	F	M
1.3	1.1	–	2.2	7.5	16.4	42.5	44.8	48.8	33.9

Men make better finance managers than women

Strongly Agree (%)		Agree (%)		Neither (%)		Disagree (%)		Strongly Disagree (%)	
F	M	F	M	F	M	F	M	F	M
–	0.5	5.0	6.0	10.0	27.3	46.3	42.6	38.8	23.0

Men are better at maintaining discipline than women

Strongly Agree (%)		Agree (%)		Neither (%)		Disagree (%)		Strongly Disagree (%)	
F	M	F	M	F	M	F	M	F	M
1.3	2.2	6.3	18.0	15.0	20.8	50.0	46.4	7.5	12.0

Women are better than men at personnel matters

Strongly Agree (%)		Agree (%)		Neither (%)		Disagree (%)		Strongly Disagree (%)	
F	M	F	M	F	M	F	M	F	M
8.8	2.2	20.0	15.3	36.3	32.8	28.8	39.3	5.0	9.8

Source: DENI (1999) (School Governors' Survey)

Note: n = 585, however, figures do not always add up to 100 per cent because of non-response.

This section illustrates that there is a clear mismatch between governors' reported attitudes to gender stereotyping and the perceptions that both teachers and Principals have of them. The next section explores gender stereotyping of just one attribute, the ability to maintain discipline, in more detail, drawing upon the results of a scenario-writing exercise completed by a sub-set of the governors' sample.

Table 11.8 Teachers' perceptions of governors' views

Governors think men are better than women at ensuring discipline in school

Strongly Agree (%)		Agree (%)		Neither (%)		Disagree (%)		Strongly Disagree (%)	
F	M	F	M	F	M	F	M	F	M
17.4	11.7	31.9	37.7	25.1	29.1	20.6	17.7	4.2	3.0

Governors think women are more suited for pastoral roles than men

Strongly Agree (%)		Agree (%)		Neither (%)		Disagree (%)		Strongly Disagree (%)	
F	M	F	M	F	M	F	M	F	M
13.6	5.1	39.7	27.4	33.6	45.5	11.0	19.0	1.1	2.0

Men are seen by governors as 'bread winners' and women's careers as secondary

Strongly Agree (%)		Agree (%)		Neither (%)		Disagree (%)		Strongly Disagree (%)	
F	M	F	M	F	M	F	M	F	M
17.4	4.0	29.7	22.8	28.8	37.5	20.6	27.4	2.8	7.4

Source: DENI (1999)

Note: Teachers' Survey, n = 1,739.

The gendering of discipline

The ability to maintain discipline is an attribute regarded as important to the role of Principal by governors, both in relation to managing staff and pupils. To explore the extent to which this is seen as a gendered construct, we invited a sub-sample of eighteen governors (reflecting broadly the characteristics revealed in the survey) to complete a scenario-writing exercise, of whom sixteen responded. Such a technique can be a useful device to tap underlying assumptions and disentangle social constructs (Guttentag and Bray 1976). It should be emphasised that the governors were presented with hypothetical situations and their own views or behaviour cannot exactly be 'read off' from their responses. The exercise seeks rather to identify what constructs have some currency in the situation described. The exercise worked well in revealing frames of reference, as the following account illustrates. The respondents were presented with this scenario and the two questions which follow it:

> You are chairing a committee set up to appoint a Principal for a secondary school in a 'rough' area. The previous Principal was encouraged to take early retirement as he had experienced difficulties in maintaining discipline. There are three appointable candidates. Ms X is already a head teacher in a similar

school in Glasgow, she is forty-five, single and wants to return to N. Ireland to be nearer her elderly parents. Dr Y is a well qualified, ambitious young man (thirty) in a hurry who is already a deputy head in a small grammar school. He has two young children. Mrs Z is fifty, has teenage sons and is deputy head of the school in question. You believe Ms X to be the best candidate but after the recent experience of the school, most of the other members of the committee feel a male Principal is needed to assert some authority.

What arguments do the members of the committee put forward to support their views?

What arguments do you put forward to support your view?

The scenario emphasised the need for the appointee to be able to address discipline issues, given the type of school and its recent history. The main issue is to deconstruct 'authority' from the arguments put forward by members of the committee. In particular, to what extent is the ability to instil and maintain authority seen as a gendered construct?

The respondents provided arguments (on behalf of the committee) as requested for the appointment of Dr Y on the grounds that a man was needed to assert authority. The arguments in favour of Dr Y were couched in terms of his sex, either alone, or combined with his age (his qualifications were mentioned by only two respondents). His 'ambition and energy' were seen as an advantage, despite the likelihood expressed by some that because of these attributes, he might 'move on'. Only one of the respondents opted to make a case for Mrs Z although the scenario only referred to 'most' of the committee feeling that a man was needed. The overwhelming response to this first question then, is that Dr Y would be the best candidate because he is a man and men are better at maintaining authority and discipline of both pupils and staff. For example:

Only male principals could exert necessary authority required to maintain discipline.

Men are better disciplinarians . . . Staff, especially women staff would accept orders more readily from a male Principal.

Why do Principals need to be male in order to instil authority in schools? This is a particularly pertinent question given that the hypothetical scenario describes the previous (male) Principal as being asked to take early retirement precisely because he was unable to provide the discipline required. Some of the responses help us to unpack this. One perspective is that male *strength* is required. This is couched as *physical* strength by some but simply as strength by others:

It would take a male to withstand physical intimidation.

Male physical strength helps to impose discipline even though there is no physical contact with students.

They feel that a man is best placed to impose the discipline that was lacking before. A woman would not be strong enough.

Believe a man to be a stronger person. Children would take orders better from a man . . . More respect for a man as head teacher.

The authority and strength of the male are couched by some respondents in terms of the *father-figure role* in families. Indeed, respondents volunteered that children need fathers and point out that Dr Y is himself a father:

He (Dr Y) will carry the weight, force and discipline of a father figure.
His physique, size and voice will be helpful.
Men are firmer disciplinarians than women. Troublesome pupils are usually male and will be less respectful to females. Most troublesome children are from one-parent (usually female) families – they need a strong male disciplinarian.
As a father, he should be aware of the need for discipline.

A further demographic factor identified in Dr Y's favour is his age. His relative youth was interpreted as meaning that the pupils would relate to him better and that this would help to underline his authority:

Nearer in age to pupils – better understanding of teenagers.
Young man: would understand the frustrations and ideas of the pupils.
Dr Y is young, and ambitious and energetic. He will relate well with children and instil the discipline that is so obviously needed.
Because he is young he is likely to understand the pupils better (less age gap).

It is interesting to note here that Dr Y's potential ability to establish rapport with pupils makes no distinction between male and female pupils. It could be that no distinction is anticipated, or that the respondents subconsciously have male pupils in mind.

A further element in the social construction of 'authority' relates to ambition. Dr Y is described in the scenario as 'a well qualified young man (30) in a hurry who is already a deputy head in a small grammar school'. The respondents (on behalf of the committee), view this ambition as a further plus factor (although later on, they express concern about potential risk of lack of commitment to the school). His ambition is interpreted as meaning that he will be well motivated to make a success of his appointment, and that this will in part be reflected in an enthusiasm to instil discipline quickly. Hence although some imagine he will be looking to move on, this too is seen positively as it is viewed as implying he will be anxious to make a good job of the post in a short space of time:

Dr Y is ambitious. He may stay a short time in the school. He may see it as a further successful step in his career ladder. He will move quickly to re-direct the school.
Will see this appointment as a stepping stone so will aim to run a successful school.

Dr Y – well qualified and ambitious. Therefore he will be motivated to make a very good impression as he will be looking to his own future.

To what extent is relevant experience conceived as an element in being able to establish authority as Principal of a school? In the scenario we have two women who have experience either of the school in question or a similar one, and Dr Y who is described as a deputy in a grammar school. This might on the face of it appear to be a weakness in Dr Y's case. However, the respondents are able to represent this as an advantage:

Coming from a grammar school he will value excellence and discipline.
He is coming from a grammar school which should give a morale boost to our school.

From the first question, then, we have established that the respondents were able to present a case for hiring a young male to be Principal, largely on the grounds of his sex, despite the difficulties of the previous male incumbent and the candidate's lack of experience in a similar school. His relative youth, and his ambition (and therefore possible short stay in post) are presented as advantages. His qualifications do not particularly feature in the discussion.

The second question relating to this scenario invited the respondents, who were told they are in the role of chairing the appointment committee, to put forward their own (given) view as to why Ms X should be appointed. It will be remembered this candidate is already head teacher in a similar school in Glasgow and we are told that she is single and wants to move back to Northern Ireland to be near her elderly parents.

Here, the overwhelming response was that the candidate should be appointed because of her experience. This was couched both in terms of her years (she is 45) and the fact that she is a head in a similar school where (we presume) she has successfully asserted her authority. Of the fifteen respondents replying to this particular question, all mentioned experience as the most positive factor. This implies that women can assert authority but have to prove that they can do so: it will not be assumed on the grounds of their sex to the same extent that we saw in relation to Dr Y:

She has a wealth of experience in a similar role in a similar school in a similar area.
She has valuable experience in a similar school in Glasgow, as Principal. She is old enough to carry authority.

In the case of Ms X, however, reference is also made to the fact that she is single and has no children: these factors are seen as advantages:

No long-term family commitments.
Miss X (*sic*) is single, she has obviously committed her life to her work.

Being single, she may be undistracted in her dedication to our school.

This is interesting as we see that while for Dr Y being a father is an advantage because it will help him to relate to the pupils, for Ms X by contrast, being single and childfree is presented as an advantage because she will not be distracted from her duties.

Ms X's motivations for applying for the post, as described in the scenario, refer to wanting to be near her elderly parents. Three respondents comment on this. Two see it as a positive factor: it implies a long-term commitment to the area. A third expresses concern that her parents may become more demanding as time goes by.

It is in responses to this question that some disadvantages of the other two candidates are posited. Two take the opportunity to point up disadvantages with Dr Y: his ambition here is presented in a more negative light as representing a lack of commitment to the school in his hurry to move on, and his experience in a grammar school is seen as insufficient to prepare him for the post in question. Ms Z (the current deputy head) is written off (at 50) as being too old and as being 'part of the discipline problem'. Her experience as a mother of two teenage sons affords her no points despite the advantage apparently accruing to Dr Y from his (presumably) much younger children.

Just four respondents take the opportunity in this question to contest the association of authority and sex. Two cite the case of the previous incumbent, one touches on the issue of physical strength and the final one postulates that strength of character is more significant than sex in asserting authority.

The responses to the two questions related to this scenario illustrate some interesting points. Authority is constructed as gendered and gendering relates to (physical) strength and the father role. Apparent disadvantages of the male candidate, such as relative youth, lack of experience both general and specific, are turned round to represent advantages. The family characteristics of candidates are not contested as legitimate concerns for an appointing panel: these work for a male parent and against a female parent. A single woman is commended for her single-mindedness and commitment to her job but there is concern about other potential caring duties.

There were two respondents who expressed some concern about this scenario: one who 'would not allow such a discussion' and another (in response to the second question) who was more concerned with management style than a matter of principle: 'I do not argue with my board of governors. I instead try to arrive with a majority consensus of opinion which I feel is much better.'

In principle, governing bodies should not, of course, allow discussions where the sex and or family responsibilities of candidates are taken into account as this can be discriminatory. The fact that only one respondent answered in this way suggests that the reality is that issues such as age, marital status and family responsibilities may well play a significant part in appointment decisions and are considered to be as relevant as experience and qualifications.

Conclusion

This chapter set out to explore some of the implications of the post-LMS changes in the role of Principals and Governors for the proportion of Principal posts likely to held by women. Governors now have a greater degree of responsibility for the appointment of Principals. The political arithmetic of Principal posts in Northern Ireland suggests that gender is an important determinant of who gets what post, as it is elsewhere in the UK. Where women are Principals, it tends overwhelmingly to be in nursery, primary or small rural single-sex grammar schools. When women apply and are appointed to a Principal post, it is more likely to follow a re-advertisement. However, the data presented here suggest a series of additional 'chill factors' are emerging which may mean women will be even less likely to apply for these posts in the future.

According to the Principals in our study, there is now more of an emphasis on external relations, and on financial and human resource management. While these responsibilities are viewed as time-consuming, they are not regarded by the Principals as particularly difficult although for some the more public nature of the role was unwelcome. The major change for Principals, they reported, was volume and diversity of work.

This perception of the changed role of Principals was to an extent shared by teachers. However, their emphasis was on what they perceived to be the stress factor in the job. The teachers tended to view governors as being more influenced by gender-stereotypes than governors' responses seemed to indicate was justified.

The increase in time needed for the role of Principal because of new or expanded responsibilities will be difficult for women with traditional domestic division of labour arrangements. The perception by teachers that the role is stressful may well be a deterrent for many women who already shoulder major domestic responsibilities. The views that teachers, particularly women, have of the extent to which governors are influenced by gender stereotypes may again act as a deterrent. The fact that only half the governors who had already made appointments had received equal opportunities training is a cause for concern: further, the scenario exercise gave some indication of subconscious gendering of the construct of 'authority' which is deemed essential to the Principal role in order to maintain discipline in schools.

While on the face of it, the record of promotion of women to Principal posts in Northern Ireland compares favourably with elsewhere in the UK, closer examination shows that there is gender segregation within the ranks. Moreover, the post-LMS changes in the role, and perceptions of those changes by teachers and governors may act as a deterrent to women considering applying for the post in the future. The Department of Education in Northern Ireland and the employing authorities are now seeking to address these issues as a key element in their commitment to monitoring and promoting equal opportunities.

Acknowledgements

This chapter draws upon a study commissioned by the Department of Education Northern Ireland on barriers to women's promotion in teaching. We are grateful to DENI for permission to publish this account of some of the findings, and to all the Principals, Vice Principals, teachers, governors and others who gave so generously of their time for the research. We are also grateful to Sara Delamont of University of Wales, Cardiff for advice on the governors' scenario.

Notes

1 The 1988 Education Reform Act covered England and Wales. The equivalent legislation for Northern Ireland was the Education Reform (Northern Ireland) Order of 1989.

2 The Guidelines on Policy Appraisal and Fair Treatment (PAFT) were issued in Northern Ireland under General Secretariat Circular 5/93 with effect from 1 January 1994. The overall aim of the PAFT initiative is to ensure that questions of equality of opportunity and equity of treatment for all sectors of the community are addressed, and inform policy-making action at all levels of government activity. The principles inherent in the Guidelines have been embraced by government departments and non-departmental public bodies.

3 The Fair Play initiative is based on Chwarae Teg (Welsh for Fair Play), a consortium brought together by the Equal Opportunities Commission in Wales with the Welsh Development Agency, Training and Enterprise Councils and local authorities in 1992. Similar initiatives were launched by the (then) Department for Employment in the English regions. Scotland, N. Ireland and, indeed, Belgium now have Fair Play consortia.

4 The contract for the study was awarded to Deloitte & Touche Northern Ireland, a management consultancy company. The research team comprised Philip Heaton and Lyn McBriar of Deloitte & Touche, with Teresa Rees of the University of Bristol as an external consultant on equal opportunities to the team. We are grateful to the Steering Group for the project and DENI who provided us with valuable comments and who have allowed this account of the research to be published.

References

Business in the Community (1996) *Opportunity 2000 Annual Report*, London: Business in the Community.

Cunnison, S. (1994) 'Women teachers: career identity and perceptions of family constraints – changes over a recent decade,' *Research Papers in Education* 9: 81–105.

Deem, R. (1989) 'The new school governing bodies – are gender and race on the agenda?,' *Gender and Education* 1, 3: 247–61.

—— (1991) 'Governing by gender? School governing bodies after the Education Reform Act', in P. Abbot and C. Wallace (eds) *Gender, Power and Sexuality*, London: Macmillan.

Deem, R., Brehony, K.J. and Heath, S. (1995) *Active Citizenship and the Governing of Schools*, Buckingham: Open University Press.

Department of Education Northern Ireland (1993) *Action Plan on Women's Issues*, Belfast: DENI.

—— (1999) *Women in Teaching: Equal Opportunities*, Final Report by Deloitte & Touche, Belfast: Department of Education Northern Ireland.

Guttentag, M. and Bray, H. (1976) *Undoing Sex Stereotypes*, New York: McGraw-Hill.

Hall, V. (1993) 'Women in educational management: a review of research', in J. Outson (ed.) *Women in Education Management*, Longman: Harlow.

—— (1996) *Dancing on the Ceiling: A Study of Women Managers in Education*, London: Paul Chapman Publishing.

Hall, V., Mackay, H. and Morgan, C. (1986) *Headteachers at Work*, Milton Keynes: Open University Press.

McKeown, P., Donnelly, C. and Osborne, R. (1996) 'School governing bodies in N. Ireland', in C. Pole and R. Chawla-Duggan (eds) *Reshaping Education in the 1990s: Perspectives on Secondary Education*, Lewes: Falmer Press.

McLaughlin, E. and Quirk, P. (eds) (1996) *Policy Aspects of Employment Equality in N. Ireland*, Belfast: Standing Advisory Commission on Human Rights, Vol. 2.

Montgomery, P. and Davies, C. (1991) 'A women's place in Northern Ireland', in *Social Attitudes in Northern Ireland*, Belfast: Blackstaff Press.

Osborne, R., Gallagher, A., Cormack, R. with Shortall, S. (1996) 'The implementation of the PAFT Guidelines in Northern Ireland', in E. McLaughlin and P. Quirk (eds) *Policy Aspects of Employment Equality in N Ireland*, Belfast: Standing Advisory Commission on Human Rights, Vol. 2.

Postscript

Since this chapter was written, the EOCNI has merged with the equality agencies for race and disability and with the Fair Employment Commission to become the Northern Ireland Equality Commission. The Standing Advisory Commission on Human Rights has become the Northern Ireland Human Rights Commission.

12 Teacher education policy and gender

Pat Mahony

Introduction

It is difficult to imagine that anybody could disagree with the belief expressed by all major political parties in recent years that 'good teachers using the most effective methods, are the key to higher standards' (DfEE 1997: 1). Such consensus probably ends at this point, however, for as soon as notions such as 'good teachers', 'effective methods' or 'higher standards' are defined, different viewpoints will emerge about the purposes, priorities and desirable ends of schooling and the best means of achieving them. In voicing some disquiet about the potentially negative impact of recent developments in teacher education policy on gender equality, I have no wish to fabricate some past golden age in which anti-discriminatory practice was the norm. In being critical of current government policy neither do I wish to disassociate myself from a commitment to wanting 'better teachers' or even 'raising standards' but as I shall try to show, the devil lies in the detail of what is meant by these terms.

The issues explored in this chapter have arisen from two projects undertaken with my colleague Ian Hextall. The first 'The policy context and impact of the Teacher Training Agency' ran from September 1995 until November 1996 and the second 'The impact on teaching of the National Professional Qualifications' began in December 1997 and is due to be completed in December 1999.[1] At the time of writing we have just completed our pilot interviews with a range of people involved in various elements of the National Professional Standards and Qualification framework.

The Teacher Training Agency

The Teacher Training Agency (TTA) was legislated into existence in September 1994 after more than a decade of Conservative govenment interventions in the organisation and 'delivery' of Initial Teacher Training (ITT) and professional development. These included: the setting up of the Council for the Accreditation of Teacher Education, the establishment of alternative routes into teaching (including licensed and articled teachers and school-centred Initial Teacher Training schemes), the development of partnership arrangements between Higher

Education Institutions (HEIs) and schools (with locally negotiated payments), the introduction of competence-based approaches to the assessment of students, the abolition of the probationary year and the devolution of responsibilities for induction to schools. Within this context the reasons for establishing the TTA makes for an interesting study in its own right (Mahony and Hextall 1997) but for the purposes of this chapter it is necessary only to draw attention to two elements of the policy context.

Education policy

First, in relation to education policy, the school effectiveness and improvement movements have been influential in defining 'effective' teachers and leaders as the linchpin of 'effective' schools (Hextall and Mahony 1998). Both the Conservative and Labour governments have attached enormous importance to the role of 'effective' schools (defined largely in terms of academic performance), in ensuring the competitiveness of UK plc in the global economy (DfEE 1995, 1997). Therefore, it is no surprise that the training of effective teachers for effective schools within the broader context of the competitive state provides a major rationale for the work of the TTA – as the following quotation from the Chief Executive demonstrates:

> everyone is now agreed that the top priority in education is the need to raise pupils' standards of learning . . . And there is a widespread awareness that, in a competitive world, constant progress is necessary just to maintain parity with other nations.
>
> (Millett 1996: 2)

This view is not without its critics: Ashton and Green (1996: 3) challenge the 'simplistic consensus' from which 'policy debates and much scholarly discussion begin' that more and better skills necessarily lead to improved economic performance; Robin Alexander has been quoted as claiming that 'there is no direct and causal link between pedagogy, attainment in literacy and national economic competitiveness' (Budge 1997: 17) and Lingard and Rizvi (1997: 3) argue on the basis of their study of the OECD that 'in the construction of policy, globalization works as an ideology just as much as it refers to direct empirical effects'.

Public policy

Seen from the more general perspective of public policy the TTA can be located in the programme of 'reinventing government' instituted in the whole of public provision in the UK. This has included the restructuring of state welfare services such as health, education, housing and community care in accordance with the principles of New Public Management (NPM) or 'new managerialism' which has involved dispersing the management, reporting and accounting approaches of the public sector and modelling them by different degrees along the lines of 'best', i.e. 'efficient' commercial practice. In pursuit of these political priorities, agencies and other non-departmental public bodies, such as the TTA, have been established.

These transformations have generated questions well beyond education about the nature, role and functioning of the public sector. As the concern with 'process' has shifted to a preoccupation with 'outcome', the definition and adequacy of criteria used as bases for performance review have been brought into question. As the definitions, nature and control of the work of public sector professionals and the impact of these on 'customers' have been reshaped, issues of inequality are beginning to emerge across the public sector as it strives to conform to the 'virtuous three Es: economy, efficiency and effectiveness' (Pollitt 1993: 59).

> consumerist and managerialist versions of diversity have been the principal forms through which social differentiation has been addressed and embedded in the new regime. In the process the social structuring of inequalities, divisions and antagonisms become flattened in their representation as either individual wants or categories of 'special' needs. This does pose a problem about what has happened to these structured differences as a result of the new regime. Has it reproduced existing inequalities? Has it redressed them? Or has it created new forms of differentiation and inequality?
>
> (Clarke and Newman 1997: 153)

Reconstructing teaching

Since its origin the TTA has been extremely active to the extent that there is now no aspect of the occupational and professional lives of teachers which is not affected by the Agency. In a recent initiative a National Professional Standards and Qualifications (NPS/Q) framework is being developed for newly qualified teachers, subject leaders, special educational needs co-ordinators and head teachers. Standards for 'advanced skills teachers' are also in the process of being developed.

The NPS/Q which will form the focus for the rest of this chapter occupies a central place in the fundamental restructuring of teaching and recomposition of the teaching force with considerable implications for social justice in its broadest terms (Griffiths 1996). Within the wider context of education policy and public policy, the development of national standards can be seen both as providing a centralised specification of 'effective teaching' and as a codification of relations between managers and managed where the former becomes locally responsible for the compliance of the latter. Occurring as it does within the centralisation–decentralisation nexus where 'policy steering' is achieved through much tighter regulation by the centre (Hoggett 1996), the NPS/Q framework represents a much more systematic control of teaching, judged according to priorities, criteria, procedures and indicators established at a distance with little scope for local autonomy.

The NPS/Q framework

At the time of writing, the standards which have to be met for the award of Qualified Teacher Status (QTS) (TTA 1997a) and head teachers (TTA 1997b) are in the very early stages of application and it is therefore not possible to do more than identify an agenda of concerns and questions which will need to be followed up in future research. The concerns Ian Hextall and I have begun to identify so far in relation to the policy text may diminish or grow as more information becomes available about how the standards are being realised in practice and their impact on the system.

The content of the standards for QTS

Documentary analysis of TTA and related literature reveals an omission which is immediately obvious – there is no explicit account of how teaching or leadership is being conceptualised, no indication that there are different representations of these activities and no justification of, or rationale, for the particular accounts implicit in the standards. The teaching community is being required to accept specific stand-ards without any account of the overall model to which these standards belong. This raises questions about what exactly has been agreed to (or not) in the various consultations undertaken by the TTA and to what extent busy people, even if they have been consulted, have noticed some significant absences and silences.

However, even if the account has not been made explicit, it is no surprise to find that the standards for QTS consist largely of achieving the subject knowledge and craft skills necessary to teach and assess the National Curriculum. This one would expect if, as has been argued, the rationale underpinning the NPS/Q framework is the demand for 'effective' teachers to secure a highly qualified work-force, within the context of 'reinvented government'. This view of 'effectivity' is very different from that expressed by the values and practices of feminist ideas about good teaching. While these are by no means homogeneous either in terms of ends or means, none the less Weiner's formulation of what is minimally involved in feminist teaching provides a useful starting point. She argues that feminism has three dimensions:

> *political* – a movement to improve the conditions and life-changes for girls and women;
> *critical* – a sustained, intellectual critique of dominant (male) forms of knowing and doing;
> *praxis-orientated* – concerned with the development of more ethical forms of professional and personal practice.
>
> (Weiner 1994: 7–8)

If we now turn our attention to the standards themselves it would seem from our pilot interviews with HEI and school staff that a range of views and practices could emerge:

some of the standards are OK, the language of others . . . for me . . . there are connotations of male ways of teaching . . . authority, discipline and control rather than the more subtle strategies you see the women developing. Some of the standards are wide open for interpretation – for good and ill. It's what's missing that's the problem and how far people will even notice it.

(Deputy Head in charge of student teachers)

Some of our interviewees included in the 'what's missing' category, the responsibility of all teachers to understand and challenge how schools both operate within and reconstitute social inequalities organised around the axes of 'race', gender, class, sexuality and disability. When pressed, they acknowledged that a training institution could decide to go beyond the standards but they were doubtful whether this was realistic given the time constraints, the pressures of inspection on courses and the fact that 'equal opportunities is not high on the agenda these days'. This issue has recently exploded in the *Times Educational Supplement*:

> The Government's chief race adviser has accused the Teacher Training Agency of 'sticking two fingers up' at anti-racism. In a blistering attack Sir Herman Ouseley, head of the Commission for Racial Equality, called the agency 'negligent' and ministers 'impotent' in their failure to put equal opportunities firmly on the teacher-training curriculum.
>
> (Ghouri 1998: 1)

In response, a senior TTA officer said that the agency was 'not prepared to prescribe' anti-racist work. This is unconvincing in a context where the National Curriculum for Initial Teacher Training does prescribe the training curriculum for primary and secondary English, Mathematics and Science (DfEE 1998).

It is difficult to avoid a pessimistic view of the likely impact of the standards on practice. Even the standard 'have a working knowledge and understanding of anti-discrimination legislation' (TTA 1997a: 11) is unlikely to yield a demand for the kinds of sophisticated anti-sexist practices we know are possible (Kenway and Willis 1998). This is because the kinds of approaches which teachers need to develop in order to satisfy even the most minimal account of non-discriminatory practice are in no way covered by the legislative framework of the relevant Acts (Mahony and Hextall 1998); schools have not yet been taken to court for consistently consigning black boys to lower ability groups (or excluding them from school altogether) nor is there any legal redress for parents who object to their daughters' education being directed to 'civilising' the behaviour of the boys or dominated by the need to deal with the continuum of sexual harassment (Mahony 1989).

Application of the standards for QTS

The Standards for the Award of Qualified Teacher Status have a double function beyond the obvious one of forming the performance criteria against which individual trainees are to be assessed. First, as from 1998, they will form the basis for the identification of 'areas of strength' and 'further priorities for development during induction' within a career entry profile. At the time of writing this initiative is about to be undertaken for the first time and data are not yet available on its impact.

The second function of the standards is to form the basis upon which institutions are inspected by the Office for Standards in Education (OFSTED). The grades awarded are important because the TTA uses them either to reward ITT providers with increased student numbers or to penalise them (the ultimate penalty being closure). Anecdotal evidence is emerging that some of the 'standards', 'competences' or 'criteria for good practice' which institutions have developed locally with their partnership schools are being swept aside by the rigidity with which some inspectors are insisting that the only legitimate criteria for the assessment of students are the national standards. Even where inspectors accept local 'standards' (provided they incorporate the national standards), the fact that institutions are assessed on the accuracy of their assessments of students *against the national standards* means that at least during the inspection process their grip is inescapable. For example, one HEI tutor during our pilot interviews said that 'we can't operate with two frameworks – ours and the national standards so the strong equal opportunities dimension in our account of what it means to teach has been eradicated'. It remains to be seen whether this is replicated nationally.

There may also be consequences for the way student teachers are taught and for what they, in turn, learn about what it means to teach young people, for it would seem that the way in which teaching is being redefined is a long way from the kind of feminist pedagogy we saw indicated by Weiner. For one HEI tutor the preoccupation with ensuring that students met each and every one of the standards was beginning to challenge her own sense of professionalism as a concern for the processes and politics of teaching and learning was replaced by the need to ensure the compliance of others:

> We're moving more and more towards a position where it almost feels like policing the students. In the past, feedback on their lessons in school was a formative and supportive process; a continuation of a professional dialogue where we explored together various options for handling a class or teaching a unit of work. Whether they were measuring up to the standards did of course form the backcloth but we didn't kick into summative assessment mode until towards the end of their practice. Now, almost from the beginning of the course, we have to show that we are setting them regular personal targets and monitoring whether they achieve them. This means we are also policing the school mentors . . . So everyone is policing everyone from OFSTED down. It's not that we used to be soft on students before but learning to teach isn't

something that develops in a linear way where you crack one thing in a week and then move on to the next . . . Somehow there's no space left to explore the dilemmas in teaching and we're pushed to present it as a shopping list of items to be acquired and any item omitted is a source of concern. In such a climate, it's a struggle to retain a non-punitive attitude when we know the results of the inspection will have such serious repercussions.

(HEI tutor)

As we shall see later, the whole issue of control and 'policing' to ensure the compliance of others is highly gendered.

The National Professional Qualification for headship

It is no coincidence that of all the many places in which the TTA could have begun its work, one of its first initiatives was directed towards head teachers. Many authorities in the school effectiveness field have identified 'leadership' as occupying a critical position in the development of effective schools. More widely across the public sector, it is being claimed that there is a growing divide between those who occupy client-related professional positions and the managers who administer the service as a whole and to whom power is seen to be shifting (Taylor-Gooby and Lawson 1993).

Commenting on the changing role of the head teacher even before the introduction of the National Professional Qualification for Headship (NPQH), Fergusson said:

the headteacher is ceasing to be a senior peer embedded within a professional group . . . and is becoming a distinctive and key actor in an essentially managerialist system, in which the pursuit of objectives and methods which are increasingly centrally determined is the responsibility of managers who must account for their achievement and ensure the compliance of teaching staff.

(1994: 94)

It is within this context that the training of heads has occupied a central place in the TTA's overall strategic vision:

We also know that effective teaching must be supported by high quality management and leadership at middle and senior levels in the profession . . . We know from OFSTED evidence that the managers and leaders in our schools need: to offer leadership; to set tone, ethos, direction and purpose; to translate purpose into plans; to implement those plans; and to check, through monitoring and evaluation, that progress is taking place. Managers and leaders also need to be accountable for that progress, at whatever level they manage.

(TTA 1996a: 9)

A flavour of what this means in practice can be given by the first two 'Key Areas of Headship' as identified in the national standards for head teachers (TTA 1997b: 6–7). Achievement of the standards is necessary for the award of the NPQH which is intended to become mandatory for new heads as from 2002. In the section on 'Strategic Direction and Development of the School', heads 'lead by example', 'provide inspiration and motivation', 'create an ethos and provide educational vision', 'create and implement a strategic plan', 'ensure that all those involved in the school are committed to its aims', 'monitor, evaluate and review the effects of policies, priorities and targets and take action if necessary'. In relation to 'Teaching and Learning', they 'create and maintain an environment which promotes and secures good teaching', 'determine, organise and implement the curriculum and its assessment', 'ensure effective teaching of literacy, numeracy and information technology', 'monitor and evaluate the quality of teaching', and 'create and maintain an effective partnership with parents'. Personal attributes include 'personal impact and presence', 'resilience', 'energy, vigour and perseverance', 'self-confidence and intellectual ability' (ibid.: 4).

As with the standards for QTS, a great deal hangs on interpretation but there are a number of reasons to be concerned.

The gendered nature of management

First, men's occupation of management positions is disproportionate to their numbers both beyond and within teaching. Collinson and Hearn (1996: 1–2) have explained that 'women comprise less than 5 per cent of senior management in the UK and US, 5 per cent of UK Institute of Directors and less than 1 per cent of chief executives'.

Schools in the UK, though significantly more gender-balanced than some of our European counterparts, also reflect a considerable gender bias in the proportion of 'managers' to 'managed' as illustrated in Table 12.1. The significance of this data lies not in the numbers of women heads compared to men but in the

Table 12.1 Distribution of male and female teachers in 1994

	Men (%)	Women (%)	Total
Primary			
Heads	10,257 (48.8)	10,779 (51.2)	21036
Deputies	5,713 (31.5)	12,418 (68.5)	18131
Classroom teachers	16,812 (10.2)	148,064 (89.8)	164876
Total	32,782 (16.1)	171,261 (83.9)	204043
Secondary			
Heads	3,440 (78.1)	965 (21.9)	4405
Deputies	5,586 (65.9)	2,885 (34.1)	8471
Classroom teachers	84,938 (48.0)	91,854 (52.0)	176792
Total	93,964 (49.5)	95,704 (50.5)	189668

Source: Calculated from DfEE (1996)

relationship between the respective totals of men and women in the profession and the numbers who are heads. In the case of men roughly a third are heads whereas, of the women, the figures show that it is only about one in seventeen.

Second, discourses of management tend to be masculinist in character. Modern management theory derives mostly from the private sector and even the most cursory inspection of popular texts reveals a great deal about the kind of 'person' represented by the modern manager or leader. Ostensibly presented as gender neutral, these texts privilege competitive, conquering, aggressive and power-seeking masculinities, either by providing examples of individual, 'successful' leaders and managers who are nearly always men or by promoting images of tough, unflinching, rational, action-orientated, analytical, objective, risk-taking, financially astute 'people' in total control both of their vision and the place of others within it. Collinson and Hearn (1996: 2–3) in arguing that there has always been a strong connection between men and management say that in the 1980s: 'Managers and senior executives were frequently depicted and portrayed themselves as "hard men", virile, swashbuckling and flamboyant entrepreneurs who were reasserting a "macho" management style that insisted on the "divine right of managers to manage".'

The 1990s, they argue, has brought an increased evaluation of managers and their performance, one criterion of which is 'the masculinist concern with personal power and the ability to control others and self' (ibid.: 3). Conventional managerial discourse has become redolent with highly (hetero)sexualised talk of 'penetrating markets' and 'getting into bed with suppliers/customers-competitors' and a considerable amount of business is conducted between male managers through networks established in male sports and clubs.

Given that the public sector has been restructured in line with 'best commercial practice', it is not surprising to find a similar version of masculinist discourse in evidence. According to John Clarke and Janet Newman:

> many public sector organisations have taken on images of competitive behaviour as requiring hard, macho or 'cowboy' styles of working. It is as if the unlocking of the shackles of bureaucratic constraints has at last allowed public sector managers to become 'real men' released from the second-class status of public functionaries by their exposure to the 'real world' of the market place.
>
> (1997: 70)

The standards for headship in no way exemplify the excesses described above. However, they do represent a dominantly hierarchical management model in which responsibility for and control of others' work are central features of the head's role. How that control will be exercised will undoubtedly vary between individuals. However, such individuals, whatever their personal politics, do not exist independently of the presumptions and expectations underpinning the context in which they work.

In claiming that there is a considerable fit between conceptions of 'the manager' (or in more recent parlance 'the leader') and particular modes of masculinity, I am not here advancing an essentialist thesis in relation to women and men, quite the opposite, and with far more potentially negative consequences. If masculinities and femininities are socially constructed, ordered and practised differently in different contexts, the problem goes far beyond the presence or absence of women and even beyond the relative positioning of women to men. What is at stake are the values, ways of understanding the world and ways of relating to others which are traditionally polarised around the binaries of 'femininity and masculinity'. If success in management is defined in masculinist terms, then, as I have suggested elsewhere (Mahony 1997), women will be pressured to conform to its dictates in ways which may create tensions between their values and their power to act in collaborative ways. As Kanter points out:

> A number of studies have shown that as women move up the organizational hierarchy, their identification with the masculine model of managerial success becomes so important that they end up rejecting even the few valued feminine managerial traits they may have endorsed.
>
> (1993: 72)

This leads us on to a third problem. We have seen how key parameters for policy are being established at the centre, partly policed by the centre through mechanisms of surveillance and regulation, but also subjected to internal, localised control. Clarke and Newman argue that this has:

> the effect of creating a 'dispersed managerial consciousness', the embedding of the calculative frameworks of managerialism throughout organisations . . . all employees come to find their decisions, actions and possibilities framed by the imperatives of managerial coordination . . . people are increasingly conscious that managerial agendas and the coporate calculus condition their working relationships, conditions and processes and have to be negotiated.
>
> (1997: 77)

There is some evidence that a 'dispersed managerial consciousness' has already developed in schools. In a recent study comparing expectations of school leadership across Denmark, England, Scotland and Australia, teachers in England placed a high emphasis on the need for 'strong leadership' or 'assertive leadership'. The good head was depicted as skilful in relation to finance and administration (reference being made to the impact on staff jobs, of poor financial management) and deemed to possess 'vision' (i.e. able to determine a clear direction). Good communication skills were also thought necessary since teachers could only follow the head's lead, if it had been communicated successfully in the first place (Mahony and Moos 1998). To this extent, the NPS/Q framework, by providing a detailed specification of the respective roles of 'leaders' and 'led', merely codify transformations which have already occurred. This is small comfort, however, for whereas the TTA treats as problematic what it sees as the 'feminisation' of teaching (TTA 1996b: 11–12), I am suggesting that a much more serious problem is the comprehensive 'masculinisation' of the profession and its values.

Application of the standards for headship

At the time of writing the first cohort of candidates are undertaking training for the NPQH and it will be some time before we know the proportions of women to men who have applied, been accepted, funded and gained the qualification. Such information may not be easily accessible, for within the NPQH documentation, which includes details on the procedures for application, training and assessment as well as the standards themselves (TTA 1997c), little focused attention is paid to issues of selection and sponsorship. At the end of the application form there is a detachable sheet for 'Equal Opportunities Monitoring' but candidates are merely invited to complete it. This is surprising given that one of the reasons cited by the DfEE for not maintaining equal opportunities monitoring of teachers was the low level of response from public bodies (Mahony and Hextall 1998).

Issues of sponsorship and selection raise questions about the extent to which dominant networks promote 'people like us' (Kanter 1993; Collinson and Hearn 1996). How LEAs, employers and other sponsoring bodies will undertake their activities, how sensitive they will be to the need to guard against their own preconceptions and assumptions in relation to who gets selected, on what basis, by what criteria, through what procedures and with what forms of redress in terms of appeals and grievance, all remain to be seen. Some may be tempted to retreat into the old refrain of 'the best person for the job' but while this has a common-sense plausibility it merely obscures issues of structural discrimination.

At a more general level it is as yet unclear what modes of articulation or models of progression are envisaged between the various elements of the NPQ framework and whether the overall framework is premised on a presumption of the male 'career' orientated teacher: 'who is single mindedly purposeful in the pursuit of career goals, following a linear progression through carefully planned steps. This model ignores the competing pressures of home and family circumstances on career' (Hall 1996: 34). These are issues which will have important implications for the opportunity structures available to teachers and there is little to suggest that the existing social distribution of such 'opportunities' is likely to be fundamentally challenged.

Conclusion

Conceptions of the 'effective teacher' and head teacher are being redefined in ways which render invisible the role of schools in contributing to the construction and maintenance of gender inequalities. Teachers' responsibilities to challenge these and other inequalities are being removed as the purposes of schooling are articulated around a narrow form of economic instrumentalism. Hence the process of occupational restructuring upon which the TTA has embarked could carry important implications for individual teachers, for the teaching profession as a whole, and for the social and ideological contextualisation of education.

Because NPS/Q initiative is at a very early stage of development, this chapter has inevitably emphasised policy text. This carries its own dangers in that any or all of the concerns expressed here could turn out to be groundless at the point of policy realisation. However, given the data which already exists in the field of education, from other public sector debates on the impact of managerialism and from many years of working with beginning and experienced teachers to develop 'anti-sexist' practice (Mahony 1995), it is difficult to remain optimistic. At the very least, given that the establishment of the framework of National Professional Standards and Qualifications has such enormous potential consequences for the shape and form of teaching and for the nature of the institutions in which it occurs, an opportunity has been missed to make it explicit that issues of social justice lie at the heart of schooling. These will continue to impact daily on present and future cohorts of teachers, on the children or students with whom they work and on the communities in which they are embedded.

Note

1 'The Policy Context and Impact of the Teacher Training Agency' (Award number R000 22 1642) and 'The Impact on Teaching of the National Professional Qualifications' (Award number R000 23 7382) have been funded by the Economic and Social Research Council.

References

Ashton, D. and Green, F. (1996) *Education Training and the Global Economy*, Cheltenham: Edward Elgar.

Budge, D. (1997) 'In search of foreign correspondences', *Times Educational Supplement*, 5 December.

Clarke, J. and Newman, J. (1997) *The Managerial State*, London: Sage.

Collinson, D. and Hearn, J. (1996) 'Breaking the silence: on men, masculinities and managements', in D. Collinson and J. Hearn (eds) *Men as Managers, Managers as Men*, London: Sage Publications.

DfEE (1995) *Benchmarking School Budgets*, London: HMSO.

—— (1996) *Statistics of Education: Teachers*, London: HMSO.

—— (1997) *Excellence in Schools*, London: HMSO.

—— (1998) *Teaching: High Status, High Standards*, Circular Number 4/98, London: DfEE.

Fergusson, R. (1994) 'Managerialism in education', in J. Clarke, A. Cochran and E. McLaughlin (eds) *Managing Social Policy*, London: Sage.

Ghouri, N. (1998) 'Race chief attacks training negligence', *Times Educational Supplement*, 3 July.

Griffiths, M. (1996) 'The discourses of social justice in schools', paper presented at British Education Research Association Conference, Lancaster, September 1996.

Hall, V. (1996) *Dancing on the Ceiling: A Study of Women Managers in Education*, London: Paul Chapman.

Hextall, I. and Mahony, P. (1998) 'Effective teachers for effective schools', in R. Slee, S. Tomlinson and G. Weiner (eds) *Effective for Whom?*, London: Falmer Press.

Hoggett, P. (1996) 'New modes of control in the public service', *Public Administration*, 74, Spring: 9–32.

Kanter, R.M. (1993) *Men and Women of the Corporation*, second edition, New York: Basic Books.

Kenway, J. and Willis, S. (1998) *Answering Back: Girls, Boys and Feminism in Schools*, St Leonards, NSW: Allen and Unwin.

Lingard, B. and Rizvi, F. (1997) 'Globalization, the OECD and Australian higher education', in J. Currie and J. Newson (eds) *Globalization and the University: A Critical Perspective*, Thousand Oaks, CA: Sage.

Mahony, P. (1989) 'Sexual violence and mixed schools', in C. Jones and P. Mahony (eds) *Learning Our Lines: Sexuality and Social Control in Education*, London: The Women's Press.

—— (1995) 'Teaching how to change and changing how to teach', in L. Boysen, K. Krogh-Jespersen, E. Lahelma and H. Ruotonen (eds) *Content and Gender: Transforming the Curriculum in Teacher Education*, Sheffield: Pavic Publications.

—— (1997) 'Talking heads: feminist perspectives on public sector reform in teacher education', *Discourse*, 18, 1: 87–102.

Mahony, P. and Hextall, I. (1997) *The Policy Context and Impact of the TTA: A Summary*, London: Roehampton Institute.

—— (1998) 'Social justice and the reconstruction of teaching', in P. Sikes and C. Vincent (eds) *Social Justice Education Policy, Journal of Education Policy* 13, 4: 545–58.

Mahony, P. and Moos, L. (1998) 'Democracy and school leadership in England and Denmark', *British Journal of Educational Studies* 46, 3: 302–17.

Millett, A. (1996) 'Chief Executive's Annual Lecture', London: TTA.

Pollitt, C. (1993) *Managerialism and the Public Services*, second edition, Oxford: Basil Blackwell.

Taylor-Gooby, P. and Lawson, R. (eds) (1993) *Markets and Managers*, Milton Keynes: Open University Press.

TTA (1996a) *Corporate Plan*, London: TTA.

—— (1996b) *A Strategic Plan for Teacher Supply and Recruitment: A Discussion Document*, London: TTA.

—— (1997a) *Standards for the Award of Qualified Teacher Status*, London: TTA.

—— (1997b) *National Standards for Headteachers*, London: TTA.

—— (1997c) *National Professional Qualification for Headship: Information for Applicants*, London: TTA.

Weiner, G. (1994) *Feminisms in Education: An Introduction*, Buckingham: Open University Press.

Part 4
Groups at the margins

13 Gender equality, the 'learning society' policies, and community education

Lyn Tett

Introduction

People learn in many different ways and contexts and if the society in which they live regards learning as a normal activity for people of all ages then everyone, rather than a limited group, is likely to be effectively engaged in some form of learning of their choice. Currently, however, participation in any post-compulsory education and training is both a highly gendered activity where 'men . . . receive a greater share of substantial employer-funded education and training for adults' (Sargant *et al.* 1997: 21), and highly classed, where those who leave education largely unqualified are unlikely to engage in learning later. It appears that if you do not succeed in the first place then you will not succeed later! On the other hand, women outnumber men by 2.5 to 1 in community-based adult education classes (*ibid*). This is particularly true of education provision in Scotland where a range of community-based adult learning initiatives succeed in engaging with women who do not normally seek out learning opportunities, often offering a first step back into education (see SCEC 1995). This is partly because there is a Community Education Service that, uniquely in Europe, offers an integrated structure for the promotion of lifelong learning which takes positive action to enable excluded people, such as educationally disadvantaged women, unemployed men and minority ethnic groups, to participate in education and training.

There are many ways in which a learning society and notions of lifelong learning have been and may be conceptualised. For example, Robert Owen in the last century, suggested that 'any general character, from the worst to best, from the most ignorant to the most enlightened, may be given to any community by application of [good education]' (Silver 1965: 61) and regarded learning as a fundamental right of all citizens, whatever their age, as a means of developing a more equitable society. In contrast, the idea of the 'learning society', that has been developed in the late 1990s, is replete with different assumptions. These were developed in European and UK policy documents, became formalised in 1996 when this was declared as the 'European Year of Lifelong Learning', and have been confirmed by the Labour government's Green Paper in 1998. These policies embody a particular conception of society that is mainly a response to an economic and employment climate where mobility and short-term contracts have become the norm with the concomitant need to constantly update knowledge and skills (see Hutton 1997).

The conception of gender equality, similarly, will affect what action is taken to address perceived problems of lack of participation in learning opportunities. Within community education there are, broadly, two contrasting perspectives on gender and equal opportunities, one which identifies inequality as a problem of equal importance to men and women and one which regards women's lack of power in the economic, political and educational structures as part of a far broader pattern of female subordination. These perspectives are generally referred to as the 'liberal' and the 'radical' approaches.

These different explanations and analysis of sexual inequalities have generated different solutions and strategies for change. Liberals have tended to focus on increasing access for women to education and employment combined with the examination of factors such as prejudice, traditional values and the lack of proper role models that act to sustain this situation. Radicals, on the other hand, have put the relationship between patriarchy, power and women's subordination at the centre of their thinking and asserted that a dominant male and subordinate female dualism is manifest at every level of society (Thompson 1983). Radicals have expressed doubts about the value of policies which deny or ignore competing educational and economic interests and have criticised policies of educational change which fail to acknowledge the constant competition for power and control, between men and women, black people and white, and between class interests. In this view expanding educational opportunity is not just a question of juggling resources or encouraging access to non-traditional occupations for women. If women are to capture a greater slice of the 'cake', men will have to give up their hold upon the system – something they are unlikely to do without a struggle. Radicals have therefore concentrated on the politics of change through an emphasis on the value of collective action, groups and networks which provide support against the hostility that radical ideas generate. In contrast, liberals have sought to generate change from the inside and adopted a consensual, professional approach which plays down the possibility of conflict.

Underpinning educational interventions from both these broad perspectives is the basic premise that women are disadvantaged by men and steps should therefore be taken to expose this disadvantage and challenge and change it. One strategy for doing this has been to develop educational interventions with both genders designed to challenge stereotypes in ways which address issues of power and inequality, both individually and structurally. Educational work with men has been justified on the grounds that by making men aware of their sexist assumptions they are able to take responsibility for challenging oppression. Educational interventions that have sought to promote greater gender equality approaches for women include programmes to encourage entry to non-traditional areas (Women into Science and Technology) or promotion in specific roles (Women into Management) at the 'liberal' end of the feminist spectrum or the education that starts from the lived experiences of women which helps them take action to change their oppression at the 'radical' end of the spectrum (see Thompson 1983).

Policies, as Ball (1990: 22) has argued, are 'statements about practice – the ways things could or should be – which are derived from statements about the world'. What is seen as legitimate in terms of policy and practice privileges certain visions and interests which embody claims to speak with authority in ways that shut out alternatives. However, although the conception of the learning society as evidenced through these policy documents may be limited, the potential exists for community educators to interpret these policies more radically. One particular difficulty in seeking such a vision has been a discourse that privileges the hegemonic view of a gender-neutral society that denigrates the values of caring and mutual support and values the economic over the social.

To explore the ways in which the policy debate has been constrained through the imposition of particular political discourses, I examine the EU and UK policy documents on lifelong learning in order to make explicit the fallacies embedded within them. I then seek to identify ways in which these policies might be challenged that would promote greater gender equality.

A European Union perspective

At EU level the term 'Lifelong Learning' first came into common parlance in the 1993 White Paper *Growth, Competitiveness, Employment: The Challenges and Ways Forward into the 21st Century* (Delors 1993). As the title suggests, the White Paper is primarily concerned with laying out a formula for economic success within the Union. However, within the introduction, the White Paper recognises 'lifelong education and training' as key to job retention and economic prosperity. It goes on to say:

> Our countries' education and training systems are faced with major difficulties . . . [that] are rooted in social ills [such as] the breakdown of the family and the demotivation bred by unemployment. Preparation for life in tomorrow's world cannot be satisfied by once-and-for-all acquisition of knowledge and know how . . . [but should be based on] . . . the concept of developing, generalising and systematising lifelong learning and continuous training.
> (Delors 1993: 16, 146)

These paragraphs enshrine many of the key concepts underpinning the European paradigm for lifelong learning. In terms of gender equality there is an unreflective and somewhat pathological view of 'the family' that has apparently 'broken down' and consequently can be blamed for a range of social ills such as delinquency, vandalism, child abuse, benefit dependency, and an implicit separation of the problems presented by individuals from the social and political order that created the problems. In many ways this approach mirrors that popularised by Etzioni (1993: 61) whose argument is that the decline of the two-parent family lies at the heart of the problems of Western society because both parents are necessary to provide mutually supportive educational involvement if children are to learn effectively.

Member States are asked to develop training policies that meet the education and training needs of the long-term unemployed, ensure increased flexibility in delivery mechanisms and decentralisation of the management of education systems. The gendered nature of the ability to participate in further education and training without, for example, adequate childcare provision (McGivney 1993; Engender 1997), is not considered.

The stated aim of a second White Paper entitled *Teaching and Learning: Towards the Learning Society* (Cresson 1995) was to address what were perceived as 'factors of upheaval' affecting Member States. These are identified as the impact of the information society, the impact of internationalisation as it affects job creation, and the impact of the scientific and technical worlds. The White Paper also prioritised education and training concerned with citizenship, personal fulfilment and the tackling of exclusion. Again, a gender-neutral society is portrayed with 'the everyday social relations of gender' (Brah 1992: 142) such as low paid employment, housework and childcare and women's exclusion from key centres of political and economic power, ignored (Walby 1997).

UK government perspectives

In December 1995 a consultative document on lifetime learning was introduced. While issues of lifelong learning had been raised in other government policies, this documented the first coherent view of government's vision of lifelong learning. The primary concern was with economic competitiveness and human resource development, however, like its European counterpart it also recognised the importance of learning in other spheres: 'The presentation and acquisition of knowledge and the ability of individuals to fulfil their personal capacity are vital signs of a free and civilised society' (DfEE 1995: 4). Despite this wide vision it is clear that learning was seen as taking place in response to market forces. An example of this is the major roles and responsibilities ascribed to individuals and the minor role ascribed to government:

> First, the learning market should be driven by customers and their choices, not by providers or other organisations;
>
> Second, demand for learning should be well informed and the result of considered plans;
>
> Third, the government should intervene only where it can effectively lower the barriers that prevent the learning market working properly or accelerate the introduction of good practice; it should not seek to distort decisions on learning. Public expenditure needs to be justified in terms of wider economic and social returns.
>
> (DfEE 1995: 40)

The consultative document embodied an assumption that it was the responsibility of the individual to engage with the learning society and the underpinning ideas were about pragmatic expediency and market principles rather than any wider egalitarian understanding. This was made even clearer by a Scottish Office document (SOEID 1997) issued following the responses to the DfEE document that stated 'Scotland's future competitiveness demands a more highly skilled and adaptable work force. To achieve this we must convince individuals of the relevance of continuing learning' (SOEID 1997: 5).

In February 1998 the New Labour Administration issued a Green Paper *The Learning Age* (DfEE 1998). It again reiterated the need 'for a well-educated, well-equipped and adaptable labour force' (ibid.: 3) but added '[learning] helps make ours a civilised society, develops the spiritual side of our lives and promotes active citizenship . . . It strengthens the family, the neighbourhood and consequently the nation' (*ibid.*: 3). Throughout the Green Paper there is an emphasis on partnership, with the government's role 'to help create a framework of opportunities for people to learn . . . [by] sharing responsibility with employers, employees and the community' (*ibid.*: 6). While there is a clear shift from the earlier emphasis on the primacy of the market, the obstacles posed by class, poverty, employment status and gender have not been explored despite the evidence provided in the earlier Fryer Report (1997) about their importance.

If the assumptions contained in these documents are to be challenged then it is important to identify a framework for critically analysing policies relating to lifelong learning in order to reveal the contradictions that leave space for counter-hegemonic actions. Policies on lifelong learning appear to draw upon a number of inter-related fallacies (see Blacke 1996) that cumulatively give the impression of a commitment to lifelong learning. However, if these fallacies are separated out and examined it becomes easier to see how they might be challenged by those committed to a more radical view. In order to do this the next section explores each in turn.

Fallacies

Fallacy: education and training are commodities in the market

If education and training are placed within the market place and as a commodity then failures in education are assumed to be because the 'producers' (educators and local government politicians) have taken over and pursue their own purposes at the expense of the needs of the 'consumers' of the service. Marketisation and the commodification of public services are thus portrayed as mechanisms for greater efficiency and increased consumer control. While the covert aim may be to undermine the power of professionals, the overt claim is that they will bring about an improvement in the quality of educational provision by creating a system in which high quality provision is financially rewarded.

However, there is little empirical evidence to suggest that removal of the power of professionals and the placing of education and training within a market context does improve efficiency or user control. For example, the incorporation of Further Education Colleges has led to less opportunities for socio-economically excluded communities rather than more (see Tett and Ducklin 1995). Rather than empowering consumers a market driven system perpetuates inequalities because, as Ranson suggests:

> The market . . . elides, but reproduces, the inequalities that consumers bring to the market place. Under the guise of neutrality, the institution of the market actively confirms and reinforces the pre-existing social class order of wealth and privilege.
>
> (Ranson 1994: 95–6)

For those marginalised by inadequate childcare, or poverty or geography, their choice will be limited by the lack of accessible provision; for those marginalised by cultural difference, excluded from current systems, it will be their lack of knowledge and understanding of the system itself which disadvantages them. There seems little likelihood that the market will do anything to improve people's dispositional barriers to learning.

Similarly, this argument suggests that within the market context, education and training are activities which will enhance the individual's ability to engage only in economic life and through this contribute to 'national culture and quality of life' (DfEE 1995: 3). Once the citizen is constructed primarily as a consumer, a very particular and limiting notion of lifelong learning follows. Indeed, as Turner (1994: 157) has pointed out, the language of citizenship, including rights discourses, has quite simply not included women mainly because of their caring role in the family.

Moreover, there is an emphasis on the individual which appears to militate against a desire to work with and for others. At the centre of the marketisation model is the individual, not as a contributor to the democratic society, but rather as self-interested, embodying 'possessive individualism' (see McPherson 1975). While human beings are not necessarily by nature possessively self-interested, markets can make them so because an intrinsically selfish motivation and competition are encouraged.

Fallacy: economic success equals eradication of deprivation and exclusion

The European Community offers the following definition of social exclusion:

> Social exclusion refers to the multiple and changing factors resulting in people being excluded from the normal exchanges, practices and rights of modern society . . . It emphasises the weaknesses in social infrastructure and the risk of allowing a two-tier society to become established by default.
>
> (Commission of the European Communities 1993)

There is a clear recognition in this document of the complexity and multifaceted nature of social exclusion and a willingness to seek measures to combat it. Within a UK context, however, inadequate skill levels within the unemployed population are seen as the causes of poverty and failures of the education and training systems to meet the needs of the economy are in turn blamed for rising levels of unemployment. At another level the impact of globalisation has been used to account for perpetuating a growing inequality but this explanation is then used as a reason why nation–states do not have opportunities to intervene (see Cockett 1996: 56).

Within the lifelong learning policy documents it is suggested that economic competitiveness is the desired goal and that economic success will have benefits for all. However, the link between education and training and economic development is complex and there is no evidence that participating in learning will necessarily lead to greater prosperity for all. Instead, lifelong learning policies should address questions about how vocational education and training will enable the most excluded to participate in a vibrant economy.

Fallacy: failure is the fault of the individual

This fallacy is intimately related to the preceding two. Given that the market is perceived as fair and equal, then failure to succeed in a market structure cannot be the fault of the system, but rather is rooted in the failings of the individual to engage appropriately. In this sense, not only educational failure, but also exclusion can be identified as individual pathologies. Placing individuals in competition with each other in a market situation also undermines any aspiration towards active citizenship in a participative democracy since, as Ranson says: 'The institution of the market demands a singular currency of transaction . . . because it simplifies human beings and denies the complexity of their individuality and interdependence' (1994: 92–3).

Within the policy frameworks offered for lifelong learning issues such as non-participation, educational under-achievement, lack of knowledge of the range of education and training opportunities, are not perceived as structural failures but rather issues of individual attitude or ability. However, as Veronica McGivney (1990: 20) has pointed out, many adults do not participate, not because of low motivation but because powerful constraints arise from cultural and social class divisions. School creates (or reinforces) sharp divisions in society, by conditioning children to accept different expectations and status patterns according to their academic 'success' or 'failure'. Through the use of imposed standards and selection, the education system traditionally rejects or excludes large numbers of the population, many of whom subsequently consider themselves to be educational failures.

If, therefore, it is the structure of society that creates inequalities, and education and training are part of that structure, then why should individuals participate in a system in which they know they start at a disadvantage? It is insufficient to just recognise inequality and strive for greater inclusion, rather, we need to look beyond that to the causes of that inequality. Moreover, if we regard education as being about responding to individual need and this is seen within a context of middle-class lifestyles, then no attention is paid to the ways in which these 'needs' are politically constructed and understood (see Tett 1993).

Similarly if it is individuals' attitudes and inadequacies that alienate them from education and training, then there is no logic in promoting lifelong learning through refinement of systems that are already failing. As Nisbet and Watt (1995: 63) state: 'tackling educational disadvantage through schools, however, faces a serious obstacle in the antagonism felt by many adults and pupils to schools and to the authority they represent'.

The fallacy that individual failings lie at the heart of either educational failure or economic success creates a convenient scapegoat for structural inequality justified through the workings of the market. This means that the 'learning society' becomes one more way of reproducing and legitimating existing inequalities.

Fallacy: education is neutral and ungendered

Participation in education could currently be described as a pyramid with women now predominating in continuing education and further education which are the least well resourced sectors. As Maggie Woodrow points out in relation to higher education:

> In all European countries, a gender breakdown of the university system [has] at the base undergraduate level [women holding] the balance; at postgraduate level it is against them; at senior lecturer and management level they are seriously underrepresented . . . In education systems as a whole women are most heavily represented on the staff of primary schools and most underrepresented in universities – this sector of course carrying the greatest status, remuneration and influence.
>
> (Woodrow 1996: 36)

Not only is participation in education gendered but the subjects studied also reflect a male/female dichotomy. A number of authors (Stromquist 1990; Thomas 1990) have argued that not only are certain subjects seen as more suitable for men than women but also these subjects in themselves seem to embody qualities which are linked to ideas about 'masculinity' and 'femininity'. 'Knowledge' as a whole becomes compartmentalised with the result that some kinds of knowledge are considered more important and this is communicated very effectively in schools and other institutions. Subject specialisation, therefore, reinforces gender distinctions. In addition, an emphasis on new technologies as a way of advancing learning opportunities risks exacerbating social and gender divisions resulting in a 'society divided between the information-rich and the information-poor' (Fryer 1997: 21). The government's Green Paper (DfEE 1998) has put particular emphaisis on the use of new technology to deliver learning but has not shown how students are to become computer literate or how teachers are to be trained in understanding the application of technology to learning, nor acknowledged the gendered differences in access to, and familiarity with, these technologies (Engender 1997).

If the gendered nature of participation in education and training is ignored and 'equal opportunities' policies are based on a meritocratic model that assumes that opportunities are not defined, interpreted and applied by those already in positions of power, then the learning society becomes just one more way of reinforcing the status quo. One effect of the gender imbalance among decision-makers is that facilities that might increase participation and study opportunities for women are seldom prioritised, particularly in terms of creche places and other provision that would make for family-friendly services. In addition, an emphasis on vocational and work-based education and training has tended to benefit men more than women partly because of women's predominance in part-time work where the majority are responsible for paying their own fees for learning (Sargant *et al.* 1997: 57).

Much of the current provision within continuing education is of programmes designed along sexually stereotyped lines which emphasise women's roles as mothers and household managers and men's as workers and providers. These messages do not convey emancipatory knowledge and may solidify values and attitudes that cause women and men to accept current gender relations rather than question them. However, people's views about the way the world works are forged in their daily experiences. For both men and women, whose experience is of a sex-segregated labour force and of a family structure which still assumes that women are responsible for most of the domestic labour (see Gaskell 1992; Engender 1997), it is hardly surprising that a culture based on gender differences is assumed to be the norm. Ideas about what is possible are rooted in experience so knowledge about what men and women do *now* suggests that this is what they must *continue* to do. So change becomes very difficult.

This means that a policy that is committed only to marginal changes will continue to preserve that world as it is. What is necessary is a 'problematising' approach (see Freire 1972) that enables oppressed groups to reflect critically on their reality in a way that enables them to alter their social relations. In particular, this should address the changes in the family structure such as the increase in women's participation in the labour force, the growth of the percentage of women who are sole carers for their children, the increase in divorce and remarriage rates, which have made the 'traditional' family of two natural parents with a mother at home unrepresentative of the current family pattern (see Walby 1997). It is a mark of the hegemonic nature of familial ideology that the so-called 'traditional' family has become the foundation of public policy in a range of areas, such as parental involvement in schools, and why its apparent breakdown is a cause for concern throughout Europe.

Challenging the arguments

I have suggested that the lifelong learning documents present a powerful policy steer precisely because they are so all encompassing that it is hard to identify and analyse cogently all the underlying fallacies. However, by deconstructing the policies it is possible to identify a number of paradoxes that throw up contradictions which in turn create spaces for challenge and alternative action. This could lead to a curriculum based on the development of a critical understanding of the social, political and economic factors that shape experience whereby learning becomes a truly lifelong process concerned with reflection on, for example, the ways in which life experiences are gendered. Individuals, at whatever stage of their lives, would be empowered to make informed choices about what they needed to learn based on an understanding of the opportunities and constraints affecting them. The choices people would be likely to make may well be about acquisition of vocational skills or qualifications but are equally likely to be about fulfilling social or cultural objectives (see Blacke 1996: 56).

Community educators need, through their daily practice, to demonstrate the efficacy of this model in action to show policy-makers and others involved in the delivery of education and training that alternative constructs for learning are effective in enabling individuals and communities to fulfil their social, economic and personal needs. The 'discourse of blame' which has already been identified may put onerous burdens on education and training but at the same time it places it in a very powerful position at the centre of debates. This is a position that community educators should be exploiting, since in times of change (the restructuring of local government, with its focus on decentralisation, and a new administration committed to promoting adult learning at home and at work), there are opportunities to use the spaces provided by these contradictions to develop a more radical practice. This would involve the valuing of learning in relation to communities and society as a whole through, for example, supporting activists to argue for change that would benefit all the community.

The way in which these policies may offer opportunities for the fostering of active citizenship creates other possibilities. By centring citizenship within a context of social justice it is possible to challenge many of the fallacies contained within the lifelong learning policies. The emphasis on the individual as a consumer and 'possessive individualism' can be challenged on the basis that it is antipathetic to fostering the sense of collective responsibility that is central to active citizenship. Learning within a market construct can be challenged for its failure to address the exclusion of certain groups and individuals in society. Positive action in favour of the less privileged can then be justified as a way of involving more people in a participatory democracy that is essential for a functioning civil society. Within this paradigm women's gendered experiences would be seen as a learning resource to be used, rather than a deficiency to be rectified.

By placing a framework of liberatory practice at the centre of lifelong learning, and re-interpreting the policies accordingly, it is possible to create real opportunities for community educators to support change in the existing social order. A 'whole life – all life' focus will place the learner's needs and experience at the centre of the development of the capacity to recognise, understand and act to change the effects of the dominant political, social, and economic order. Practice placed in this framework can demonstrate to other providers and policy-makers its effectiveness in addressing learning needs in the broadest sense, using the government's own rationale to justify what is done.

Education can act as an emancipatory force which causes both men and women to question accepted gender roles. This has been demonstrated by a number of women's groups and, recently, one or two men's groups, who have introduced into the educational discussion issues such as abortion, authoritarianism in the family, and men's violence to women and children. It is likely that these groups can be a force for educational change especially if they start

> from the problems, experiences and social position of excluded majorities, from the position of the working people, women and black people. It means working up these lived experiences and insights until they fashion a real alternative.
>
> (Johnson 1988: 813)

Lifelong learning and the opportunities it represents can be used as a unifying force, not only between providers but also between different interest groups, in ways that ensure that this process of unification is in itself dialogical and challenges oppression and exclusion. The learning society might then be an intrinsically more democratic one in so far as its citizens would be more actively able to develop critiques of the power inherent in the social infrastructure. This will involve the nurturing of an education and training system whose function is not to reflect and reproduce gendered inequalities in society but rather one that prioritises provision for those whose earlier educational and socio-economic disadvantage would give them a first claim in a genuinely lifelong learning system.

References

Ball, S. J. (1990) *Politics and Policy Making in Education*, London: Routledge.

Blacke, F. (1996) 'Life long learning: The incomplete project', unpublished MEd dissertation, Heriot Watt University, Edinburgh.

Brah, A. (1992) 'Difference, diversity and differentiation', in R. Donald and A. Rattansi (eds) *'Race', Culture and Difference*, London: Sage.

Cockett, R. (1996) 'Thatcher's final victory: a Labour win', *New Statesman* 20 December, pp. 56–7.

Commission of the European Communities (1993) *Background Report: Social Exclusion, Poverty and Other Social Problems in the European Community*, ISEC/B11/93, Brussels: European Commission.

Cresson, E. (1995) White Paper: *Teaching and Learning: Towards the Learning Society*, Brussels: Commission of the European Communities.

Delors, J. (1993) *Growth, Competitiveness, Employment: The Challenges and Way Forward into the 21st Century*, Brussels: ECSC., EC., EAEC.

Department for Education and Employment (1995) *Lifetime Learning: A Consultation Document*, Sheffield: DfEE.

—— (1998) *The Learning Age: a Renaissance for a New Britain*, London: The Stationery Office.

Engender (1997) *Engender Audit*, Edinburgh: Engender.

Etzioni, A. (1993) *The Spirit of Community: The Reinvention of Modern American Society*, New York: Simon and Schuster.

Freire, P. (1972) *Pedagogy of the Oppressed*, Harmondsworth: Penguin.

Fryer, R.H. (1997) *Learning for the Twenty-First Century* London: DfEE.

Gaskell, J. (1992) *Gender Matters from School to Work*, Buckingham: Open University Press.

Hutton, W. (1997) *The State to Come*, London: Vintage.

Johnson, R. (1988) 'Really useful knowledge, 1790–1850', in T. Lovett (ed.) *Radical Approaches to Adult Education: A Reader*, London: Routledge.

McGivney, V. (1990) *Education's for Other People: Access to Education for Non-Participant Adults*, Leicester: NIACE.

—— (1993) *Women, Education and Training*, Leicester: NIACE.

McPherson, C.S. (1975) *Democratic Theory: Essays in Retrieval*, Oxford: Clarendon.

Nisbet, J. and Watt, J. (1995) *Educational Disadvantage in Scotland: A 1990's Perspective*, Edinburgh: SCEC.

Ranson, S. (1994) *Towards the Learning Society*, London: Cassell Education.

Sargant, N. with Field, J., Francis, H., Schuller, T. and Tucket, A. (1997) *The Learning Divide*, Leicester: NIACE.

SCEC (1995) *Scotland as a Learning Society: Myth, Reality and Challenge*, Edinburgh: Scottish Community Education Council.

Silver, H. (1965) *The Concept of Popular Education*, London: MacGibbon and Kee.

SOEID (1997) *Lifelong Learning: The Way Forward*, Edinburgh: The Scottish Office.

Stromquist, N. P. (1990) 'Gender inequality in education: accounting for women's subordination', *British Journal of Sociology of Education* 11, 2: 137–53.

Tett, L. (1993) 'Education and the market place', *Scottish Educational Review* 25, 2: 123–31.

Tett, L. and Ducklin, A. (1995) 'Further education colleges and educationally disadvantaged adults', *Scottish Educational Review* 27, 2: 154–64.

Thomas, K. (1990) *Gender and Subject in Higher Education*, Birmingham: SRHE and OU Press.

Thompson, J. (1983) *Learning Liberation: Women's Response to Men's Liberation*, London: Croom Helm.

Turner, B. (1994) 'Postmodern culture: modern citizens', in B. van Steenburgen (ed.) *The Condition of Citizenship*, London: Sage.

Walby, S. (1997) *Gender Transformations*, London: Routledge.

Woodrow, M. (1996) *Project on Access to Higher Education in Europe: Part 1 – Synthesis and Recommendations*, Strasbourg: Council of Europe.

14 Gender and exclusion from school

Gwynedd Lloyd[1]

Introduction

The 'New Labour' government has indicated its desire to tackle social exclusion and it is evident that school exclusions are one of the earliest points at which pupils become detached from the mainstream. Attention has turned to the fact that not only is exclusion from school increasing, but that far more boys than girls are excluded from school. When this is acknowledged in the literature, it tends to be through a focus on the majority boys and rarely on the smaller but still significant numbers of girls excluded. This chapter will focus on disciplinary exclusion from school as a gendered process through a discussion of findings from a recent Scottish research project on 'Exclusion from School and Alternatives'. It will show that exclusionary processes in Scotland are similarly gendered although this aspect may not often be explicitly recognised or considered by the participants in the process. There is very considerable variation between schools in the proportion of girls excluded, pointing to a complex pattern of gendered construction of deviance and raising questions about the relationship between gender and school ethos. The chapter suggests the usefulness of comparative research on the impact of different policies and practice in varied cultural contexts north and south of the border.

Scotland: the context

In Scotland, unlike England and Wales, there has not been a national reporting system on exclusion nor has recent legislation defined the process of exclusion other than in general terms, the law on exclusion being found in a number of different Acts and regulations (Cullen *et al.* 1996a). Information on pupils excluded was collected from education authorities through the data on non-attendance at school, exclusion paradoxically under the heading of unauthorised absence. Several authorities objected to this and failed to submit figures. In any case the lack of standardised exclusion definitions and processes meant that those figures which did appear were highly inaccurate. In 1998 following the publication of the research discussed below and after a period of national consultation the Scottish Office published national guidelines on exclusion (SOEID 1998).

There are other key features of the Scottish context which may be relevant to a discussion of the process of exclusion. Some, such as the development of a quasi-market structure for the delivery of educational services and significant curriculum changes, are common to Scotland and other parts of Britain but the character of the change, it may be argued, has been different. Strong Labour-controlled local authorities, with almost no schools opting out, a teacher trade union representing most teachers, and vocal parental and professional organisations meant that there was perhaps more of a balance with central government, although the effect of the recent restructuring of local government into thirty-two smaller authorities has still to be seen (Riddell and Brown 1994). Scottish education has perhaps always been a smaller and more homogeneous system, with curriculum change managed through the use of national guidelines in contrast to the more prescriptive National Curriculum. Scottish education ministers and HMIs in the last few years rarely engaged in public criticism of teachers.

Further relevant features of Scottish society are, first, the relatively small proportion of children from ethnic minority communities, very few from African-Caribbean families and, second, the higher level of children living in poverty than in the rest of Britain (Lloyd and Riddell 1997). Out of school there has been a broad consensus on the value of the welfare-based Children's Hearing System where decisions are made by a lay panel about children considered to need compulsory measures of care and/or control. This system is based on a structural separation between the legal establishment of guilt and the consideration of issues of care and welfare and reflects a concern to deal with children under 16 in terms of welfare even when the grounds of referral are offence based (Schafer 1992). Most Scottish authorities also have policies and structures, often referred to as youth strategies (Kendrick 1995), to promote inter-agency working and to maintain children, where possible, in their local schools and communities.

In the early 1990s there was, however, a sense of increasing pressure on schools and concern over what seemed to be increasing numbers of pupils being excluded. The research reported below was commissioned by the Scottish Office in order to provide a picture of exclusion policy and practice in Scotland.

Exclusion in Scotland: the research

The aims of the study were to map policy and practice of exclusion in Scotland and to explore in-school alternatives to exclusion. The project had three phases: a study of education authority policy and procedures across Scotland, a survey of head teachers about their exclusion policy and practice; and case studies of schools offering contrasting practices. The first phase found considerable variation in the ways authorities defined, counted and kept exclusion figures and variation on the kind of exclusion allowed and the length of time permitted.

In stage two information about numbers of excluded pupils was collected from 176 schools, 60 primary and 116 secondary, that is 3 per cent of primary schools and more than a quarter of all secondary schools in Scotland. In addition, 120 of the schools provided detailed written information about each pupil who had been excluded over an eight-month period. They do not constitute a representative sample as 60 per cent of the schools had been selected by their education authority, not randomly, but as being either high or low excluding in the context of their authority (Cullen *et al.* 1996b). Nevertheless, the data collected from these schools does provide an illuminating snapshot of Scottish practice.

In the third stage of the project, detailed interviews were carried out with a range of school staff, other professionals, parents and pupils in twelve schools, eight secondary and four primary, selected as matched pairs of 'high' and 'low' excluding but with broadly similar pupil populations. Some eighty-four interviews were conducted in total at this stage. We had some difficulties in gaining access to pupils and parents in some schools, particularly in the primary sector. Some head teachers seemed reluctant to disrupt the carefully balanced relationship they felt they had negotiated with parents of excluded pupils. Some interviews were conducted in school, others in places where pupils or parents felt more comfortable, for example in homes. One was even conducted in a supermarket cafe. So the findings discussed in this chapter derive from the interviews with head teachers and their written data on exclusion in stage two and on the more detailed interviews in the case study schools in stage three of the research project.

The overall picture of exclusion

Some 25 schools reported no exclusions during the previous 8 months, of these, 21 were in the primary sector. The 39 primary schools reporting exclusion figures had excluded 202 pupils in total while the secondary schools (110) had excluded 3,562 pupils. Three primary schools and 24 secondary schools had excluded more than 5 per cent of their population at least once during this period. In addition to exclusion, a further 959 pupils from the survey schools had been informally sent home, some in authorities where procedures did not officially allow this. Analysis of the detailed information provided showed that 64 per cent of excluded primary pupils and 69 per cent of excluded secondary pupils had been excluded on only one occasion during the study period. There was a substantial variation in both policy and practice between the Scottish authorities and a wide disparity between schools in numbers of pupils excluded and of days lost as a result of exclusion. These variations along with exclusion data for boys and girls are discussed in the remaining sections of the chapter.

Excluded pupils and socio-economic disadvantage

As catchment area or socio-economic status are not easily identified the project used two proxy measures for this; these were the percentage of pupils eligible for free school meals and the head teachers' estimation of the socio-economic status of the pupils:

> as the percentage of pupils eligible for free school meals increased, exclusion from school tended to increase but there were substantial exceptions. Some

13 per cent of the schools had both a high exclusion rate and the lowest percentage of pupils eligible for free school meals.

(Cullen *et al.* 1996b)

Conversely, 20 per cent of the schools had disadvantaged catchment areas but made less use of exclusion than some schools in prosperous areas.

Table 14.1 indicates that the secondary pupils who had been excluded were not overwhelmingly those eligible for free school meals, whereas seven out of ten excluded primary school pupils were eligible. The relationship between exclusion and poverty is therefore complicated. The data indicates that there were higher rates of exclusion in more disadvantaged areas but that other factors to do with the character of schools are clearly very important.

Gender and exclusion from schools in Scotland

Table 14.2 shows that boys were far more likely to have been excluded than girls, particularly from primary school. At the secondary level boys were excluded more often and for longer periods than girls. Overall, boys were between three and four times as likely than girls to have been excluded. For single exclusions boys outnumbered girls by three to one but were not excluded for longer periods than girls. For multiple exclusions boys outnumbered girls by just over four to one and were also more likely to be excluded for a higher total of days than girls.

Our findings are not statistically generalisable to the rest of Scotland but these

Table 14.1 Excluded pupils' eligibility for free school meals

Eligibility	Primary school pupils N = 184		Secondary school pupils N = 2,526	
	n	*%*	*n*	*%*
Eligible	134	73	824	33
Not eligible	50	27	1,198	47
No information	0	0	504	20

Table 14.2 Sex of excluded pupils

Sex	Primary school pupils N = 184		Secondary school pupils N = 2,518	
	n	*%*	*n*	*%*
Boys	169	92	1,934	77
Girls	15	8	584	23

Note: Overall numbers shown in the tables vary as a result of incomplete information provided in some categories by schools.

figures, if repeated across the country, would suggest that the proportion of girls excluded from secondary school, i.e. 23 per cent, could be somewhat higher in Scotland than in the rest of Britain. Studies of exclusion in England and Wales have all found disproportionately larger numbers of boys to have been excluded and in particular African-Caribbean boys. Boys are between four and five times as likely to be excluded than girls (Blyth and Milner 1996). At primary school level the proportion of boys is even larger (Parsons *et al.* 1995; Hayden 1997).

The findings of this study also support the argument that although girls are a smaller proportion they are still excluded in numbers – just about 600 girls from 120 schools in our study! Yet a discussion of the experience of girls rarely features in the literature. Nor does it stand out as an important issue in the perspectives of head teachers. When the 176 head teachers interviewed in phase two of the research project were asked an open question about what they saw as the salient issues about exclusion, only two mentioned gender. The unquestioning acknowledgement of the gender differences is exemplified by the acting head teacher of a secondary school when providing a list of excluded pupils:

> I don't mind if you take this away and do a boy/girl thing, for example. You're very welcome to it. I'm not going to do it because I don't have the time but you'll find boys grossly outweigh girls in this . . .

It might be argued that the most significant finding of our project is perhaps the way in which the gender differences are largely taken for granted by respondents.

Analysis of our case study interview data does, however, point us to some ideas which may be helpful in exploring gendered patterns of exclusion. These are:

- that girls' deviance in school may be different from boys';
- that schools have gendered models of deviance;
- that schools respond differently to girls' deviance;
- that schools employ different strategies with boys and girls;
- that teachers respond differently in classrooms;
- that the ethos and culture of the school are gendered;
- that commitment to equal opportunities affects how schools respond to deviance.

In the British literature on exclusion, as suggested earlier, where exclusion is considered in terms of gender this tends to focus on boys. By implication therefore girls are not excluded as often simply because they are not boys. Boys offend more than girls, are identified more often as having 'emotional and behavioural difficulties', or 'conduct disorders'. Therefore the disparity is 'normal' and unproblematic and explanations characterised by an implicit biological reductionism.

More sociologically based arguments suggest that although girls may be as 'needy, disruptive and prone to problems as boys . . . they present less of a challenge in schools' (Crozier and Anstiss 1995: 44). Girls' disruptiveness is seen to be linked to their gender identity and to be less overtly confrontational. The accounts of girls themselves of getting into trouble at school often refer to persistent everyday misbehaviour such as talking, smoking, not wearing 'suitable' clothes, lateness, absence and reflect an awareness of a negotiation over the boundaries of acceptable behaviour (Lloyd 1992). This negotiation implies a recognition by pupils of the gendered constructions of teachers' perceptions of boys' and girls' deviant behaviour (Davies 1984).

A number of interviewees in our study argued that the character of girls' deviance was different: 'In third year especially it's bullying, falling out with their friends, usually over some boy' (Educational welfare officer). Several mentioned the particular importance of friendships to girls and also that girls might be more likely than boys to get into trouble as a result of responding to 'slagging':

> They [i.e. other pupils] call you names and nag at you and you just end up striking back because you get sick of it, then it's not the other person that gets into trouble it's me.
>
> (Girl, secondary school)

> It doesn't mean we haven't had girls in the past who have caused a fair degree of worry but we don't just now. I can't even think of any who maybe have the potential. They pose us different worries. I think the girls' worries are relating to things like attendance. They're maybe being kept at home to look after younger ones.
>
> (Primary school head teacher)

The various participants in this study argued that the reasons for exclusion would be different: 'There would be considerably more boys excluded than girls but there are certainly girls in living memory who have had a short-term exclusion, mostly for language, more so than anything else' (Assistant head, secondary school).

Analysis of the reasons given in written data by schools for the exclusion of pupils (in stage two) of our study, however, indicates that a very similar pattern of reasons was given for boys and girls.

Figure 14.1 shows that the largest number of exclusions from school are for what the schools see as fighting or assault between pupils (for assaults on staff see below), followed by generally disruptive behaviour. Vandalism was given as a reason much more often for boys than for girls, 11:1 whereas the small figures for truancy as a reason for exclusion showed the largest proportion of girls, 15 girls to 24 boys. So the reasons given by schools for exclusion of boys and girls suggest that, although boys and girls are excluded in very different proportions, they are excluded for similar reasons.

Of course the kinds of reasons given are themselves open to considerable interpretation. When fighting between pupils is considered serious, or when fighting becomes characterised as assault, depends on the perception or judgement of the staff. What these finding do not directly indicate is whether when boys and girls are excluded, for example, for disruptive behaviour, what assumptions about

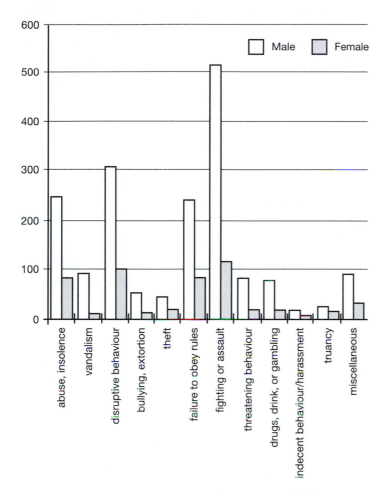

Figure 14.1 The reason for exclusion identified by schools

Notes: Reasons identified here were provided by schools in the phase two survey. Primary school
pupils N = 184, secondary pupils N = 2,250.

gender and disruptiveness may be implicit in the construction of the behaviour as
sufficiently disruptive to warrant exclusion.

Truancy in relation to exclusion of girls was raised on a number of occasions by
respondents.

> I know one girl just runs rings round you and she appears, she disappears and
> she is just basically raising her fingers to the system, so although it looks like
> it's for persistent truancy it's for persistent disregard for any system the
> school has for discipline. She's cheeky to staff when she's here – it's just a
> mess – but one of the things it goes down as is truancy.
>
> (Assistant head, secondary school)

This suggests that the important aspect is not the failure to attend but the implied challenge to the authority of the school. The use of exclusion in relation to girls who truant was raised by two external professionals. An educational welfare officer talked of working to get a girl to return to school but of her exclusion on her first day of return. She also saw the problem as lying in the girl's apparent attitude to authority. She described her as having been in trouble with the police. 'It was more her attitude that got her into it, she wouldn't even get out of bed to talk to them.' A Reporter to Children's Hearings, when discussing a secondary school girl with a pattern of exclusion and truancy, also raised the problem 'of dealing with children who don't want to be in school and when they do arrive are excluded anyway'. The girl's mother saw the issues as related. 'She's been excluded a lot, mainly for her behaviour, and as a result of that she's been doing a lot of truanting as well . . . I think it's more boredom than anything else.' She said that her daughter was often excluded for disruptiveness in class:

> She seems to take over the class, sort of thing. She gets other kids to . . . She can disrupt the class easily . . . I think I would say that she's one of the leaders, you know, because she's not one of the sheep. Everybody more or less sort of copies her and then that's the teacher sort of left, you know . . .

The attendance officer involved with the family above also talked about the greater maturity of girls like this, who have not officially reached school-leaving age, but have actually moved on from it. The earlier maturity of girls was mentioned by a social worker in a secondary school based project:

> Teachers complain about very immature boys and girls coming in, especially boys I think – first year boys they basically behave like primary three or four pupils who are not ready to accept the discipline of 'That's your desk, that's your chair and you stay in it!'

Interviews in our case study schools showed that there were variations in the concept of an 'acceptable' pupil, in particular in the primary schools they identified some pupils as difficult but 'savable'. Factors seen to be important to this definition included age, level of achievement, personal and relationship skills, parental contact with the school, parental and home circumstances and length of the time the problem had persisted. Gender was not mentioned as a factor despite the huge disparity in the figures. The apparently greater maturity of girls, however, may be significant in that they may be seen by teachers to have considerably more developed social and relationship skills. The teachers in the primary schools suggested that often excluded pupils were seen to have been those who had

> challenged the teacher's competence and status by questioning, contradicting, wasting time or hindering or bothering others in the class. The impact of

other pupils in the teachers's judgment of whether or not a pupil at risk of exclusion could be saved should not be underestimated.

(Cullen *et al.* 1996a)

So the school's definition of a 'savable pupil', boy or girl, may also be influenced by the views and the actions of their peers (Marshall 1996).

It is clear that one important factor affecting how schools view deviant behaviour is the extent of explicit challenge to the school or to individual teachers. Related to this is the question of how girls and boys respond to correction or attempts to impose discipline by staff. A teacher of English in a secondary school, when discussing a girl who had been in trouble in the school argued in her favour that: 'she doesn't answer back, she takes a telling off, not very graciously but she doesn't answer back'.

Girls may be more effective in defusing challenge by 'taking a telling off'. Girls were also more likely than boys to be excluded only once which may suggest that if exclusion does act as an effective deterrent, and this is not the only possible way of looking at this, then it may be more effective for girls.

There was some suggestion of greater leniency towards girls as the account from an excluded boy illustrates: 'In the class just after I came back from exclusion there was a lassie swearing and the teacher didnae bother but when I got caught I got chucked out' (Boy, secondary school). A mother's view also reveals the same perspective on girls' deviance: 'If it had been a boy that was doing what Isobel was doing, I don't think they would have given him so much space.'

It could be argued that girls may be treated with greater leniency or chivalrousness when they offend in ways considered typical for girls but with greater harshness when they are considered to be behaving in unfeminine ways, more typical of boys, for example, using violence. This has been well established in the criminal justice system. Further, it may be that decision-making is influenced by other aspects of the girl's life, again with greater harshness if her actions are not acceptably compatible with her female destiny (Gelsthorpe 1989; Hudson 1989; Samuel 1994). This may lead to a consideration together of indiscipline and morality for girls but not for boys. Social work staff interviewed in this project saw non-attendance at school as providing a gender-specific risk for girls, expressed in terms of the notion of moral danger: 'They're going out of control, they're in danger, in moral danger often' (Social worker).

So, the interviews with professionals involved in the exclusion process do suggest that gender is an important, although often implicit, factor in making sense of why girls *may* be excluded and of why they *may not* be excluded. Their accounts suggest that schools have highly gendered models of deviance.

Violence, power and decision-making

The small numbers of pupils excluded for violence towards teachers are shown in Table 14.3 along with figures for drug and offensive weapon related exclusions. Here the number of girls excluded for these reasons is even smaller. This is

Table 14.3 Pupils excluded for physical assault on staff, offensive weapons or drugs

Reason for exclusion	Boys excluded				Girls excluded				Total excluded	
	Primary N = 169		Secondary N = 1,726		Primary N = 15		Secondary N = 524		N = 1,434	
	n	%	n	%	n	%	n	%	n	%
Physical assault on staff	7	4	18	1	0	0	1	0.2	26	1
Drugs	1	0.6	38	2	0	0	6	1	45	2
Offensive weapons	4	2	14	0.8	0	0	1	0.2	19	0.8

paralleled in the criminal justice sphere where the proportion of women convicted of the most violent crimes is smaller than their general representation in the crime statistics. Such women may, however, be treated more harshly than equivalent men by the criminal justice system because their crime is not only violent but, worse, is unfeminine and therefore more 'abnormal'.

An assistant head of a secondary school described an incident involving a 'bad' girl:

> We had a girl recently who broke another girl's nose in the dining hall. The girl is standing in a queue in the dining hall. This one with about twenty of her chums comes through the dining hall, goes up to the girl, breaks her nose – premeditated, cast of 400 watching. Put her out, formally exclude, on the basis that if I was the parent of the victim I wouldn't want my daughter to go back into a place where this girl was. The authority wouldn't let us do that. We had to bring the kid back but I think the outcome will be that the other kid moves so we lose the nice kid because we are not allowed to formally exclude the bad kid.

This sounds like an action any school would find unacceptable. It is not clear, however, whether this was seen as particularly bad behaviour because it was a girl and perhaps because it was a girl engaging in violence with her peer group, a type of behaviour usually seen to be more typical of boys.

Decision-making in issues of exclusion is made, as it is made in the criminal justice system, largely by men. Scottish law defines exclusions as the responsibility of the head teacher. In our study only two of the secondary school head teachers were women. Even in primary schools, numerically dominated by women teachers, more than a third of heads were men. One assistant head in a secondary school described the decision-making on exclusion in the school board of studies, consisting of the Rector (i.e. head teacher) the Depute Rector and four Assistant Rectors, only one of the latter female. It may be argued that decision-making must be imbued with gender. Our data do not allow us to consider this in any depth. Other literature does look at relations of power in schools and in class-rooms in gender terms, and in terms of the sense of power felt by teachers.

Robinson describes the disciplinary structure of the schools in her research as authoritarian and sees this as perpetuated through an ideology of 'hegemonic masculinity' (Robinson 1992). Male and female teachers were seen to employ different classroom disciplinary strategies and to vary these according to the gender of their pupils. It may be that some male teachers are less threatened by disruptive behaviour in girls and are therefore more willing to accommodate them. One secondary guidance teacher described a case of exclusion that in his view could have been avoided. Two girls were outside and were told by a teacher to go into the classroom and sit in the middle:

> So they had taken him literally. They went into the classroom and sat in the middle of the floor. Now I would have gone Grrrrrr or whatever and they would have got up and have gone and that would have been the end of the matter. But, no, they end up suspended for three or four days.

So whether behaviour is considered sufficiently disruptive for exclusion may depend on the limits of tolerance, and the gendered conceptions of acceptable behaviour, of the individual teacher and the school staff with power to exclude. These limits are, however, themselves also circumscribed by school and authority policy.

Schools make a difference

Exclusion rates vary considerably from school to school. It is well established that these differences cannot be explained simply in terms of the individual character of pupils or the socio-economic characteristics of the schools' intake (Galloway *et al.* 1985; McLean 1987; McManus 1989; Blyth and Milner 1996). Our study, as outlined earlier, supports the view that the school itself does make a difference. While economic disadvantage was related to exclusion rates, there were none the less, schools with high exclusion rates in prosperous areas and schools with low exclusion rates in disadvantaged areas. The study does suggest that there is a need for research which would lead to more understanding of the cultures of working-class and middle-class boys and girls.

Comparison of schools with similar catchment areas and very different exclusion rates indicated that there were characteristics of the schools which tended to make them more inclusive or excluding. More inclusive schools tended to emphasise both social and academic goals rather than narrowly academic aims, to be characterised by more flexible and open pupil–teacher and school–home relationships, to have strong interprofessional relationships, a supportive senior management and a responsive local authority. If differences in overall exclusion rates between schools can be partly understood in terms of the culture and ethos of the school, then we need to ask questions about how these may be gendered.

School exclusion rates vary also in the proportion of boys and girls excluded. If such proportions reflected any simple distinction between the deviant behaviour of boys and girls then one would expect the rate to be constant. We, however, found like Daniels (1996) that this was not the case and that there was a big range across schools. One secondary school had excluded ten girls and no boys. In other schools, although there was always a majority of boys, the proportion varied considerably; in some schools the proportion was as high as 9:1, in others half of those excluded were girls. Both these groups of schools included urban and rural areas and disadvantaged and more affluent catchment areas. The rate of exclusion by gender was not associated with the overall rate of exclusion of the school. So how do we make sense of such large variation? Why should the exclusion process in some schools be more gendered? Our study raises more questions than it provides answers although there are indications of areas which could fruitfully be further explored. Local and national monitoring of exclusion statistics would fail to address some important differences in exclusion rates of boys and girls if they were analysed only in global terms which mask the considerable variations at school level.

Interviews with secondary school staff suggested that support strategies employed by the schools may sometimes be differentiated according to gender. Selection of support strategies is clearly influenced by the teacher's conception of the underlying reasons for the child's difficulties (Cullen *et al.* 1996a). The main reasons offered by teachers as explanations for behaviour problems included difficulties in domestic background, underlying difficulties in learning, psychological problem, socio-economic deprivation, and general disaffection with school. Other literature points to the greater tendency of girls' behaviour to be constructed in terms of emotional or individual psychological difficulties (Hudson 1989). If disruptiveness in boys is more likely to be seen in schools as 'normal', then it may be that disruptiveness in girls may be constructed as more abnormal and, as argued earlier, responded to with greater harshness. Alternatively, it may be that it is understood as an indication of an emotional difficulty and dealt with less punitively, for example through counselling rather than exclusion. Teachers' interpretations of girls' and boys' deviance mean that various support strategies and punitive processes may be happening in different schools and often within the same school.

Another area which could be further explored concerns the impact of equal opportunities policies on exclusion rates. Several interviewees suggested that there was a pressure to identify girls who might require additional support. Girls may be experiencing various 'difficulties' but because they may not express them in such a directly confrontational way as boys they are not offered formal support. So an equal opportunities strategy may encourage schools to actively identify girls to include in support services:

> But then that's one of the issues we try to look at in youth strategy, coming from the other side of the fence is that girls must have the same problems as boys, so we must look for girls here, because girls just don't present in the same way, in the same disruptive way as boys do, yet they must be under the same pressures, so they just sit quietly.
>
> (Behaviour support teacher, secondary school)

It's been a strange thing recently. One of the performance indicators that we have is that we are supposed to work with as many females as males and just over the last couple of years, not by any one of ourselves, but at the last count up we were 59 per cent female and 41 per cent male.

(Social work groupworker, working with secondary school)

This position, in part, stemmed from the acknowledgement that when girls were offered support this often involved their participation in activities where they were always in the minority, for example, groupwork often takes place with two or three girls to a group of eight or nine boys. When girls are referred to out of school provision they often find themselves in the same situation. One reason then, for girls to be more included is to create a more balanced atmosphere which is not dominated by the interests of boys. However, this may also draw more formal attention to girls who may therefore move more quickly through the tariff system of the school.

If equal opportunities policies encourage those working with pupils identified as deviant in school to include more girls, what impact will this have on exclusion rates? Does gender equity mean that more girls will be excluded?

Conclusion

Our study confirms that while there are major gender differences in the process of exclusion from school, these differences are often left implicit in the discussion of the issue of exclusion by school staff. Where these issue are addressed, they suggest a gendered model of deviance in school and, conversely, a gendered notion of acceptable pupils. It may be that schools and teachers are using different strategies with boys and girls, at both classroom and school level. It points to important questions still to be asked by researchers and policy makers about how gendered conceptions of behavioural difficulties may be reflected in exclusion rates. What characterises schools with high and low rates of exclusion of girls? How do more inclusive schools conceptualise behavioural difficulties and how are these gendered? How is school ethos gendered? Are schools with active equal opportunities policies processing more girls into disciplinary routes? We need to explore the processes of disciplinary decision-making and look at how structures of support are used for boys and for girls. The views of girls, and their families, are not strongly visible in the literature and should be more actively sought.

There are wider issues over the relationship between overall higher attainment rates and lower exclusion rates for girls and whether strategies to reduce rates of exclusion and engage boys more effectively in schools could lead to proportionately more excluded girls. The policy dilemma for schools over the balancing of the needs of the individual difficult child against the needs of the more compliant majority can also be viewed in gender terms. Differences in exclusion rate mean that sometimes this may be understood as the needs of disruptive boys versus those of compliant girls.

There would be very interesting questions also in trying to make sense of why Scottish schools might seem to be excluding more girls than their equivalents in England and Wales and whether the overall pattern and rate of increase of exclusion in Scotland may be different. Increasing rates of exclusion in England have been related to the increasing marketisation of education, with the greater autonomy of head teachers combined with greater central pressures over the curriculum. Parental choice widens social distance between schools and means that schools which are full need not consider admitting excluded or 'difficult' pupils. In Scotland too parental choice has widened differences between schools, particularly in the cities but there has been virtually no opting out of local council control. League tables of examination results have also increased pressures on schools. However, strong council policies of inclusion support those schools which are attempting to reduce their exclusion rate.

Guidance on exclusion has recently been issued by the Scottish Office (SOEID 1998). These guidelines, which follow from the research reported here and from the consultation with local authorities undertaken afterwards, have a very different flavour from equivalent DfEE documents. They emphasise that exclusion from school is seen as a last resort, that the educational needs of excluded pupils must continue to be addressed, that multi-agency approaches should be used and they refer to the series of pilot projects being funded on alternatives to exclusion. They explicitly encourage an inclusive approach. They argue that, while uniformity across the country is undesirable, some degree of consistency is needed, but leave the principal responsibility for the management of exclusion with the local councils. They do not, however, specify stages of exclusion in days or the nature of grounds for exclusion. They do ask for the completion of an incident report form for each exclusion, to form the basis of local and national monitoring. This will allow, in future, a more detailed analysis of patterns of exclusion by gender and the correlation of gender with other factors in exclusion, such as social class and ethnicity.

Further research, and reflection by authorities and by schools, are needed to explore how they construe and respond to deviant behaviour in both boys and girls. The restructuring in 1996 of local government into thirty-two smaller from twelve large regional authorities may be increasing a greater local diversity of practice with respect to exclusion and to alternatives. However, the development of the Scottish Parliament may create a counter-move towards more centralisation of educational policy and practice. These developments support a strong case for more cross-border research focusing on the impact of social and educational change on the educational experience of pupils, boys and girls.

Note

1 The research on which this chapter is based was funded by the Scottish Office Education and Industry Department and carried out by Mairi Ann Cullen, Margaret Johnstone, Pamela Munn and the author.

References

Blyth, E. and Milner, J. (eds) (1996) *Exclusion from School*, London: Routledge.

Crozier, J. and Anstiss, J. (1995) 'Out of the spotlight: girls' experience of disruption', in M. Lloyd-Smith and J. Dwyfor Davies (eds) *On the Margins. The Educational Experience of Problem Pupils*, Stoke on Trent: Trentham.

Cullen, M.A. and Lloyd, G. (1997) *Alternative Educational Provision for Excluded Pupils*, Report to the Scottish Office Education and Industry Department, Edinburgh: Moray House.

Cullen, M.A., Johnstone, M., Lloyd, G. and Munn, P. (1996a) *Exclusions from School and Alternatives 1. Educational Policy and Procedures*, Report to the Scottish Office Education and Industry Department. Edinburgh: Moray House.

—— (1996b) *Exclusions from School and Alternatives 2. The Headteachers' Perspective*, Report to the Scottish Office Education and Industry Department, Edinburgh: Moray House.

—— (1996c) *Exclusions from School and Alternatives 3. The Case Studies*, Report to the Scottish Office Education and Industry Department, Edinburgh: Moray House.

Daniels, H. (1996) 'Equal to the challenge', *Special!* Autumn edition.

Davies, L. (1984) *Pupil Power: Deviance and Gender in School*, Lewes: Falmer Press.

Galloway, D., Martin, R. and Wilcox, B. (1985) 'Persistent absence and exclusion from school: the predictive power of school and community variables', *British Educational Research Journal* 11, 1: 51–61.

Gelsthorpe, L. (1989) *Sexism and the Female Offender*, Aldershot: Gower.

Hayden, C. (1997) *Children Excluded from Primary School*, Buckingham: Open University Press.

Hudson, A. (1989) 'Troublesome girls: towards alternative definitions and policies', in M. Cain (ed.) *Growing Up Good: Policing the Behaviour of Girls in Europe*, London: Sage.

Kendrick, A. (1995) 'Supporting families through inter-agency work: youth strategies in Scotland', in M. Hill, R. Hawthorne Kirk and D. Part (eds) *Supporting Families*, Edinburgh: HMSO.

Lloyd, G. (1992) *Chosen with Care? Responses to Disturbing and Disruptive Behaviour*, Edinburgh: Moray House Publications.

Lloyd, G. and Riddell, S. (1997) 'Scotland', in C. Day, D. Van Veen, and G. Walraven (eds) *Children and Youth at Risk and Urban Education: Research, Policy and Practice*, Leuven-Apeldoorn: Garant.

McLean, A. (1987) 'After the belt: school processes in low excluding schools', *School Organisation* 7, 3: 303–10.

McManus, M. (1989) *Troublesome Behaviour in the Classroom: A Teacher's Survival Guide*, London: Routledge.

Marshall, W. (1996) 'Professionals, children and power', in E. Blyth and J. Milner (eds) *Exclusion from School*, London: Routledge.

Parsons, C., Benns, L., Howlett, K., Davies, A. and Driscoll, P. (1995) *National Survey of Local Education Authorities' Policies and Procedures for the Identification of, and Provision for, Children who are Out of School by Reason of Exclusion or Otherwise*, Final Report to the DfEE, Canterbury: Christ Church College.

Riddell, S. and Brown, S. (eds) (1994) *Special Educational Needs Policy in the 1990s*, London: Routledge.

Robinson, K. H. (1992) 'Classroom discipline: power, resistance and gender: a look at teacher perspectives', *Gender and Education* 4, 3: 273–87.

Samuel, E. (1994) 'Gender and differential treatment in the criminal justice system: a review of the research literature', in S. Asquith, and E. Samuel (eds) *Criminal Justice and Related Services for Young Adult Offenders*, Edinburgh: HMSO.

Schafer, M. (1992) 'Children's hearings and school problems', in G. Lloyd (ed.) *Chosen with Care? Responses to Disruptive and Disturbing Behaviour*, Edinburgh: Moray House Publications.

SOEID (1998) *Guidance on Issues Concerning Exclusion from School*, Circular No. 2/98, Edinburgh: Scottish Office.

15 Caring, consuming and choosing

Parental choice policy for mothers of children with special educational needs

Heather Wilkinson

Introduction

This chapter is based on a longitudinal study of the experiences of twelve mothers, of primary-aged children with special educational needs (SENs),[1] as they went through the statementing[2] and school choice process following the introduction of parental choice policy through the 1988 and 1993 Education Acts. Their experiences are illustrative of some of the problems which have arisen in the area of special educational needs policy in the 1990s and of wider tensions reflected in social welfare in England in the 1990s, as central government policy has influenced the domestic division of labour (David 1991). In turn, these individualised decisions about children's education can affect wider collective patterns of integration. Although parental responsibility for a child's education was already strongly gendered, the introduction of parental choice policy through the 1988 Education Act emphasised the need for someone to take on the responsibility of school choice. Research suggested that this became part of the existing domestic division of labour. For families where a child has SENs this responsibility became additional to that of carer, with both these roles usually undertaken by women. Mothers now take on the work involved in both statementing and choice of school and in this chapter I explore these themes of choice, caring, and work in relation to these activities.

Recent developments in parental choice and SEN policy

The 1980s was a period of fundamental change in social welfare and policy in England and Wales as consecutive Tory governments attempted to reduce public expenditure through critiques of dependency culture. An examination of the main legislation during the period illustrates the wider changes, with the New Right introducing market ideologies and a gradual shift away from egalitarian measures based on universal access to welfare provision to the notion of market selectivity as the solution to the perceived crisis of the welfare state. These changes were reflected in a number of social policy areas including health, public housing and social services. Loney *et al.* (1991) noted three main aspects of this reconstruction of welfare beginning with the 'rolling back of the state' which saw a reduction in state provision and an encouragement of a 'mixed economy of welfare' with a variety of public, private and voluntary service providers. Second, new patterns of control were created through an internal reorganisation of state services resulting in both increased central control and more localised control through competition. Finally, a rebalancing of state and private provision left state provision in some areas as the point of last resort, 'the choice of those who have no other choice' (ibid.: 4).

While education policy reflected all of the wider changes detailed above, the 1988 Education Reform Act (ERA) placed a much greater emphasis on the role of direct consumer choice through parental choice provisions than did any of the other newly created social markets (Gewirtz *et al.* 1995). From an ideological perspective, 'choice' is a difficult concept to argue against being apparently empowering and positive for all, but Stalker (1997) suggested that within the notion of choice it was possible to identify two distinct meanings or 'antimonies'. Thus choice might refer to a progressive idea of self-determination or to the operation of the consumer in the market place: 'Thus two different conceptualisations are contained – or perhaps concealed – within the one word. Such a juxtaposition blurs differing ethos in current policy initiatives, yet succeeds in winning unanimous approval for the concept' (ibid.: 6).

In the sphere of education, choice was sold to parents as offering greater opportunities for individual freedom, but in reality they were placed in the role of consumer, with limited options available. Competition and choice were seen to be the fundamental mechanisms by which education would be improved and what became clear from early research on parental choice (Brown 1990; Ball 1994; David *et al.* 1994) was that the responsibility for a child's education, in a system that could mean the success or failure of their individual child, was firmly placed with individual parents.

In the area of special educational needs the introduction of the market had particular implications for the consumer. Prior to the 1993 Education Act, a fundamental difficulty raised by special education professionals was the increased demand from schools and parents for pupils to be statemented at a time of extreme pressure on resources. LEA professionals were given the task of controlling this increased demand and the 1993 Education Act increased the in-school assessment stages. Stricter criteria and monitoring were clearly intended to limit and control demand but such a response was short term and did not address the underlying difficulties behind the increased demand.

The 'local' markets for parents of children with SENs became increasingly complex since it involved choice between mainstream and special schools. Mainstream schools varied in their reaction to children with special educational needs, but concerns centred on the effects of these children on budgets, league tables and marketing strategies. This is not surprising since markets leave little room for considerations based on social justice principles. Gewirtz *et al.* comment:

The education market (like all markets) is intended to be driven by self interest: first, the self interest of parents, as consumers, choosing schools that will provide the maximum advantage to their children; second, the self interest of schools or their senior managers, as producers, in making policy decisions that are based upon ensuring that their institutions thrive, or at least survive, in the marketplace.

(1995: 2)

Parents of children with SENs were likely to find themselves pulled between the conflicting advice of special and mainstream education professionals.

In the next section I draw on the experiences of the twelve case study[3] mothers to examine some of these issues in greater detail. This work was carried out in two Local Education Authority (LEAs) areas, one predominately rural and the other a large metropolitan area. Each mother was interviewed several times over a period of between seven and fifteen months, from the point of initial referral for assessment for a statement of special educational needs until the final statement was received and a school place confirmed. I also attended important meetings, case conferences and assessment meetings as an observer and accompanied mothers on school visits during these periods. Interviews were also carried out with the senior LEA personnel responsible for special needs policy and with the professionals involved with each case, including speech therapists, physiotherapists, educational psychologists and teachers. This chapter focuses on the experiences of the mothers. The purpose of the interviews with the mothers and other professionals was to understand the process of decision-making.

The gendered nature of choice

In focusing on the policy and process of parental choice in the research process it became clear, from the initial interviews, that the 'job' of choosing a school and taking care of the child's educational needs, was located very much in the domestic realm and, given the domestic division of labour, was therefore the responsibility of the mothers. It has long been implicitly assumed in policy that women take the central responsibility within the family for the education of their children. As women's economic activity has increased, their role in the family has also changed, but this has not been fully recognised by policy-makers. David commented:

The 'education reforms' developed throughout the 1980s do not seem to have taken account of these particular family changes especially in women's roles as mothers. Rather they have assumed a continuing traditional family form of two parents, with clear gender differentiation, albeit only alluded to implicitly and not explicitly.

(1991: 441)

As 'parents' were required to be more actively involved in securing a school place for their child, this consumer role reinforced the mother's role and responsibility, even more so for mothers of children with special needs. The recent work of David *et al.* (1994: 131) found that 'mothers are almost invariably involved in those processes and procedures whatever the kind of family and child'.

Of the twelve case study families, eleven had fathers living in the home yet paternal involvement was limited in both the choice of primary school and their wider participation in the statementing process. As the element of caring increases for parents of a child with special needs (Baldwin 1985), it was the mothers who were more likely to be in contact with or have more experience of other children with whom they could compare their own child's development. Also, once a child was at school, the mothers were more likely to be in regular contact with the teacher when dropping off or collecting the child, so the mother tended to be the first point of contact for discussion and therefore tended to have greater insight and information on the child's needs. They were also the most likely of the parents to be attending child development clinics, their GPs, health checks, and so on and were therefore the first point of contact for the initial diagnosis and ongoing interventions.

When making decisions several of the mothers would go and look at a school then describe it to the father afterwards:

Interviewer: . . . and did he [father] go and look at the schools too?
Mother: No, but I told him about each one and I didn't say which one I preferred and he said, well, the first one sounds better. (Chloe)

Mother: It was a joint decision between myself, Andrew's first teacher, Mrs Host, and Mrs Conner. They both sat down and said, 'Look, at the end of the day a statement's going to be best'. (Lydia)

This is part of a historical pattern of the domestic division of labour which has changed relatively little as David *et al.* (1994: 47) argue: 'It certainly seems to be the case that mothers are expected to be entirely responsible for a child's development before the age of compulsory schooling especially in terms of health and daily child care'.

In addition to running the home, caring for the children and meeting the extra demands of a child with special needs, seven of the twelve mothers were also in some form of paid employment (see Table 15.1). Despite this, most of the mothers, when questioned, felt education was their responsibility, especially if their partner was involved in full-time employment:

He's self-employed my husband so he can't take time off to come to these schools, I find that I'm doing it on my own. (Ann)

I didn't go to any meetings, but if the school needs to see me they'd either pop a letter in Andrew's bag and it may not be that week I can see her but

Table 15.1 Employment and marital status of the mothers

Mother	Child	Marital status	Employment status
Lydia	Andrew	Married	Full time
Alison	Becky	Married	Full time
Sally	Neil	Married	Part time
Jenny	Harry	Married	Part time
Lucy	Adrian	Married	Part time
Jane	William	Married	Part time
Emma	Mick	Married	Part time
Penny	Jake	Married	Not in paid work
Rosa	John	Married	Not in paid work
Sue	James	Single	Not in paid work
Ann	Sophie	Married	Not in paid work
Chloe	Ellie	Married	Not in paid work

obviously if I've got a slack period at work or haven't deadlines, well, then, you can organise. It is quite flexible. (Lydia)

In summary, despite the fact that parents of children with special educational needs have traditionally played a marginal role in decision-making on special educational needs, they are now expected to play a much more central role. The 1993 Education Act reinforced these changes, putting in place tribunals and appeals systems for parents of children with SENs. Parents of children with special educational needs now expect greater involvement, but these expectations are shaped by the class, geographical, ethnic and religious characteristics which each parent brings to the process (Gewirtz *et al.* 1995). However, the policy of parental choice masked the underlying gendered assumption that it would be mothers, as the main care providers, who would take on the additional responsibility for securing a school place. The gendered nature and complexity of the work involved lead on to the next section which looks at the nature of the work involved in securing a school place for a child with special needs.

The unpaid work of caring and choosing

Caring for a child with special educational needs tends to be a demanding task. It is construed that parents undertake these unpaid caring tasks through an emotional obligation (Thomas 1993) but in some cases the work involved in caring for a disabled child is recognised as work through the payment of a carer's allowance. Five of the mothers (Sue, Ann, Jenny, Chloe and Penny), received Carer's Allowances in recognition of the high level of care their child required. For mothers of children with special needs, their obligation to choose a school and the importance invested in this task meant that their caring activity extended beyond the private domestic sphere of the home and into the public realm of the educational psychologist's (EP's) office, the case conference, the special needs nursery, and so on.

Both the process of assessment prior to the opening of a Statement of Needs and the choice of school require active engagement in decision-making (David *et al.* 1994) and I have described this as 'work' requiring a certain degree of organisation, understanding and committed activity. To participate in these processes the mothers required a significant amount of time to attend meetings, visit schools, read the school literature and spend time discussing and considering the options. Several of the children in the study had to attend speech therapy, physiotherapy and hydrotherapy sessions, often in different locations. All the mothers in the study had to attend a range of additional meetings associated with the assessment process and were involved with professionals such as physiotherapists, occupational therapists, speech therapists and home support professionals including Portage[4] and health visitors, as well as voluntary involvement in support groups and information groups.

Mothers were assisted considerably by having access to a car, telephone, photocopiers, and so on, to make the 'work' easier and more effective:

> I wouldn't like to think that I was not in the position that I'm in. I mean, I work as a secretary so I've got my word processor and I've got the time and everything else. I wouldn't like to think I was a mum at home having to do that. And I imagine as well that there are some parents that aren't as bright as you might need to be to understand the process if you like. But, as I say, for me it was not too bad because I have all my equipment at work and the facilities to do everything.
>
> (Jenny)

Some mothers openly viewed the process as a work-based task paid off in terms of securing the best education for their child: 'Getting Adrian statemented was just another part of the business really' (Lucy). All these responsibilities required a great degree of energy and co-ordination at a stressful time. Additionally, most of the mothers had other children to care for, a home to run and several were also engaged in part-time or full-time paid work (see Table 15.1):

> It took quite a while to get into the system but then I was 9 months pregnant when we moved. He [younger child] was born 10 days after we moved in here, so time to organise her, organise having a baby, organise a new house . . . it was impossible.
>
> (Chloe)

However, other mothers found the process more problematic and several were left confused and frustrated. These frustrations were closely related to the lack of negotiation available to the mothers. Those who attempted to influence the process found themselves in a position of disadvantage since the professionals had prior knowledge of available resources and places in schools and special units and therefore the possible outcomes. The agenda was set for and by the professionals, who were themselves locked into market constraints. Mothers needed the cultural resources (Bourdieu 1984) to be able to speak at meetings, to make their points known, especially if they were in disagreement. This was particularly difficult as 'parents it seems are not perceived as being experts' (Cornwall 1987: 50). The professionals perceived the mothers' knowledge as 'private' knowledge based on their domestic experience and therefore not as relevant or important as their own 'expert' knowledge. The mothers had to convince the professionals of their ability and knowledge before they could play a more active role: 'I can't tell you exactly what his needs are because I'm just the mother, I'm not a professional' (Jenny).

Despite three of the twelve case study mothers being actively involved in the processes, only one managed to gain some foothold of influence in the process and she remained concerned at just how far her influence would make a difference:

> I've been fairly frustrated by it all . . . obviously I wanted to retain sort of good relationships so it's just a case of trying as tactfully as possible to ensure things progress. There are some guidebooks to help you understand the process better but because they've [the professionals] got the final decision, you never felt really confident because the way everything is worded. As I say, you feel until you get that letter anything could happen.
>
> (Alison)

These frustrations resulted in a gradual change in the self-identity of the mothers. While expecting, and being expected, to participate in the process, the mothers underwent a shift when their initial feelings of wanting to choose the best for their child were eroded as they felt increasingly marginalised. They realised that most of the decision-making and negotiating power rested with producers, especially the educational psychologist, and ultimately the schools. Penny was probably one of the most involved and aware mothers in the sample, yet she reflected negatively on her own experiences:

> I don't think there is any choice. I think it's very misleading because yes, it does say parental choice, you can choose, but I felt that my hands are tied, that I don't really have very much choice because if the 'expert' says that this is going to be, you know, be suited, or you should go and have a look, I mean even if they don't say go and have a look at this school, it's like only saying, you know that is the best one. You know, regardless of whatever I have in mind before.
>
> (Penny)

The tensions illustrated by the experiences of these mothers highlight the difficulties where the balance of power remains in favour of the producers. Despite the parental choice rhetoric and policy, the system remains highly bureaucratic, operating within a formal structure, involving techno-official language, written reports and communication, and expert knowledge. It is extremely difficult for the mother to detect the hidden agendas of professionals and schools. To be able to access these effectively a mother has to be aware of her own individual situation but also how it is located within the operation of a local education market situated in a wider allocative system.

Choosing between special and mainstream: tensions between individualised and collective solutions

The mothers in this study were making complex choices between particular options, often between a special and a mainstream placement. They were influenced by a variety of discourses of disability, drawn from the media, schools, formal and informal networks and from their own backgrounds and previous experiences of the education system. Previously location was supposedly based on level of need and where best those needs could be met, and in the main (but by no means consistently) mainstream schools were increasingly seen as being the better option especially following the 1981 Education Act which recommended mainstream provision, albeit with caveats based on efficient use of resources. In some LEAs, depending on opinion and economics, a number of special schools had been closed and this was true of the metropolitan LEA, but much less so in the rural area.

Of the twelve children, five gained a mainstream school placement and seven ended up in a special school. Table 15.2 illustrates some of these choices and, from the mother's perspectives, some were more straightforward than others.

The most straightforward cases were William, Andrew and Neil who remained at their local mainstream primary school following the opening of a Statement of Needs with between two to five hours per week additional classroom support. John was given a place in his local mainstream school with full-time non-teaching assistant (NTA) support, which was his mother's choice. However, these children had comparatively minor support requirements and their assessments were carried out prior to the 1993 changes in assessment procedures. It is possible that these children would not be given a Statement of Needs post-1993 under the new arrangements for assessment.

Harry was also given a mainstream school placement, the choice of his mother, Jenny, who had been to look at some special schools in the local area but felt they were not ideal for Harry:

Table 15.2 School placements and the preference of the mothers

Mainstream school	Mother's preference	Special school	Mother's preference
William	yes	Jake	no
Andrew	yes	Adrian	yes
John	yes	Becky	yes
Harry	yes	Sophie	unsure
Neil	yes	Ellie	yes
Michael	yes	James	no

> I went to [local special school] an excellent school for children with special
> needs. They've got everything. They've got all the equipment. They've got
> everything. But honestly looking at Harry and looking at the children there,
> I thought their needs were far greater than Harry's. I would really like Harry
> to go to a mainstream school and accept that he's a bit different.
>
> (Jenny)

Many mothers remained unsure over the placement of their child in a special
school. Several of the mothers saw the special schools as providing a range of
services and facilities which they felt their child would benefit from and would not
be able to access as easily through a mainstream placement.

> I'm not one of these people that I want her to go to a mainstream school for
> the sake of it. If I think a special school can provide what she wants, then
> that's where she'll go.
>
> (Ann)

It was evident that many of the mothers were unaware of wider debates on integration and disability, with some still referring to 'handicapped' children and
expressing concerns around sending their child to a mainstream school. 'If she's
capable I would love her to go to a mainstream school but then I know how cruel
children can be' (Chloe). In considering the special schools it was also evident
that some of the mothers had made decisions based on their own needs too.
Chloe had visited both Lane and Valley, the two local special schools in the rural
area:

> I went to see the Valley School first and it was fantastic. They had every-
> thing you could think of, but because it was for the more severely handi-
> capped I thought, well, everyone keeps saying how well she is doing, I'll
> look at the other school. And I went down to Lane School and it was as if I
> was a problem being there. 'That's that, that's that and you can't go in
> there and if you want to see us again give us a ring and we'll see if we can fit
> you in.' And I thought, well, I don't want her going there . . . Valley
> School was just so much better, better equipped and everyone was so
> friendly there.
>   The Valley School, he was so nice and caring which is what I feel a special
> needs teacher should be, that extra bit of caring, and that school was
> fantastic.
>
> (Chloe)

Jenny, Harry's mother, was also very impressed by non-educational reasons by
the first mainstream school she visited.

> The headmistress there is lovely, really nice, really helpful. She took us down
> to see the nursery and she told us she had no objections whatsoever to taking

in a special needs child. And she was so nice. Because I was so happy with Lowtown School I thought, well, what's the point in trailing around.

(Jenny)

A few months later, during a follow-up interview, Chloe recognised that her original choice had been based on her own need for support and initial perception of the school than purely on the educational needs of Ellie:

I think I would make more effort, not with her, but with the choice of schools. I chose for her to go to Valley School because I personally preferred it. Whereas teachers there said she would be better off at Lane School as she was ahead of everyone else in the class. And Lane School was just for slight learning difficulties and Valley for very severe learning difficulties . . . Looking back on it now, I would have put her in Lane School for the simple reason it was more geared towards her educational needs than Valley School.

(Chloe)

Her experience illustrates how the first approach from the school can impact upon the mothers, especially if the mothers were feeling confused or marginalised by the statementing process.

What can be seen as diversity for individual parents can have a negative effect on wider patterns of mainstreaming, resources and equity. The examples cited above illustrate the notion of the 'hidden hand' of the market (Jonathon 1990) where positive individual actions can adversely effect the collective group. However, it is important to examine the mothers' reasons for choosing special schools. These were more likely to be based on pragmatic, personal or medical/professional reasons such as the atmosphere and approach of the school with several case study mothers experiencing the 'push' from mainstream schools and the 'pull' of special schools. Professional recommendations and knowledge gleaned from informal networks were also rather more important than political reasons around the politics of integration.

Conclusion

In this chapter I have used the experiences of twelve case study mothers to highlight the tensions and difficulties created for them by the policy of parental choice. The changes brought in by the 1988 ERA were based on an ideal, a notion that market forces would solve the economic, social and political problems by shifting the balance of power from producer to consumer through the creation of a purchaser–provider split with increased opportunities for choice and competition. Now schools, in control of their own budgets, compete for students funded on a per capita basis and parents are expected to take on the responsibility for their child's education by choosing the 'best' school from the range available, using information from league tables and testing; schools as producers should respond to the parental demand and standards should improve.

Mothers of children with special needs were often unsure about the 'best' placement for their child and were influenced by the competing advise of a range of professional groups. These mothers incurred significant caring responsibilities and were also expected to take on the additional work of negotiating both the statementing and parental choice processes. As the user part of the market equation, mothers can only make choices within the limitations imposed by the system, resources, geography and their own level of cultural capital (Ball *et al.* 1996) and involvement. The conditions of choice are not under their control since the apparent mechanisms of choice are all limited in one way or another as professional power remains pervasive at a local level. The ideal of a market with a diversity of providers from which mothers can choose does not exist for most mothers of children with special needs. Their choice is often restricted to one mainstream or special school. If a choice is available between mainstream schools, this will often be dependent upon the individual school's attitude towards pupils with SENs. The reforms extending parental choice to parents of children with SENs did not offer a fundamental rethinking of the inherent problems of limited resources and increasing numbers of claimants on these resources. For a group already marginalised, the promises of consumerism, for the most part, remain empty.

Notes

1 For the purpose of this study the term 'SEN' was accepted to mean children with additional educational needs but excluded children defined as gifted.
2 'Statementing' is a process of assessment by a range of professionals to determine a child's educational needs and recommend a way of meeting these needs in school.
3 All names in the chapter are pseudonyms.
4 Portage is a home-based intensive therapy for disabled pre-school children. It is provided through the health service and varies according to the needs of the child, but includes work on walking, motor skills, toilet training and speech.

References

Baldwin, S. (1985) *The Costs of Caring: Families with Disabled Children*, London: Routledge and Kegan Paul.

Ball, S.J. (1994) *Education Reform: A Critical and Post Structuralist Approach*, Buckingham: Open University Press.

Ball, S.J., Bowe, R. and Gewirtz, S. (1996) 'School choice, social class and distinction: the realisation of social advantage in education', *Journal of Education Policy* 2, 1: 89–112.

Bourdieu, P. (1984) *Distinction: A Social Critique of Judgement and Taste*, London: Routledge and Kegan Paul.

Brown, P. (1990) 'The Third Wave: education and the ideology of parentocracy', *British Journal of the Sociology of Education* 11, 1: 65–85.

Cornwall, N. (1987) *Statementing and the 1981 Act: The Process of Decision Making*, Cranfield: Cranfield Press.

David, M. (1991) 'A gender agenda: women and family in the new ERA', *British Journal of the Sociology of Education* 12, 4: 433–64.

David, M., West A., and Ribbens, J. (1994) *Mothers' Intuition? Choosing Secondary Schools*, London: Falmer Press.

Gewirtz, S., Ball, S. and Bowe, R. (1995) *Markets, Choice and Equity in Education*, Buckingham: Open University Press.

Jonathon, R. (1990) 'State education service or prisoner's dilemma – the "hidden hand" as a source of educational policy', *Educational Philosophy and Theory* 22, 1: 16–24.

Loney, M., Bocock, R., Clarke, J., Cochrane, A., Graham, P. and Wilson, M. (eds) (1991) *The State or the Market: Politics and Welfare in Contemporary Britain*, London: Sage.

Stalker, K. (1997) 'The antinomies of choice in community care', in S. Baldwin and P. Barton (eds) *Needs Assessment and Community Care: International Perspectives*, Oxford: Butterworth Heinemann.

Thomas, C. (1993) 'Deconstructing the concepts of care', *Sociology* 27, 4: 649–69.

16 Class, race and collective action

Carol Vincent and Simon Warren

I think the concern is that we can see that the research shows that a lot of our youngsters [African/Caribbean] are being expelled from school, we can see that we're sort of at the bottom of the league tables, whatever table comes out we seem to be at the bottom, except for unemployment and crime, we're top of those.

(Jean, African/Caribbean mother)

Introduction: parents and the education market

The introduction of a quasi-market in education in the late 1980s provoked a symbolic shift in the way in which parents related to the education system. Parents were no longer clients of a traditional welfare state service, but rather, in a re-positioning which reflected similar developments in other public sector services, located as consumers of a newly restructured education system. However, it has been frequently argued that parents' new found 'powers' in relation to schooling do not, by and large, translate into their relationships with particular schools. On the contrary, parents' consumer 'powers' tend to diminish once the choice of school is made. When a child starts at that school, the dominant discourse becomes that of 'partnership' with the professionals, a discourse which can often result in parents being positioned as the subordinate party (Vincent and Tomlinson 1997). Parental rights and abilities to voice their opinions and views in school vary depending on individual situations, but it is rare to find examples where this is encouraged by a school on a sustained basis. The cultural and social resources to which parents have access also require consideration. Some groups of parents may be better at presenting themselves and framing their concerns and opinions in ways which teachers recognise as valid. It is, in part, for these reasons, that we set out to study parents' groups and organisations which operate independently of any one school. We wanted to see what kind of support and experiences these groups gave to the parents who became involved with them. In particular, what are the characteristics, in terms of gender, race and social class, of those parents who become involved with different groups and organisations? To what extent could these groups help encourage the articulation of individual and/or collective parental voices? The focus of this chapter is a small, self-help support group of

African/Caribbean mothers. We hope that an analysis of the work of this group will highlight the complex interaction between race, social class and gender in influencing parent–teacher relationships, and parents' success in reaching and maintaining a status quo in these relationships which they find satisfactory.

The research project

The self-help group is one of four case studies which participated in this research project[1] exploring parent-centred organisations (PCOs). PCOs is a term we have coined to describe locally based initiatives that are run by professionals for parents, or by parents for other parents. In brief, PCOs seek to intervene in the relationship between parents and the education system. They may do this by offering parents information, support and, in some cases, advice and advocacy, on education issues. The research explores the extent to which these groups disseminate attitudes, values and beliefs about the 'appropriate' role for parents in relation to the education system and parents' responses and reactions to this. The other three case studies were an *advice centre* offering parents information and support with regard to special educational needs provision; a *parent education group* offering parents an accredited practical skills course which involved the students in making educational materials suitable for early years children; and a *pressure group*, campaigning for enhanced educational funding. The four case study groups differed considerably in their orientation and their focus of activity. Their variety is indicative of the ways in which parents get involved in educational issues, other than, or in addition to, their relationship with their own child's individual school. Clearly, the PCOs are all influenced by the introduction of a competitive, quasi-market framework into education. However, the four are affected and they respond in different ways depending on their particular orientation. The campaigning group, for instance, challenged the assumption made by the last Conservative government of a positive relationship between the improvement of learning outcomes and leaner, apparently more efficient educational units. The self-help group, on the other hand, as we go on to demonstrate, was concerned to enhance its members' ability to act as consumers of education.

In terms of the overall project analysis, we identified a Gramscian framework as providing a useful starting point, focusing, in particular, on the concepts of hegemony, civil society, and a third idea, that of 'structures of feeling', which is derived from Gramsci's work (Holub 1992). PCOs operate within civil society, a sphere Gramsci saw as crucial because it was where 'values and meanings are established, where they are debated, contested and changed' (Kumar 1993: 383). That process by which 'cultural authority [is] negotiated and contested' (Fraser 1992: 53–4) is essential to Gramsci's concept of hegemony which emphasises the formulation – and possible *re*formulation – of dominant social meanings. Thus our starting point for the project as a whole was to explore hegemonic understandings of the role of parents that are utilised and disseminated in a range of PCOs and to explore the processes by which these are maintained or challenged by the groups themselves and by members or clients (the terminology differs depending on the group under consideration). How are race, social class and gender implicated in such hegemonic understandings, and reactions and responses to them? In addition, do the groups disseminate specific ideas, and beliefs concerning the way in which parents should position themselves in relation to the education system? If yes, then, what are these ideas, and how are they received? A key element here is the role of PCO staff. Renate Holub (1992), using Gramsci's work, argues that those we would now call professionals (e.g. doctors, priests and teachers), are particularly effective at disseminating hegemonic beliefs because of their (partial) access to their clients' *structure of feeling* (that is, the assumptions, ideas and values that structure communication between members of a community.)[2] They can utilise that access to propound values that support the status quo. However, Gramsci argued that counter-hegemonic ideas can also be produced through the same structures. (See Vincent 1997 for a fuller account of the theoretical framework.)

As the project proceeded, the social movement literature provided further theoretical input. Education as a site of collective lay activity is largely overlooked, yet there is evidence of much activity on educational issues, although this remains largely unquantified and unmapped. Examples include local, voluntary groups organising over special education issues, one-off campaigns (e.g. over school closure) and the vigorous, but often neglected terrain of community-based supplementary education. We were particularly interested in the way in which much of the sociological analysis in this area concentrates on the potential of groups to initiate social transformation. The role of social movements in redefining, creating and challenging social meanings and dominant understandings is referred to by several analysts (e.g. Castells 1983; Melucci 1988; Johnston and Klandersmans 1995). This approach has obvious resonance with our interest in the potential of PCOs to create or encourage counter-hegemonic discourses. Elsewhere, we have argued that analysis of small, local groups such as the PCOs, problematises our understanding of social movements (Vincent and Warren 1997b). The grandiose claims of some analysts that social movements are progressive, radical groupings intent on creating 'symbolic challenges' (Melucci 1988) to dominant hegemonies is not substantiated by the incrementalist, limited, somewhat marginal, work of small-scale, local PCOs. Thus much social movement analysis 'misses' such groups. An exception is the work by Ian Taylor (1996) on 'suburban social movements', small, local groups of a conservative nature, such as NIMBY campaigns and Neighbourhood Watch. However, the project PCOs do not fit into this classification either, being neither as conservative nor as insular as Taylor's examples. Rather, we would argue that the case study groups *are* involved in attempts, albeit they are tentative, fragile and partial, to create new meanings and understandings concerning parents' roles in relation to education.

There is a further point to make concerning the dominant paradigms within social movement analysis, one that is particularly relevant to this analysis of the self-help group. Class is a major issue in much social movement writing (e.g. the collection by Maheu 1995); race and, in particular, gender, are given much less prominence. Heidi Safia Mirza extends this argument in her writing on black collective action. The dominant understanding here, she maintains, recognises only particular *masculine* forms of collective action:

> Urban social movements, we are told, mobilise in protest, riots, local politics and community organisations. We are told that it is their action, and not the subversive, covert action of women that gives rise to so-called 'neo-populist, liberatory, authentic politics' (Gilroy 1987: 245). This is the masculinist version of radical social change; visible, radical, confrontational, collective action, powerfully expressed in the politics of the inner city, where class consciousness evolves in response to urban struggle.
>
> (Mirza 1997: 272)

Mirza's argument is that black women's collective action, which in so far as it has been the focus for analysis at all, has been understood as 'resistance through accommodation', is actually far more complex than such theories would suggest. She uses the organising and running of supplementary schools as an example, highlighting the apparent paradox of these schools, established by black communities as substitutional strategies operating outside of the mainstream, and yet adopting pedagogies and curricula which appear formal, conformist and conservative (see also Reay and Mirza 1997). She explains this by reference to a process of 'strategic rationalisation':

> For black women strategies for everyday survival consist of trying to create spheres of influence that are separate from, but engaged with existing structures of oppression . . . Their desire for inclusion is strategic, subversive and ultimately far more transformative than subcultural reproduction theory suggests . . . In certain circumstances, *doing well can become a radical strategy*. An act of social transformation.
>
> (1997: 276, 270, 274, original emphasis)

In this chapter, we will apply Mirza's insightful analysis to the self-help group, and also focus on an important, additional element – social class. Apparently little attention has been paid to class differences within minority ethnic groups. Black people in the UK for example are still routinely seen as all working class (Aziz 1997). A recent report for the Policy Studies Institute (PSI) surveying the position of ethnic minority groups in Britain in the mid to late 1990s discusses the socio-economic positions of Asian, Caribbean and white groups when compared to each other, but only briefly alludes to differences within groups (Modood *et al.* 1997). As part of the post-modern emphasis on the multi-faceted and shifting nature of identities, there has been a decisive move away from seeing black groups as homogeneous, connected by common experiences of racism (Mirza 1998). Consequently, analyses of identity have increasingly sought to highlight specificity and difference. We suggest that it is particularly class differences within non-white groups that remain unexplored, whereas ethnic differences between black groups and gender differences have received some attention (e.g. Gillborn and

Gipps 1996 and Modood *et al.* 1997 on ethnicity; Reynolds 1997 on gender). We wish to consider the salience of the self-help group's race, class and gender, to explore the interaction of these dimensions and how they influence the characteristics and nature of the group and its work. We will do this in two ways, first, through a profile of one of the core activists in the group, and, second, by considering the group as a whole. We continue by discussing whether the group should be seen as either radical or conformist, and conclude with some suggested avenues for further action. But first we turn to a description of the self-help group.

The group

The self-help group was a small group of black parents, all of whom were women, who 'offer[ed] support and guidance to parents of children at school ... and network with agencies and departments within the [City] Education department' (promotional literature). The group has been in operation since 1992. During that time membership has fluctuated considerably. At one point it had nearly 100 members on its mailing list. In 1997, during the period of study, that number was down to just over fifty. Meetings were held every four to six weeks in a community centre. Turn-out varied, but regular attendees numbered about ten to twelve, and responsibilities tended to fall on a core group of three to four. As is the case with most social movements, particularly those that are local and small in scale like the self-help group, achievements were the result of commitment and considerable personal expenditure in terms of time and effort.

During the second half of 1996 and the first half of 1997 we interviewed seven members of the group (all female). We also interviewed one man who was not a member of the group but who attended a course run by the group's co-ordinator, Annie, which was aimed at encouraging more black people to become school governors. The respondents were a self-selecting group, in that they all volunteered to be interviewed as part of the research project, and they are amongst the more consistently active members of the self-help group. Their views are therefore not necessarily representative of all the group's members. Half of those interviewed were professionally involved in education, a further two respondents work in schools in non-teaching capacities. Only two respondents did not work within the education system. All of them were also involved with other community activities, largely within the African Caribbean community. Three were participating in some form of further education.

Annie, the group's co-ordinator, was employed by an education charity, which provided the group with some funding. She was involved in governor training, and placed particular emphasis on encouraging black parents to become governors. According to its members, the self-help group had two main functions:

- providing information and a forum for debate, as well as offering skills and support to individual parents who were experiencing difficulties with their children at school;

- improving parent–teacher relationships and expanding parents' views of their appropriate role in relation to schools.

Forum for debate

Issues discussed included:

> [from] basically what to do with a difficult five year old . . . to where was the nearest riding club . . . what options there are at 11+ . . . about your normal comprehensive or about selective schools or grammar schools, what each can offer, why it might not be a good reason to go to a grammar school or vice versa.
>
> (Mother, currently unemployed)

Issues of behaviour and discipline in school, school choice and forms of parental participation seemed to be recurring themes for the group as these were ones that parents regularly raised, or as one mother (a teaching assistant) put it:

> Yes, I know the eleven plus is on the agenda to actually talk about that, or the on-going thirteen plus and twelve plus that some [secondary schools] actually do, that's on the agenda for probably the next meeting, I think, to talk about, and universities, or where to go from sixteen onwards, and misbehaviour in school and how parents can actually get involved in the school and governors, school governors.
>
> (Mother, school ancillary staff)

Information giving

Information can be useful in giving shape and form to parents' previously diffuse concerns. One of the members of the group who was not involved professionally in education, expressed this in the following terms: 'I'm always concerned about it [her daughter's education] in many ways, but I can't sort of pin-point it . . . The group has opened up my eyes . . . it's through this group that I learned about the governors' course' (Mother, school ancillary staff).

Information could also give shape and form to parents' vague sense of concern in another way – by drawing attention to the structural discrimination at work within the education system:

> That was part of the aim, to make the black community aware of what was going on . . . actually getting some of the parents, I suppose, to acknowledge what was going on, because it is easy to, sort of, you know, sweep everything under the carpet. As long as your child was going to school and they weren't getting into any serious trouble, that was enough, but we were saying, it isn't enough. Research was saying that children, especially black children, were doing quite well, but something was happening when they went to secondary school.
>
> (Annie)

The self-help group was involved in acquiring and disseminating informal, local opinion between friends and acquaintances, as well as official, written information (what has been referred to elsewhere as *hot* and *cold* knowledge (Ball and Vincent 1998)). The number of education professionals involved in the self-help group meant that the group was characterised by this mixture, this fusion, of hot and cold information. The professionals were, of course, knowledgeable about the workings of the education system in the city, but their knowledge was passed on to other parents, not through 'official' public channels, but in the private, informal surroundings of a self-help group:

> We're making parents more aware of what is going on in the City and that there is a support network there, that they're not on their own, and also that we all face the same problems, whether we're professionals or not.
>
> (Mother, education administrator)

Support

As well as providing general information through seminars, conferences, leaflets and the group's own meetings, members would also try and provide help and advice to individual parents with a particular problem. In this, they used their considerable combined knowledge of the local education system to guide parents through to the appropriate individual or to suggest a possible course of action.

Promoting black involvement in governance

This aim was part of an attempt to expand parents' views of their appropriate role. Group members felt that it was important for local black people to be involved in schools' governance and decision-making processes.

'Appropriate' parenting

The group's understanding of 'appropriate' parenting was clearly articulated. According to one of the key activists in the group, the main function of information and support is to 'guide [parents] through the system: rather than saying "oh the school is wrong", or "you are wrong", because I don't think that helps anybody, because what we're trying to do is build the relationship, not destroy it' (Mother, education administrator).

Similarly, asked what role the group would like black parents to play in schools, this key member suggested a 'supportive' one of black parents going 'into schools more regularly, and help[ing] out on a voluntary basis because . . . you have a totally different perception when you're in the class and you see the difficulties about teaching'. However, the group did not subscribe to a passive role for parents, but rather a model that could be described as that of a *critical friend*. One member described this in the following terms:

I'd also like to see parents questioning more, especially when you go to Parents' Evening and it's the usual thing, 'oh, your child has potential' . . . And I'd like to see more parents say, 'Well, what do you mean by this? What can I do to help? Do you actually understand that my child might be good at, I don't know, singing, so why is she never Mary in the school play?' . . . things like that. Also the debate about putting . . . African history, Caribbean history, different arts [into the curriculum] . . . It's only going to help the child's self-esteem . . . So those are the things I think I'd like parents to be doing, asking questions, and supporting the school when it's necessary, because, you know, all schools aren't bad.

(Annie, group co-ordinator)

This suggests that the group aims to support black parents in making the education system work well for their child, partly by making apparent their own interest and readiness to be involved. However, it is likely that the questioning approach advocated by the mother quoted above, is one with which only a few parents will feel comfortable. It is much easier for someone to adopt if they have high levels of confidence and knowledge about the education system (the self-help group is, of course, trying to support other black parents while they acquire these attributes). It is also, as it is presented here, very much an individual strategy: if the school ignores the constant questioning of one parent, then that individual can be effectively marginalised.

Another member pointed out that the group's task was to change people's ideas about where the boundaries of school control were:

[If] people feel that education is what schools do, and it's something that happens nine 'til three thirty, then they are not going to get involved until their child is ill, hurt or in trouble. If parents only respond when there is a problem, then the group will not be able to attract people when there isn't an immediate problem to be resolved, so it's about *selling the support for education.*

(Mother, social worker; our emphasis)

Overall, we suggest that the role of *critical friend* contains a number of elements:

- parents as 'consumers' of education needing the appropriate information to make rational choices between different types of educational provision;
- parents as 'informed partners', supporting the education of their children through helping in the classroom or curriculum support at home;
- parents as 'managers' of local educational provision through participation as governors;
- parents as 'cultural activists' seeking greater understanding of the cultural values and experiences of the African Caribbean community by the education system.

By and large, the first two aim to encourage black parents to get the best from the existing education system, although it requires their acceptance, their fitting in to existing arrangements. However, the latter two have the potential to more radically alter relations between black parents and the education system, a point to which we return in the Conclusion.

The idea of parents taking up a role as 'critical friend' serves to emphasise the importance to the self-help group of parents making their own views and opinions known within school. This had implications for the way in which group members viewed the 'official' discourse of parents as consumers. Parental choice was important to members. They felt that one of the group's functions was to ensure parents had adequate information with which to make their choice of school, whether that be a selective, grant-maintained or local authority school. Despite this emphasis on the provision of information and parental choice, the language of consumerism was not widely adopted within the group. Consumer powers tend not to address the right to have a voice within an organisation. However, the concept of 'critical friend' disseminated by the self-help group placed a high premium on voice. As a result, their commitment to consumerism was heavily qualified.

Unpacking subjectivities

In this section, we wish to look at the way in which race, gender and class interact to shape the workings of the group and the setting of its priorities. As Davies puts it, we are trying to understand the 'multiple positionings that any one person takes up in their day to day life' in an attempt to conceptualise 'the relation between each individual's day to day existence and social structures' (Davies 1989: 8). Elsewhere (Vincent and Warren 1997a), we have illustrated this concept with reference to 'Jean' one of the group's core members. We attempted to show how different facets of her identity, as a mother of two boys, a black woman and an education administrator, located her in a particular set of relationships with the education system. It was a position of relative symmetry of power with her children's teachers; she was, as she said, 'sympathetic from that side', and this allowed her a degree of access into the school, which other less informed parents might not have. In addition, she had been a school governor, and had been asked by the school to conduct some in-service training: 'I feel confident obviously, and informed enough to go in and not exactly challenge, but be supportive of the teacher because I am sympathetic from that side.'

Her relation to the school as a parent was very much framed by her role as an education professional. It also located her somewhat differently to other black parents whom she felt 'are under stress because they don't know what's going on in education, they don't know what's happening to their children'. Her response to this was to put her 'insider' knowledge at the service of other parents:

> I feel I've got a part to play in that group because of the background I have in education and I feel I can support the group as a whole, but I can also

support individual parents . . . I haven't got all the knowledge, but what I usually do is pass them on to somebody who I feel will do it, or phone this person first, and say 'look, expect a parent to ring you, and these are the main concerns,' so that you know, they're getting that support from the people in the know. I don't pretend I know everything.

Jean saw this task as a personal responsibility, that is a responsibility to, as she termed it 'give something back' to support the education of the next generation of black children (see also Reay and Mirza 1997). This sense of responsibility is realised and enacted in a particular way, however, for she clearly sees her role as mediating between black parents and the education system:

I sort of guide them through the system, rather than saying 'oh, the school is wrong' or 'you are wrong', because I don't think that helps anybody, because what we're trying to do is build the relationship not destroy it.

Jean subscribed to the underlying rationale for the group, that it was a collectivist response to the inadequacies of the present education system, not least of which is the generally distant relationships between black parents and teachers. Some of her words may give the impression that Jean was encouraging parents to seek an accommodation with the school which may work to parents' disadvantage, given the imbalance in power existing between the two 'sides'. However, the context in which the group operated is important here. The group was a network of which she was a member, not, as was the case in one of our other case studies, an advice centre in which she was a worker. Instead of a traditional professional–client model, the emphasis was much more on mutual support, as self-development took place within a *reciprocal* network:

I think the idea of a network is that it's a self-support group and that there are people within the group who are sort of supporting each other from their own personal experience. Sometimes I think the danger of having an organ-isation that says 'we will solve your problems', well, some of the problems can't be solved . . . We all face the same problems, whether we're profes-sionals or not, whatever we classify ourselves as . . . we've all got children, and I'm no expert in bringing children up, and nor are they, but we can always support each other.

(Jean, mother, education administrator)

Much of her motivation came from her close identification with group members, in this case as a black mother:

I do that [attend meetings] more for love than money . . . When I go on a Saturday, I don't wear my City cap at all, and I think that's important for the parents to know, but on the other hand, the information is still in my head somewhere and so that helps them, and so I do go as a black parent to this group.

She had a particular concern, as the mother of two sons, about the treatment of black boys within the education system. This aspect of her identity positioned her within relationships with the education system that were potentially more asymmetric and conflictual, than when her role as education professional was paramount:

> I think that when you look at especially young lads nowadays, I think they really start from a minus, minus. People feel threatened by black lads . . . I think black girls, we tend to be a little bit more resilient, and we'll give and take a little bit more . . . The black lads are being demoted because they're standing up for themselves; now black girls do stand up for themselves, but you find that more black lads, teachers see them as aggressive . . . and I think they are made to fail because of some of the situations around them. That's why I keep a very tight rope on my boys, because if I felt that any teacher was sort of looking at them as being aggressive, or whatever, then I'd be going in and I'd be the aggressive person because I'd be saying, 'come on, give him a chance'.

This is an inflection framed more by her identity as the mother of boys who are part of a group routinely experiencing discrimination, than her role as educational professional.

Within and without the system

Our brief profile of Jean is intended to illustrate how the interaction of race, gender and class contribute to her subjectivity. In this section, we impose an (admittedly artificial) distinction between those three dimensions, in order to consider how they shape and influence the work of the group.

Gender

It is common for mothers, rather than fathers, to take the major role in their child's education, regardless of variations in social class or ethnic background (David 1993). This reflects hegemonic discourses around mothering which emphasise the mother's responsibility for their children's social, emotional, moral and intellectual development. Several commentators have traced the impact of this total responsibility on mothers as their children develop from babies (Urwin 1985) through the pre-school years (Walkerdine and Lucey 1989) to school (Griffith and Smith 1991; Ribbens 1994; Reay 1998). This situation appears to describe the experience of the majority of families from all social classes and ethnic groups. Even in families where both parents have paid work, the primary responsibility for childcare often still lies with the mother (Brannen and Moss

1991; Jordon *et al.* 1994). Recent studies of school choice have shown that most of the work involved in the choice process is undertaken by the mother (Gewirtz *et al.* 1995; David and West 1994). The women we interviewed in the self-help group described the group's femaleness as reflecting the traditional and still predominant division of labour between men and women. There was no evidence that they particularly approved of this state of affairs, but it was accepted as 'the way things are':

> maybe it's reflective of what the family, the family's constitution, which is mainly females on their own trying to bring up the children, and the father is around, but not around, if you know what I mean.
>
> (Mother, social worker)

> [fathers] seem to have this view that it's the woman's role to play and they don't see that the education has something to do with them, it sort of comes in with the cooking and cleaning really.
>
> (Mother, teaching assistant)

> I'm not being stereotypical, but it's usually the mothers who are more interested, they have more of an interest in the educational side of their children's development.
>
> (Mother, education social worker)

> well that's probably because the mothers are the parents, both the father and mother.
>
> (Mother, social worker)

There has been a tendency for some accounts of motherhood to highlight its oppressiveness, downplaying the emotional satisfactions, and rewards (Ribbens 1994; Vincent and Warren 1998). We would also suggest that although hegemonic discourses concerning 'appropriate' mothering can be very constraining for women (e.g. 'sensitive mothering', described by Walkerdine and Lucey 1989), mothering can also offer women opportunities for agency, action, and a renewal or growth in their personal confidence (Jetter *et al.* 1997). There is evidence for this with regard to particular women in all four of our case study groups, although the degree of agency differs depending on the particular context.[3] In relation to the self-help group, Mirza's comment that black women have a history of playing a major role in determining and influencing educational provision for their children (Mirza 1997) is apposite. The women portrayed themselves as assertive and confident:

> We've had the odd man come in, but I think we've frightened them off. We're quite assertive women as you can see . . . I think black women are more, I don't know, pushy in that way, to support their children.
>
> (Jean)

Interestingly, men were better represented on the black governors course. Asked to explain this, the informant quoted above replied, '*Power*'.

> I mean it's a management post isn't it, and I think probably men would probably see themselves more as, I mean, going to a parents' group probably sounds a bit wishy washy to men, whereas if you say I'm going to be a school governor, it's a different light.[4]

Race

The group itself operated as a space in which black women (and theoretically, men) could meet together to discuss issues of common concern; a space where 'whiteness was displaced and blackness seen as normative' (Reay and Mirza 1997):

> I think that [for] black people dealing with situations of authority has not always been that positive for them, so it's about alleviating the barriers, . . . a forum to let them talk freely without feeling that they are going to be picked up on or ridiculed in some way. And I think there's certain issues, certain understandings that people, black people, go through, no matter where they're from, you know, there's a commonality that gives them that initial ease. I mean, later on as you go on, you may find there's differences between people and I think it's that initial comfort making, relaxing situation . . . I think there are certain things that can be discussed with black/white, but then there's a history that perhaps they won't share . . . It's like men and women wouldn't perhaps be asking the same questions, so I do think that even though there may be a lot of things that are the same, it's the differences, I feel, creates a problem.
>
> (Mother, social worker)

For some members, belonging to a black group helped reinforce a sense of 'self' and 'community':

> I often felt that being brought up in [part of city] we were actually losing out in a sense in mixing with the black community because, you know, being the only black girl in the class, and looking around at other black families and I've always wanted to be more involved in the community
>
> (Mother, social worker)

Another said:

> You can't be too black [if you're to succeed] . . . I don't know how you define 'too black', there's got to be some conformity . . . the higher we move up . . . a little bit more of yourself you have to give up in order to fit in, because you've got to be able to fit in.
>
> (Mother, education social worker)

We are suggesting therefore that their location as black women supplied the group members with the impetus to create a forum with a strong, affirmative sense of identity, in which individuals could, with collective support, demonstrate agency and activity over their child's education. However, the intensity of their common identity as black women meant that core group members rarely mentioned social class differences between themselves and other black mothers.

Class

To the members of the group who were themselves education professionals the idea of 'giving something back' to 'the black community'[5] was an important motivator (see example of Jean above). Despite differences in levels of education and current occupation, these professional women felt that their common origin and identity as African/Caribbean meant that they had, at least partial, access to the 'structure of feeling' of other black parents. When they spoke of 'other' black parents, they spoke of lack of knowledge about the education system, sometimes even 'ignorance', and a lack of confidence with which to challenge the system, characteristics which, by and large, the professional members of the group did not share – at least to the same degree. There was no suggestion that there were fundamental differences in priority or perspective between themselves and other, non-professional black parents, concerning education.

Rootes (1995) suggests that social movements are dominated by the 'higher educated', those who by virtue of their education move into middle-class, professional jobs, often in the public sector. As so many of the key members were education professionals, the self-help group clearly fits into this category.

The self-help group can be characterised by members' generally positive approach to the current education system. The professional members of the group had, after all, succeeded both in terms commonly employed by the education system, and on their own terms: 'We've got to be able to make the best of what we have, and it can work. Here I am as an example, I came through that system' (Mother, education social worker).

Another, talking about her own generation of black parents, said:

> So a lot of parents, a lot of the parents who are parents now, are letting all that come out, their anger and frustration at the system, and their children you know . . . I guess if you're not within the system and can actually see how it works, you tend to feel that there is definitely them and us, but it isn't.
>
> (Mother, social worker)

This immediately raises the question of whether professional interpretations of events and procedures will be accepted by those parents whose experience of educational institutions has led them to conclude that there is indeed a 'them' and 'us' situation, and that power is firmly accrued by 'them'. As we noted earlier, the professionals in the self-help group explained the non-involvement in school of other black parents in terms of their lack of knowledge and confidence, and of schools not being welcoming. They did not, however, foreground the degree of alienation which characterises the relationship of some parents, both black and white, to educational institutions (Vincent 1996).

We wish to argue that class is a crucial factor, influencing (although not determining) the nature and form that collective action takes. Therefore it seems to us that the dominance of education professionals amongst the core members of the self-help group means that the direction the group takes, and its attitudes and views towards schooling are infused with a broadly positive reformist approach to the education system, a desire to work *within* the system to affect change.

It is important to note that we are not in any way suggesting that the black women in the group have had their critical faculties blunted by incorporation and socialisation into a professional culture. Rather, they were vociferous in their criticisms of many aspects of the system, and, in particular, the way black children are treated. They were all too aware of the discriminatory elements in the functioning of the education system. Indeed, the self-help group provided a space for these professionals to act in a way they cannot within the constraints of their particular occupations. This is illustrated by Annie's comments on the genesis of the group:

> Many issues came out, and there were a lot of, I suppose, professionals on the [governors' training] course, who were in education and they were quite aware of some of the issues, but weren't in a position to do anything about it in their particular roles, their professional roles, and I guess myself as well felt that we could do something more concrete, if you like, in a voluntary capacity, a self-help capacity. So we thought that if we met regularly and tried to discuss the particular issues, contact various people as [a group], rather than as a teacher or an education officer or something, that we might get more done . . . If we met regularly as a proper group, got some funding, maybe we could start having conferences, having seminars, and, you know, bring the debate to the public and carry on from there.

However, despite their criticisms, group members did not dismiss the system in its entirety. Their concern was to help as many parents as possible support their children as they navigated a path through educational institutions, hopefully to emerge, successful, at the end. Thus we are suggesting that the strategies they chose to adopt are a result of, and particular to their identities as black, professional women.

Radical or conformist?

We have outlined some of the ways in which race, class and gender can be said to have shaped the imperatives and ethos of the self-help group. Moreover, we have argued that the professional identities and concerns of the key activists encourage a largely positive, slowly reformist approach to the education system which may fail to engage with the experiences of working-class, non-professional parents.

However, we do not intend to label the group as 'conformist'. The radical–conformist binary is, in fact, unhelpful to capture the multi-faceted and dynamic nature of this group. We will elaborate by referring to an earlier paper, in which we considered the relationship between professionals and clients in two of the project case studies – the advice centre and the parent education group (Vincent and Warren 1997a). The professionals here, we argued, saw themselves as a 'different kind' of professional, able to negotiate and establish more supportive, sympathetic and apparently more egalitarian relationships with their clients because of their access to their client's structures of feeling, based on their sharing of similar class or ethnic backgrounds. These professionals, were, we concluded, 'active accommodators', generally accepting the limits of what they could do within their organisations, but also using the spaces available to them to develop these positive relationships with their clients. We contrasted the example of Jean with these other professionals, arguing that it was she who provided the most marked example of a 'different kind' of professional. The location of the self-help group as an independent forum acting outside the mainstream education system was a key factor in this. Her identity as a professional educator and administrator informs the directions in which she guided other parents, and explains her emphasis on accommodation and mediation. In that sense, she too is an active accommodator. However, taking her professional knowledge to a self-help group has more radical implications. Reay and Mirza (1997) comment on the limits and constraints for teachers that hinder the likelihood of them taking up positions as 'transformative intellectuals' (Giroux) within the existing education system. The constraints, we suggest, are the same for other professionals. The self-help group was the way in which these black women professionals chose to develop a base for mutual support and for collective action. Action, that is, that did not consist of high profile protests, but rather a concern to present teachers and schools with an alternative understanding of black children from that which they see as the dominant one (see epigraph), and to encourage other black parents to support their children through a white dominated education system. As Heidi Mirza says:

> Research on black women in education shows that there is much evidence to suggest that black women do not accept the dominant discourse, nor do they construct their identities in opposition to the dominant discourse. They redefine the world, have their own values, codes and understandings, *refuse* (not resist) the gaze of the other.
>
> (1997: 276)

Thus we suggest that the radical and transformative potential of the self-help group lies in its ability to produce:

> alternative frameworks of sense . . . Concrete concepts such as efficacy or success could be considered unimportant. This is because conflict takes place principally on symbolic grounds, by the challenging and upsetting of dominant codes upon which social relationships are founded in high density

informational systems. The mere existence of a symbolic challenge is in itself a method of unmasking the dominant codes, a different way of perceiving and naming the world.

(Melucci 1988: 248)

Conclusion

We have argued that membership of the self-help group allows its core activists to negotiate the different demands placed upon them as black women, as mothers, and as education professionals. Despite the apparently reformist emphasis of the group, guiding parents through the existing education system can also be, as Heidi Mirza argues, a radical strategy, encouraging the success of black pupils in a white-dominated education system, and also providing a different understanding of black youth to the negative portrayal described in the opening quotation.

The self-help group provides support and information for parents at risk of being positioned as 'on the margins' of school life by virtue of their social class and/or race. It helps these parents access schools and other educational institutions more effectively, but currently is only able to do this in a limited way. The group provides individual members with a network of support, but currently that network takes little collective action. Instead the support of the collective is directed at achieving largely individual ends. This strategy, with its enduring emphasis on individual goals, is clearly a result of the pressures upon the resources of a small group of individual activists. However, we suggest that this way of working may also be a response to the uncertainty and sense of struggle that accompanies the precarious position of the emerging black middle class (Landry 1987). We will conclude by asking whether the tendencies towards individual support and problem-solving which characterise the current work of the self-help group may act against its more radical potential. There is a risk, for example, that non-professional parents, instead of becoming fully involved as group members may simply adopt a *band-aid* approach. By this, we mean parents using the expertise of core members to solve particular problems *for* them (not *with* them), and then breaking their contact with the group. It is a term we have used to describe strategies adopted by some parents in their relationships with workers at the case study advice centre. In this case, we described such behaviour as a rational approach by parents in the face of what they saw as greatly differential resources (material resources, and those of time, information and cultural capital) between themselves and the paid advice centre workers. It is not, however, an approach which provides for an egalitarian relationship between members of a mutual support group, the model which provides the rationale for the self-help group.

Another possibility for future development would be for the self-help group to adopt a more pro-active campaigning role on key issues of importance to black (and other) parents – achievement and exclusions, to name but two.[6] Currently, the group encourages individuals to become critical friends, to be more assertive in their relationships with their children's particular schools, thereby seeking to challenge the (im)balance of power between *individual* teachers and parents. The adoption of a campaigning element would develop a public and collective, rather than a private and individual, model for change. It may also help attract and involve a wider group of parents. As a result, the self-help group may be able to mount a collective challenge to hegemonic discourses which still define black and working-class families as a problem.

Notes

1 The project, award no. R00022 1634, was funded by the ESRC.
2 A structure of feeling is a distillation of many elements, feelings and assumptions: the elements of place, history, economics, feelings of belonging, exclusion, or 'ownership', and assumptions of values and beliefs that translate into 'mental maps', attitudes and actions (Taylor *et al.* 1996). Raymond Williams (1977) also used the concept in this way.
3 For example, women in the campaigning group and the parent education group both claimed that their involvement led to a growth in their personal confidence. They used a varied range of examples, however – from addressing very large public meetings to entering their children's classroom – the diversity of which shows that perceptions of 'confidence' are not uniform, but socially constructed.
4 An interesting parallel was provided here by the gender make-up of the pressure group. It was noticeable that activists at the level of individual schools were over-whelmingly female. Men were more involved at regional and national level.
5 When asked about this phrase, most respondents noted that it presented an essentialist and reified view of a diverse grouping.
6 However, the constraints of time and funding loom large. It is worth noting again that all this group has achieved has been the result of the hard work and dedication of a small number of women.

References

Aziz, R. (1997) 'Feminism and the challenge of deviance', in H. Mirza (ed.) *Black British Feminism*, London: Routledge.

Ball, S. and Vincent, C. (1998) ' "I heard it on the grapevine": hot knowledge and school choice', *British Journal of Sociology of Education* 19, 3: 377–400.

Brannen, J. and Moss, P. (1991) *Managing Mothers: Dual Earner Households after Maternity Leave*, London: Unwin Hyman.

Castells, M. (1983) *The City and the Grassroots*, London: Edward Arnold.

David, M. (1993) *Parents, Gender and Education Reform*, Cambridge: Polity Press.

David, M. and West, A. (1994) *Mothers' Intuition? Choosing Secondary Schools*, London: Falmer Press.

Davies, B. (1989) 'Education for sexism: a theoretical analysis of gender bias in education', *Educational Philosophy and Theory* 21, 1:1–19.

Fraser, N. (1992) 'The uses and abuses of French discourse theories', in N. Fraser and S. Bartsky (eds) *Revaluing French Feminism: Critical Essays on Difference, Agency and Culture*, Indianapolis: Indiana University Press.

Gewirtz, S., Ball, S. and Bowe, R. (1995) *Markets, Choice and Equity in Education*, Buckingham: Open University Press.

Gillborn, D. and Gipps, C. (1996) *Recent Research on the Achievement of Ethnic Minority Pupils*, London: HMSO.

Gilroy, P. (1987) *There Ain't No Black in the Union Jack*, London: Hutchinson.

Griffith, A. and Smith, D. (1991) 'Constructing cultural knowledge: mothering as discourse', in J. Gaskell and A. McLaren (eds) *Women and Education: A Canadian Perspective*, 2nd edition, Calgary, Alberta: Detseilig Enterprises.

Holub, R. (1992) *Antonio Gramsci: Beyond Marxism and Postmodernism*, London: Routledge.

Jetter, A., Orleck, A. and Taylor, D. (eds) (1997) *The Politics of Motherhood: Activist Voices from the Left to Right*, Hanover, NH: Dartmouth College Press.

Johnston, H. and Klandersmans, B. (1995) 'The cultural analysis of social movements', in H. Johnston and B. Klandersmans (eds) *Social Movements and Culture*, London: UCL Press.

Jordon, B., Redley, M. and James, S. (1994) *Putting the Family First*, London: University College Press.

Kumar, K. (1993) 'Civil society: an inquiry into the usefulness of an historical term', *British Journal of Sociology* 44, 3: 375–95.

Landry, B. (1987) *The New Black Middle-Class*, Berkeley, CA: University of California Press.

Maheu, L. (ed.) (1995) *Social Movements and Social Classes: The Future of Collective Action*, London: Sage.

Melucci, A. (1988) 'Social movements and the democratisation of everyday life', in J. Keane (ed.)*Civil Society and the State*, London: Verso.

Mirza, H. (1997) 'Black women in action: a collective movement for social change', in H. Mirza (ed.) *Black British Feminism*, London: Routledge.

Mirza, M. (1998) ' "Same voices, same lives?": revisiting black feminist standpoint epistemology', in P. Connolly and B. Troyna (eds) *Researching Racism in Education*, Buckingham: Open University Press.

Modood, T. *et al.* (1997) *Ethnic Minorities in Britain: Diversity and Disadvantage*, London: Policy Studies Institute.

Reay, D. (1998) *Class Work*, London: University College Press.

Reay, D. and Mirza, H. (1997) 'Uncovering genealogies of the margin: black supplementary schooling', *British Journal of Sociology of Education* 18, 4: 477–99.

Reynolds, T. (1977) '(Mis)representing the Black (Super)woman', in H. Mirza (ed.) *Black British Feminism*, London: Routledge.

Ribbens, J. (1994) *Mothers and their Children*, London: Sage.

Rootes, C. (1995) 'A new class? The higher educated and the new politics', in L. Maheu (ed.) *Social Movements and Social Classes: The Future of Collective Action*, London: Sage.

Taylor, I. (1996) 'Fear of crime, urban fortunes and suburban social movements: some reflections from Manchester', *Sociology* 30, 2: 317–37.

Taylor, I., Evans, K. and Frazer, P. (1996) *A Tale of Two Cities*, London: Routledge.

Urwin, C. (1985) 'Constructing motherhood: the persuasion of normal development', in C. Steedman, C. Urwin, and V. Walkerdine (eds) *Language, Gender and Childhood*, London: RKP.

Vincent, C. (1996) *Parents and Teachers: Power and Participation*, London: Falmer Press.

—— (1997) 'Community and collectivism: the role of parent-centred organisations in education', *British Journal of Sociology of Education* 18, 2: 271–83.

Vincent, C. and Tomlinson, S. (1997) 'Home-school relations: a swarming of disciplinary mechanisms?', *British Educational Research Journal, Special Edition: A Reflexive Account of Educational Reforms* 23, 3: 361–7.

Vincent, C. and Warren, S. (1997a) 'A "different kind" of professional? Case studies of the work of parent-centred organisations', *International Journal of Inclusive Education* 1, 2: 271–83.

—— (1997b) 'Social movements and education: a case study', paper presented at the Parental Choice and Market Forces Seminar, Kings College, London, October.

—— (1998) 'Becoming a "better" parent?' *British Journal of Sociology of Education* 19, 2: 177–94.

Walkerdine, V. and Lucey, H. (1989) *Democracy in the Kitchen*, London: Virago.

Williams, R. (1997) *Marxism and Literature*, Oxford: Oxford University Press.

Conclusion
Gender policy and educational change

Jane Salisbury and Sheila Riddell

The chapters in this volume in their different ways and foci have thrown considerable light upon issues broadly themed around gender, policy and educational change. Some chapters have been concerned to enhance knowledge about contemporary education and schooling, other contributors have set out to identify knowledge *for* schooling. Embedded in all contributions is a concern for social justice and in particular about improvements in young people's educational, social and economic situations, particularly those of girls and women.

In the mapping out and descriptions of change over time provided in some chapters readers can see how agendas have shifted and emphases altered in relation to equal opportunities policy-making and practice. As Miriam David and her colleagues point out, the equal opportunities culture of the mid-1990s is narrowly focused and fuses social justice issues with performance, standards and improvement. A strong emphasis on the latter is evident in the creeping discourses of performativity and new managerialism which several contributors explore. To date, the 'New' Labour government appointed in 1997 shows little sign of subverting the agenda of performativity which preoccupied the previous Conservative administration.

The impact of educational reforms on gender equality is one of the regional issues confronting both national governments and the European Union. This is especially crucial in the context of sharp differences in social and economic conditions between European regions. There is a dearth of knowledge of how European, national and regional policies are interpreted and mediated at institutional levels. Several contributors have demonstrated that geography does matter! The tacit theme underlying chapters in Part 1 is that of the *dis*United Kingdom. In Northern Ireland for, example, the impact of the marketisation of education was significantly different than in other UK regions such as Scotland, as over half the Northern Irish schools are outside the jurisdiction of LEAs. Open enrolment did, however, lead to a rise in the number of pupils going to grammar schools. In parts of rural Wales geographical distances between schools means that for many parents, 'choice' is not an option. Thus the Right's policy thrust to 'marketise' education and increase competition between schools has had varied effects which have been shaped by different local conditions.

Clearly, shifts observed in the wider social and economic arena have shaped to some degree, girls' improved examination participation and performance. To what extent labour market and cultural transformations have led to changed vocational aspirations for girls and boys remains unclear. Gallagher *et al.* argue that a key explanation for the change in entry and attainment patterns is pupil expectation. In particular, the changes in educational choices for girls appeared from the qualitative data to be best explained by changes in girls' perceptions of the opportunities available to them in the wider society. It is a moot point that students in the late 1990s seem more aware and sensitive to changing cultural expectations; some of the young women portrayed in Macrae and Maguire's chapter for example, demonstrate 'poverty of aspiration' (Sharpe 1976) and remain caught up in the shackles of 'heterosexualised feminity' (Thorne 1993) which position them in subordinate relationships to males. These authors point out that factors of social class in particular, as well as 'race' do impact upon female achievement. It is salutory to note that though girls are achieving more GCSE examination passes at 16, their post-16 choices remain gendered in the old 'trad-itional' way. Females are still more likely than males to be following arts and humanities at A level and pursuing 'feminised' vocational courses such as child development or hair and beauty GNVQs/NVQs (EOC 1998).

A number of authors have expressed a concern that the current attention on emergent patterns of attainment may divert attention from the continuing cur-ricular differences between boys and girls at school, as well as beyond it. Curricu-lar changes associated with the recent decade of educational reforms, in particular the National Curriculum, have enabled more students to participate in the wider curriculum though their 'choices', as Croxford shows us, lead boys and girls to gender-differentiated areas of the curriculum. The 'slimmed down' National Curriculum introduced after the Dearing Review (1994) needs close scrutiny for its impacts upon gendered participation.

Collection of data on entry and performance in statutory attainment tests and public examinations has been used by researchers, politicians and feminists in various ways. Numerous questions for research have been generated from this type of numerical data which ostensibly assists regional governments in monitor-ing performance against the National Educational and Training Targets (NACETT 1995). As performance indicators, these types of data are now used by schools, colleges and their governing bodies, to inform 'target setting' and action planning and to raise standards and in promotional materials. A content analysis of contemporary 'glossified' school prospectuses and mission statements would reveal how the vocabularies of commercial business marketing have permeated and transformed, what used to be friendly introductory handbooks for new pupils and parents! What Clarke and Newman (1997) call 'dispersed managerial con-sciousness' has already developed in schools as several contributors to the volume show.

It is an urgent priority identified by feminist scholars in this volume, that research into educational *processes* as well as performance is undertaken. The social processes occurring in the various educational settings of schools and classrooms need closer exploration as Duffield's observational data demonstrate. There is some evidence to suggest that the 'setting' of pupils has been increasing in recent years (OHMCI 1997; Boaler 1997) with allocation to sets earlier than was the case five years ago. Moreover, it is argued that in deciding set placements, too little account is taken of assessment data from primary schools. Pupils are often 'locked' into bands and sets which lead to 'tiered-grade limited' GCSE examinations. Thus school organisation may have a significant influence upon subsequent patterns of entry and achievement (Salisbury *et al.* 1998). Similarly, as Murphy's chapter shows, various modes of assessment are also implicated in the differential perform-ance of boys and girls. Indeed, further research is needed to investigate the impacts of different forms of literacy upon the attainments of boys and girls as Millard's (1997) recent work suggests that 'gendered literacy' may be a crucial determinant.

The powerful and reflexive account provided by David *et al.* discusses how research undertaken for the Equal Opportunities Commission (EOC) – a body with its own strategic policy aims and responsibilities – created tensions for the feminist research team involved. David and her colleagues raise a number of serious questions arising out of their experiences. Their critical evaluation of the shifts, in the last decade, from 'pure academic' to 'policy-oriented' research illus-trates well the 'altered landscape of research'. Much of the research presented in the current volume has adopted a dual function of both exploring and promoting gender equality in education. The variously funded projects (ESRC, SOIED, DENI, EOC, etc.) reported in the four Parts of the volume belong to a new research industry in which pure, policy-orientated and strategic research are enmeshed and difficult to disentangle.

Researchers' voices, evident in all chapters, convey a clear and unambiguous message – the need for further closely focused research on gender. Many of the concluding paragraphs send out, hopefully to other cue conscious researchers, a sense of 'unfinished business'. There is an open acknowledgement, urgency even, that the numerous policy and practice issues identified need to be rendered more visible via both qualitative and quantitative approaches. Feminist writers like Mahony remind us that as researchers we have a responsibility to understand and challenge how schools both operate within and reconstitute social inequalities around the axes of race, gender, class, sexuality and disability.

In conclusion, if one were to pick out a single over-riding theme from this collection, it would probably be the title of Macrae and Maguire's chapter, 'All change, no change'. Gender relations, both within and outwith the sphere of education, have, in some respects, changed radically and in other ways not at all. This may be linked to wider features of social reproduction which embrace class, ethnicity and disability as well as gender. Writers such as Beck (1992) have sug-gested that individual choice within a market-led economy has led to the dimin-ution of traditional social structures and identities. Ball (1998), discussing the transitional experiences of young people in London, and drawing on Bourdieu's notion of habitus, suggests:

> For some young people (mainly working class) there is a maladjustment to position, a loss of that sense of placement, of a sense of positioning . . . For

others (mainly middle class) their symbolic capital is under threat of devaluation, their 'sense of place' is threatened but for them, it could be said, the logic of practice is reinforced rather than transformed.

Social class, gender, ethnicity and disability all retain a central role in influencing the way in which young people engage with education and the labour market. But they certainly do not produce pre-determined individual identities and outcomes. The authors in this collection have all engaged with the way in which gender continues to exert an influence upon but not determine lives, within a changing political context shaped both by the market and by equality agenda reflecting both individualised and collective concerns.

References

Ball, S. (1998) 'It's becoming a habitus: identities, youth transitions and socio-economic change', paper delivered to the British Educational Research Association Conference, Belfast, 27–30 August 1998.

Beck, U. (1992) *Risk Society: Towards a New Modernity*, trans: M. Ritter, London: Sage.

Boaler, J. (1998) 'Reclaiming school mathematics: the girls fight back', *Gender and Education* 9, 3: 285–305.

Clarke, J. and Newman, J. (1997) *The Managerial State*, London: Sage.

Dearing, R. (1994) *The National Curriculum and its Assessment: Final Report*, London: SCAA.

EOC (1998) *Gender and Differential Achievement in Education and Training: A Research Review*, Manchester: EOC.

Millard, E. (1997) *Differently Literate: Boys, Girls and the Schooling of Literacy*, London: Falmer Press.

National Advisory Council for Education and Training Targets (NACETT) (1995) *Report on Progress*, London: NACETT.

OHMCI (1997) *The Relative Performance of Boys and Girls*, Cardiff: OHMCI.

Salisbury, J., Gorard, S., Rees, G. and Fitz, J. (1998) 'The comparative performance of boys and girls in Wales: an alternative view of the gender gap', paper presented to the ECER Conference, Ljubjana, 15 September 1998.

Sharpe, S. (1976) *Just Like a Girl: How Girls Learn to be Women*, London: Penguin.

Thorne, B. (1993) *Gender Play: Girls and Boys in School*, Buckingham: Open University Press.

Index